Memory and Violence in the Middle East and North Africa

T0341977

EDITED BY
USSAMA MAKDISI
AND
PAUL A. SILVERSTEIN

Memory and Violence in the Middle East and North Africa

INDIANA UNIVERSITY PRESS
Bloomington and Indianapolis

In memory of Edward W. Said

This book is a publication of

Indiana University Press
601 North Morton Street
Bloomington, IN 47404-3797 USA

http://iupress.indiana.edu

Telephone orders   800-842-6796
Fax orders   812-855-7931
Orders by e-mail   iuporder@indiana.edu

© 2006 by Indiana University Press

The paper used in this publication meets the minimum requirements of American National Standard for Information Sciences—Permanence of Paper for Printed Library Materials, ANSI Z39.48-1984.

Manufactured in the United States of America

Library of Congress Cataloging-in-Publication Data

Memory and violence in the Middle East and North Africa / Edited by Ussama Makdisi, and Paul A. Silverstein.
    p. cm.
    Includes bibliographical references and index.
    ISBN 0-253-34655-X (cloth : alk. paper) — ISBN 0-253-21798-9 (pbk. : alk. paper)
    1. Violence—Middle East—History. 2. Violence—Africa, North—History. 3. Political violence—Middle East—History. 4. Political violence—Africa, North—History. I. Makdisi, Ussama Samir, date II. Silverstein, Paul A., date
    HM886.M46 2006
    303.6'0917'5927—dc22

                                                                                2005016784

1 2 3 4 5 11 10 09 08 07 06

Contents

Preface and Acknowledgments

Questions of memory, violence, and reconciliation in the Middle East and North Africa are no more pertinent than today, when U.S. military efforts to instantiate the neoconservative vision of "A New American Century" have wreaked havoc throughout the region, causing countless deaths and casualties in Afghanistan and Iraq, and veritably tearing these societies asunder. American military violence has been matched by growing networks of armed resistance that simultaneously invoke a regional history of anti-imperialism and a religious duty of *jihad*. Seeking to understand the logic and motivations behind this violence and counterviolence, the international public is only offered limited and often intentionally misleading answers: on the one hand, a partisan rhetoric that masks geopolitical and economic interests in a language of democratization and a global "war on terror"; on the other hand, an equally hackneyed academic discourse of an essentialist "clash of civilization" in which a secular–rational West is forever poised against an Arabo–Islamic East bent on the former's destruction.

Memory and Violence in the Middle East and North Africa seeks to transcend ideological cant and reified sociogeographic categories. It situates current struggles in a longer history of confrontation that cannot be reduced to facile cultural oppositions between secularism and religiosity, between Western and Islamic expansionism. In examining processes of memory, violence, and reconciliation as they take place during and in the aftermath of the Franco-Algerian war, the Lebanese civil war, and the Arab-Israeli conflict, this volume demonstrates the lingering effects of past struggles on present confrontations throughout the region. This is merely the beginning of the investigation, and many arenas of past conflict and present implication (including the legacies of the Ottoman Empire, World War I, the Armenian genocide, and the British colony in Iraq) await further exploration. Without taking into account the multiplicity and impact of such memories of conflict, the prospects for future peace and reconciliation are drastically limited.

The essays in the volume were originally written for a workshop on the theme of "Memory and Violence in the Middle East and North Africa" held at Rice University on 23–25 March 2001. The essays were subsequently revised in response to questions that arose during the workshop, particularly regarding the tension between the often conflicting imperatives of conflict resolution, nationalism, and reconciliation. The contributors have gone to great lengths to reach beyond the narrow audience of Middle East specialists; they address a wider international audience whose interest in the issues of violence and reconciliation is far from merely theoretical. For this, and all their hard work and patience throughout the long process of writing, presenting, and revising their chapters, we are most grateful.

We also want to extend our deep gratitude to the workshop's original sponsors at Rice University: the James A. Baker III Institute for Public Policy, the Center for the Study of Cultures, the Office of the Dean of Humanities, and the Department of History. Many colleagues, including As'ad Abu Khalil, Bernard Arésu, Peter C. Caldwell, John Collins, James Faubion, Werner Kelber, Najwa al-Qattan, Julie Peteet, Paula Sanders, Christoph Schumann, Daniel Sherman, Susan Slyomovics, Gale Stokes, Sarah Thal, Keith Watenpaugh, and Lora Wildenthal, generously offered their time and energy to participate in the workshop and provide their helpful commentary on the papers published in this volume. Edward Djerejian deserves special recognition and thanks for the unflagging support that he extended to the project since its inception many years ago.

We further wish to acknowledge all of the engagements we have had with readers of parts or all of the book manuscript over the past years. In particular, Lisa Hajjar and an anonymous reader for Indiana University Press made numerous comments and suggestions that productively challenged our conceptualizations and pushed us to refine and strengthen our convictions. We cannot reciprocate their efforts. Rebecca Tolen and the editorial staff at Indiana University Press have moreover been a source of editorial inspiration throughout the long process of transforming a set of rough essays into a publishable book. We can only blame ourselves if the resulting volume does not live up to their hopes and expectations.

Earlier, shorter versions of several of the chapters appeared elsewhere. We thank the publishers for permission to reprint portions of the following texts:

Glenn Bowman, "The Two Deaths of Basem Rishmawi," *Identities* 8 (1): 47–82. Copyright 2001. Reproduced by permission of Taylor & Francis, Inc. http://www.taylorandfrancis.com.

Yael Zerubavel, "Krav, Hakrava, Korban: Tmurot Be-Idi'ologit ha-Hakrava ha-Patriotit be-Israel," in *Patriotism,* ed. Avner Ben-Amos and Daniel Bar-Tal (Tel Aviv: Dyonon & Hakibbutz Hameuchad, 2004), 57–95. Reprinted with permission.

Shira Robinson, "Local Struggle, National Struggle: Palestinian Responses to the Kafr Qasim Massacre and Its Aftermath, 1956–66," *International Journal of Middle East Studies* 35 (3): 393–416. Copyright 2003 Cambridge University Press. Reprinted with permission.

Gabriel Piterberg, "Erasure," *New Left Review* 10: 31–46. Copyright 2001 Independent News Collective. Reprinted with permission.

Nadia Abu El-Haj, "Instituting Archaeology" and "Terrains of Settler Nationhood," in *Facts on the Ground: Archaeological Practice and Territorial Self-Fashioning in Israeli Society* (Chicago: University of Chicago Press, 2001), 45–98. Reprinted with permission.

Note on Transliteration

Arabic words and names have been transliterated according to a simplified system based on the *International Journal of Middle East Studies* (IJMES). All diacritical marks have been omitted. We have retained the (ʿ)ayn and the hamza(ʾ). We have not changed the transliterations of names adopted by authors who write in either English or French or of those individuals or places that are commonly known by specific transliterations (e.g., Geagea, not Jaʿjaʿ, Beit Sahour, not Bayt Sahur). Arabic words in common usage in English such as *Beirut* or in French such as *Maghreb* remain in the common form.

Memory and Violence in the Middle East
and North Africa

Introduction: Memory and Violence in the Middle East and North Africa

Paul A. Silverstein and Ussama Makdisi

This book explores the intersection of memory, violence, and reconciliation in the Middle East and North Africa. It takes as its point of departure the thesis that the myths and narratives that found and sustain modern national polities are situated at the intersection of competing collective memories of violence. Focusing on twentieth-century politics in the Middle East and North Africa, the book examines how processes of colonization and decolonization, of sectarianism and secularism, of state-building and communal loss produce a multiplicity of imagined communities that define themselves in relation to a common set of lionized (or demonized) individuals, memorialized places, and visceral events. Whether represented as trauma or destiny, the historical domain of violence becomes the basis for the constitution of collective narratives of origin, loss, and recovery, as well as the precondition for any future reconciliation. Rather than being unitary and stable, such narratives are always contested, and constantly are reworked and rewritten in relation to the political experiences and requirements of each successive generation.

As a region, the Middle East and North Africa has largely been defined by the fractious legacy of Western colonialism. But the region has also been defined by a range of ostensibly precolonial identities and postcolonial conflicts that greatly complicate any unipolar explanations of causality for violence. European colonialism undeniably created the physical borders of almost all the area's nation-states through treaties (such as San-Remo and Lausanne of the early 1920s) that partitioned the defeated Ottoman Empire. Colonialism has also precipitated several ongoing conflicts, the Arab-Israeli being the most salient, but its legacy has been powerfully affected by (as much as it has affected) other historical forces such as religion, gender, ethnicity, and localism. If the Arab-Israeli conflict is obviously derivative from British and Zionist colonialism, the civil war in Lebanon and the near ubiquitous state repression of internal dissident groups across the region indicate more than one narrative that explains the emergence and elaboration of memory and violence.

The current U.S. occupation of Iraq, and the resistance this occupation has engendered, is a prime example of this. The situation in Iraq today underscores the overlapping and mutually entrenching influences that give shape to a complex dynamic of memory and violence: from the uncanny similarities in rhetoric and actions between the U.S. occupation forces and their British colonial predecessors of the early 1920s that are highlighted by Arabs but denied by American officials, to the Shiʿi rhetoric of resistance that calls upon a longstanding narrative of the martyrdom of Husayn at Karbala at the hands of the Sunni Umayyads, but that also draws on contemporary far more recent Iraqi nationalist memories of British imperialism and of Iraqi resistance to it.

This complexity, this deep entanglement of myth and memory, is forged by the confluence of the powerful legacy of a late, and in some instances still ongoing, colonialism and the deliberate policies pursued by postcolonial governments. Together, these have been critical in defining the Middle East and North Africa as a region where the processes of putative reconciliation remain evidently weak despite several state-sponsored efforts to effect such reconciliations or to unilaterally impose resolutions. Why and how this has occurred, and how precisely the distinction between putative conflict resolution and actual reconciliation are played out in different historical, geographical, and cultural contexts across the region, are major themes taken up in this volume which seeks to cast the problems of memory and violence in the Middle East and North Africa within wider international contexts.

The interplay between memory and violence, and the limits of reconciliation it imposes, was nowhere more graphically illustrated than in the wake of the events of 11 September 2001. The terrorist attacks and the American military response in Afghanistan and Iraq have been repeatedly scripted in Manichean terms—as a war of "us" and "them," "good" and "evil," "democracy" and "terrorism," the Christian "West" and the Muslim (Middle) "East"—commanding the world to choose sides: "Either you are with us, or you are with the terrorists."[1] The violence, as both challenge and riposte, solidified, reified, and idealized inherently fragmentary and unstable ethnic, religious, and national communities, transforming, in the immediate wake of 11 September, an American "nation divided" into a "nation united."

Such processes of reification operate in and through the manipulation of social memories of past conflicts and the fabrication of historical parallels. In the hours that followed the collapse of the Twin Towers, U.S. news anchors searched for a precedent for the seemingly unprecedented. Initially they settled on Pearl Harbor, an image that seemed to resonate with the American public due to its enduring memory as the last attack on U.S. soil, made all the more manifest by a veritable rebirth of the World War II nostalgia industry in the late-1990s and the serendipitous release of the eponymous Hollywood blockbuster *Pearl Harbor* during the previous summer.[2] However, the Pearl Harbor analogy proved short-lived, made almost irrelevant by President George W. Bush's declaration that the "war on terrorism" would be fundamentally unlike the nation-state based wars of previous generations, that it would proceed in a fashion without boundaries and even without an end—implying that the new war was effectively outside of history yet thoroughly informed by a certain hegemonic reading of U.S. history. In this reading, the violence inflicted by the United States on millions of others—Indians, Japanese, Germans, Vietnamese, Arabs—has consistently been framed by a discourse of fundamental U.S. innocence and goodness that began with the Puritan attempt to establish a "City on a Hill," and continues with the current ostensible effort by the United States to both promote "peace in the Middle East" and more recently to instill "democracy" there as well.

In this regard, the work of the emeritus professor of Ottoman history Bernard Lewis (see 2004) has done more than anyone else to explain and answer the question of "why do they hate us" to an American public. Time and again he has reminded U.S. audiences that what is at stake in the current "war against terrorism" is nothing less than a "clash of civilizations," a struggle whose immediate irruptions reflect a *long durée* of world rivalry between Islam and the Judeo-Christian West. Hence Lewis moves across centuries to explain current violence, deliberately collapsing the vital distinction between the uneven unfolding of history, with all its junctures and contradictions, and the crystalline historiographies composed of memories and narratives that do indeed sweep smoothly across huge spans of time. At its base, Lewis's argument rests on a notion of a stark opposition between a Judeo-Christian West and an Islam that has been unable to come to terms with its own decline. Singular, monumental, and epochal, the roots of contemporary violence, Lewis insists, lie in a Muslim rage against modernity, nourished by an allegedly millennial memory of, and an utterly irreconcilable yearning for, past glory. Such an argument has resonated deeply with a U.S. public precisely because it does not infringe upon—indeed it affirms—a dominant narrative of U.S. innocence that has no memory, no place, for the actual role of the United States in the Middle East.

Meanwhile, other pundits and publics have understood the U.S. "war on terror" in terms of a different set of world historical tropes, rhetorics, and narratives. Motivated by a similar Manichean logic and by Bush's own promise of a "crusade against the evildoers," certain Islamists scripted the American military campaigns against the Taliban and Saddam Hussein governments into a unilinear narrative of Christian aggression against Muslim lands: from the Crusades to the Reconquista to nineteenth-century European imperialism to the establishment of the State of Israel to the Soviet invasion of Afghanistan to the second Gulf War through the present. For example, Ayman al-Zuwahiri, a leader of the al-Qaʿida terrorist network, routinely refers to the Americans as "crusaders"; in the process, he, like Lewis, collapses history and historiography, playing to what he recognizes is a well-known and accepted narrative in the contemporary Arab world that equates the unjust (but transient) crusades with unjust imperialism, and that conflates medieval Muslims with modern Arabs. Although the term "the Crusades" (*al-hurub al-salibiyya*) was not coined in Arabic before the nineteenth century in the context of an increasingly aggressive European colonialism of the Ottoman Empire, Zuwahiri's deployment of the term today refers to a supposedly enduring testament of the perfidy of the West and the absolute justness of those self-styled defenders of Islam. The innate and ahistorical goodness of the American people thus finds a corollary in the innate and ahistorical justness of the Muslim nation or *umma*. This deployment of a millennial "memory" of unjust war, however, is not only directed against the "infidel" West, but also at those at home. It is thus part of a bitter struggle against a secular Arab interpretation of the Crusades, and indeed, against a secular Arab world (cf. Maalouf 1984).

The very contested and polyvalent meanings of referenced historic events like "the Crusades"—the fact that they have emotive salience in particular yet mutually opposed ways for large numbers of people in the United States as well as in the Middle East—makes them ideal grist for the ideological mill of the various nationalisms and ethno-religious sectarianisms and fundamentalisms that mark our present condition. Likewise, the multiplicity of such historical narratives recalls the fact that the post–11 September "war on terror" is but one moment within larger processes by which memory, violence, and processes of peace and reconciliation are conjoined in the Middle East and North Africa. As the fates of postwar Afghanistan and Iraq were being decided, the larger region was marked by ongoing open warfare between the Israeli state and Palestinian groups, and between the Algerian military and armed Islamist forces. In what became known as the al-Aqsa *intifada,* a new generation of Palestinians picked up the mantle of the 1980s struggle and violently enacted their resistance to continued Israeli occupation and domination, to a "peace process" that largely left unresolved decades of conflict and dispossession. In the meantime, Algerian Islamist fighters—many of whom were popularly known as *afghanis* for their previous participation in the war against the Soviets in Afghanistan—described themselves as the new *mujahidin* in the unfinished war against (neo-) colonialism, against Western economic domination and cultural hegemony symbolized by the Francophone military state.

These wars were conjoined in the region with low-intensity struggles for civil rights and the freedom of cultural expression in places as diverse as Turkey, Iran, Egypt, Lebanon, the Gulf States, and Morocco. Feminist and ethno-cultural movements throughout the Middle East and North Africa drew on past heroes and martyrs to advance their causes. Amazigh (pl. *Imazighen*) activists in Morocco and Algeria, for instance, reference and retroactively make martyrs of mytho-historical figures like the king Jugurtha who led Numidia to war against Rome, or the Berber queen Kahina who fought against seventh-century Arab invaders, as well as coteries of more recent militants killed by "*le pouvoir*" or Islamists, in their struggles for linguistic and cultural rights in North Africa. Indeed, one might say, with Marx (1963: 15), that "the tradition of all the dead generations weighs like a nightmare on the brain" of today's "freedom fighters"—"jihadis" and "secularists" alike—in the region today.

At the same time, while terror, torture, and the suppression of civil liberties continue to stereotype the region as a bastion of human rights violations, efforts and processes of truth and reconciliation accompany those of redress and revenge. Although the violence of everyday domination and surveillance remains ever-present for millions of people living under state and occupier regimes in the region, the character of this domination for many is defined not by interstate armed confrontations, but rather by the internal sphere of civil war, minority uprisings, and militarized police interventions. Such domestic violence has developed a number of "peace processes" and efforts of "truth and reconciliation." In Israel/Palestine, this has involved various efforts at diplomatic negotiation for the Israeli withdrawal from the occupied territories and the creation of a Palestinian entity that emerged from the 1993 Oslo Accords, and continued with the U.S.-backed "Road Map" even after the 2002 reoccupation of much of the West Bank and Gaza Strip. In Algeria, President Abdelaziz Bouteflika attempted to bring a halt to the ongoing civil war by signing a "civil concord pact" in 1999, granting amnesty to members of one of the major guerrilla groups, the Islamic Salvation Army, though remaining silent concerning other militias. Under pressure from local and international human rights group, newly enthroned King Mohamed VI of Morocco created a Commission of Arbitrage and Indemnification in August 1999 that paid out $84 million U.S. to the families of 3,700 victims of state torture and disappearance during the so-called *années de plomb* ("years of lead") before it was dissolved in January 2004 and replaced with an Institution for Equity and Reconciliation charged with definitively "turning the page" on that period.[3]

Unfortunately, these attempts to normalize civil relations and bring an end to violence by fiat have proved largely unsuccessful in ending domestic struggles. Bolstered by the post–11 September global "war on terror," military actions, targeted assassination, and police roundups of suspected "terrorists" continued apace in the name of "state security." All in all, state-directed efforts at "truth and reconciliation" tended to ignore the roots of the civil conflicts—the extant political and socioeconomic inequities that frequently map onto internal class, ethnic, and religious divides. Moreover, they operated without public expiation or recognition of responsibility, and as such left unquestioned both the particular legitimacy of the regimes in place and the more general nationalist myths that justify their rule.[4] Indeed, the peace processes in question often amount to little more than self-bolstering speech acts performed for an international audience by states and their elite interlocutors. In unilaterally declaring the termination of hostilities, empowered political actors like Bouteflika sought to reclaim a monopoly of violence and hence of control. The fact that such acts have been rarely successful in promoting lasting peace—and indeed have often fueled further violence in the region—is a dilemma that this book seeks to address.

State-driven efforts at reconciliation thus dovetail with larger practices through which, as Ernest Renan (1990 [1882]) reminds us, amnesia is made the condition of possibility for the nation. In some cases, the nation is constructed through the violent erasing of inconsistent historical artifacts, as Nadia Abu El-Haj and Gabriel Piterberg discuss respectively in their chapters in this volume on Zionist archaeological practice and the post-1948 literal plowing under of Palestinian history by the Israeli military (cf. Abu El-Haj 2002). In other cases, as Saree Makdisi and Anja Peleikis argue in their chapters on the lacunae of official memory in post–civil war Lebanon, national unity is built on an official refusal to address the details of the conflict. The contemporary Lebanese state, with certain notable exceptions (namely the 1994–1996 trial of the former leader of the rightist Lebanese Forces Samir Geagea), embarked on a policy of the physical reconstruction of Lebanon based on an idealization of prewar intercommunal harmony that ignored questions of the particular responsibility among militias for the fifteen years of violence (Rowe and Sarkis 1998; S. Makdisi 1997; Khalaf 2002). In still other cases, as James McDougall and Benjamin Stora write of in their chapters on historiography and the Franco-Algerian war, the revolutionary and later ruling National Liberation Front's fetish of nationalist violence during the war glossed over internal divides, leading to a postwar representation of a universal sharing of suffering, blame, and heroism by members of the national polity. The postrevolutionary Algerian state honored the "martyrs" (*shuhada*) of the war of national liberation and provided reparations for their families, constructing a national myth that commemorated "one hero, the people" (Silverstein 2000; Stora 1995, 1991). Yael Zerubavel's analysis of the literary representation of military funerals in this volume similarly indicates how the Israeli nation has been historically reconstituted through the scripting of individual soldiers' deaths as "patriotic sacrifice" (see Zerubavel 1995).

In contrast, local commemorative practices contest such official historical amnesia and reification by publicly memorializing particular moments or individuals in conflicts. Much to the chagrin of state actors, they transform "victims" into "martyrs," "terrorists" into "heroes," and "soldiers" into "assassins" (and vice versa) through a variety of rituals and iconographies of remembrance —from funeral processions, to domestic altars for slain family members, to pilgrimages to massacre sites, to unofficial museums for disappeared villages or groups.[5] As rituals, they are clearly occasions for "collective effervescence" in the Durkheimian sense (cf. Durkheim 1995 [1912]: 220–221)—for the representation and performative enactment of group solidarity and identity. At the same time, however, they are also occasions for "metasocial commentary" (Geertz 1973: 448), for a critical discussion (often on the symbolic plane) of social relations and values. Rituals of commemoration can thus underwrite alternate narratives of temporality and belonging that are often at odds with state-endorsed histories.

Moreover, these subaltern narratives of violence are themselves subject to change and revision. Shira Robinson's description of the history of the Palestinian commemoration of the 1956 massacre at Kafr Qasim, in her chapter in this volume, demonstrates that it is not only the official Israeli story of the massacre and its victims that is at stake, but the ritual of remembrance as well. Successive retellings of the deaths of villagers at the hands of Israeli soldiers reference previous commemorations and the politics surrounding them. In the end, the contemporary memorials serve as much as a protest against the circumscribed conditions for public remembrance under occupation, as against the historical fact of the massacre itself.

In a similar manner, the death of Beit Sahour resident Basem Rishmawi, as

Glenn Bowman documents in his chapter, held different significance before and after the Oslo Accords, as the agency of resistance shifted from young rock throwers to the structures of the Palestinian Authority. During the first *intifada,* Palestinians treated his death as an assassination by the Israeli Defense Forces, whereas under the rule of the Palestinian Authority—governed by the regulations of the Oslo Accords—the death was re-presented as an honor killing by a member of a rival *hamula* (clan, or extended family). However, such efforts to erase martyrdom are balanced by rival Palestinian attempts that multiply martyrs. For instance, Palestinian funeral processions for victims of the Al-Aqsa *intifada* have been contested not only by the Israeli state that fears their incitement of organized protest, but also by different Palestinian groups (Fatah, Hamas, etc.) each trying to claim ownership of the victim.[6] In this sense, past violence is constantly being rewritten in the terms of the present conflict.

In exploring these processes, this volume seeks to explore how such memories of violence and violence of memory frame contemporary politics and the possibilities for the resolution of current conflicts in the Middle East and North Africa. It questions how official and unofficial histories of struggle are variously produced, consumed, and reproduced in the forging of national and transnational polities. How are personal, affective experiences of violence co-opted and appropriated in the construction of political ideology? What is the role of operations of erasure and amnesia in the constitution of collective memories and imagined communities? How do memories of past violence underwrite both the enactment and understanding of contemporary conflict? Does state power require a monopoly on historical narration, and if so, how is that hegemony maintained? What alternative institutions to the national state exist for containing and combating divisive memories? To what extent can the participation of other actors, from internal communities to non-governmental organizations (NGOs) to international monitors, promote processes of truth and reconciliation? The remainder of this introductory chapter will begin to address these basic questions by theoretically situating the book in terms of the themes of violence, memory, and reconciliation.

Violence

Although the Middle East has long been stereotyped as a region of primordial and endemic religious violence, in recent years a number of provocative works have indicated how the violent enactment of communal identity is a decidedly modern phenomenon tied to the (colonial) formation of and (postcolonial) tensions within nation-states.[7] Sectarianism does not, in other words, precede national politics and state creation, but rather is largely the effect of these processes. The assumed link between territory, history, and the body—at the basis of both sectarian and nationalist claims—remains uncertain, as territories demarcate multiple, conflicting histories and bodies betray multiple descents. Indeed, one of the effects of violence is to inscribe ethnic and religious determinacy onto such unstable, embodied social fields and spaces (Appadurai 1998:

234). As Lisa Malkki (1995: 88) has argued in regards to the history of genocidal violence against Hutus in Burundi, "through violence, bodies of individual persons become metamorphosed into specimens of the ethnic category for which they are supposed to stand."

One place to examine this process of violent subject formation is the late-colonial Algeria described by Frantz Fanon. In his essay "Concerning Violence," Fanon asserts with characteristic bluntness that colonial history is a history of violence; the "first encounter [of the settler and the native] was marked by violence and their existence together—that is to say the exploitation of the native by the settler—was carried out by dint of a great array of bayonets and cannons" (1963: 61). Moreover, if colonization, for Fanon, is violence, so too must be decolonization: "The violence which has ruled over the ordering of the colonial world, which has ceaselessly drummed the rhythm for the destruction of native social forms . . . that same violence will be claimed and taken over by the native at the moment when . . . he surges into the forbidden quarters" (1963: 40). It is this deep history of violence that continues to bind former colonizers and colonized together in the postcolonial period. Today's violence, exemplified poignantly by the Algerian civil war, largely finds its roots in past struggles and unresolved conflicts over territory, resources, and identity.

Fanon's insights are directly applicable to the study of conflict in the Middle East and North Africa, particularly his observation that subjectivities are to a large extent the products and not the causes of violence, and that these subjectivities are written in space and time. In Fanon's reworking of the Hegelian master-slave dialectic, native and settler create each other in and through violence. If the settler comes into being through the rape of native soils and bodies, "for the native, life can only spring out of the rotting corpse of the settler." (1963: 93). Colonial Algeria has indeed provided a paradigmatic case where, as James McDougall discusses in his chapter in this volume, the construction of a singular Algerian national polity from a multi-ethnic, multi-lingual, multi-religious population precipitated in large part from resistance to French colonialism. However, as Ussama Makdisi (2000) has demonstrated in the case of Ottoman Lebanon, this dialectical process of the construction of sectarian identity through violence has occurred also in situations where categories of *colonizer* and *colonized* are less evident. Indeed, the current situation of protracted violence in Israel/Palestine, as Shira Robinson and Glenn Bowman's essays in this volume attest, needs to be largely understood as a particularly virulent example by which "Jews" and "Arabs" become dialectically constituted as singular and reified communities in the course of historical struggle.

Moreover, this violent dialectic manifests itself spatially, as "a world divided into compartments": the settler's town and the native's town—the former as a place of modernity, of technology and sanitation; the latter as a place of backwardness, of poverty and filth (Fanon 1963: 38–39). Existing in "reciprocal exclusivity," these two areas are often seen as being inhabited by "two different species" (Fanon 1963: 39–40), with high walls, no-man's lands (*cordons sanitaires*), and military forces maintaining their absolute difference. As we know from studies of colonial urbanism, urban policy in the Middle East and North Africa directly maintained this spatial "apartheid," establishing "modern," European cities at a safe distance from the "traditional," native *medinas* (cf. Abu-Lughod 1980; Çelik 1997; Rabinow 1989; Thompson 2000; Wright 1991). The current Israeli construction of a separation wall around Palestinian territories follows directly from these same concerns over "security" and racial integrity.

Allen Feldman, in his study of Protestant–Catholic violence in Belfast, Northern Ireland, has built on these Fanonian insights to describe "novel subject positions [that] are constructed and construed by violent performances" (1991: 20). Rather than understanding violence as a "derivative symptom" of ideological divergences, he treats it as "an institution possessing its own symbolic and performative autonomy" that "emerges as mnemonic for historicizing space and spatializing history" (1995: 21, 27). In other words, it is through violent acts that territory becomes ethnically demarcated, that Catholic and Protestant Belfasts are established, that the various lines between Israel and Palestine come to be drawn.

What makes these ethno-spatial divides real is not a history of habitation based in competing claims of ancient ownership that defy any lived memory, but rather a more recent history of violence and territorial expropriation experienced by generations still alive. Nadia Abu El-Haj and Gabriel Piterberg's chapters demonstrate how land—subject to exploration, destruction, and reconstruction —formed the object *and* means of struggle in the constitution of the Israeli nation-state. Territory, in this respect, comes to function as a repository of past violence, a landscape filled with anger, sorrow, and jubilation. As in the northern Lebanon described by Michael Gilsenan (1996: 32), violence and its narratives are "enshrined on the landscape," inhabiting hillocks, villages, and valleys (cf. Abu-Lughod et al. 1999). The struggles over territory that mark the Al-Aqsa *intifada* and the Israeli reoccupation thus inscribe themselves in a longer history of appropriation and expropriation; today's martyrs quite literally walk in the footsteps of martyrs past. Violence in every case plays itself out as historical reenactment, always—to borrow Marx's famous formulation—both tragic and farcical. It is through such ongoing repetition and recurrence, and not as primordial unities, that ethnic and religious communities of "Israelis" and "Palestinians" (not to mention "Arabs," "Imazighen," and "Kurds") gain substance.

Memory

Violence as a pragmatic process of community construction is further iterated and mediated through a politics and discourse of memory. In order to understand the resurgence of past conflict into the contemporary political culture of the Middle East and North Africa, it is necessary to focus on contentious histories and structures of commemoration. As Maurice Halbwachs (1980) and other more contemporary scholars have averred, memory work is intimately tied to social (re-) production, as individual memories of cultural practices and events are socialized and transmitted, preserved and forgotten, ritualized and performed.[8] These processes effectively pluralize the category of social memory, insofar as multiple memories and "counter-memories" always exist in mutual conflict within any given social formation.

Treating social memory as a polyvalent object of scholarly analysis has several important implications. In the first place, it dispenses with the arbitrary distinction between "history" as a universal, singular, and normative category and "memories" as popular, disparate, and multiple (cf. Nora 1984: xix). Moreover, it necessitates looking beyond the "nation" as the privileged locale of social life. Nadia Abu El-Haj's contribution is especially critical of the ways in which academic studies of commemorative practices often end up parroting the ideological commitments of the social actors whose memories they analyze, without interrogating the colonial genealogies of their modes of remembrance and the underlying power relations embedded within them. While such criticism is particularly pertinent in cases where the sciences of memory (archaeology, folklore studies, etc.) dovetail with the construction of national ideologies, as in the case of Israel, one finds similar processes of national reification at work in the cases of Algerian national historiography and post-war Lebanese reconstruction, as James McDougall and Saree Makdisi detail in their respective chapters.

As a plural object of study, social memory dovetails with the larger social category of historical consciousness, i.e., codes of temporality intrinsic to the production of particular subjectivities (cf. Comaroff and Comaroff 1992). What is at issue is how particular temporal schemes underwrite the imagination of self and the practice of politics. Not only are the diacritics by which Israelis, Palestinians, Lebanese, Algerians, Imazighen, and so on define themselves the products of a history of past social actions, but the very historical frameworks employed to understand these past productions are themselves social and historical constructions. As Marshall Sahlins has argued, cultural logics of history can vary dramatically, including, among others, modes of "mytho-praxis" (the eternal recurrence of creation events), "heroic history" (the determination of all historical events from the actions of a single leader), and chronology (the commensurability of all moments in time). Or, as he avers, "other cultures, other times" (Sahlins 1985: 32–72). Rather than stable frameworks, these historicities are subject to transformation of both subtle and radical nature, as groups encounter each other and internal hierarchies rise and fall. Basem Rishmawi's life and death, as Glenn Bowman shows, takes on a completely different course when narrated through the temporality of the *intifada* (i.e., as but a moment in a perpetual struggle) or the Palestinian Authority (i.e., as a step toward intercommunal reconciliation). In the process of such changes, subjects and groups are created and recreated.

Such shifts in historical consciousness can be traced by focusing on the production of historical narratives of particular events and struggles. Narration involves the restructuring of the temporal sequence in order to resituate a current predicament and enable future action. As Edward Bruner has elaborated, "the present is given meaning in terms of that anticipated present we call the future and the former present which we call the past" (1986: 142). In addition to dealing with the multiple deaths of Basem Rishmawi, the essays by Robinson and Zerubavel likewise chronicle the multiple deaths of Kafr Qasim victims and Israeli soldiers as their struggles are renarrated under different historical presents of the Israeli state. Of particular interest in these cases is the flexibility of narration, its ability to expand and contract, and to appropriate particular events and de-center others. As history only exists as a narrated sequence, the opposition between history and memory can be heuristically bracketed.

Memory (understood as historical imagination) and narration play important roles in the constitution of national and postnational consciousness.[9] As early as 1889, Renan indicated the centrality of memory in his subjective vision of the nation as a "soul, a spiritual principle." For Renan, however, national memory proved to be very selective, with lacunae and aporias—"forgetting"— as a particularly "crucial factor in the creation of a nation" (1990: 11, 19). Absence of memory, as Makdisi and Stora respectively recount in the cases of postwar Algeria and Lebanon, becomes the condition of possibility for forging unity in the aftermath of violent disunity.

Benedict Anderson has taken these insights further, arguing that the "daily plebiscite" Renan sees mediating national belonging does not solely depend on the particular events selected (i.e., the content) in the narration of a nation's past, but in the parameters (i.e., the context) of the narration itself, in other words in the narrativity. Focusing on the rise of print capitalism, he argues that modern, civic nations required the desacralization of language and temporality that had underwritten religious and dynastic communities. In this regard, he has highlighted the newspaper and the realist novel as conveyors of a "homogenous empty-time" through which readers can imagine their simultaneity with their conationals in daily "mass ceremonies" of reading (1983: 35). Following the essays of Abu El-Haj, McDougall, and Zerubavel, one might expand these national "texts" to include plays, histories, and even museums.

In both Renan and Anderson's accounts, what remains important is the profound tension between history and cosmology at the heart of national imagination (Renan 1990: 11; Anderson 1991: 36). It is this ambivalence between a nation's heroic, immemorial past and the everyday (and violently extreme) exigencies through which it is continually recreated (cf. Bhabha 1990: 1), that is crucial. Indeed, it is the discrepancy between official nationalism and extant conditions of marginality that continues to haunt contemporary Israel and Lebanon, and particularly the lives of the Yemeni Jews and southern Shiʿa described respectively by Gabriel Piterberg and Anja Peleikis. What mediates this tension is exactly the work of memory in all its multiple, multivocal, and mutually conflicting narrations.

Memories of particular historical events within the Algerian War, the Lebanese civil war, the Palestinian *intifada,* and other national conflicts have been variously appropriated and narrated in the imagination of different forms of postcolonial community that both coincide with and challenge that of the nation. In examining the various representations of these national conflicts, the contributors to this volume demonstrate how the return to past moments of violence has in fact paved the way to the constitution of a multiplicity of post-colonial (if not postnational) subjectivities.

Reconciliation

This politics of memory is particularly evident in the public and official processes of reconciliation enacted thus far in countries of the Middle East and North Africa. The efficacy of departure from active violence—and moves toward national or international reconciliation—depends almost entirely on a confluence of different historical factors: from the historical context of reconciliation itself, to the vision and credibility of the leaders involved in its making, to the active participation of ordinary people in the process. For this reason, this volume deliberately eschews a universal liberal or legal perspective on reconciliation in favor of a recognition of the different histories and possibilities that promote or hinder reconciliation. Because reconciliation by definition depends on compromise, all processes of reconciliation depend on a partial "forgetting." But as the chapters of this volume demonstrate, it is not forgetting, or amnesia, that is important per se, but how this forgetting happens, how and by whom it is desired and received, and how it is imposed and resisted.

What this volume explores in historical and ethnographic detail is how systems, codes, languages, and administrations of reconciliation seek to assert their own form of hegemonic memory, a memory that can often be acknowledged to be flawed, can be seen to be incomplete, can be viewed as partial, yet at the same time is invariably understood as necessary by peoples involved in conflict. Rather than see or explain processes of reconciliation in dualistic terms of lies versus truth, this volume asks how multiple and often irreconcilably contradictory memories of conflict coexist with single supposedly hegemonic state-sponsored regimes of reconciliation. Seeing this tension as historically produced and contingent, this volume investigates the dialectic between accommodation and repression, between state-sponsored reconciliation (be it enshrined in documents, enacted in commissions, or erected in monuments) and unofficial truths and memories in cases such as Lebanon, Algeria, and Israel.

The processes of reconciliation underway in the case of South Africa and other countries such as Chile, Spain, and Mexico provide fascinating counterpoints to what has, what is, and what may well unfold in the Middle East. Generally speaking, there seem to be two distinct and antithetical paths toward reconciliation following violent civil conflict. The first involves some sort of recounting of past violence, either through the establishment of a formal commission of inquiry, or through the selective declassification of government documents relating to a specific period or policy. This category includes different attempts to "tame" the relationship between memory and violence, to defuse sectarian, class, racial, national, or ethnic grievances by providing information about the dead or disappeared, answering lingering questions, and acknowledging past violence, for which there must be some degree of accountability, or at least, recognition. Some governments—most famously South Africa's—have established commissions with specific mandates and powers to help uncover the "truth" behind various acts, policies, and time periods. Others, most recently Mexico under Vicente Fox, have refused to establish commissions and instead have declassified select documents relating to the so-called "dirty war" during the 1970s and early 1980s. In almost all cases, however, the politics of openness and recognition is limited by the constraints of power, by the modality of transition from civil conflict to civil peace, and by the often irreconcilable pulls of accountability and reconciliation.

The second model is that of a general amnesty and what can loosely be called a politics of amnesia. Rather than acknowledging the past by delving into it (in however tentative a fashion), the politics of amnesia acknowledges the past by ostensibly ignoring it, by looking forward rather than backward. The presumption in the second model is that there can be no acknowledgment of past violence without a return to that violence; that memories of violence are necessarily too difficult and divisive and therefore must be dispensed with along with the violence itself. Ethnic or religious divisions are considered not as problems that can be finally resolved, but as problems that must be actively managed. The selective "forgetting" of the past is deemed indispensable to any prospect of reconciliation. Rather than see a truth commission as the key to reconciliation, the second model insists that certain truths must be the first casualties of peace, and in the process often blurs the lines between reconciliation and the status quo.

Without doubt, however, the boldest experiment in truth and reconciliation in recent years comes from post-Apartheid South Africa, with establishment of the Truth and Reconciliation Commission (or TRC) in 1995. As Bishop Desmond Tutu put it, the great challenge of South Africa was to "balance the requirements of justice, accountability, stability, peace, and reconciliation. We could very well have had justice, retributive justice, and had a South Africa lying in ashes—a truly Pyrrhic victory if ever there was one. Our country had to decide very carefully where it would spend its limited resources to the best possible advantage" (1999: 23). The TRC, according to Tutu, was established very self-consciously as a refutation to other forms of coming to terms with the legacy of violent conflict. It was seen by its founders as an alternative to the victor's justice evinced at the Nuremberg trials, but also to the politics of amnesia and blanket amnesties that have manifested themselves in post-Franco Spain (Rigby 2001) and in post–civil war Lebanon. Precisely because the TRC sought to come to terms with the violence of the past was a blanket amnesty rejected, and yet because of the fact that South Africa's transformation from Apartheid rule to democratic rule was a result of a negotiated settlement rather than a total military defeat of the Apartheid regime, victor's justice was deemed not only immoral but impracticable. As Tutu put it,

> Our country's negotiators rejected the two extremes and opted for a "third way,"
> a compromise between the extreme of the Nuremberg trials and the blanket amnesty or national amnesty. And that third way was granting amnesty to individuals

in exchange for a full disclosure relating to the crime for which amnesty was being sought. It was the carrot of possible freedom in exchange for truth and the stick was, for those already in jail, the prospect of a lengthy prison sentences, and for those still free, the probability of arrest and prosecution and imprisonment. (1999: 30)

Yet for all its achievements, the TRC has demonstrated how notions of reconciliation and justice, often conflated, are rarely in harmony (Nuttall and Coetzee 1998). One of the most cogent criticisms of the TRC comes from the Nigerian novelist and Nobel laureate Wole Soyinka who noted the evident absence of restitution and the lack of remorse on the part of the perpetrators of Apartheid's dirty work. Soyinka, like Tutu, reflected on the cathartic possibilities inherent in discovering what happened under Apartheid, particularly for its victims. "Memory obviously rejects amnesia," stated Soyinka, "but it remains amenable to closure that, apparently, is the ultimate goal of social strategies such as Truth and Reconciliation" (Soyinka 1999: 20). But he also asked: "Truth as prelude to reconciliation, that seems logical enough; but Truth as the justification, as the sole exaction or condition for Reconciliation?" (20). Soyinka goes on to question the equation of truth and reconciliation, turning to the utility of the South African model for other cases in Africa, such as Idi Amin, Sanne Abbacha, and Mobutu, as well as to cases such as Pol Pot in Cambodia and Pinochet in Chile.

> We know that strategies for the transformation of society often demand a measure of pragmatism or, to put it crudely, deals. Secret, sometimes unrecorded, but deals nevertheless, a guarantee between the lines, legible only to signatories to the public document. Indemnity is often granted to the undeserving in order to minimize damage to the structure of society and even preserve lives—Argentina, Chile, these are all pertinent examples that nevertheless constitute an outrage to the moral sense and stress the limits of our humanity. Ideally, we wish that the Galtieris, the Pinochets of the world would encounter nothing less than the fate of the Nicolae Ceaucescus, the Sergeant Does, and other human pollutants of the planet. Despite that recognition, however, despite the realization that South Africa is, like any other zone of state-engendered anomie, unique in the intricacy of motions—both internal and external—that led to her liberation, there remains a sense that the adopted formula for the harmonization of that society erodes, in some way, one of the pillars on which a durable society must be founded—Responsibility. And ultimately—Justice. (26-27)

Using Tutu's advocacy and Soyinka's criticism of the TRC as a point of departure, the essays in the volume ask a series of questions: What are the differences in the relationship between justice, memory, and reconciliation in the cases of civil war, as opposed to international conflicts such as the Arab Israeli conflict? How does a process of reconciliation take place in one conflict in a region plagued by several ongoing and now interdependent conflicts? How do national memorializations affect the possibility of reconciliation between warring national groups? How does realpolitik affect, circumscribe, limit, influence, and postpone the possibility of reconciliation?

The death in 2002 of Elie Hobeika in Lebanon reveals the extraordinary interplay and complexity of these questions. The Maronite Christian Hobeika was widely accused of having perpetrated, with Israeli collusion, the massacre of over a thousand unarmed and defenseless Palestinian civilians, mostly old men, women, and children, at the refugee camps of Sabra and Shatila following the Israeli invasion of Lebanon in the summer of 1982. The invasion was led by Ariel Sharon, now the elected prime minister of Israel, and it occurred amidst a Lebanese civil war that is now officially over. Hobeika, like many other militia leaders, took advantage of a general 1991 Lebanese amnesty law that forgave the vast majority of political crimes committed during the civil war under the rubric of letting bygones be bygones. No warlords save one were prosecuted; they were immune from censure and thrived on what Soyinka has described (in the Nigerian case) as a "culture of impunity" (Soyinka 1999) because the civil war amnesty had come at the price of a total evisceration of any pretense of justice for the victims of civil war. Postwar Lebanon has been dominated by a politics of forgetting (letting bygones be bygones) without amnesia, a "deal" between warlords, a deal that reflected not only the realpolitik of Lebanon, but also the exhaustion of a war-weary Lebanese people who seemed overwhelmingly (and quite naturally) to want to put the civil war "behind" them. It is in this context, then, that Hobeika became a minister (at different times, of social affairs and the handicapped, of the displaced, and of water and electricity); the price paid for Lebanese "reconciliation" and an end to civil war included the forgetting of the crimes committed by Elie Hobeika. He scuba dived, drove fancy cars, and lived the good life.

Until, that is, his assassination in January 2002. A car bomb killed him, three of his bodyguards, and a civilian. Here the process of Lebanese reconciliation with its own seemingly insurmountable official wall of silence around what happened during the civil war and why (in the name of national unity and civil peace) directly clashed with an altogether different process at work, that of the manifestly unresolved Palestinian-Israeli conflict. In the two years preceding Hobeika's death, Palestinian and Lebanese survivors of the Sabra and Shatila massacre, led by a Lebanese Maronite lawyer, filed a suit against Ariel Sharon and others, including Hobeika, in a Belgian court. According to a 1993 Belgian law, Belgian courts arrogated to themselves universal jurisdiction over crimes against humanity, regardless of where the crime itself had been committed or by whom (King-Irani 2003). As the case slowly inched forward despite vehement Israeli protests, Hobeika repeatedly announced that he was prepared to testify before the Belgian court. He insisted that he was innocent and that he would "reveal the truth" about what happened at the Sabra and Shatila camps.

In the meantime, Ariel Sharon had provocatively "visited" the Haram al-Sharif (Temple Mount) in September 2000, thus setting off the second Palestinian *intifada*, and had then gone on to become the democratically elected prime minister of Israel. Hobeika's assassination by unknown agents brings all the contradictions of the process of memory, violence, and reconciliation to the fore. An alleged mass murderer is killed. Is this justice? Hobeika was posthumously awarded the National Order of the Cedars with the rank of commander. Lebanese "reconciliation" demanded silence on the largest single massacre of Palestinian civilians in the history of the Arab-Israeli conflict; yet Palestinian memories of this massacre sparked not only Israeli concern regarding the indictment by a European court of their prime minister—who had a very different memory of Sabra and Shatila, namely, that he was not responsible for supposedly age-old Lebanese tribalism and that, in any event, there had been several hundred Palestinian "terrorists" hiding in the camps—but also threatened to undermine the very basis of the Lebanese sectarian deal on reconciliation.

It is clear from Hobeika's history as well as, for example, from the cases examined by Makdisi, Robinson, and Peleikis in this volume that all processes of reconciliation putatively involve a taming of the violent politics of memory. Yet it is also manifestly clear that the qualitative aspects of processes of reconciliation are shaped by the credibility of its agents. In the case of South Africa, the towering figure of Desmond Tutu genuinely believed that the Truth and Reconciliation Commission had, in fact, a "marked therapeutic effect" on the victims of Apartheid who were allowed to testify because they were integral to the "healing truth" that the commission led by the independent Tutu sought to produce (Tutu 1999: 26–27). Susan Sylomovics (2001) has demonstrated that the Moroccan amnesty law and truth commission lacks a credible figure such as Tutu to lead the process, and is designed from the outset to shield the government rather than to expose its crimes. Unlike the TRC model that advocates openness with all its limitations, we see in the Middle East that the processes of reconciliation have been engineered to be closed and highly staged. This also reflects a balance, or rather an imbalance, between the forces of an open civil society and transparency and the far more powerful forces of the illiberal state. Hence in Lebanon, Hobeika can be awarded the National Order of the Cedars, and can be eulogized by the Maronite Patriarch as a man who "never closed his heart to those in need" (*Daily Star* 28 January 2002). Hence justice for his alleged crimes and those of the current Israeli prime minister had to be sought outside the countries in the Middle East, in Europe, and specifically in a country that had itself (until pressured by the United States to gut its law in June 2003) sought to apply the principle of universal jurisdiction to make partial amends for its own excessively violent and unaccounted for colonial past in Africa.

What needs to be asked is why this difference between the TRC, with all its limitations, and the cynical Lebanese model which is based on Soyinka's "culture of impunity"? One answer may lie in identifying the role of defeat, the perception of defeat (or lack thereof), the acknowledgement of defeat or the refusal to do so, following a violent conflict. Here the case of postwar Japan (Dower 2000) illustrates how a perception of defeat shapes a process of postwar reconciliation, albeit not between equals but between victors and vanquished.

John Dower has used the evocative phrase "embracing defeat" to indicate how Japanese were forced to structure their memories of the unprecedented violence of World War II and the unimaginable destruction of Japan around the U.S. military occupation of their country. As with the Germans following the defeat of Nazism, the Japanese were forced by the Americans to confront their recent past, but as Dower proves, within the constraints of American Cold War politics and American racial assumptions about allegedly inferior Asian cultures. The Japanese government, for example, was aware of the "victor's justice" played out at the Tokyo Tribunals, which led to the hangings of several hundred Japanese; they also participated in creating a sense of what Dower has described as "loser's justice" (2000: 474–484). Taking stock of the general parameters set up by the American prosecutors at the Tokyo Tribunals, postwar Japanese governments and society sought to limit the memories of Japanese militarism to a small clique of wartime leaders, thereby exculpating the Japanese emperor himself. They also sought to limit the memory of crimes to those committed against the ultimately victorious Allies but not against the hundreds of thousands of so-called Korean "comfort women." Similarly, although the modality of the South African TRC reflected the fact that the transition to democracy in South Africa was the result of a negotiated settlement, the TRC's existence was only possible with the total discrediting of the Apartheid system. The contradictions of the TRC reflected the total defeat of the Apartheid idea of racial segregation but also the fact that the Apartheid system was not overcome militarily but politically.

In the Middle East, no such total defeats of ideas or structures have yet been acknowledged. Of course the Palestinians have been the main losers in the Arab-Israeli conflict, but they have neither accepted nor reconciled themselves to total defeat. Indeed their very national aspirations are premised on a remarkably successful overturning of the Zionist narrative that has actively denied their presence or coherence as a national people, as Piterberg demonstrates in his essay on the Israeli language used to describe the so-called "refugee problem" following the 1948 war. The process of Palestinian–Israeli reconciliation, if it is ever to come about, might well have to be based on a "negotiated surrender" of the Palestinians as Marc H. Ellis (1999) has written. This manner of "embracing defeat" might acknowledge at some level the irreversible nature of the 1948 defeat without acquiescing to the current Israeli occupation, and without forfeiting a Palestinian right to compensation or return. This, in turn, might lead the way to a sharing of historic Palestine between Israelis and Palestinians.

In the case of Lebanon, the civil war officially ended by the invoking of former Lebanese prime minister Saeb Salam's famous dictum of "no victor, no vanquished," which explicitly tied a notion of reconciliation to an understanding of war without victors. Yet as Peleikis writes, this notion of reconciliation—symbolized in the Beirut downtown reconstruction project overseen by the private company Solidere that has attempted to efface all traces of the civil war—is confronted daily with its own failure as villagers and city dwellers remember the war, with victors and vanquished, without necessarily articulating this memory verbally, coherently, or singularly.

In the end, then, what is at issue is the tension between the deconstruction of official memories of violence and the realpolitik of processes of conflict resolution and reconciliation. Whereas social critics operate under a moral imperative to examine state-imposed politics of amnesia in order to reveal those popular memories of struggle written out of the history books, their criticism can often run counter to the needs for closure that underwrite pragmatic concerns of terminating conflict and/or postwar state-building. Memory projects that rake the coals of the forgotten run the risk of rekindling the dying embers of past conflicts. When victims of colonial expropriation become reinterpreted as martyrs to a present *intifada*, the groundwork for unending conflict is laid. How many deaths, Bowman wonders in his essay in this volume, must Basem Rishmawi—the Beit Sahour resident perhaps killed by Israeli security forces or by a member of a rival *hamula*, depending on which story one is to believe—suffer? An interminable number, perhaps, until a hegemonic narrative of the Israeli-Arab conflict is internalized into the everyday practices and historical consciousness of Israeli and Palestinian citizens alike. Whether a middle ground exists between the hegemony of memory and the brutality of violence in the context of the illiberal state regimes of the Middle East remains an open and productive question that the essays in this book seek to address.

Organization of Chapters

The contributors to this volume explore the enduring character of individual and group experiences of violence and struggle from a variety of geographic perspectives and theoretical angles. They draw on a wide variety of ethnographic, historical, and literary materials in the analysis of particular conflicts. While the chapters focus individually on the Franco-Algerian war, the Lebanese civil war, and the Arab-Israeli conflict, the volume emphasizes the more general processes of memory, violence, and reconciliation that link these separate cases, that bind the Middle East and North Africa as a region. Rather than any ascribed primordial cultural or religious commonality of the region, it is precisely these historical processes—as situated in the context and legacy of Ottoman and European imperialism and their aftermath—that constitute the southern and eastern shores of the Mediterranean as a single object of contestation and, hence, analysis. In this respect, as the volume argues implicitly, the Arab-Israeli conflict cannot and should not be treated as an isolated case, but rather needs to be understood as part of a larger dynamic of struggle over the representation and ownership of history and territory that affects the Middle East and North Africa as a whole.

The organization of this volume underlines this unity of regional concerns, clustering chapters around the overlapping themes of "violence and sacrifice," "resolution and reconciliation," and "the archaeology of memory." This thematic order reflects a temporal movement from enactment of violence, through the efforts of resolution, to the practices of commemoration. Clearly, these distinctions are not absolute, and individual chapters often address the very interpenetration of processes of violence, reconciliation, and memory in particular historical and ethnographic instances. Nonetheless, the clusters—in each grouping together essays focusing individually on Israel/Palestine, Lebanon, and Algeria—do illustrate how instances of conflict across time and space within the region continue to inform each other and determine larger prospects for resolution, if not reconciliation. Such prospects are not always positive, and the book expresses a certain amount of pessimism about the role of state actors in promoting the perpetual peace about which Immanuel Kant dreamed so many years ago. That said, by exploring the persistence of plural memories and the numerous local-level efforts at addressing past wrongs and promoting future rights, the chapters that follow indicate areas where at least partial peaces are in the making.

Notes

1. Glenn Bowman (1994a, 1994b, 2001) has noted the role of violence in fomenting Manichean logics of identity in Palestine and the former Yugoslavia. See also his chapter in this volume.

2. In addition to *Pearl Harbor*, one could cite Steven Spielberg's *Saving Private Ryan* and Tom Brokaw's coffee table book, *The Greatest Generation*, as underwriting a renewed nostalgia for unproblematic American patriotism. Indeed, the irreality (or perhaps hyperreality) of the live television images of the attack bore distinct features of the *déjà-vu*, as a monstrous concatenation of clichéd images drawn from Hollywood disaster films and Tom Clancy techno-spy thrillers. Slavoj Žižek similarly noted this play of the "real" and the "irreal" in American nationalism in his Web article, "Welcome to the Desert of the Real!" (2001), written three days after the World Trade Center attack.

3. For Palestine, see Said 1999, 2000. For Algeria, see Stora 2001 and chapter in this volume. For Morocco, see Slyomovics 2001.

4. Compare to public apologies by Germany to the Jewish people for the Holocaust, by the U.S. President Bill Clinton to African Americans for slavery, and by Japan Prime Minister Miyazawa to Korea and the Philippines for the bonding of military sex slaves ("comfort women") during the second World War. On the contested politics of Holocaust memory and the larger process of German reparations (*Wiedergutmachen*), see Bartov 1996; Cole 1999; Finkelstein 2000; Friedlander 1993; Hartman 1994; LaCapra 1994, 1998; Novick 1999; Pross 1998; Vidal-Nacquet 1992; Wiedmer 1999; Young 1993. On the American debate over slavery reparations, see Horowitz 2001; Robinson 2000. On "comfort women" in the Japanese military, see Choi 1997; Hicks 1995; Tanaka 2001; Yoshimi 2000.

5. For a study of village-level commemorative practices in Israel/Palestine, see Slyomovics 1998. For a foundational anthropological discussion of memory in relation to an earlier period of Palestinian national activism, see Swedenburg 1995.

6. See Allen 2004 for an engaging ethnographic account of the polyvalent politics of Palestinian martyr funerals.

7. These works range in approach from the phenomenological (Appadurai 1998;

Das 1990, 1997; Feldman 1991; Malkki 1995; Scarry 1985) to the semiotic (Brass 1997; Daniel 1996; Gilsenan 1996) to the transactional (Roy 1994; Tambiah 1996) to the statist (Rejali 1994) to the historical (Makdisi 2000; Nirenberg 1996).

8. Previous scholars have examined how social memory comes to be embodied in public performances (Connerton 1989; Fentress and Wickham 1992), landscapes (Nora 1984), literatures (Fischer 1986), images (Matsuda 1996), ideologies (Gluck 1987), monuments (Sherman 1999), and even domestic architecture (Bahloul 1996 [1992]). Moreover, drawing on contexts of conflict and struggle, they have explored the relationship between memory, violence, and structures of power (Boyarin 1994, 1996; Rappaport 1990; Werbner 1998).

9. For a discussion of the narrative construction of nationness, see Homi Bhabha's introduction to his collection, *Nation and Narration* (1990). For a discussion of the "postnational" and its relation to imagination and fantasy, see Appadurai 1996.

References Cited

Abu El-Haj, Nadia. 2002. *Facts on the Ground.* Chicago: University of Chicago Press.

Abu-Lughod, Ibrahim, Roger Heacock, and Khaled Neshaf. 1999. *Landscape in Palestine: Equivocal Poetry.* Birzeit: Birzeit University Press.

Abu-Lughod, Janet. 1980. *Rabat: Urban Apartheid in Morocco.* Princeton: Princeton University Press.

Allen, Lori. 2004. The Polyvalent Politics of Martyr Funerals in the Palestinian Intifada. Unpublished manuscript.

Anderson, Benedict. 1991. *Imagined Communities: Reflections on the Origin and Spread of Nationalism.* London: Verso.

Appadurai, Arjun. 1998. Dead Certainty: Ethnic Violence in the Era of Globalization. *Public Culture* 10 (2): 225–247.

———. 1996. *Modernity at Large: Cultural Dimensions of Globalization.* Minneapolis: University of Minnesota Press.

Bahloul, Joelle. 1996 [1992]. *The Architecture of Memory.* Cambridge: Cambridge University Press.

Bartov, Omar. 1996. *Murder in Our Midst: The Holocaust, Industrial Killing, and Representation.* New York: Oxford University Press.

Bhabha, Homi K. 1990. Introduction: Narrating the Nation. In *Nation and Narration,* ed. Homi K. Bhabha, pp. 1–7. New York: Routledge.

Bowman, Glenn. 2001. Thinking the Unthinkable: Anthropological Meditations on the Events of 11 September 2001. *Anthropology Today* 17 (6): 16–19.

———. 1994a. Xenophobia, Phantasy and the Nation: The Logic of Ethnic Violence in Former Yugoslavia. In *Anthropology of Europe: Identity and Boundaries in Conflict,* ed. Victoria Goddard, Llobera Josep, and Chris Shore, pp. 148–171. Oxford: Berg Press.

———. 1994b. "A Country of Words": Conceiving the Palestinian Nation from a Position of Exile. In *The Making of Political Identities,* ed. Ernesto Laclau, pp. 138–170. London: Verso.

Boyarin, Jonathan. 1996. *Palestine and Jewish History.* Minneapolis: University of Minnesota Press.

———, ed. 1994. *Remapping Memory: The Politics of TimeSpace.* Minneapolis: University of Minnesota Press.

Brass, Paul. 1997. *Theft of an Idol: Text and Context in the Representation of Collective Violence.* Princeton: Princeton University Press.

Bruner, Edward M. 1986. Ethnography as Narrative. In *The Anthropology of Experience,* ed. Victor W. Turner and Edward M. Bruner, pp. 139–155. Urbana: University of Illinois Press.

Çelik, Zeynep. 1997. *Urban Forms and Colonial Confrontations: Algiers under French Rule.* Berkeley: University of California Press.

Choi, Chungmoo, ed. 1997. *The Comfort Women: Colonialism, War and Sex.* Durham: Duke University Press.

Cole, Tim. 1999. *Selling the Holocaust: From Auschwitz to Schindler, How History Is Bought, Packaged, and Sold.* New York: Routledge.

Comaroff, Jean, and John Comaroff. 1992. *Ethnography and the Historical Imagination.* Boulder: Westview Press.

Connerton, Paul. 1989. *How Societies Remember.* Cambridge: Cambridge University Press.

Daniel, E. Valentine. 1996. *Charred Lullabies: Chapters in an Anthropography of Violence.* Princeton: Princeton University Press.

Das, Veena. 1997. Language and Body: Transactions in the Construction of Pain. In *Social Suffering,* ed. Veena Das, Arthur Kleinman, and Margaret Lock, pp. 67–91. Berkeley: University of California Press.

———. 1990. *Mirrors of Violence: Communities, Riots and Survivors in South Asia.* Delhi: Oxford University Press.

Dower, John W. 2000. *Embracing Defeat: Japan in the Wake of World War II.* New York: Norton.

Durkheim, Emile. 1995 [1912]. *The Elementary Forms of Religious Life.* Trans. Karen E. Fields. New York: Free Press.

Ellis, Marc H. 1999. *O, Jerusalem: The Contested Future of the Jewish Covenant.* Minneapolis: Fortress Press.

Fanon, Frantz. 1965. *A Dying Colonialism.* New York: Grove Press.

———. 1963. *The Wretched of the Earth.* New York: Grove Weidenfeld.

Feldman, Allen. 1991. *Formations of Violence: The Narrative of the Body and Political Terror in Northern Ireland.* Chicago: University of Chicago Press.

Fentress, James and Chris Wickham. 1992. *Social Memory.* Oxford: Basil Blackwell.

Finkelstein, Norman. 2000. *The Holocaust Industry: Reflections on the Exploitation of Jewish Suffering.* London: Verso.

Fischer, Michael M. J. 1986. Ethnography and the Post-Modern Arts of Memory. In *Writing Culture: The Poetics and Politics of Ethnography,* ed. James Clifford and George E. Marcus, pp. 194–233. Berkeley: University of California Press.

Friedlander, Saul. 1993. *Memory, History, and the Extermination of the Jews of Europe.* Bloomington: Indiana University Press.

Geertz, Clifford. 1973. Deep Play: Notes on the Balinese Cockfight. In *The Interpretation of Cultures.* New York: Basic Books.

Gilsenan, Michael. 1996. *Lords of the Lebanese Marches: Violence and Narrative in an Arab Society.* Berkeley: University of California Press.

Gluck, Carol. 1987. *Japan's Modern Myths: Ideology in the Late Meiji Period.* Princeton: Princeton University Press.

Halbwachs, Maurice. 1980. *The Collective Memory.* New York: Harper and Row.

Hartman, Geoffrey, ed. 1994. *Holocaust Remembrance: The Shape of Memory.* Oxford: Blackwell.

Hicks, Geroge. 1995. *The Comfort Women: Japan's Brutal Regime of Enforced Prostitution in the Second World War.* New York: Norton.

Horowitz, David. 2001. *Uncivil Wars: The Controversy over Reparation for Slavery.* San Francisco: Encounter Books.

Khalaf, Samir. 2002. *Civil and Uncivil Violence in Lebanon: A History of the Internationalization of Communal Contact.* New York: Columbia University Press.

King-Irani, Laurie. 2003. The Sabra and Shatila Case in Belgium: A Guide for the Perplexed. http://www.indictsharon.net. Accessed on 11 August 2004.

LaCapra, Dominick. 1998. *History and Memory after Auschwitz.* Ithaca: Cornell University Press.

———. 1994. *Representing the Holocaust: History, Theory, Trauma.* Ithaca: Cornell University Press.

Lewis, Bernard. 2004. *From Babel to Dragomans: Interpreting the Middle East.* New York: Oxford University Press.

Maalouf, Amin. 1984. *The Crusades through Arab Eyes.* New York: Schocken Books.

Makdisi, Saree. 1997. Laying Claim to Beirut: Urban Narrative and Spatial Identity in the Age of Solidere. *Critical Inquiry* 23 (3): 661–682.

Makdisi, Ussama. 2000. *The Culture of Sectarianism: Community, History, and Violence in Nineteenth-Century Ottoman Lebanon.* California: University of California Press.

Malkki, Liisa H. 1995. *Purity and Exile: Violence, Memory, and National Cosmology among Hutu Refugees in Tanzania.* Chicago: University of Chicago Press.

Marx, Karl. 1963. *The Eighteenth Brumaire of Louis Bonaparte.* New York: International Publishers.

Matsuda, Matt K. 1996. *The Memory of the Modern.* Oxford: Oxford University Press.

Nirenberg, David. 1996. *Communities of Violence: Persecution of Minorities in the Middle Ages.* Princeton: Princeton University Press.

Nora, Pierre, ed. 1984. *Les lieux de mémoire.* Paris: Gallimard.

Novick, Peter. 1999. *The Holocaust in American Life.* Boston: Houghton Mifflin.

Nuttall, Sarah, and Carli Coetzee. 1998. *Negotiating the Past: The Making of Memory in South Africa.* Cape Town: Oxford University Press.

Pross, Christian. 1998. *Paying for the Past: The Struggle over Reparations for Surviving Victims of the Nazi Terror.* Baltimore: Johns Hopkins University Press.

Rabinow, Paul. 1989. *French Modern. Norms and Forms of the Social Environment.* Cambridge, Mass.: MIT Press.

Rappaport, Joanne. 1990. *The Politics of Memory: Native Historical Interpretation in the Colombian Andes.* New York: Cambridge University Press.

Rejali, Darius. 1994. *Torture and Modernity: Self, Society and State in Modern Iran.* Boulder: Westview Press.

Renan, Ernest. 1990 [1882]. What Is a Nation? In *Nation and Narration,* ed. Homi Bhabha, pp. 8–22. London: Routledge.

Rigby, Andrew. 2001. *Justice and Reconciliation after the Violence*. Boulder: Lynne Rienner.

Robinson, Randall. 2000. *The Debt: What America Owes to Blacks*. New York: Plume.

Rowe, Peter G., and Hashim Sarkis. 1998. *Projecting Beirut: Episodes in the Construction and Reconstruction of a Modern City*. Munich: Prestel.

Roy, Beth. 1994. *Some Trouble with Cows: Making Sense of Social Conflict*. Berkeley: University of California Press.

Sahlins, Marshall. 1985. *Islands of History*. Chicago: University of Chicago Press.

Said, Edward. 2000. *The End of the Peace Process: Oslo and After*. New York: Pantheon.

———. 1999. Truth and Reconciliation. *New York Times Magazine*, January 10.

Sherman, Daniel. 1999. *The Construction of Memory in Interwar France*. Chicago: University of Chicago Press.

Silverstein, Paul. 2000. Franco-Algerian War and Remembrance: Discourse, Nationalism, and Post-Coloniality. In *Francophone Studies: Discourse and Identity*, ed. Kamal Salhi. Exeter: Elm Bank Publications.

Slyomovics, Susan. 2001. A Truth Commission for Morocco. *Middle East Report* 218: 18–21.

———. 1998. *The Object of Memory: Arabs and Jews Narrate the Palestinian Village*. Philadelphia: University of Pennsylvania Press.

Soyinka, Wole. 1999. *The Burden of Memory, the Muse of Forgiveness*. New York: Oxford University Press.

Stora, Benjamin. 2001. *La guerre invisible. Algérie, années 90*. Paris: Presses de Sciences Politiques.

———. 1995. *L'Algérie en 1995. La guerre, l'histoire, la politique*. Paris: Editions Michalon.

———. 1991. *La gangrène et l'oubli. La mémoire de la guerre d'Algérie*. Paris: Editions La Découverte.

Swedenburg, Ted. 1995. *Memories of Revolt: The 1936–1939 Rebellion and the Palestinian National Past*. Minneapolis: University of Minnesota Press.

Tambiah, Stanley J. 1996. *Leveling Crowds: Ethnonationalist Conflicts and Collective Violence in South Asia*. Berkeley: University of California Press.

Tanaka, Toshiyuki. 2001. *Japan's Comfort Women: Sexual Slavery and Prostitution during World War II*. New York: Routledge.

Thompson, Elizabeth. 2000. *Colonial Citizens: Republican Rights, Paternal Privilege and Gender in French Syria and Lebanon*. New York: Columbia University Press.

Tutu, Desmond Mpilo. 1999. *No Future without Forgiveness*. New York: Doubleday.

Vidal-Nacquet, Pierre. 1992. *Assassins of Memory*. New York: Columbia University Press.

Werbner, Richard, ed. 1998. *Memory and the Postcolony: African Anthropology and the Critique of Power*. London: Zed Books.

Wiedmer, Caroline. 1999. *The Claims of Memory: Representing the Holocaust in Contemporary Germany and France*. Ithaca: Cornell University Press.

Wright, Gwendolyn. 1991. *The Politics of Design in French Urban Colonialism*. Chicago: University of Chicago Press.

Yoshimi, Yoshiaki. 2000. *Comfort Women: Sexual Slavery in the Japanese Military during World War II*. New York: Columbia University Press.

Young, James Edward. 1993. *The Texture of Memory: Holocaust Memorials and Meaning in Europe, Israel, and America*. New Haven: Yale University Press.

Zerubavel, Yael. 1995. *Recovered Roots: Collective Memory and the Making of Israeli National Tradition.* Chicago: University of Chicago Press.

Žižek, Slavoj. 2001. Welcome to the Desert of the Real. *Re:constructions: Reflections on Humanity and Media after Tragedy,* 15 September. http://web.mit.edu/cms/reconstructions/interpretations/desertreal.html.

Part One.

Violence and Sacrifice

1 A Death Revisited: Solidarity and Dissonance in a Muslim-Christian Palestinian Community

Glenn Bowman

Many observers of—as well as many participants in—the first Palestinian *intifada* (literally "shaking off") saw the harbingers of a new Middle East in the radical forms of social and political organization thrown up by West Bank and Gazan Palestinians against the continuation of Israeli dominion over their homeland. Edward Said saw the disappearance of social fragmentation, the marginalization of old forms of social organizations, and the elevation of women in the struggle to roles equivalent to those of men as "momentous changes . . . [which will] surely have an effect throughout the Middle East as the twentieth century approaches its end" (Said 1989: 21). Such enthusiasm, however, began to erode as the *intifada* changed character in its latter years and after the *intifada* was called off following the secret Oslo Palestinian-Israeli negotiations. Glenn Robinson's *Building a Palestinian State: The Incomplete Revolution*, written in 1995, expresses in its title the frustration felt by many as the Palestine National Authority began to consolidate its rule and halt that early radicalism's already faltering momentum. By 1998, Lisa Taraki was noting that, despite the radical reworkings of Palestinian society affected by widespread communal mobilization against the occupation, the changes were not irreversible: "Traditional forces may assert or reassert themselves in different times and different forms. . . . There are some indications that there may be a revival of the *hamula* [clan or extended family][1] structure in the areas of social support and political life" (Taraki 1998: n.p.). This essay gives particular attention to "the revival of the hamula structure" in the dynamics of everyday life in the period between the first and second *intifada*s, and shows how political decisions on the national and international level shaped and constrained local political decisions so as to defeat moves toward using radical *intifada*-period means of envisaging community and dealing with conflict. In stressing that the ascendancy of traditional forces in community life was—and continues to be—deeply contested, I seek to show the local community as an active, deeply political arena for assessing situations and engendering solutions and suggest that there is nothing inherently stable about the current hegemony of the "traditional." To once again cite

Taraki's assessment of the state of contemporary Palestinian society, the "hegemony [of traditional forces] over political life is not a matter that has been settled, even in the short term" (Taraki 1998: n.p.).

* * *

The sheer brutality of the events remains. Sometime between 8 P.M. and 9 P.M. on 23 March 1981, Basem Rishmawi left his fiancée's home in the West Bank town of Beit Sahour to walk the short distance to his family's house. He never arrived. Five days later a late night call from the Bethlehem offices of the Israeli military police announced to his family that Basem's body had been found on 25 March in the vicinity of the town dump. According to the Shin Bet officer who called, a military investigation had revealed that Rishmawi had been killed while preparing a bomb that had exploded prematurely. He announced that the body would be delivered that night to the Greek Orthodox church for interment. Soldiers, arriving before the body, allowed perhaps only a dozen people—immediate family members and a priest—into the church and it was these who were able to briefly examine the corpse when it was delivered at approximately 1:30 A.M. on 29 March. It was immediately clear that there was something wrong with the officer's story; although the body had been dismembered by an explosion, there seemed to be no connection between the damage that force had caused and other wounds such as heavy bruising on the face, multiple penetration wounds, and deep gouging—seemingly caused by brutally tight binding—on the wrists. As the mourners whispered amongst themselves that it appeared as though a bomb had been set off in or next to the body after death, armed soldiers watched over the brief funeral and the subsequent entombment in the family plot.

* * *

I first encountered Basem's name and image in January 1990 after members of one of the town's numerous *intifada* "committees" had smuggled me into the town past roadblocks erected by the military authorities to enforce a siege imposed in response to Beit Sahour's protracted maintenance of a tax strike.[2] Hung in a place of honor on the wall of the reception room of a house that my "guides" had brought me to was a picture of a solemn-looking young man. When I asked about it, I was told the story of Basem's killing, and it was made clear that—although no one knew whether he had been killed by Jewish settlers or by Israeli soldiers—he was an arbitrarily chosen victim of Israeli oppression of Palestinians: "it could have happened to anybody, and by chance the victim was Basem."[3]

I would come across Basem's picture again and again in the following days as I interviewed people whose houses and shops had been stripped by squads of soldiers led by tax collectors, whose husbands, fathers, sons, or daughters had been imprisoned or were moving from house to house avoiding arrest, and whose will to revolt was fanned by the government's attempts to break a town that Palestinians in Jerusalem characterized as "tougher than Gaza." During that week, informants repeatedly asserted that all Beit Sahouris—and by extension all Palestinians—were rendered the same by the hostile activities of a occupying force that did not distinguish between Muslim or Christian, male or female, young or old, rich or poor. A Christian shopkeeper told me, "There is no difference; we are under the same conditions, the same oppression, the same hopes, the same policy . . . the occupation does not differentiate between Muslim and Christian," and later a Muslim schoolteacher said, "We live together as the same people; we feel there is another one who is enemy to us both."

Basem—who had apparently been kidnapped, tortured to death, and then dismembered by his Israeli captors so that his remains could bear the brand "terrorist"—stood as a sort of Palestinian Everyman. He—like other Beit Sahouris before him—had already suffered the martyrdom Palestinians under occupation could see as their fate so long as the logic of the Zionist occupation of Palestine held sway. When a soldier dropped a building block from a guard post on the roof of a three-story building onto the head of Edmond Ghanem on 18 July 1988, Beit Sahouris saw yet more evidence of a systematic program of extermination mobilized against them and strengthened their resolve to protect themselves by uniting to fight the common enemy. Symptomatic of this collectively espoused resolve was the 1993 calendar published by the Arab Orthodox Club displaying, beneath an image of Beit Sahour with its mosque and Catholic and Orthodox churches, photographs of seventeen Beit Sahouris who shared not their religious affiliation but the fact that they, Muslim and Christian alike, had been martyred (six in 1992) by the forces of occupation.[4]

The idiom of martyrdom became the language of community during the early days of the *intifada*. One man, speaking of hearing of the Gaza killings that had sparked the *intifada*,[5] claimed that his first thought was "why am I not this man?" He knew Israeli soldiers killed Palestinians simply because they were Palestinians, and as a Palestinian he was sure it was just an accident of time and place that prevented him from being one of the victims: "We see that one day it is one person, and the next day another. The following day it may be us, so we say *hellas* [enough] and begin to work to stop it." The soldier's (or settler's) undifferentiating gaze here creates a defensive "Palestinian" identity out of a society that, without that antagonism, might not have discerned a unity within the congeries of identities constituted by allegiances to family, class, religion, and locale (Bowman 2003: 322–327).

Loss and victimization at the hands of the collective enemy became, in the context of the *intifada*, elements of a prestige economy. As I stood in the midst of scattered clothing, bedding, and broken furniture left behind after a tax raid on the apartment of a couple who ran a small electrical goods shop, the woman told me that "The people who have not had their things confiscated by the tax men are envious of those who have; it's like building a new house." In this *potlatch*-like counter-economy[6] status accrued to those who "gave freely" (and aggressively) to the enemy (Mauss 1969: 31–45), and "new houses"—stripped and desecrated by predatory military assaults—took the place of the tidy apartments and small houses of the pre-*intifada* years. Over the previous twenty years, Beit Sahour had extensively developed an infrastructure of small local industry (much of it finishing clothing for the Israeli market) that had considerably raised the general standard of living above that of other West Bank communities. In 1990, however, people prided themselves in throwing back at the Israelis the wealth that had come to seem no more than payment for accepting occupation. Beit Sahouris played a vanguard role in the uprising by refusing to pay taxes to the occupying government and by systematically disengaging from the Israeli economy. The Israeli response was draconian, but a recently plundered pharmacist told me that "If the Bedouin can live in tents, so can we. We have our agriculture and it is very good. The *Jerusalem Post* called us the 'Japan of the Palestine/Israel' but we can lose all that and go back to the fields."[7]

Landscape, history, sectarianism, and social organization were reworked in popular discourses that circulated through and constituted the self-professedly revolutionary community of that period. Parts of the town that had previously been designated by topographic features or by the names of important persons or families who had lived in the area were renamed so as to resonate with the myths of Palestinian resistance. The town's highest sector (previously known as the *ras* or "head") was renamed "Shqif Castle" so as to recall a famed Palestinian victory, while other sectors of the town became "Tall al-Za'tar" and "Shatila" to evoke militant refugee camps in Lebanon.[8] When people spoke of local history they accentuated stories of coordinated resistance by the townspeople to earlier oppressions. I collected numerous accounts of Beit Sahour's resistance to the Ottoman draft during World War I, of Muslims and Christians marching together to the shrine of Nabi Musa to oppose the British Mandate, of an Orthodox priest who cached arms to fight the British during the 1936–1939 revolt, of Baathist, Nasserite, and finally Communist demonstrations against the Jordanian occupation, and of the long history of Beit Sahour's support for the Popular and Democratic Fronts during the period of Israeli hegemony. In these, the *we* of an historic and enduring community was reified and affirmed.[9] Underplayed in—or simply excluded from—these narratives were past clashes with local Bedouin communities (the *ta'amra*), disputes over landownership, struggles between classes, feuding between family groups, and the divisive responses of local Christians and Muslims to the differentiating policies of the various colonizing powers that had dominated the town.

These stories celebrated Beit Sahour's overcoming of the temptation to divide along the lines provided by the townspersons' various religious affiliations. In 1984, the Beit Sahouri population stood at 8,900 persons, of which 17 percent were Sunni Muslim, 67 percent were Greek Orthodox, 8 percent were Roman Catholic, 6 percent were Greek Catholic, and 2 percent were Lutheran (Pena 1984).[10] An Orthodox member of the medical committee that had smuggled me into town (itself composed of a Muslim, two Orthodox Christians, and one Latin) made the following representative statement:

It is you outside who try to make a difference between the Christians and the Muslims. We are a people, we all go to each other's feasts, we visit with each other, we live the same life. We are one people.

That intercommunality was evident in public manifestations of solidarity such as the annual joint Christian–Muslim scout marches on Christmas day and the decision of the committees organizing the "Day of Prayer for Peace" on 5 November 1989 to invite Shaykh Saʿid al-Din al-ʿAlami, Mufti of Jerusalem and head of the Islamic Council, to announce from the pulpit of Beit Sahour's Orthodox Church a *fatwa* (religious ruling) against the purchase of confiscated Sahouri goods that Israeli tax officials were putting up for auction in Tel Aviv. The municipality erected a nondenominational municipal shrine over the site of recent apparitions of the Virgin Mary (Bowman 1993: 448–451). That shrine's caretaker, an Orthodox man employed by the municipality, asserted, "we are here Muslim and Christian, there are two Christian groups. The Municipality builds for all the people and the people all own and use the well."

During the *intifada,* local political activities were organized by thirty-five "neighborhood committees" representing that same number of neighborhoods. The activities of these committees were coordinated, and issues pertaining to the whole of the town were dealt with by the *sulha,* a parallel municipal authority established in 1989. Previously, Beit Sahour's internal political structures had been based on those of the town's clans. Issues arising within a family or between families were debated in family forums and then forwarded through a clan elder to the municipal council (constituted of representatives of the eight major families, six of which were Christian and two Muslim). This familial locus ensured that municipal engagement in local issues pertained either to interfamilial or intersectarian disputes. Neighborhood committee membership was, however, decided by local elections that—in a town whose considerable twentieth-century expansion had ensured that most neighborhoods were made up of two or more clan groupings—blunted the salience of *hamula* groupings and focused committee discussions on concerns determined by place rather than kin affiliation; healthcare, security, water, electricity, food, income for the families of people killed, injured or imprisoned, and so on. The *sulha*'s executive was elected by representatives of the twenty-two major political, cultural, and social organizations in the town and was concerned with issues pertinent to the town's entirety: raising money to support the needy, settling disputes, coordinating responses to *intifada* situations, and so on (Robinson 1997: 80–81). Thus the idiom of identity shifted from one of *hamula* and sect to one of political struggle and nation.

Basem Rishmawi, although he was Greek Orthodox and a member of the al-Qazaha *hamula,* was throughout the years of *intifada* a symbol for Sahouris of what it meant to be a Palestinian under Israeli occupation. His martyrdom was a spectacular instance of what Palestinians learned from Likud's Sharon and then from Rabin's "iron fist policy" (with its policy of breaking the bones and bulldozing the houses of stone throwers); they realized that this was the fate they too could expect if the occupation were to continue. Basem's sad yet severe gaze joined those of other Sahouri martyrs gazing from the secular iconostases of the poster-bedecked streets, the walls of portrait-dense household reception rooms, and the illustrated calendars (where the dates of martyrs' deaths seemed simultaneous with those of people's presents and futures) over the people of Beit Sahour as they struggled to find ways of celebrating Palestinian identity without following Basem's path to a terrible death in a back road dumping ground.

*   *   *

Basem's name began to circulate again two years after the Oslo Agreements had brought the *intifada* to a close. In the summer of 1995, soon after Israeli troops withdrew from the Bethlehem region (leaving it under the control of the Palestine National Authority), a Sahouri by the name of Faez Qumsiyya was arrested by Palestinian security for nonpolitical criminal activities. Under interrogation, Faez confessed to having been involved—along with his cousin Samer Qumsiyya and a local Muslim—in Basem Rishmawi's murder.

This marked the second time that events related to the death of Basem Rishmawi engaged Beit Sahour: one woman told me, "It was like he had been killed again, and all the Rishmawis and much of the rest of the town went into mourning." This time, however, the story of his killing did not circulate in the midst of burgeoning nationalist mobilization but instead accompanied a "winding down" of commitment and solidarity. Since the heady days of the tax strike, Beit Sahour's fervor had been substantially diminished by the failure of the Palestine Liberation Organization to bulwark commitment in the face of fiercely punitive measures:

> [T]he PLO in Tunis [had] failed to support Bayt Sahur's campaign, as it feared the political consequences of such grassroots initiatives. . . . [Sahouris felt that] Tunis not only did not support Bayt Sahur's efforts but actually tried to thwart them by privately urging others to pay their taxes and by more closely aligning itself with members of the old elite. (Robinson 1997: 88–89)

Communal solidarity was unraveling as those who had already lost considerable amounts of property grew increasingly aggrieved at others who, fearful of finding themselves in similar penury, began covertly to pay their taxes.

After the March 1990 arrests of the remaining committee members of the underground grassroots United National Leadership of the Uprising (which had coordinated *intifada* strategy), the leadership of the uprising was directed from outside by various external groups (Fatah, Democratic Front for the Liberation of Palestine, Popular Front for the Liberation of Palestine, Palestine People's Party) all of which operated semiautonomously under the PLO umbrella. From then on, political activity in Beit Sahour, as elsewhere in the Occupied Territories, was coordinated and carried out by competing political factions paid for their activism and remunerated for their losses by the outside organizations. Many argued this took the revolution away from the people and gave it to the politicians who destroyed it: "The *intifada* was made by those on the street and broken as soon as they began 'throwing stones for money.'" Tendencies toward fragmentation were aggravated by the Oslo settlement. While this failed to ameliorate day-to-day deprivations,[11] it removed Israeli soldiers from the streets and hid the operations of the Israeli security apparatus behind the proxy Palestinian "Preventative Security Force." Everyday evidence of "another one who is enemy to us both" virtually disappeared, and the collective solidarity with which Beit Sahour had faced its enemy began to dissipate as the focus that antagonist had provided diffused.

To understand the role of the antagonist in the formation—and maintenance— of Palestinian identity, one must comprehend the ways in which politicized identities develop out of those forms of identity characteristic of the everyday exchanges of communal life. In the development of Palestinian solidarity, differential aspects of identity—based on religion, class position, *hamula* affiliation, party membership, and even to some degree age and gender—were *subsumed* within an enveloping political and public identity. A contingent political identity came to seem essential, while more ingrained and enduring identities were perceived as secondary or limited in salience. During my fieldwork in Jerusalem's Old City between 1983 and 1985, I observed a discursive shift as Palestinians were forced by increasing hostile attention from soldiers, settlers, and tax collectors to recognize that their communality as "Palestinians" was more salient than the differences religious affiliation opened between them. People who in the early months of my fieldwork had called themselves "Palestinian Christians" or "Palestinian Muslims" pointedly began to reverse the order of the substantive and the adjectival so as to say, "I am not a Palestinian Christian; I am a Christian Palestinian," or, "I am a Palestinian first, then a Muslim" (Bowman 1986: 5).

Outstanding in such identity transformations is the perceived presence of an antagonist that dissolves the differences between those it threatens. What creates the space of perceived communality are not the routines of everyday life structuring and manifesting systems of difference and orchestrating relations between the variant vertical and horizontal role positionings of age, class, gender, education, appearance, and religion, but the presence of an antagonism perceived to threaten all within its purview with either physical extermination or the wholesale extirpation of their differentiated, subsumed identities. Thus, in an example cited by Ernesto Laclau and Chantal Mouffe, "it is because a peasant *cannot be* a peasant that an antagonism exists with the landowner who is expelling him from his land" (1985: 125); without land the practices that make up the *habitus* of a peasant's life are impossible to enact. In such situations the multiplex "being" the antagonism threatens with impossibility shapes itself into an overarching political identity uniting all those who feel themselves at risk.

Although the threat of death figures centrally in the rhetoric evoking antagonism, it is the danger that communal identity will be destroyed that is more significant than actual bodily destruction. The threat Palestinians came to perceive the Israeli state as posing to them was not necessarily the threat of whole-sale genocide (although as incidents in Lebanon showed such genocide was not beyond belief) but what Baruch Kimmerling has recently called "politicide" (Kimmerling 2003: see also van den Berghe 1990). Thus in the Palestinian in-stance, as elsewhere (see Pettigrew 1997), the death of a martyr is powerful be-cause it prefigures the potential extermination of the social body for which the martyr's body stands.

Identity formation through antagonism had been evident in Beit Sahour long before the outbreak of the first *intifada*. However, by the time Faez Qumsiyya confessed to killing Basem Rishmawi, consensus on Israel's antagonism was be-ing eroded not only by factionalization but also by the sense of many that the Palestine National Authority's establishment was the first step of an inexorable progress toward Palestinian statehood. That perception transformed the Israeli state from a force with the disallowing of a Palestinian state and people as its *modus vivendi* to a partner in mutually beneficial contractual relations with a Palestinian entity. *Palestinian*—when no longer the marker of a domain at risk but instead the collective label of those gathered within the embrace of a terri-torially defined state—loses its defensive salience, and new articulations of iden-tity, spawned by new perceptions of antagonism operating *within* the Pales-tinian community rather than *against* that community as a whole, can begin to emerge (see Bowman 1994). It was in such a context that the "second death" of Basem Rishmawi would be interpreted, and acted upon, in ways very different from those that followed on his "first death."

The significant difference between the knowledge which circulated after Basem's "first death" and that which followed his "second" is that while the per-petrators of the "first" were thought to be national "others" (either soldiers or settlers) those who killed Basem the "second" time were Sahouris. The devas-tating implication of that emerges strongly from the response of one informant to my query about the possibility of a revenge killing: "No one in Beit Sahour kills others in Beit Sahour."[12] The fact that the second killing showed precisely that Beit Sahouris could kill Beit Sahouris not only invalidated that adage but threatened to dissolve the community itself.

The description of Basem's killing that emerged was particularly ugly. As Basem got into a car that had stopped to offer him a ride, he was overcome and bound with wire by Faez Qumsiyya, Faez's cousin Samer, and an unnamed man, a Muslim. The three then drove him to a nearby valley where he was subjected to torture motivated not by any desire for knowledge but by a combination of sheer sadistic pleasure and the fact that Samer Qumsiyya felt that Basem had once slighted him. Basem was beaten and his face, arms and body burned with cigarettes. He was cut in his stomach, arms and legs, and chained to the bumper of the car and dragged along the road. Finally he was stabbed to death. The body was disposed in valley's rubbish dump as an intentional gesture of degradation and shaming.

It is difficult to discern the source of these details as it seems unlikely that Faez—except under extreme duress—would have divulged such information.

Many attributed the knowledge to a file alleged to have been left behind when Israeli security abandoned the Bethlehem police station. This was said to indicate that the three men, under instructions from Samer's father, Bishara Qumsiyya, had kidnapped and executed Basem because of Basem's association with Fatah. Regardless of whether or not the file existed, no one doubted Bishara Qumsiyya's involvement. Bishara Qumsiyya was, throughout the 1980s, leader of the Bethlehem region "Village League"[13] and commanded an Israeli-armed "militia" of thugs and criminals that imposed a reign of terror on Beit Sahour and neighboring sites of nationalist sentiment such as Bethlehem University. The League was well known for collaboration and acts of intimidation; in 1987 League members raked the Arab Orthodox Club with gunfire. One of the great victories of Beit Sahour's *intifada* was the defeat of the Village League; in March 1988 Bishara Qumsiyya was forced to mount the pulpit of the Orthodox church to confess his collaboration before a capacity crowd and to renounce any further association with the military government.

Rishmawi's murder fitted the Village League agenda perfectly. Unbeknownst to most at the time of the "first death," Basem had, six months before his killing, joined Fatah and been trained, during a putative family visit to Jordan, in Syrian guerrilla camps. It is not clear, in light of this, why Sahouris did not assess the killing as a straightforward (albeit mediated by proxies) act of the Israeli military. Yet despite clear indications that Basem had been executed by agents carrying out an explicit Israeli policy of eliminating PLO operatives in the Occupied Territories, the town took the killing as very much an intracommunal concern.

The town had been given little choice. The Palestinian officials who had overseen Faez's confession refused to try Faez and his accomplices for collaboration and murder, and instead instructed the Rishmawi and Qumsiyya families to settle the case between them by ʿatwa, or tribal law. Many Beit Sahouris believe that unpublished agreements behind the Oslo Accords prevented the Palestinian judiciary from prosecuting important collaborators. Bishara had been named in Faez's confession and would have been implicated had a trial been allowed to proceed. As the families involved knew of Faez's confession (he had repeated it to his parents and asked them to arrange reconciliation with Basem's family), the only way to quiet the case and its dangerous ramifications was to hand it over to them, through the medium of tribal law, for extrajudicial settlement.

The problem posed to the town if the case was being handled under tribal law, rather than through governmental channels, is that the former refers to collective responsibility whereas the latter deals with individuals. ʿAtwa negotiates the payment of blood money in cases of intergroup rivalries so as to effect a reconciliation between two groups forced into hostilities by the actions of individual members.[14] Beit Sahour, however, did not represent itself as constituted by separate groups, and many were aware of the implications of treating the acts of individual agents under the rubric of collective responsibility. Relations within Beit Sahour—particularly amongst the Christian families—were tightly imbricated, and although one could distinguish nominally between distinct *hamulas* (and within each of them between individual *ʿaʾilas*, or constituent extended families), the interrelations between these were formally and informally dense. While any murder in a small town is potentially explosive, the murder of a Rishmawi by a Qumsiyya was particularly divisive insofar as both were *ʿaʾilas* of the al-Qazaha *hamula* (to which 40 percent of the town's population belongs) and both families are almost exclusively Greek Orthodox (the religious community to which two-thirds of the town's population is affiliated). Were extended family loyalties to predominate over wider communal loyalties, a wedge would be driven through the midst of one of the town's two major clans and—insofar as intermarriage between members of the two *ʿaʾilas* is not uncommon—nuclear families would be riven. Furthermore, although parallel cousin marriages occur in Beit Sahour, marriages between Christian families often not only cross *hamula* boundaries but also knit together couples (and thus families) across sectarian divides.[15] People stressed that almost every Christian in the town was related—directly, through ties of godparenthood, or both—to the Qumsiyyas and Rishmawis. The children of one of my primary informants (who was of the Al-Jaraysah clan) were godparented by Rishmawis, while his brother's children were god-parented by Qumsiyyas. A feud between Rishmawis and Qumsiyyas would impede, if not block, the operation of a number of kin and patronage networks linking Christian Beit Sahouris across a multitude of fields. The Orthodox community, which currently shares a single church, would risk a split. The Arab Orthodox Club, with representatives of each of these *ʿaʾila* in its governing positions, would be seriously disrupted by hostilities and, if it survived, would no longer represent the whole of the (male) community. Finally, the town itself—which has a minority Muslim population yet is sited in a region with a Muslim majority—might be placed at risk if the issue of the third man—whom no one would name and many would not even indicate was Muslim—opened hostilities between Muslims and Christians.

As a result, when representatives of the families of Faez and Samer Qumsiyya[16] approached the Rishmawis to request a truce so that negotiations over blood money could be initiated, a number of moves were made by townspersons and community organizations to bridge the gaps prized open by the violence of the events. The elders of other Qumsiyya families in the town renounced Faez Qumsiyya and reiterated their 1988 rejection of the family of Bishara and Samer.[17] Although it was generally held to be inconceivable that anyone other than a "psychopath" would think of taking vengeance on the families, form was followed and the delegations approaching the Rishmawi elders to sue for peace did not include Qumsiyyas but were made up of spokesmen from other Sahouri families through which the families of the killers had chosen to speak. The guarantors confessed the guilt of their clients and promised that an agreement on blood money payment would be reached. In response, elders from the Rishmawi family guaranteed that no revenge would be taken.

The Rishmawi response was far from unanimous. The Rishmawi *ʿaʾila* is large, and in the crowded *majlis*[18] in which the representatives of its many households gathered, discussion went on far into the night over how the case would be handled. The divide lay between two camps. One, which contained many *intifada* activists, argued that the killing was a political act carried out against "the nation." Negotiations should therefore be handled by a committee made up of representatives of the political parties active in the town. The other camp was made up of two groups with distinct agendas that could be met by facing the matter as a family affair. The larger was concerned to ensure that Basem's family got the greatest possible settlement out of the negotiations. Basem, his parents' eldest son, would have been their chief support, and the family—since his death—had been impoverished by his father's subsequent stroke. This group was concerned that while a settlement between the Qumsiyyas and a bloc made up of the national parties would serve to "build bridges" and reduce the threat of factionalization, it would result in only a nominal payment to Basem's family of blood money, leaving them little better off than they were at present. The other party was that of the traditionalists, and, although their "antinational" stance was neither popular nor powerful, it was held by several old men who felt their authority had been eroded through the years of popular mobilization.[19] They wanted things done "properly," and were anxious to prevent yet another "coup" by the political forces they felt had usurped power belonging to the community's traditional leadership.

As it was, this latter group "settled" the issue by taking it out of the hands of the family. After a night of unresolved argument, some of its members drove to the neighboring Bedouin village of Taʿamra where they told its elders, who traditionally would have served as *qudah* (judges), that the national bloc within the Rishmawi family had insulted them. The Taʿamri demanded an apology, implying that without one they would not be available as *qudah* for Beit Sahour in the future. When the representatives of the national grouping heard this, they walked out of the negotiations in disgust.

These events made it impossible to deal with the case directly in national political terms. Nonetheless, despite the translation of the terms of the dispute into the traditional familial idiom, the community—including all Qumsiyyas not in Faez and Samer's immediate families—remained fervently opposed to those implicated in the killing. Over the next several days, men representing various non-familial collectivities in the town (the Orthodox Club, the political parties, the churches, the unions, the scout groupings, and so on) met with Rishmawi family elders to familiarize them with the implications of the case for their groups, for the town, and for the national cause in general.

Anxiety escalated as the conditions for the *sulha* (reconciliation ceremony) were discussed because of fear that the amount of blood money the Rishmawis would demand might prove so high that the Qumsiyyas would refuse to pay, thereby breaking the truce and initiating feud. *ʿAtwa* is not a coercive system backed by state power but a system of reconciliation grounded on the assumption that those who embrace it consider continued sociality to be more important than the occasional expenses accrued in maintaining it. Traditionally, blood money payments ensure peaceful relations between groups placed in a state of potential war. They disarm the warring groups by establishing commensality between them, binding them with formal ties of obligation through the arrangement of a number of deferred payments that, it is hoped, will in time be replaced by less onerous ties of friendship and even marriage (see Peters 1990: 64–65, 170). In this instance, the severity of the crime was exacerbated by the extremely long delay between the crime's commitment and the approach of the delegates of the Qumsiyya families to the Rishmawi *majlis*. While the calculated infliction of pain and humiliation rendered the crime more heinous than either an undeliberated act of passion or, as is often the case behind blood money negotiations, a simple accident,[20] the long delay between when the murder was carried out and when its perpetrators confessed (or, as many suspected, were forced to confess) suggested that the perpetrators' commitment to peace with the Rishmawis was at best pragmatic in its motivation. It was clear that the spirit of desired reconciliation that should accompany *ʿatwa* was absent, and many feared that the Rishmawis would respond with what would in effect be a compensatory act of violence by demanding full compensation for the loss and dishonoring.

On the night of the *sulha,* the "whole town" gathered in the hall of the Greek Catholic convent because "everyone—even [other members of the Qumsiyya] family—had suffered badly under the league" and all were concerned about how the affair would be resolved. The meeting was convened under the jurisdiction of a noted *shaykh* from Hebron, a major Palestinian city twenty miles to the south, who had been chosen to act as *qadi* (judge) by the Rishmawis with the agreement of the representatives of the Qumsiyyas.[21] The size of the meeting, its public character, and the prestige of its arbitrator were all unusual, as was the character of the negotiations. Usually arbitration was simple, quickly effected, and, finally, convivial:

> Normally, even when a person was killed, the killer's representatives would go to the family of the person killed, apologise profoundly (how can you refuse when the old men are humbling themselves and the entire family is putting itself in your debt? . . .) and then work ritually through "we need a million shekels," then "and here is 100,000 for Mohammed and 100,000 for Jesus" until there was nothing to be paid. This is about good will and needs to be done within at most three days. (see also Granqvist 1965: 122–123; Haddad 1920: 107)

Here, however, good will was lacking. The Rishmawi family made an initial demand that, while high, would have allowed a series of reductions to a price that could easily be paid, even by Faez's family which—unlike Samer's—was not well off. In response, however, the representative of Faez's family and that of Samer and Bishara made a counteroffer that was ludicrously low for intentional murder (i.e., 9,000 Jordanian dinars or $12,750). This hostile bargaining breached convention and threatened negotiations. After interventions by the extrafamilial spokespersons, an agreement was finally reached (and approved by the *qadi*) that each Qumsiyya family would pay 20,000 Jordanian dinars[22] as a first payment, with subsequent payments adding up to no more than 18,000 dinars each. Faez's negotiators spoke with his father and returned to announce his agreement. Those who spoke for Samer left the hall to relay to Bishara the *qadi*'s decision and returned a few minutes later to announce that Bishara claimed Samer had been beaten into confessing, that he had not been involved, and that the family would pay nothing.

The response was immediate collective outrage. Bishara's initial representatives as well as the negotiators he appointed had repeatedly admitted that the family accepted Samer's guilt and its own responsibility for making blood payments. The last-moment renunciation broke the truce, and while some said the *qadi* announced that any Rishmawi had the right to kill any of the males of Bishara's immediate family, others claimed there was no need to announce this since everyone knew it. En masse the crowd—including other Qumsiyyas—broke from the church hall and headed for Bishara's house to burn it down. A neighbor who worked for the Palestinian security forces knew that women were living in the house and, fearing they might be killed, hid in a field in front of the house and fired his machine gun in the air. The crowd—assuming Bishara and armed supporters were in the house—dispersed while Palestinian National Authority (PNA) forces came in to clear the house and establish order.

For the next few weeks an uneasy peace reigned. Arrangements had been reached with the father of Faez Qumsiyya and, although he was unhappy at having to sell land to pay blood money, there was no feud between his family and the Rishmawis. Bishara, from within Israel, "sold" his house to his son-in-law so as to protect it from feud vengeance. Samer, though safe in prison, was, like his father, liable to be killed by any Rishmawi who saw him.[23] No one spoke of the third man other than to say he was safe in a collaborators' village in Israel. Most, if not all, of the 20,000 dinars was given to the parents of Basem.

Two weeks later, Faez died in prison. The official PNA version was that he died of natural causes, but Beit Sahouris believed that Bishara had had him killed to lift the onus from his son and, indirectly, from himself.[24] Faez's father claimed, regardless of who had killed Faez (and he implied it was a Rishmawi), that Faez's death satisfied the principle of "blood for blood"—a death had been followed by a death. He demanded, even before Faez's funeral, that the Rishmawis return his 20,000 dinars.

The Rishmawi response was furious. The negotiations in the church hall had left them substantially slighted, not only by the initial Qumsiyya offer of 9,000 dinars and the violation of ritual that offer effected but also by the relatively small settlement agreed upon. Faez's father's demand that the blood money be returned came across as more violence against the concept of community underlying both *ʿatwa* and Beit Sahour. As one Beit Sahouri insisted, "The point of blood money is not about the cost of a crime (for instance the medical care of a victim) but about making a statement of apology and reconciliation. Faez's family's demand for the money is an obscenity." This event was, for some Rishmawis, the last in a series of provocations directed toward their family by the Qumsiyyas and they increasingly voiced the opinion that the killing and the events that followed were neither political nor criminal but antagonistic expressions of one "lineage" toward another.

One impediment to feud, however, was the presence of a substantial number of Qumsiyyas in the bloc mobilized against Samer, Bishara, and Faez. Qumsiyyas had been as much persecuted by the activities of the Village League as other Beit Sahouris, and one informant told me that Bishara—in the heyday of his powers—had made a particular point of refusing favors to kin to show that he was beholden to no one. For the identity politics of the situation to move fully into the idiom of family and lineage such situationally drawn delineations had to be effaced, and this erasure was effected during Faez's funeral by a Rishmawi who photographed the Qumsiyyas who attended and then circulated the "incriminating" photographs amongst the Rishmawis. According to the photographer, and those who took him seriously, the presence at Faez's funeral of a large percentage of the town's Qumsiyyas was testimony to the fact that they were loyal to Faez despite having escaped responsibility for the murder by renouncing him. The photographer's charges seemed to be given even greater credence by the fact that those Qumsiyyas who had been ostentatiously photographed leaving Faez's funeral were understandably nervous about attending the funeral two days later of an elderly Rishmawi.[25] Claims were made that Qumsiyyas had chosen to attend the funeral of a killer of Rishmawis rather than to offer condolences to the Rishmawis for the loss of one of their family.

Despite the fact that not all Rishmawis and Qumsiyyas accepted their allocated places in the newly polarized social terrain, the charge served to constitute two antagonistic camps made up respectively of all Rishmawis and all Qumsiyyas. Those Rishmawis who felt that family honor had suffered in the course of the *sulha* and what ensued were able, through mobilizing a rhetoric of hostility to "those" who had humiliated them, to reassert the strength and honor of the Rishmawis (see Stirling 1960 for an analogous case). The members of Faez's immediate family, who resented being left to carry the financial burden of paying off the Rishmawis, in turn found it in their interest to implicate other Qumsiyyas in the burgeoning feud so that the money Faez's father had been forced to pay would be returned as a consequence either of a strong bloc of kin support consolidating behind him or because an eventual outbreak of feud violence would abrogate the terms of the settlement.

Between 1995 and the outbreak of the second *intifada,* violence broke out at several points between Rishmawi and Qumsiyya youths, and while careful counsel prevented these eruptions of underlying hostilities from developing into more extensive feuding nothing was resolved. Faez's father continued to demand his 20,000 dinars back while the Rishmawi elders continued to assert not only that the demand was a violation of the *sulha* agreement but also that the failure of Faez's family to make the final payment (*teyba*) programmed into the agreement means that the reconciliation process had broken down. Things rested, in effect, in abeyance, and although no substantial violence between Qumsiyyas and Rishmawis broke out (causing the suspended antagonisms to coalesce into open feud), neither had any move by nationalist or transfamilial forces in the town succeeded in breaking the deadlock and restoring commensality between those involved.

* * *

Throughout my research into the way Beit Sahouris negotiated the dilemmas thrown up by the murder of Basem Rishmawi, none of my informants would tell me the name of the "third man" implicated in the killing. It is not that people did not know who he was, or where he had lived, or where he was at present; it was just that people did not want to talk about him. The "third man" was beyond the bounds of the story, and his family had not been called to account in the course of the *sulha* negotiations. People would say he was not important either because he had lived outside Beit Sahour or because he had disappeared and could not be tried for the crime. Others would, however, let slip in passing that he was a Beit Sahouri who had lived quite near to Bishara Qumsiyya and had recently been seen living in a collaborator village on the road between Jenin and Afula. When I repeated this information to those who contended he was not locatable, or when I played the devil's advocate by reminding them that according to the rules of ʿatwa it did not matter whether or not the culprit could be located if his family could, they would look uncomfortable and change the subject.

In the summer of 1999, I met with a friend who, in the course of gossiping, asked me if I had heard about an episode that had occurred that winter which "had the whole town in an uproar." A Beit Sahouri woman—"a bad woman, but Orthodox"—had surreptitiously married a Muslim man (whose name or provenance was not proffered, although the location of the place where they lived immediately after the marriage implies he was Beit Sahouri). When her family found out, it tried to get her back, but she and her husband fled to Taʿamra, where they took shelter with a Bedouin family. Elders from her family, along with the town mayor, went to the PNA in Bethlehem to complain and were told by the authorities (who are very sensitive to Muslim–Christian issues) that they had no right to interfere. My informant concluded:

> The Sahouris see this as an expression of the threat to them of the Muslims. It used to be that we were separated by the mountains from Obadiya [a neighboring Muslim village] but now its mosques are on our borders, the Jews are on Jabal Abu-Ghneim, and Bethlehem is mixed. Everyone is taking over, and now they are beginning to take the women.

In this discourse, Beit Sahour has become a very different place from that described in the discussions related in the first part of this paper. There, Beit Sahour was a Palestinian village made up of Christians and Muslims who shared in everything, and particularly in their solidarity in the face of the national enemy (who was "Israeli," not "Jewish"). Here, on the other hand, "we . . . the Sahouris" are Christian and deeply threatened by other religious communities ("Muslims" and "Jews") pressing on our borders from all sides and now, most frighteningly, "beginning to take the women."

What are invisible in this discourse are the Beit Sahouri Muslims who constitute a minority population within the borders of a largely Christian town, itself located within a national territory in which Muslims are the majority population. The man in this story, who has stolen the daughter of his Christian neighbors and, by marrying her, turned her into a Muslim, is, like the third man in the killing of Basem Rishmawi, the internal trace of an antagonism that Beit Sahouri Christians rarely discuss, and then only as something "outside." Neither of the two, however, acted from "outside"; it was from within Beit Sahour that they had effaced Christian identities through murder and seduction.

Throughout my notebooks dating as far back as my earliest *intifada* work in Beit Sahour, there is a shadow discourse haunting Sahouri assertions of strong commensality and communality between Muslims and Christians. Christian Sahouris spoke—in tones that in 1990 were hushed and somewhat embarrassed yet which, by the late 1990s, had become more open and assertive—of the threat of the Muslims elsewhere in Palestine, of their covetousness about Christian wealth, of their intolerance for religious and cultural difference, and of the impossibility of coexistence with them. This material was always just under the surface, but it did not predominate and only served to organize perceptions (and assertions) at certain moments—and then only in relation to Muslims outside of Beit Sahour. Even today it is extremely rare to hear a Beit Sahouri Christian make a negative comment about a fellow townsperson who is Muslim, and when they do so, it is as a criticism of particular individuals that link them to a generalized *outside* collectivity (e.g., "so and so is like a Khalili [Hebronite]"). I have never heard a Beit Sahouri Muslim criticize a Beit Sahouri Christian *as* a Christian.

The unnamed and unpursued "third man," like the unnamed and unlocalized Muslim husband about whom everyone in Beit Sahour was allegedly talking (but not to me), is a reminder of what must not be brought into the open. Although Sahouris had always been Christian Sahouris and Muslim Sahouris, a chilling realization was growing in the late 1990s as the threat of Israeli military dominion appeared to recede. Without the presence of "an enemy who is enemy to us both" forms of self- and communal assertion that had previously been sublimated in the interest of asserting solidarity were coming to serve as "models of" and "models for" the social (see Geertz 1973: 93–94). To be reminded that the antagonism between Muslim and Christian, which the ideologues of both religions increasingly assert, is not simply an antagonism between an inside and an outside but even more saliently an antagonism within Beit Sahour, is to be reminded of the impossibility of community. That counterfactual knowledge is simultaneously known by all, and is universally disavowed.

*   *   *

I have attempted through this ethnography to show how "ways of telling" shape the possibilities of response to events in the life of a community. The "first death" of Basem Rishmawi articulated, for the majority of inhabitants of Beit Sahour, a model capable of giving shape to a Manichaean world made up of an imagined community and another grouping antagonistic to that community. It impelled strategies of social consolidation and resistance appropriate to the maintenance of the community that it had helped to bring into conscious being. However, as the context in which that story circulated was transformed by political and social developments, so too was the story's significance. Although one might argue that what happened in 1995 was that "people got their facts right" and therefore a "true story" replaced a "false story," what I have tried to show is that the rectification of the "facts"—the realization that Palestinian collaborators working for the Israelis killed Basem rather than Israelis themselves—would have had little if any effect had there not already been a very substantial shift in the perspectives of Beit Sahouris on issues of politics, identity, nation, and community. Within the terms of nationalist discourse, the question of whether an Israeli soldier following the orders of his superiors kills a Palestinian or whether a Palestinian collaborator following the orders of his Israeli superiors does the deed, is moot; in each instance, the deed is a political assassination carried out by an agent of the national enemy in accordance with that enemy's plans to eradicate the nation. That the "second death" of Basem Rishmawi came instead to be, for many, an expression of the antagonism of one Beit Sahouri family grouping for another demonstrates the ascendancy of a different mode of interpretation. Antagonism, which I have argued serves to construct solidarities among those who perceive it as threatening, came to be seen as interfamilial in the post-Oslo context, and the ascendancy of that idiom "muted" interpreters who continued to argue that the real antagonism came from the Israeli state. That muting, however, did not simply silence voices but engendered situations in which a nationalist response was seen as inappropriate and extraneous.

The hegemonization of the familial idiom of interpretation and the overturning of the nationalist idiom was not a simple matter of will, choice, and the fickleness of interpreters. Through the details of the story that I have relayed above, we can see the operations of the convoluted logic of contingency. The contexts within which various interpretations of the torture and murder of Basem Rishmawi are situated and elaborated are themselves dense with the accretion of a multitude of other articulations as well as with the institutional structures (some active, some latent) that have taken shape as persons in the past and present have used those articulations as models for activities. An event in the process of being interpreted and fixed in its meaning by consensus has to "negotiate" a multitude of switching points, and at each of these shifts can be affected in the way the event is interpreted and in the consequences it will come to have. If the inequities of power underlying the Oslo Accords had not led to the PNA's vow not to prosecute collaborators . . . , if the old men in the Rishmawi family *and* of the Ta'amra had not been resentful of the undermining of traditional structures of authority . . . , if Faez had not died in prison . . . , if the photographer had not had the equipment or the will to photograph the persons at the Qumsiyya funeral . . . things would not have developed as they did. Some of those "switching points" are more stable than others; the decision of the PNA to turn the case over to tribal law inserted the deliberations on the significance of the case into a traditional structure that could only work in familial terms. The translation of the events into the idiom of family, which that time-honored institution had effected, can in turn be seen to overdetermine the far more idiosyncratic decision of the photographer to extend the borders of the antagonism to the limits of the Qumsiyya ʿaʾila.

Although after more and more interpretative decisions are made the range of options is substantially reduced, the force of contingency still prevails. Although over the period narrated in this chapter the logic of events substantially closed down the ways in which the community could negotiate the implications of the murder of Basem Rishmawi, the historic context in which that logic operates still retains the power to transform its course and meaning. During my last bout of fieldwork in Beit Sahour, in the summer of 2003, the various tellings of Basem Rishmawi's killing were still in occasional circulation, but their salience had been blunted by Israel's violent reoccupation of the territory, by its building of the massive settlement of Har Homa on the town's borders, and by the land loss, impoverishment, and social isolation effected by Israel's erection of "the wall" through and across the municipality (see Bowman 2004).

Against this backdrop, the story of Basem's death (the site of the dumping ground is now beneath "the wall") seems not so much inconsequential as disjunctive, as though it deals somehow with a place and time to which one cannot get from the present. The latent feud, though still unresolved, was clearly in abeyance, and no one was talking of tensions or hostilities between Muslim and Christian Sahouris. This was not, however, a return to the community of the first *intifada;* although, even more than then, the antagonism of the Israeli occupation was visible to all, there was little sense of political solidarity outside the offices of institutional groups dependent for support on the "outside." It appeared as though the logic of fragmentation that had begun to operate when "people began throwing stones for money" had ineluctably carried on to the point where nuclear families were struggling, with little help from others, to find a way to survive in the face of a state machinery set on exterminating them not only as Palestinians but even as individuals. Although it is likely that the telling of the "second death" of Basem Rishmawi played some part in weakening the bonds of Sahouri community, it is also possible that the lesson of his "first death" will be recalled, and a new solidarity in the face of "one who is enemy to us both" will emerge.

Notes

Field research was primarily funded by the Wenner Gren Foundation for Anthropological Research although a short field trip to Beit Sahour in January 1990 was paid for by the Middle East Research Information Project. My greatest appreciation goes, of course, to the people of Beit Sahour, although I am as well deeply indebted to colleagues in

Israel/Palestine, the United States and the United Kingdom who have read and commented on this paper.

1.   See Rothenberg 1999 on the Palestinian *hamula*.
2.   See Hunter (1991: 121–128) on the *intifada* tax revolt strategy in general and Robinson (1997: 66–93) for Beit Sahour's role in it.
3.   Insofar as the disputes raised by this case have not been resolved, I do not mention informants by name other than when their identities are already commonly known.
4.   As of July 2003 the Arab Orthodox Club was still the principle site of men's social gathering in Beit Sahour; Christians, Muslims, and atheists are welcomed. Its name refers far less to the neighboring Greek Orthodox church than to an early twentieth-century protonationalist movement through which Palestinians struggled to wrest control of the church and its substantial properties from a "foreign" (Greek) priesthood (Bowman 1993: 436, n. 8).
5.   On 8 December 1987, an Israeli tank transport vehicle swerved across the road at a checkpoint to flatten a carload of Palestinian workers waiting for clearance to cross to work in Israel; four residents of the Jabaliyya refugee camp were killed. The driver claimed to have killed the men in revenge for the previous day's knifing of an Israeli tax collector in Gaza city.
6.   Potlatch designates a competitive system of gift exchange practiced among northwest coastal American Indians, in the course of which lavish gifts were often destroyed in the pursuit of prestige (see Mauss 1969: 31–45).
7.   This assertion of the ease with which Beit Sahour could return to its "agricultural roots" is somewhat idealized, although townspersons did attempt to do so during the first *intifada* to escape dependency on Israeli markets (see Frankel 1994: 42–66; Hunter 1991: 144–145, 211–212; Schiff and Ya'ari 1990: 247–248; and Robinson 1997: 74–76).
8.   Shqif is Beaufort Castle in South Lebanon. Fatah held it from 1970 until 1982, even during the Israeli invasion of 1978. Tall al-Zaʿtar resisted a several month siege by Maronite militia in early 1976 (Rosemary Sayigh, personal communication). Shatila is, of course, one of the two sites of the notorious Sabra and Shatila massacre discussed in the introduction.
9.   Nonetheless, the constant emphasis on the town's resistance to the Israeli occupation indicated that it was in this particular struggle that the community realized the quiddity of its identity.
10.   Townsfolk, Christian and Muslim alike, consistently stated that the Muslim population was between 25 and 30 percent. The 1997 census, which collected but did not publicize figures on religious affiliation, shows a population of 11,250, of which 3,278 were under twelve and 620 over 65 (Palestinian Central Bureau of Statistics 1999: 50, 55).
11.   The Oslo Agreements barred access to Jerusalem to all but the very few who could attain permits from the military authorities, etiolated trade links between West Bank businesses, and forced un- or alternative employment onto many workers who had after 1967 become dependent on working in Israel.
12.   I was told in 1994, before the "second death," that, "No Christian or Muslim has ever been killed by another here."
13.   The Harakat al-Rawabit al-Filistiniyya (Movement of Palestinian Leagues) was established in 1981 by the Orientalist Menahem Milson, whom the new

Likud government appointed head of the West Bank Civil Administration. The leagues simultaneously functioned to mediate between the military government and local communities (providing family reunion permits, travel permits, driving licenses, jobs in the civil service, building permits, abrogations of house demolition orders, intercessions on behalf of jailed relatives, and reductions in prison sentences) and to organize and run proxy military units dedicated to the destruction of the PLO and the intimidation and closure of institutions providing civil alternatives to Israeli structures of governance (Tamari 1983; see also Aronson 1990: 248–253).

14. The details of procedure and terminology in tribal law pertaining to murder are laid out comprehensively in Aref el-Aref's *Bedouin Love, Law and Legend* (1944: 86–115) and elaborated in Hilma Granqvist's study of traditional dealings with matters of unnatural deaths in the village of Artas, which borders Beit Sahour (1965: 110–132). See also Cohen 1965: 139–145 and Ginat 1987 for blood disputes in Israel/Palestine; Peters 1990: 59–83 for feud amongst segmentary North African Bedouin; and Black-Michaud 1975 for Mediterranean examples.

15. A Catholic informant told me: "It is standard practice to take daughters from the Orthodox and return them to the Orthodox." This arrangement, while not prescriptive, is quite common. Christian–Muslim marriages are rare, usually only involving Beit Sahouris "outside" in diaspora (but see below for a recent case and its consequences). See Holy 1989, Donnan and Gibb 1993, and Geertz 1979 on the logic and function of parallel cousin marriage.

16. Although the murder had happened fourteen years earlier, the adult males of Faez's and Samer's immediate families went into hiding since—according to ᶜatwa—they were liable to vengeance killing by Rishmawis until the terms of a truce were reached. Faez and, by then, Samer were in prison (and Bishara in Israeli-controlled Jerusalem), but according to ᶜatwa all males from the killer's clan over twelve and not elderly are vulnerable to attack (Haddad 1920: 105). However, not only did the town's ethos militate against anything more than nominal observance of the rules but the other Qumsiyyas' denunciations of the crime were seen to absolve them of responsibility.

17. Such a declaration by members of the extended ᶜaʾila of their rejection of the killer is called iᶜlan baraʾa (see Cohen 1965: 144, n. 1); among the Bedouin with whom El-Aref worked it is called tuluᶜ (El-Aref 1944: 88).

18. The *majlis* is the traditional reception room of a Palestinian house (see Gilsenan 1982: 181–187 for Lebanese parallels). In situations such as those described above, the *majlis* of the elder representative of the family group will serve as the meeting point of all family representatives and those "outsiders" they host.

19. The accuracy of their feeling is testified to by the statement of one Rishmawi, a member of the national camp, who told me, "Since the early sixties we had been working to diminish the authority and influence of the *hamula*."

20. Cohen (1965: 68–71) and Granqvist (1965: 117–123) provide examples of accidental deaths necessitating negotiations and payments.

21. The qadi's religious status is analogous to that of other blood money arbitrators such as the Cyrenaican *marabtin biʾl baraka* (Peters 1990: 64) and the Berber *igurramen* (Gellner 1969).

22. The sum was $28,170 at the September 1995 rate of exchange. This was a low settlement considering the nature of the crime. It can be compared with the 12,000 dinars that a local factory owner was forced by arbitration to pay one of his workers when his gun accidentally went off and grazed the man's neck.

23. Although the other adult males of Bishara and Samer's family were legitimate targets, townsfolk claimed that only Bishara and Samer were liable to be murdered, "because they have not attempted to resolve the case."

24. Within a week, Samer was released from prison, allegedly because there was no one alive and in reach of the PNA who could testify in the cases for which he had been held.

25. Informants claimed that in the past all Beit Sahouris had attended all marriages, baptisms, and funerals, but now people "are required to go [only] to funerals," treating all else as family affairs. Observation reveals that now only friends, families, and members of the same religious community attend funerals, but Qumsiyyas and Rishmawis are members of the same *hamula* and are affiliated to the same church; consequently, failure to attend each other's funerals is a visible assertion of division.

References

Abed, George, ed. 1988. *The Palestinian Economy: Studies in Development under Prolonged Occupation.* London: Routledge.

Aronson, Geoffrey. 1990. *Israel, Palestinians, and the Intifada: Creating Facts on the West Bank.* London: Kegan Paul International.

Black-Michaud, Jacob. 1975. *Cohesive Force: Feud in the Mediterranean and the Middle East.* New York: St. Martin's Press.

Bowman, Glenn. 2004. About a Wall. *Social Analysis* 48 (1): 149–155. Also http://electronicintifada.net/v2/article2872.shtml.

———. 2003. Constitutive Violence and the Nationalist Imaginary: Antagonism and Defensive Solidarity in "Palestine" and "Former Yugoslavia." *Social Anthropology* 11: 319–340.

———. 1994. "A Country of Words": Conceiving the Palestinian Nation from the Position of Exile. In *The Making of Political Identities,* ed. E. Laclau, pp. 138–170. London: Verso.

———. 1993. Nationalizing the Sacred: Shrines and Shifting Identities in the Israeli-Occupied Territories. *Man: The Journal of the Royal Anthropological Institute* 28 (3): 431–460.

———. 1986. Unholy Struggle on Holy Ground: Conflict and Its Interpretation. *Anthropology Today* 2 (3): 4–7.

Cohen, Abner. 1965. *Arab Border-Villages in Israel: A Study of Continuity and Change in Social Organization.* Manchester: Manchester University Press.

Donnan, Hastings, and Camilla Gibb. 1993. Marriage among Muslims: Preference and Choice in Northern Pakistan. *Journal of the Anthropological Society of Oxford* 24 (2): 180–181.

El-Aref, Aref. 1944. *Bedouin Love, Law and Legend: Dealing Exclusively with the Badu of Beersheba.* Jerusalem: Cosmos Publishing Company.

Frankel, Glenn. 1994. *Beyond the Promised Land: Jews and Arabs on the Hard Road to a New Israel.* New York: Simon and Schuster.

Geertz, Clifford. 1973. Religion as a Cultural System. In *The Interpretation of Cultures: Selected Essays by Clifford Geertz,* pp. 87–125. New York: Basic Books.

Geertz, Hildred. 1979. The Meaning of Family Ties. In *Meaning and Order in Moroccan Society: Three Essays in Cultural Analysis,* ed. C. Geertz, H. Geertz, and L. Rosen, pp. 87–125. Cambridge: Cambridge University Press.

Gellner, Ernest. 1969. *Saints of the Atlas.* London: Weidenfeld and Nicolson.

Gilsenan, Michael. 1982. *Recognizing Islam: An Anthropologist's Introduction.* London: Croom Helm.

Ginat, Joseph. 1987. *Blood Disputes among Bedouin Rural Arabs in Israel: Revenge, Mediation, Outcasting and Family Honor.* Pittsburgh: University of Pittsburgh Press.

Granqvist, Hilma. 1965. *Muslim Death and Burial: Arab Customs and Traditions Studied in a Village in Jordan.* Helsinki: Commentationes Humanarum Litterarum 34 (1).

Haddad, Elias N. 1920. Blood Revenge among the Arabs. *Journal of the Palestine Oriental Society* 1:103–112.

Holy, Ladislav. 1989. *Kinship, Honour and Solidarity: Cousin Marriage in the Middle East.* Manchester: Manchester University Press.

Hunter, F. Robert. 1991. *The Palestinian Uprising: A War by Other Means.* Berkeley: University of California Press.

Kimmerling, Baruch. 2003. *Politicide: Ariel Sharon's War against the Palestinians.* London: Verso.

Laclau, Ernesto, and Chantal Mouffe. 1985. *Hegemony and Socialist Strategy: Towards a Radical Democratic Politics.* Trans. Winston Moore and Paul Cammack. London: Verso.

Lustick, Ian. 1980. *Arabs in the Jewish State: Israel's Control of a National Minority.* Austin: University of Texas Press.

Mansour, Antoine. 1988. The West Bank Economy, 1948–1984. In *The Palestinian Economy: Studies in Development under Prolonged Occupation,* ed. G. Abed, pp. 71–99. London: Routledge.

Mauss, Marcel. 1969. *The Gift: Forms and Functions of Exchange in Archaic Societies.* Trans. Ian Cunnison. London: Routledge and Kegan Paul.

Morris, Benny. 1990. *1948 and After: Israel and the Palestinians.* Oxford: Clarendon Press.

———. 1987. *The Birth of the Palestinian Refugee Problem, 1947–1949.* Cambridge: Cambridge University Press.

Palestinian Central Bureau of Statistics. 1999. *Population, Housing and Establishment Census 1997, Census Final Results—Summary: Bethlehem Governate.* Ramallah: Palestinian Central Bureau of Statistics.

Pappe, Ilan. 1992. *The Making of the Arab-Israeli Conflict, 1947–1951.* London: I. B. Tauris.

Pena, Ignazio. 1984. *Christian Presence in the Holy Land.* Jerusalem: Christian Information Center.

Peters, Emrys. 1990. *The Bedouin of Cyrenaica: Studies in Personal and Corporate Power.* Cambridge: Cambridge University Press.

Pettigrew, Joyce, ed. 1997. *Martyrdom and Political Resistance: Essays from Asia and Europe.* Amsterdam: VRIJE Universiteit Press.

Robinson, Glenn. 1997. *Building a Palestinian State: The Incomplete Revolution.* Bloomington: Indiana University Press.

Rothenberg, Celia. 1999. A Review of the Anthropological Literature in English on the Palestinian Hamula and the Status of Women. *Journal of Arabic and Islamic Studies* 2: 24–48.

Sahliyeh, Emile. 1988. *In Search of Leadership: West Bank Politics since 1967.* Washington, D.C.: The Brookings Institute.

Said, Edward. 1989. Intifada and Independence. In *Intifada: The Palestinian Uprising against Israeli Occupation,* ed. Zachary Lockman and Joel Beinin, pp. 5–21. Boston: South End Press.

Schiff, Ze'ev, and Ehud Ya'ari. 1990. *Intifada: The Palestinian Uprising—Israel's Third Front.* New York: Simon and Schuster.

Shapira, Anita. 1992. *Land and Power: The Zionist Resort to Force, 1881–1948.* Trans. William Templer. Oxford: Oxford University Press.

Shlaim, Avi. 2000. *The Iron Wall: Israel and the Arab World.* London: Allen Lane.

Stirling, Paul. 1960. A Death and a Youth Club: Feuding in a Turkish Village. *Anthropological Quarterly* 33: 51–75.

Tamari, Salim. 1983. In League with Zion: Israel's Search for a Native Pillar. *Journal of Palestine Studies* 12 (4): 42–56.

Taraki, Lisa. 1998. Contemporary Palestinian Society. http://home.birzeit.edu/wsi/Status%20Report.htm

van den Berghe, Pierre, ed. 1990. *State Violence and Ethnicity.* Niwot: University Press of Colorado.

2 Martyrdom and Destiny: The Inscription and Imagination of Algerian History

James McDougall

> This generation has not only fought colonialism, but has known the signal honor of achieving victory. There resides the difference between ourselves and our ancestors.
>
> —President Houari Boumédienne[1]

> I settled in the city of my ancestors [Algiers], the cradle of heroism and of struggle, the city whose nourishment is sacrifice and martyrdom. I took up the struggle again with temerity, revolt in my soul, there where the image rose before me of those forefathers who have marked this pure earth with their blood, where I could almost sense in the air the perfume of their souls which they employed in the service of God and the Homeland, for the good of Islam and of the Muslims.
>
> —Ahmad Tawfiq al-Madani (1981: 357)

Naturalized Violence: The Sense of the Past in Algeria's Present

Algerian history would seem to be particularly, even pathologically, violent. Accounts of the country's modern experience are structured by a sequence of suffering, an unrelieved succession of conquest, colonization, and war. Algeria's contemporary history remains overshadowed by the epic armed struggle that, having triumphed with independence, was memorialized as the birth rite of the state but then horribly resurrected, in the 1990s, in a ghastly epilogue that seemingly plunged an irremediably terrorized/terrorist Algerian subject back into the cycle of reprisals. This story is so well known that there is no need to reiterate it here. Besides, that is precisely not my intention. The apparent inescapability of recurrent violence in the Algerian past and present, as a persistent feature of historical narrative and historical consciousness, however, itself presents us with an important problem that we must address if we are to analyze the foundational categories and teleological structures of Algerian politics and history, and connect them meaningfully to their social conditions of production.

A critical approach to this problem requires us to interrogate the normative categories that structure this particular national(ist) history, and to examine the processes of the social production of knowledge and power themselves through which such categories are formed, systematized, deployed, and manipulated. Such processes are crucial in the continual reformulation of the meanings with which the social world is endowed, and thus in the continual recomposition of societal worldview and political action. This occurs in the positions and strategies adopted by social actors in the world they inhabit, strategies derived from and reproducing the structures of knowledge or understanding into which members of the community are socialized and that enable them meaningfully to situate themselves, their judgments, and actions, in a particular conjunction of time (history) and space (geography/politics). This social, and socializing, process of the constitution of history as self-knowledge, in turn, is simultaneously both a factor in shaping the form of social struggles, and a crucial object of struggle, in which the goal of each antagonist is to gain the cultural authority to exercise "the force attached to the legitimate enunciation of history's meaning" (Carlier 1997: 160).

From the mid-1960s, the reappropriation and "decolonization" (Sahli 1965) of Algerian history was a major preoccupation not only for Algeria's intellectuals but, more crucially, for a state system whose legitimacy, ratified neither by universal suffrage nor by tradition, remained inseparable from its mythologized, "legendary and populist" origin in resistance and revolution. From the internecine struggles at the moment of independence in the summer of 1962, the historical register was constantly subjected to "rediscovery, reinterpretation and reutilization" (Étienne 1971: 101). The seizure of this same register of revolutionary legitimacy by the ideologues of a utopian Islamism, in the context of the political, economic, demographic, and social crisis of the mid- and late 1980s (and particularly in the aftermath of the October 1988 disturbances, when troops of the "people's army"[2] fired on protesters in Algiers) in part underlies the last decade's civil conflict (Labat 1995: 296ff).

But does this story, and the constantly reiterated past of which it seems a regeneration and in terms of which it is often scripted, simply express yet again a cyclical, structural violence inherent to North Africa and written into its natural order, from Ibn Khaldun to patrilineal segmentation theory via a colonizer's history of successive, transient "civilizational" invasions and immutably "barbaric" primitive rebellions? Was Algeria always, and does it simply remain, "an intensely violent society"?[3] Hardly. A stereotype is not an analysis. This persistent "naturalization" of violence is itself our problem.[4] Its solution lies, partly, in accounting for the centrality of an historical domain of "authentic violence" in Algeria's nationalist imaginary.

A structuring principle of the narration of history, employed for specific reasons in the production of an anticolonial historical knowledge that served to ground a vision of an "authentic Algerian self" in a reappropriated past, this notion has profoundly influenced the shaping of legitimate discourse and notions of social–historical meaning that have governed both the reading of history and the conceptualization of legitimate political action. Never "natural," Algeria's memory of violence has been naturalized in the process of giving a coherent, unifying and politically mobilizing meaning to a modern history marked, indeed, by only too many acts of violence. Each of these, to be adequately understood, must be accounted for as the result of a specific strategic choice resulting from a specific conjuncture of circumstances. Their naturalized historical meaning, though, narrated as epic and as hagiography, contributed to the creation of structures of understanding and historical self-location that instead inscribed and imagined historical violence as uncompromising "authenticity." The "authenticist" vision offers a history of sacralized struggle in which the recourse to violence is not a legitimate, if tragic, strategy, a necessity of last resort in pursuit of this-worldly political aims, but the only worthy means of struggle, the heroic continuation of a perennial historic mission in defense of the community's "essential self," rooted in the memory of martyred ancestors and promised to the fulfillment of a utopian destiny.

The real question, then, from this point of view, hinges on the presence of the past as a system of meaning and its effective force in shaping political understanding, programs, and action. This immanent past is not inherent but on the contrary is constructed, a cultural artifact (like the "nation" itself). Instead of continually reiterating past violence in pseudo-explanation of the present, we should rather consider the structures of historical understanding that underlie such reiterations. These structures, while most immediately grounded in the recent memory of the revolution (1954–1962), in fact have a longer genealogy, which ought to be traced back to the very beginnings of Algerian nationalist historiography in the "renaissance" of the arabophone intellectual elite between the two world wars.

Inscription, Creation, and Expropriation

Modern Algerian historiography in Arabic begins with two related but dissimilar figures, Shaykh Mubarak ibn Muhammad al-Mili (1897–1945) and Ahmad Tawfiq al-Madani (1899–1983).[5] Both are important figures in the intellectual and cultural history of Algeria in the first half of the twentieth century, as founding members of the Algerian branch of the wider movement for Islamic "reform" (islah, also referred to as the salafiyya movement, from its privileging the "original" Islam of the "pious ancestors," al-salaf al-salih) which reshaped Islamic thought and practice throughout the Arab world in the early twentieth century. Forerunners of this movement existed in Algeria as early as the 1870s, but it took coherent form in the mid-1920s before becoming embodied in the Association of Algerian Muslim ʿUlama (Jamʿiyyat al-ʿulamaʾ al-muslimin al-Jazaʾiriyyin / Association des Ulémas Musulmans Algériens— AUMA) founded by ʿAbd al-Hamid ibn Badis and his associates in Algiers in 1931. From 1931 on, the AUMA provided an organizational base for the reformists' campaign to gain exclusive control of the cultural authority to define "the true religion" in Algeria, an aim that would be ratified after independence when the reformists' Islam became the religion of state. Their objective in the religious field was part of a total social project that placed the ʿulama at the heart of the task of "resurrecting" Algerian Muslim society, a task in which education and socialization were the central themes. Both al-Mili and al-Madani clearly shared this broader concern. Although al-Mili's single historical work, a two-volume *History of Ancient and Modern Algeria* (1929, 1932)[6] is frequently considered the first modern, national history of Algeria, it was in fact preceded by two years by the first sustained historical text written by al-Madani, who would go on to produce a series of historical and geographical studies of Algeria, ranging from antiquity through the Ottoman era to his own present day.

Al-Madani, whose work we will briefly examine, was born in Tunis into a substantial bourgeois family of Algerian origin that had emigrated after the catastrophic Algerian rebellion of 1871. He was schooled in a *kuttab* (Qurʾanic school) before attending the Zaytuna, Tunis's great mosque and university, and the Khalduniyya, a modernist educational association that had been created at the end of the nineteenth century. He was a precocious political activist and journalist, writing his first articles for the Algiers newspaper *al-Faruq* in 1914 and imprisoned in Tunis in 1915 for the duration of hostilities for what seems to have been a wildly ill-conceived attempt to organize a revolt in the Tunisian south. From 1920 he was heavily involved in the "old" Destour (the Free Tunisian Constitutional Party, from which Bourguiba and his allies would later split) and in political journalism, becoming editor of the review *al-Zuhara* and publishing widely both in the press and in pamphlet form on international affairs. On 6 June 1925, he was expelled from Tunisia by the protectorate's police. Settling in Algiers, al-Madani turned most particularly to writing works of history and geography. He later became editor-in-chief of *al-Basaʾir*,[7] the reformists' official press organ, and was AUMA Secretary-General at the outbreak of the revolution in 1954. After the ʿulama rallied to the Front de Libération Nationale (FLN)[8] in 1956, he became a spokesman for the revolution in the Middle East, publishing a book on the Algerian question in Cairo and serving as the FLN's emissary in Indonesia, Sudan, and Syria. He became the token representative of the ʿulama in the first Provisional Government of the Algerian Republic in September 1958, as Minister of Culture and Religious Affairs, and held the same post in the first independent government, under President Ahmed Ben Bella, in 1962. Serving his country as a diplomat after leaving the government, he continued to publish works of history into the 1970s, when he also wrote his three-volume memoirs.

His first work, published in Tunis in 1927,[9] is a short history of North Africa (geographically concentrated on classical Ifriqiya and Numidia, or modern Tunisia and eastern Algeria) from the stone age to the Islamic conquest, conceived of as the story of "Carthage through Four Ages," *(Qartajanna fi arbaʿat ʿusur)* or the Punic, Roman, Vandal, and Byzantine periods. In fact, the latter two of the eponymous "four ages" are dealt with only summarily. The heart of the work is devoted to the history of Carthage, counterposed to the imperial Roman period. This past, doubtless exceedingly distant and foreign to the North African reader of the late 1920s, is retold by al-Madani as an exemplary, authentic national history. Al-Madani himself announces his understanding of the story at the outset. He addresses the reader as "O noble Maghrebi, son of Mazigh and Qahtan!" (1986: 7).[10] The attribution of this double genealogical ascendance, Berber and Arab, to the subject, and addressee, of the story, is already a programmatically unifying statement. The nation is founded on a primordial ancestry of heroism reaching back into the mists of time:

> Truly, this country of yours is possessed of a flourishing history, one which traverses the ages even to thirty centuries' distance and beyond, and gathers up in its pages the record of abundant, prodigious events and great works. This history announces to you great tidings, for it has known you faithfully, and studied you truly, before ever it knew your like among the nations who today fill the ends of the earth with their renown. (1986: 7)

Beyond (and subverting) the obvious intention of establishing a pedigree for the nation stretching back to a point anterior to the reach of the colonizer's history, two particular points should be made about this text. The first is that this book, like the same writer's later works, is manifestly born out of an intense intellectual and cultural dialogue with colonialism. Far from reaching back into some "pure" autochthonous cultural tradition for the proofs of a primordially flourishing national past, al-Madani engaged with the intellectual production of a French academic establishment that, from the middle of the nineteenth century on, had discoursed prolifically on the ancient, medieval, and modern history of North Africa. The "Algiers school" established in the colony's capital and its first college exercised not only a significant intellectual power in the French academy,[11] but also exerted a massive epistemological force on the young intellectuals emerging in Algerian Muslim society in the first quarter of the twentieth century. The reformist ʿulama, just as much as their Francophone "Young Algerian" contemporaries,[12] were obsessed with the evident power of the colonial state's modernity, and consistently sought to integrate the types of thought they encountered in the conquerors into their own cultural system. For al-Madani, not only the form but also the content of the colonizer's discourse had to be appropriated. Concerned to redeem the ancient past of his homeland and people from colonialist knowledge and domination, but having no independent access to this past, he was compelled to rely on precisely this knowledge as his principal authoritative source. He laments the neglect shown by previous Arab historians to "these . . . centuries filled with the great and the illustrious" (1986: 7), and having decided to address them himself, declares: "[T]his history which is now before you [. . .] I took from the books of the Western historians; it is they who have devoted substantial research to this period, and who have taken great pains over it. They have given life back to this dead period" (1986: 8).

Al-Madani's material, his access to the ancient Latin authors and to archaeological discoveries, as well as his categories and procedures (the use of *race* as a foundational category, the authority of physical anthropology, the systematic tripartite divisions of his orderly exposition of Maghrebi geography), his modes of argumentation, and even his conception of what constitutes valid history, are all provided by the colonizer's knowledge. European historians are cited liberally as authorities for al-Madani's statements, and, particularly in the discussions of the personalities of the "great men" of his stories, from the Berber kings of antiquity to the Ottoman rulers of the eighteenth century, European sources are quoted at length, as it were, as character witnesses. The constant insistence on the painstaking thoroughness of his research and his willfully pedagogical style of argumentation must be read, too, as a desire to mark "scientific" credentials, understood very much in terms of a dominant Occidental paradigm of knowledge production. Finally, the limited, but clearly deliberate, use of illustrations—photographs, line drawings, reproductions of European paintings—is a further device signaling his texts as modern in conception and production and scientific in method; the illustrations are not simply decorative, but are adduced as evidence in support of argument.

The second point to note is the place that the Islamic conquest itself holds in al-Madani's work. In turning to a long-neglected, pre-Islamic ancient history, al-Madani is accomplishing an important ideological task:

> The whole of North African history comprises two great ages. The first age is the purely Berber age, which begins with the first knowledge of history and runs to the arrival of the Arabs. The second age begins when the sons of Ya^{c}rab and the sons of Mazigh shook hands. The Maghrib became an Islamic country inhabited by the conjoined race of the Berbers and Arabs. (1986: 8)

This overarching two-stage structure, in which a progressive development of civilization sealed by racial fusion is set forth as the "total meaning" of North African history, raises several points.

First, all of Antiquity and the early medieval period up to the Islamic conquest is reinscribed as "the purely Berber period," thus erasing colonial historiography's fundamental notion of a Latin North Africa in the long Roman–Byzantine era. This was a notion much relied upon by the ideologues of colonization as a civilizing work seen not only as bringing the Maghreb into the modern, enlightened age but also as returning it to its authentic history, with France as the natural heir of Rome, a conception widely propagated in the late nineteenth and early twentieth centuries.[13]

Secondly, the categorical division of the Maghreb's inhabitants into "Arabs" and "Berbers" is recuperated and turned on its head, the uniqueness and immutability of "the Berber" (a trope of colonial ethnography) being accepted, but only in order to make Berber history the first "great age" of a three-thousand-year national past, continuous with the complementary history of Berbers and Arabs "conjoined," two races, but one nation, after the coming of Islam:

> Arabs and Berbers . . . became one nation, without the Berbers having greatly changed their ancient customs or the Arabs adopting those of the Berbers—they

were brought together by their unity of religion, of morality and of interests. . . . The two peoples were of one inclination and one sentiment, and they shared a love of honor and glory, a passion for freedom, and the custom of greatly honoring guests. This commonality of inclination and morality broke through the barriers which the Romans, Vandals and Byzantines were unable to pierce. The Berbers became the strongest auxiliaries of the army of Islam. (1986: 15)

Here, the colonial constitution of the native subject as racially/culturally "fenced in" since the earliest times by walls of immutability, barriers to the penetration of the "progress" and "civilizing" influence of the West, as dangerously fanatical and easily fanaticized, is subversively redeployed as a "proof" of Arab–Berber unity through the innate qualities shared by both. Islam, the perfecting salvation of the Berber race, brings to this people, already distinguished by their "great and illustrious" history of struggle and sacrifice, the true "moral" or "spiritual" civilization (*madaniyya adabiyya* or *akhlaqiyya*) of which the Arabs are the bearers. This "spiritual Orient" is counterposed to the "material civilization" (*madaniyya madiyya*) exemplified by ancient Rome and its would-be successor, modern France. This is the third achievement of the text, with the Islamic conquest itself being placed at the very center of the entire story, an archimedal point around which the destiny of the nation turns. From the point of view adopted in *Qartajanna fi arbaᶜat ᶜusur,* the conquest is not, as we might tend to think of specifically Arab–Islamic historiography, the beginning of history, but rather an end of history, a culminating telos in which the perfection of "the Maghrebi nation" is achieved. Thereafter, no further ultimately meaningful change is possible: history from this point on is only the further expansion of the nation's glory, or its long struggle to return, against the forces of decline and oppression, to this age of purity.

The moral theme of the narrative glimpsed here (the opposition of a free, "spiritual" civilization to an oppressive "material" one) is a constant feature of this historiography. The whole of al-Madani's history, as of much of the imperial European narrative from which he draws and against which he seeks to write, is structured by recurrent confrontations of opposed civilizations, facing each other across a Manichaean moral geography that bisects the Mediterranean world, opposing the "races" of Oriental origin (Berbers, Phoenicians, Arabs) to those of the West. "These were the days of the Berbers, proud sons of Mazigh. They inhabited the plains of this land and its hills. And they acquired, from all who came to them, the lights of civilization" (1986: 8). The ancient Berbers are imagined here in a "pure" state; initially "in the shadows," they are progressively "civilized" by their genealogical cousins from the east. Acquiring the rudiments of knowledge from the ancient Egyptians on their posited prehistoric migration from Mesopotamia, they are first acquainted with civilizing influence in the form of the Phoenicians who found Carthage, and finally by the Arabs, who complete the Punic civilizational mission with the light of Islam.

While progressively enlightened from one side of the divide, however, the ancient people of North Africa are constantly menaced by imperialist aggression from the other (Rome). The complementary structure of positive and negative "civilizations" encroaching on the Maghreb from east and west is, then, supplemented by the parallel constant of violent aggression and resistance. This theme of aggression and resistance is articulated around what is perhaps the key theme of al-Madani's first book, as of his later works:[14] the people's innate "love of independence," their uncompromising defense of "their independent life" and of their civilizational "character": "[The Berbers] surpassed other peoples in many priceless qualities, the most important of which are total [devotion to the] defense of their existence, inflexible firmness in defence of their independence, and the absence at any time of their assimilation by any other race" (1986: 13).

Here again, al-Madani's narrative strategy has a problematic relation to the colonial knowledge that is his invariable point of reference. The narrative of a succession of transient conquests, perennially resisted by a constant "native xenophobia," was held by the less progressive of colonialists to prove that Algerians were simply immutable, "unimprovable," and responsive only to spectacular shows of force. This was a standard historical theme for those who disbelieved the liberal colonialist notion of "emancipating" the *indigènes* by progressive "assimilation." The liberal paradigm of "improvement" was itself, of course, a paternalist myth, a "humanism which failed to recognize itself as cynicism";[15] nonetheless, it structured most political action in Algeria from the mid-nineteenth century into the 1930s. Predicated on the continued permanence of the colonial system but imagining that it could be reformed, political strategies appealing to republican, democratic France in the terms of its own ideological mantra of liberty, equality, and fraternity, united the major currents of Algerian Muslim intellectuals and activists of the interwar period. For most of them, independence—a separate, political independence through revolution, the program espoused by the radical–populist workers' movement born in the mid-1920s[16]—was a dangerous fantasy. The deeply humanist and fiercely anticolonial liberal Algerian leader, Ferhat Abbas (who would also, for want of an alternative, eventually join the revolutionary movement) wrote after the massacres at Sétif and Guelma in May 1945, which repressed an abortive attempt at a local insurrection with spectacularly disproportionate carnage, that "the use of violence is a crime against the people."[17] Nor did al-Madani, in his social conservatism and political elitism, subscribe to revolutionary action—indeed, it seems to have been with some reluctance, and only when there was clearly no alternative, that he and his movement would rally to the revolution in 1956.[18] And yet, ignoring the subtly reformist line theorized by Ben Badis, which allowed for distinct "political" and "ethnic nationalities" (a mutable, contingent *jinsiyya siyasiyya* overlaying an essential *jinsiyya qawmiyya*), his historical thesis of racial purity and separation aligns him, paradoxically, with the colonial thesis most intransigent toward the political program of partnership dominant among leading Algerians of his social group and his own movement. His insistence on the essential, genealogically predestined and immutable inassimilability of the North African shares (while inverting its values), the beliefs of colonial racism, where Europeans and Africans occupy a racially predestined place in a recurrent struggle of civilizations. The moral force of this narrative of conflict prescribes normative roles and attributes the "judgment of History" accordingly:

> The Berbers excelled from the earliest times by their sacrifice and desperate striving in the path of freedom, and by their passionate love of independence. They never submitted to a conqueror, nor ever turned to resignation, and if [ever] they yielded for a time under the rule of force, [it was only until] a propitious opportunity seemed good to them for the destruction of their enemies. (1986: 18)

If al-Madani, as an historian, was obliged to deal in terms of a dialogue with European history, and in a context of cultural production marked by the violence of the colonial system and the dominance of its forms of knowledge, it is hardly surprising that a structure of recurrent "civilizational" violence should be found at the centre of his narrative. Undoubtedly, the history of recurrent confrontation that he found in the colonial narratives of the Maghrebi past provided a framework for his own recuperation of those figures and events in a foundational history of the origins of "the nation of North Africa and its complete civilization." Instead of a stagnating immutability, locked in the backwardness of an Islamic "Dark Age,"[19] though, he found the constantly progressing but consistently "self-same" Maghrebi people, rooted in the East and civilized by Islam, whose story is three thousand years of heroic resistance and patriotic martyrdom. In the idiom that became dominant in Algerian cultural politics after independence, he discovered Algeria's "authenticity."[20]

What is most striking is the consistent, unambiguous presence of violence as recurrent and inescapable, in a text produced by a writer who would remain, into the second year of the Algerian revolution, opposed to "this slaughter which our religious convictions reprove, since on both sides the innocent are its victims."[21] Transcribing and inverting the perceptions of a colonial mythology, al-Madani constructs a historical system of absolutely antagonistic, total and immutable civilizational systems, while himself being unmistakably an intellectual and cultural product of their interpenetration. A member of a bourgeois, reformist, culturalist movement aiming at a more equal coexistence, he articulates a language of radical and violent, epic-heroic and "purist" separation. There can be little doubt that he considered this history as an exemplary moral lesson for his own time, and that its normative values of struggle, resistance, and sacrifice were intended for the audience that he, along with the other Islamic reformists from the 1920s onwards, was so eager to educate in what they defined as "cultural authenticity." The resurrected memory of the ancient ancestor-heroes, the values with which they were invested, and the Manichaean worldview within which their story was told, were all part of this project.

The point of this excavation of the themes of the earliest Algerian nationalist history is not, however, to account for the violence of the revolution itself. I have already indicated the problematic stance of al-Madani and his associates toward the escalation of an armed struggle that lay outside their control, and the actual influence of the Islamic reformist intelligentsia on the *maquisards* of the FLN is certainly not to be found here.[22] What is significant here is the way in which the *salafi* narrative, of ancestral purity and unremitting resistance-unto-death against an equally unremitting civilizational onslaught, prefigures, and perhaps provides an early model for, the later, postrevolutionary imagination of a national past understood very much in these same terms.

The creation of this national historical vision, however, has another important dimension, one related to its constitutive affinities with colonial knowledge. Even as it was composed in the as-yet-undecided political context of the interwar period, when many still believed fervently in the possibility of a reformed, multi-confessional and "fraternal" Algeria, to be created through the non-violent means of an appropriation of genuine democracy against the expropriating dominance of colonial minority rule, the constitutive logic of the emerging nationalist history was already, not a contribution to that emancipatory effort, but the logic of a new, and different, form of domination.

In the absence of the negotiated, democratic solution longed for by Ferhat Abbas (and, for example, by Albert Camus), what occurred was the transition from a colonial to a nationalist authoritarianism. In this transition, the mastery of history would prove to be important at each stage. History, in the first instance, was a resource for cultural resistance to the hegemonic, legitimate knowledge of the colonizer (whose version of history was, too, a part of the means of domination) through the medium it afforded for the assertion of a present difference rooted in the past. In the second instance—the revolutionary moment—the history being made in the resort to arms had to be inscribed as a legitimate course of action; indeed, as *the only* legitimate course of action. Revolution was necessitated, not by a failure of vision or of will, but by an inflexible and unremitting historical oppression, on the one hand, and by the historical destiny of the People (as Nation) on the other, to achieve emancipation and autonomy. It is crucial to note here that the possibility of any solution to the colonial situation other than its violent overthrow is irrevocably suppressed. Whether or not there ever was, in fact, such an alternative possibility becomes irrelevant, as the destiny of the nation in rupture and separation achieves the axiomatic status of doctrine. In the third moment, the process of establishing a "new state" (or of appropriating, more or less intact, the colonizers' state), and of distributing positions in the radically reconfigured social hierarchy, would anchor its legitimacy in references to historical roles assumed by each group and individual, now judged according to a scheme of values (the "lucidity" of each, as the Algerian National Charter of 1976 would put it, regarding "the national question") that, unquestionably vindicated by the Verdict of History, would become a resilient system of historical understanding. Thus, certain categories formed in the revolution are central to the social order thereafter, as witness the powerful institutions of access and patronage in Algeria,[23] organized around the historical roles of *mujahid* (revolutionary fighter) and *shahid* (martyr), and the abiding anathema of the term *harki* (member of the auxiliary counterinsurgency troops recruited by the French army, and condensing the notions of treachery, collaboration, savagery, dishonor, etc.).

At each moment, a multiplicity of historical possibilities is suppressed, and the complexity and heterogeneity of positions, choices, and actions are reduced to a binary classification finally encoded in the repressive categories of hero/ traitor; resister/collaborator, and so on. It is instructive to note how, in the first of these moments, that of the creation of an anticolonial history, the subjects of the story were already expropriated from the fluid, undetermined context of their own action and reinscribed in a thoroughly new, inflexible, and racially/ civilizationally predetermined system of understanding. To be sure, this nascent nationalist history also began the work of expropriating the colonizer, whose domination of history, both as knowledge and as process, it contested. But I have emphasized this double expropriation in order to insist upon the paradoxical nature of an anticolonialist, nationalist historiography that, while creating a narrative of resistance and emancipation, also signals the birth of a new exercise of power. This power is brought into being, first, over the objectified subjects of past history reconstituted as exemplars of normative values (struggle, resistance, sacrifice; treason, collaboration, dishonor) in a new context of meaning. It would then be brought to bear on other, still living, people, who found themselves "fixed," categorized, and judged by these tyrannical standards. For "national" history, posing as the voice, the image, and the "authentic past" of the People (singular), in fact imposes itself on people (plural), willing them to conform to its "glorious" prescriptions, and condemning to anathema those who fail to do as their destiny requires.

Imagination, Commemoration, and Reproduction

Revolution, for the radical–separatist Algerian nationalists whose political engagement began in the 1940s and who would go on to found the FLN, was a conscious choice considered also as a necessity—a strategy dictated by the objective conditions of the colonial situation and the evident bankruptcy of reformist politics after World War II, most particularly after the massive repressive violence that swept the districts of Sétif and Guelma in the northeast of the country on and after 8 May 1945. The declaration of the revolution itself on 1 November 1954 was the manifestly voluntarist act of a radical few whose success was by no means guaranteed. Algerian politics in the interwar period, and—though in a more febrile climate, a more blatantly repressive administrative context, and over a much greater radical–revolutionary groundswell than had been the case before 1945—up to 1951,[24] had operated primarily as negotiation within the system. The vast majority of Algerians in this period, preoccupied with the often near-impossible task of making a living, doubtless continued, whatever their innermost hopes or aspirations, in the daily attempt to "work the system to their least disadvantage" (Hobsbawm 1973–1974; Scott 1985). Many would continue to do so through the upheavals of the revolution, including those who, principally, no doubt, in order to provide for their families,[25] would join the French army's counterinsurgent forces as *harkis*. For Algeria's national(ized) history after independence, however, an integrating, mobilizing memory of the past was required, one that could not only legitimate the new political order, but could also deal with the exceptionally traumatic recent past in which Algerians had been subjected to seven years of sustained revolutionary violence and repressive counterinsurrectionary warfare. The acute sufferings and massive upheavals of the revolution, symbolized since 1962 by the mythical figure of "one and a half million martyrs,"[26] had to be somehow integrated into a cohesive logic of memory and forgetting, naturalized as a meaningful common heritage. In the social production of this history, there is a certain homology, if not a direct relationship, to be traced between the principal structures and topoi of *salafi* historiography and the social imaginary of "national" history that has continued to relate the past, and to relate itself to the past, in much the same terms.

Mustapha Haddab (1984: 400), noting that "history in today's Algeria remains a means of social and political struggle," has also suggested that, largely for this reason, "Arabic-language historiography in Algeria since independence has remained, to a considerable extent, indebted to the type of relationship to history which emerged in the arabophone intellectual milieux" (Haddab 1984: 387) of the first third of the twentieth century. History as a cultural–political resource, as "overpoliticized" and having "little chance of achieving autonomy from the [political] powers in place" (Soufi 1997: 293) has continued to carry a heavy weight of significance in the political field. There remained, in the political and media discourse of the decades after independence, and in a newly urgent fashion during the 1990s, a consistently pressing preoccupation with the representation of the past, with social memory, and then with the management of the "history of the present" being created daily in a new context of civil violence. History as an intellectual discipline and profession, on the other hand, has a decidedly subordinate social status, its graduates finding work principally in the undervalued field of secondary school teaching and finding itself, in spite (or, perhaps, because) of its political valorization, relatively impoverished in the hierarchy of the university (Haddab 1995). The main weight of "the presence of the past," then, is concentrated in the public preoccupation with "our National History" (Djender 1970), and with the public–political, rather than critical–intellectual, importance of achieving "a global understanding of the nation's past" (Djender 1970: 5). After independence and well into the 1980s, this public importance of history, reappropriated and decolonized, as the means of defining the community's vision of itself and its future was undiminished:

> It is only to the extent that we understand the events of the past, and know even its most distant reaches with the greatest objectivity and clarity, that we can also discern the horizon of the future with the greatest confidence and equanimity. (Saidouni 1984: 39)

This was written in late 1984. A survey of university students of history in 1985 found that the primacy of a "decolonization" of historical knowledge for achieving such "objectivity and clarity" was still very much in force—65 percent believed that it was "necessary to pursue the process of decolonizing history"

(Haddab 1995: 31), suggesting, at least, that the perception of an insidious colonialist influence, and the programmatic rhetoric of nationalism, were still lively a full generation after independence. The world oil price dramatically collapsed that same year, and the ensuing crisis led eventually into a maelstrom of political violence in which history would again become, not a means for the serene anticipation of the future, but a site and instrument of conflict. In accounting for the unraveling of the sociopolitical fabric and the resort to extremes of violence on all sides (army, special security forces, armed Islamist groups, self-defense groups), there has often been a resort to the invocation of Algeria's past, "inhabited by violence,"[27] a putatively constant structure "constitutive of Algerian history and culture."[28] In the Middle East, as well as in Europe, one is told that Algerians are "a violent people,"[29] that the Algerian "temperament is, so it is said, shaped by [its] particular history and culture [of violence]."[30]

It is important to insist that the new war in Algeria was not dictated by some inflexible, metahistorical fate. As Hassan Remaoun remarks :

> A social phenomenon must first be approached in terms of the social conjuncture itself prevailing at the moment of its appearance. [There] would be no need to repeat this [simple principle], were it not for the thousands of texts written on Algeria in recent years [which resort to the "violent past" in explanation of the present]. If the recent or distant past cannot directly explain the current Algerian crisis, there is, nonetheless, a memory of violence which, sacralized and never yet demystified, has been integrated through the socialization process to such an extent that it appears to constitute part of the "habitus" of Algerians. This fact is yet more striking in that the holders of political power, for purposes of legitimation . . . put their institutional resources at the disposal of this culture, exaggerating, in the dominant political discourse and through the mass media and schools which the state controls, the role of violence in the constitution of contemporary Algeria. (Remaoun 2000: 41–42)

This "legitimacy" of violence, grounded in structures of historical understanding, propagated through a dominant official discourse in the school system and mass media (see Ghalem and Remaoun 1995; Remaoun 1994; Soufi 1997), and informing the interpretation of the social world and the elaboration of political action, returns us to the question of the constitution of a "national historical imaginary." Education, and cultural authority over the social imaginary of the community, were at the heart of the Islamic reformist project, and, while the ex-AUMA current was thoroughly marginalized and dominated by the military power elite issued from the revolutionary army after independence, its project remained alive and assertive, most particularly in the domains of education and culture. Their flagship was the Arabization program—a concern already addressed by al-Madani, as Minister in the first independent government, in a project presented to the Arab League in 1962—but there was a more general, more widespread influence inherited from this current and traceable in the discourse of cultural "authenticity" (*asala*) that permeated independent Algeria from the late 1960s through to the 1980s. In opening the university year 1966–

1967, Ahmed Taleb Ibrahimi,[31] Minister of National Education, insisted in the presence of President Boumédienne that, "All study must [...] offer the possibility for developing, in our students, the sentiment of belonging to a country, a people, a culture, a history. This defence of our personality, this quest for authenticity, must be one of our major preoccupations."[32]

In a historical imagination that defines the meaning of "the nation," the state's need for constant relegitimation is fused with the cultural "authentication" of a singular, authoritative Algerian "personality"—a contemporary cultural artifact and discursive construct which is posited, and poses as historically "rooted" and immemorial. This mode of representation of the past has a close correlation with the structures and figures of the heroic, "recovered," and expropriated past of the early *salafi* historians. For the generations socialized in national(ized) history, the foundational epic is the revolution, 1 November 1954 marking an epochal break, whose story is that of a heroic feat of arms that mythologizes the exercise of revolutionary violence as the founding act of the community (see Harbi 1984; Remaoun 1995, 1997; Stora 1991). The founding revolutionary epic is equally, though, the culmination of a perennial, unceasing history of aggression and resistance. The revolution and its fallen heroes hold pride of place in an epic martyrology of armed struggles stretching back over millennia. The task of "national history" is to enshrine each with the others in a coherent story. The *maqam shahid,* the Martyr's Monument that dominates the Algiers skyline, is juxtaposed with the "Museum of the *mujahid*" beneath its colossal cement palm fronds; their narrative elides pre-modern warriors and *mahdis* with the soldiers of the revolutionary army (and the present-day state policemen who maintain a conspicuous presence around the site, which is an object of Islamist anathema). Nationalist history naturalizes the revolution as the inevitable outcome, not only of modern colonialism, but of the totality of an Algerian history narrated down the ages as struggle, resistance, and sacrifice. This story illustrates the unending defense of a purist, perfectly *salafi* notion of "collective personality":

> National history is the story of the works of [our] ancestors, glorifying their heroic actions, their sacrifices for the Nation and for all its citizens. History has, in Algeria, a very clear influence on the preservation of the Algerian personality and the deep understanding of its authenticity.[33]

In the integrative reinscription of the traumatic and divisive immediate past of the revolution, state and society confounded in the new nation reconceived the act of rupture represented in the emblematic date of 1 November 1954 as a final, climactic reactualization of the people's never-ending struggle, as the inevitable, "authentic" expression of the nation's destiny. The *milyun shahid* of the war could be honored as the last and greatest of Algeria's authentic patriots, while "the People," now emancipated, were instantly objectified as a unitary and unanimous actor, the difficult choices and constant compromises of "working the system" for over a century forgotten. Above all, the violence of revolution, a dangerous "fantasy" in the 1930s, became a permanent, structural fact;

the mythical People (as opposed to merely real persons) had always resisted, had never ceased to resist since the beginning of the conquest in 1830, just as they had always resisted every aggression throughout their three-thousand-year history.

The real history of the everyday necessity of "living the system" under colonialism, and the political strategies engaged in to better the lot of Muslim Algerians from the early twentieth century through to 1956 (when the recalcitrant parties rallied to the FLN), were occluded or, in the latter case, reconceived as "political resistance," thus achieving a retrospective homogeneity they never possessed, and totalized into the narrative of ineluctable armed revolution that, at best, finalizes and surpasses the "sterile game of politics" and, otherwise, shows it as redundant, foredoomed, a mere interlude between the primary popular resistance of the nineteenth century and its *reprise,* as if nothing had meanwhile changed, in 1954, by the People's "sole guide" and incarnation, the FLN. Thus the conjuncture, the conscious choice and strategy—and the actual, massive effort involved in the making of the armed struggle, whether considered as heroic, or tragic, or both—is obliterated in the structure, as not only inevitable, but also predestined. This naturalization of violence, announced by the earliest nationalist historiography, was, after 1962, sacralized at the heart of an official Algerian historical imaginary of "national memory."

In the crisis of the 1990s, history would be torn from this totalizing, homogeneous mold and fractured among the different currents competing for legitimacy in a destabilized social and political context where positions had to be redefined for the first time since 1965.[34] History has been constantly redeployed as a site and as an object of struggle. This has occurred, on one level, as a conflict between Islamists reinventing the revolution as a *jihad* whose goal is supposed to have been the establishment of an "authentically" Islamic state, and the army, as "repository of the memory of the heroes of the War of National Liberation" (Martinez 1998: 276), in defense of the republican state formed by the historic FLN. Beyond this most immediate struggle, however, the conflict over history is carried on, too, throughout the newly constituted public sphere of associative groups and the private press. A review of declarations, speeches, manifestos, and press articles dealing with the burning memory of the immediate history being made in the 1990s would demonstrate the suffusion of the "discourse of the present" with the register, the terms, and the "heritage" of the past. This heritage is employed as a common language, constantly reinterpreting the meaning of "national history" itself,[35] while also attempting to seek anchorage in the past for an understanding of the events of the last decade. This type of public, historical discourse, mobilized above all in the political sphere, and anchored in the politicized register of "epic," heroic, and "authentic" history, retains the moral force invested in it by the *salafi* project, contestatory in the 1920s and 1930s, and celebratory in the 1960s and 1970s. This force serves, in the current situation, to articulate on all sides concurrent claims to legitimacy, to an "authenticity" that each actor in the crisis wishes to claim as an exclusive right.

The Algerian conflict since 1992 has, then, in a sense been expressed as a struggle over inheritance. At the outset of the war, and at least up to 1994–1995, all "sides continue[d] to draw on the register of the war of independence" (Stora 1998: 154). In the discourses produced in the war of words and legitimation, titles of nobility and savagery were constantly disputed: citizens in arms[36] under the name of "patriots" and *"résistants,"* as well as soldiers—"guardians of national sovereignty"—fought to save "the integrity of the Republic" and denounced their opponents as "new *harkis*" or as "the sons of *harkis.*" The latter in their turn claimed the legitimacy of armed struggle in the reconquest of communitarian "identity" and "authenticity" against the "party of France"[37] and the neocolonial "apostates" of *le pouvoir* (the regime); all are *mujahidin* and speak in the same register of liberation and salvation. History, the absent past, has been constantly revived, re-presented in the conflict over its meaning, and over that of the present crisis and its resolution. Strategies of violence adopted in the recent conflict have also been grounded in history as a "necessity," not only as a legitimate course of action, in the face of the failure of a political strategy, but as the only legitimate course, reconnecting the present to its "authentic," heroic past. What is in reality a conjunctural choice, a strategy, is thus imagined and expressed, naturalized and legitimated, as a structural inevitability. Institutionalized in public discourse and interiorized through socialization, "the extreme valorization of the principle of armed struggle . . . ended up by creating dangerous 'automatisms' among the younger generation" (Stora 1998: 154). The many forms of struggle and their myriad possible outcomes were reduced, in the "naturalizing" inscription of history and its sacralization in the national imagination, to martyrdom and destiny.

Displacement?

When faced with an implacable social or political structure of violence—of which the colonial system was only one paradigm—people may feel compelled to adopt a strategy of violence as their only means of emancipation. This was as true of revolutionary Algeria in the 1950s as it was of South Africa in the 1960s, or of Palestinians in exile in the 1970s and in the Occupied Territories in 1987 and again in 2000. The recourse to violence considered as the only means of breaking out of a system of domination is a properly tragic step and is testimony to the terrible hypocrisies and intractabilities of the system thus contested. In its naturalization, though—which may also be a necessary social process—the meaning of this tragic choice is disfigured as the only legitimate means of contesting the system, testimony to the glory and "authenticity" of popular struggle, grounded in centuries of uniformly violent resistance to uniformly violent aggression. Revolutionary victory as the culmination of a continuous, substantially undifferentiated heritage of struggle, as that which marks the difference-in-resemblance between "this [victorious] generation" and its ancestors, which, I think, is what Boumédienne, in my epigraph, meant, reduces the complexity and heterogeneity of historical action, the myriad positions adopted and strategies enacted by real historical actors, to monochrome uniformity. Such naturalized history thus does violence to own subjects.

As the inscription and imagination of violence not as strategy but as structure, this mode of historical representation also sets up a "national imaginary" of the authentic past that, politicized and instrumentalized in processes of legitimation, informs the new strategic decisions taken by actors in new historical conjunctures. The resort to violence in the present is then understood, experienced, and expressed (and, on the outside, interpreted) as the reactualization of a structural constant. This (mis)representation has tended to color our whole view of Algerian history and politics.

The *salafi* reformists never intended to advocate armed struggle. Falling well short of any such idea, their cultural project—which, in theory, might perfectly well have been integrated into some kind of cohabitational, binational state—undoubtedly, though, benefited from a strong ancestor-hero discourse, intended to "revive" the Algerian community under their spiritual–cultural leadership. What actually happened was that their reconceptualization of the "national" past in terms of recurrent civilizational aggression and resistance, "depersonalization," and "authenticity," was recuperated and fused into a legitimation of a much more radical program by the revolutionary FLN. After independence, it provided the conceptual framework for the officialized inscription and commemorative imagination of the revolution. In the recomposition of the political sphere after 1992, it provided "automatic" grounding for the conceptualization of new political action.

The fragmentation of the single historical field of nationalism in a new war, however, has allowed both a new liberalization of the understanding of the past (the opening of debates firmly shut since 1962), and its radicalization. As of 1994–1995, there appears to have been a rupture in the Islamist camp between the leaders of the Army of Islamic Salvation (AIS), the armed wing of the Islamic Salvation Front (FIS),[38] who remained loyal to their imprisoned political leaders and open to the possibility of a political solution, and the "emirs" of the more radical Armed Islamic Groups (GIA) engaged in an escalated violence exercised, especially in the summer of 1997, as collective massacres of civilians. This seems to have indicated a change in the referential base of the latter, for whom, from this point on if not earlier, the war was conceived not in terms founded in the heritage of the Algerian Revolution, but as a *jihad* reimagined in terms of more recent theorizations of "sacred struggle." The most immediate reference for these is the Afghan experience, in which a number of GIA militants were first engaged. It is nonetheless a question, here, of political action founded on a certain type of historical understanding claiming to act in accord with, and in search of, "authenticity." The radicals' newly refigured meaning of *jihad* traces the roots of cultural identity and "legitimate" political order in a notion of community that now circumvents and displaces "national" history focused on a territorial *watan* (national homeland) to resituate itself in terms of a greater, utopian, and chiliastic political *umma islamiyya* (Islamic community).[39]

Perhaps most significant, the "authenticist" vision of nation founded by the *salafi* project has itself become questionable. It is only in the extremities of a new war that the myth of the authentic, unanimous Nation has been decentered and displaced, by a newly vocal and assertive (though undoubtedly small and fragile), pluralist and potentially democratic civil society on the one hand, and (more vocally and more viciously assertively) by an ultraradical conception of Islamic government, whose references are a mythical age of righteousness and the Afghanistan of the Taliban, on the other. The underlying "ethico-normative values" (Moussaoui 2001: 58) of struggle, resistance, and sacrifice remain. Invested since independence by the mythologized revolution, these structural topoi of historical understanding are perhaps now being re-founded in new representations, born out of a new, and reimagined, war.

Notes

The first version of this essay was written at the Maison Méditerranéenne des Sciences de l'Homme, Aix-en-Provence. I should like to thank the staff and faculty of the MMSH for making my stay there so productive and enjoyable.

1. From a speech made in 1976, quoted in Remaoun 1997: 317.
2. Sacralized in the 1976 constitution (art. 82) as "shield of the Revolution," the *Armée Nationale Populaire* roots its own legitimacy, as the central institution of state, in its putative direct descent from the revolutionary *Armée de Libération Nationale*.
3. A revealing throwaway comment, made by a distinguished analyst of Maghribi politics at a seminar in Oxford, February 2004.
4. On "naturalization" (in geography, "ethnic" categories, class, etc.), i.e., the refiguration as "nature" of what is perceptual, conjunctural, essentially arbitrary, see Bourdieu 1991: 105–106, 223; Balibar 1991.
5. The reformist historians are accorded brief mention in Merad 1967. Other studies include Bencheneb 1956, Desparmet 1933, Haddab 1984, Shinar 1971, and Touati 1997. In Arabic, see Murtad 1969.
6. *Taʾrikh al-jazaʾir fi ʾl-qadim wa ʾl-hadith.* The text of the original edition deals with the period from antiquity to the end of the Ziyanid dynasty in the sixteenth century.
7. Published in Constantine for the first time on 27 December 1935, it resumed publication after the war in 1947 and ran until 1956.
8. The FLN, an insurrectionary political and military front, was created in 1954 by dissident nationalist militants for the prosecution of the war of liberation.
9. I have referred to the second edition published in Algiers in 1986, and page references are to this printing.
10. "Mazigh" relates to the Berber word *amazigh* (pl. *imazighen,* contemporary Berberophones' own name for themselves as an *ethnie*). Al-Madani, following Ibn Khaldun, has Mazigh as an eponymous ancestor, the son of Kanᶜan

(Canaan), son of Ham, son of Noah. Qahtan is one of the canonical progenitors of the pre-Islamic Arabs of the Arabian peninsula.

11. Its number included the prodigiously productive Stéphane Gsell, author most notably of an *Histoire Ancienne de l'Afrique du Nord* in eight volumes, appearing between 1914 and 1928, and who would go on to a chair at the Collège de France, and the geographer-historian Emile-Félix Gautier, long an established authority on North Africa and a major influence on Fernand Braudel, who also taught in Algeria before World War II.

12. On the liberal, francophone élite, termed "Young Algerians" after the "Young Turks" and other similar movements in the Middle East, see Ageron 1964, and Ruedy 1996.

13. Particularly in the work of Louis Bertrand, director of the review *Afrique Latine*. See the discussion in Lorcin 1995.

14. Among the later texts, *Al-Muslimun fi jazirat Siqiliyya* extols the civilizational progress brought to medieval Europe by the (North African) Muslims in Sicily; *Muhammad ʿUthman Basha, dey al-Jazaʾir* paints a heroic portrait of the great works and war making of the late Ottoman regency of Algiers; *Kitab al-Jazaʾir* recounts the nation's never-ending defense of its liberty and calls (in the early 1930s) for the struggle to be taken up again; *Harb al-thalathamiʾa sana bayna ʾl-Jazaʾir wa Isbanya* tells of the "three hundred years' war" waged by Algeria, "bulwark of *jihad*" against early modern Spanish imperialism.

15. "What is particular to [colonial] Algeria is the coexistence of a cynical discourse with a humanist one; or more frequently a humanist discourse which is in fact a cynicism, or at least perfectly instrumental, but which fails to recognize itself as such" (Colonna 1975: 197).

16. Focused in the increasingly successful clandestine Parti du Peuple Algérien (PPA, founded in 1937 and banned in 1939) and its legal cover, the Mouvement pour la Triomphe des Libertés Démocratiques (MTLD), heir of the Etoile Nord-Africaine (ENA) founded among migrant workers in Paris in 1926. It was former militants of this current who would create the FLN in 1954.

17. See his manuscript "Mon Testament politique," published in Ageron 1994.

18. I have given a brief account of this in McDougall 2004.

19. The notorious phrase of Gautier (1927) in his classic treatise on the Islamization of North Africa.

20. For the ideology of "authenticity," see Ibrahimi 1973; for an analysis, see Deheuvels 1991.

21. Speech to the AUMA congress, January 1956, reported in Note, Police des Renseignements Généraux, Algiers, 9 January 1956 (241). Archives d'Outre Mer, Aix-en-Provence; Archives du Département d'Alger, 4I/14/2.

22. There was, no doubt, some such influence of the Islamic reformist movement on the *maquisards*, but it was more diffuse, concerned with a certain vision of Islamic orthodoxy and with the more general cultural orientation of an "essentially Arab-Islamic" national community. Even in this regard, the direct influence of the ʿulama themselves was to be much more significant after the revolution than it had ever been before or during the war.

23. The "revolutionary family": the ONM (Organisation Nationale des Anciens Mujahidin), ONEM (Organisation Nationale des Enfants de Mujahidin), and ONEC (Organisation Nationale des Enfants de Chouhada) (*chouhada/*

*shuhada*²—"martyrs"). The benefits accruing to members of these institutions include the availability of building land, housing, employment, bank loans, and imported goods. I am grateful to Abderrahmane Moussaoui for pointing out the significance of these institutions.

24. The last legislative elections in Algeria, shamelessly rigged by the Administration, were held in June 1951.

25. There is no necessity to fall once more into the trap of ideologizing (in terms of "loyalty" or otherwise) choices made for the most part, in most cases, in order to meet immediate difficulties and solve immediate problems (cf. Migdal 1974). The number of Algerians engaged in various capacities in French uniform is hotly disputed, but is supposed to have peaked at between 178,000 (Ageron 1993: 11) and 210,000 (Pervillé 1993: 305) between April (Pervillé) and November (Ageron) 1960.

26. This figure, symbolizing Algeria's war dead, has long been recognized by historians as exaggerated, but is still regularly quoted in academic as well as political writing. The true figure is impossible to ascertain with any precision but would seem to be around three hundred thousand (Ageron 1993, Yacono 1982).

27. Youssef Nacib, quoted in Remaoun 2000: 32.

28. Ahmed Rouadjia, quoted in Remaoun 2000: 32.

29. Personal communication (from a Sudanese Arabic teacher). There is also a saying current in Tunisia : "If an Algerian says to you: 'I'll kill you!'—he really will kill you."

30. William B. Quandt, quoted in Remaoun 2000: 32.

31. The son of Shaykh Bashir al-Ibrahimi, a founding member of the AUMA, who became the association's president after the death of Ben Badis.

32. Speech delivered on 15 November 1966, quoted in *Annuaire de l'Afrique du Nord* 5 (1966): 311.

33. A text written in 1972 by ʿAbd al-Malik Mukhtar (quoted in translation in Deheuvels 1995: 29).

34. On 19 June 1965, the "redressive movement," a military coup d'état led by Defense Minister Colonel Houari Boumédienne established the political order in place from then until October 1988.

35. Notably in the lifting of the taboos which covered the discrepant aspects of the "unanimous national revolution," embodied most potently in the figures of Ferhat Abbas and, even more so, Messali Hadj. The latter, historic leader of the radical–independentist current (ENA-PPA-MTLD), refused to sanction the FLN and his parallel movement, the MNA (Mouvement National Algérien) fought a "war within the war" against the FLN, leading to his eventual anathematization as "traitor." He died in exile in France in 1974. It is worth noting that the new crisis has also seen the recognition, by the French state, of its "operations for the maintenance of order" in Algeria as having constituted a "war" (June 1999), and, by some key figures of the colonial army (notably General Jacques Massu), of the torture routinely employed by the French in Algeria (summer 2000).

36. Note in particular the members of "GLD," Groupes de Légitime Défense, usually referred to as *patriotes*, armed by the state to protect themselves against Islamist terrorism. These groups have also been accused of the extrajudicial killing of civilians and of practicing the same tactics as their adversaries.

37. Hizb Fransa, the supposed neo-colonial "fifth column" sometimes claimed to be at the heart of the Algerian state.
38. The Islamist FIS coalition was created in 1989 and banned after 1992, when its first-round victory in the national legislative election was rescinded by the military's interruption of the process.
39. Here too, it remains necessary to rediscover a legitimate, authentic heritage, since, even for the most extreme acts conceived by the terrorists as "legitimate" acts of war (rape, the murder of pregnant women and of children, etc.), there is a need to find precedents in a tradition that can permit the sacralization of what, otherwise (and certainly for the vast majority of Algerians who, of course, refuse such "legitimation") remains an atrocious crime. It would be necessary to examine, here, the role played by the *fatawa* ("judicial" opinions) of the "emirs," and the narratives they employ, which doubtless claim to be founded on the acts of the Prophet and his Companions. I am indebted to Abderrahmane Moussaoui for discussion of developments among the Islamist factions.

References

Ageron, Charles-Robert, ed. 1997. *La guerre d'Algérie et les Algériens, 1954–1962*. Paris: Armand Colin.

——. 1994. "Mon testament politique" de Ferhat Abbas. *Revue Française d'Histoire d'Outre Mer* 81 (303): 181–197.

——. 1993. Pour une histoire critique de l'Algérie de 1830 à 1962. In *L'Algérie des Français*, ed. Charles-Robert Ageron, pp. 7–13. Paris: Seuil.

——. 1964. Le Mouvement 'Jeune Algérien' de 1900 à 1923. In *Études maghrébines: Mélanges Charles-André Julien*, ed. Jacques Berque et al., pp. 217–243. Paris: Presses Universitaires de France.

Anderson, Benedict. 1991 [1983]. *Imagined Communities: Reflections on the Origin and Spread of Nationalism*. London: Verso.

Balibar, Etienne. 1991. Racism and Nationalism. In *Race, Nation, Class: Ambiguous Identities*, ed. Etienne Balibar and Immanuel Wallerstein, 37–67. London: Verso.

Bencheneb, Saadeddine. 1956. Quelques historiens arabes modernes de l'Algérie. *Revue Africaine* 100: 475–499.

Bourdieu, Pierre. 1991. *Language and Symbolic Power*. Cambridge: Polity.

Carlier, Omar. 1997. Scholars and Politicians: An Examination of the Algerian View of Algerian Nationalism. In *The Maghrib in Question: Essays in History and Historiography*, ed. Michel Le Gall and Kenneth Perkins, pp. 136–189. Austin: University of Texas Press.

Colonna, Fanny. 1995. *Les versets de l'invincibilité: Permanences et changements religieux dans l'Algérie contemporaine*. Paris: Presses de la Fondation Nationale des Sciences Politiques

——. 1975. *Instituteurs algériens, 1883–1939*. Paris: Presses de la Fondation Nationale des Sciences Politiques.

Deheuvels, Luc. 1995. Histoire et épopée littéraire dans les courants fondamentalistes algériens contemporains durant les années soixante-dix. In *Les Arabes et l'histoire créatrice*, ed. Jacques Chevallier. Paris: Presses de l'Université de Paris-I, Sorbonne.

———. 1991. *Islam et pensée contemporaine en Algérie. La revue al-Asala, 1971–1981*. Paris: CNRS.

Desparmet, Joseph. 1933. Naissance d'une histoire "nationale" de l'Algérie. *Bulletin du Comité de l'Afrique Française*, July: 387–392.

Djender, Mahieddine. 1991 [1970]. *Introduction à l'histoire de l'Algérie*. Algiers: ENAL.

Étienne, Bruno. 1971. Le vocabulaire politique de légitimité en Algérie. *Annuaire de l'Afrique du Nord* 10: 69–103.

Gautier, Emile-Félix. 1927. *Les siècles obscurs du Maghreb*. Paris: Payot.

Ghalem, Mohamed, and Hassan Remaoun, eds. 1995. *Comment on enseigne l'histoire en Algérie*. Oran: CRASC.

Haddab, Mustafa. 1995. Statut social de l'histoire: Éléments de réflexion. In *Comment on enseigne l'histoire en Algérie*, ed. Mohamed Ghalem and Hassan Remaoun, pp. 15–34. Oran: CRASC.

———. 1984. Histoire et modernité chez les réformistes algériens. In *Connaissances du Maghreb: Sciences sociales et colonisation*, ed. Jean-Claude Vatin et al., pp. 387–400. Paris: CNRS.

Harbi, Mohammed. 1984. *1954, la guerre commence en Algérie*. Brussels: Complexe.

Hobsbawm, Eric. 1973–1974. Peasants and Politics. *Journal of Peasant Studies* 1: 3–22.

Ibrahimi, Ahmed Taleb. 1973. *De la décolonisation à la révolution culturelle, 1962–1972*. Algiers: SNED.

Labat, Séverine. 1995. *Les islamistes algériens entre les urnes et le maquis*. Paris: Seuil.

Lorcin, Patricia M. E. 1995. *Imperial Identities: Stereotyping, Prejudice and Race in Colonial Algeria*. London: I. B. Tauris.

al-Madani, Ahmad Tawfiq. 1986. *Qartajanna fi arbaʿa usur, min ʿasr al-hijara ila al-fath al-islami*. 2nd ed. Algiers: SNED.

———. 1981. *Hayat kifah: Mudhakkirat*. Vol. 1. French trans. *Mémoires de combat* by Malika Merabet. Algiers: SNED.

Martinez, Luis. 1998. *La guerre civile en Algérie, 1992–1998*. Paris: Karthala.

McDougall, James. 2004. S'écrire un destin : l'Association des ʿulama dans la révolution algérienne. *Bulletin de l'Institut d'Histoire du Temps Présent* 83 (1): 38–52.

Merad, Ali. 1967. *Le réformisme musulman en Algérie, 1925–1940. Essai d'histoire sociale et religieuse*. Paris: Mouton.

Migdal, Joel S. 1974. *Peasants, Politics, and Revolution: Pressures toward Political and Social Change in the Third World*. Princeton: Princeton University Press.

Moussaoui, Abderrahmane. 2001. Du danger et du terrain en Algérie. *Ethnologie Française* 31 (1): 51–59.

Murtad, Abd al-Malik. 1969. *Nahdat al-adab al-ʿarabi al-muʿasir fi al-Jazaʾir, 1925–1954*. Algiers: SNED.

Pervillé, Guy. 1993. La guerre d'Algérie: L'abandon des Harkis. In *L'Algérie des Français*, ed. Charles-Robert Ageron, pp. 303–311. Paris: Seuil.

Remaoun, Hassan. 2000. La question de l'histoire dans le débat sur la violence en Algérie. *Insaniyat* 10: 31–43.

———. 1997. Pratiques historiographiques et mythes de fondation: Le cas de la guerre de libération à travers les institutions algériennes d'éducation et de recherche.

In *La guerre d'Algérie et les Algériens, 1954–1962,* ed. Charles-Robert Ageron, pp. 305–322. Paris: Armand Colin.

———. 1995. Sur l'enseignement de l'histoire en Algérie, ou la crise identitaire à travers (et par) l'école. In *Comment on enseigne l'histoire en Algérie,* ed. Mohamed Ghalem and Hassan Remaoun, pp. 47–68. Oran: CRASC.

———. 1994. Enseignement de l'histoire et conscience nationale. *Confluences Méditerranée* 11 (Summer): 23–30.

Ruedy, John. 1996. Chérif Benhabylès and the Young Algerians. In *Franco-Arab Encounters: Studies in Memory of David C. Gordon,* ed. L. Carl Brown and Matthew S. Gordon, pp. 345–369. Beirut: American University of Beirut.

Sahli, Mohammed. 1965. *Décoloniser l'histoire: Introduction à l'histoire du Maghreb.* Paris: Maspero.

Saidouni, Nasreddine. 1984. "Nahwa nazra jadida li-taʾrikhina al-Jazaʾiri." *al-Thaqafa* 84 (November–December): 39–54.

Scott, James C. 1985. *Weapons of the Weak: Everyday Forms of Peasant Resistance.* New Haven: Yale University Press.

Shinar, Pessah. 1971. The Historical Approach of the ʿUlema in the Contemporary Maghreb. *Asian and African Studies* (Jerusalem) 7: 181–210.

Soufi, Fouad. 1997. La fabrication d'une mémoire: Les médias algériens (1963–1995) et la guerre d'Algérie. In *La guerre d'Algérie et les Algériens, 1954–1962,* ed. Charles-Robert Ageron, pp. 289–303. Paris: Armand Colin.

Stora, Benjamin. 1998. Algérie: Absence et surabondance de mémoire. In *Les violences en Algérie,* ed. Gilbert Grandguillaume et al., pp. 145–154. Paris: Odile Jacob.

———. 1991. *La gangrène et l'oubli: La mémoire de la Guerre l'Algérie.* Paris: La Découverte.

Touati, Houari. 1997. Algerian Historiography in the Nineteenth and Twentieth Centuries: From Chronicle to History. In *The Maghrib in Question: Essays in History and Historiography,* ed. Michel le Gall and Kenneth Perkins, pp. 84–94. Austin: University of Texas Press.

Yacono, Xavier. 1982. Les pertes algériennes de 1954–1962. *Revue de l'Occident Musulman et de la Méditerrannée* 34 (2): 119–133.

3 Patriotic Sacrifice and the Burden of Memory in Israeli Secular National Hebrew Culture

Yael Zerubavel

Modern nationalism is intimately linked to the ethos of patriotic sacrifice. Individuals' readiness to die for their nation is a social and moral act that defies their instinct for personal survival in the name of the future of the collectivity. This form of "altruistic suicide," to borrow Emile Durkheim's term, stems from intense identification with societal values and norms and a sense of moral obligation toward the collective (Durkheim 1951: 217–240). Idioms such as "to die on the altar of the country" and "sanctified death" reveal the sacred character of patriotic sacrifice as an important expression of "civil religion," highlighting the contribution of the sacrificial act as a symbolic reaffirmation of a nation's transcendental value (Bellah 1970: 168–186). The extreme character of patriotic sacrifice nonetheless introduces the need to curb the possible emergence of an excessive zeal that might lead to unnecessary loss of human life. "Patriotic sacrifice" therefore requires the fulfillment of certain conditions: that the call to arms is justified and the military action involved is critical for the nation's survival, and that fallen soldiers are believed to have been aware of the risk to their lives and were ready to die for this cause (Bar-Tal 1993).

In the idealized configuration of altruistic suicide, then, the individual functions in the unique position of serving as both the sacrificer and the sacrificed.[1] Such an extreme act of giving leaves the nation indebted to the fallen soldier for presenting it with the most significant gift possible. In return, the nation cultivates the memory of fallen soldiers through a variety of commemorative acts such as military funerals and burial in military cemeteries, posthumous citations and medals, annual memorial rituals for fallen soldiers, and monuments. The nation thus turns the fallen soldier into a collective representation and a national symbol.[2]

Patriotic sacrifice opens an exchange relationship between the individual and the nation that evolves into a complex system of moral, economic, and social obligations between the bereaved family (as the symbolic extension of the fallen soldier), and the state (representing the nation).[3] A soldier's death brings his family into the community of the bereaved, and the state assumes the responsibility to act in the deceased's place as a provider for the family. While the state supports the family in providing for the loss of income and the struggle to cope with the death, the bereaved family reaffirms the importance of the nation by its participation in official commemorations and activities of the bereaved families' community. The patriotic ethos assumes that the fallen soldiers' families and the state agree on the supreme significance of the sacrifice and form harmonious relations, united by their commitment to the dead and the values for which the fallen soldiers died.

The present chapter focuses on the attitude toward the ethos of patriotic sacrifice within the national secular Israeli culture from 1948 to the late 1990s. This ethos was an important foundation of Hebrew culture since the early years of Zionist settlement and struggle for the foundation of a Jewish state. Though it has remained central to Israel's defense ideology since 1948, it has also undergone significant changes in recent decades. The chapter begins with a discussion of the hegemonic attitude toward death for the country and the commemoration of the dead during the formative years of Israeli society and the first decades of the state. The discussion draws on the analysis of select literary texts and popular expressions. It then goes on to examine changes in the attitude toward the sacrificial act within the framework of relations between the state, the fallen soldier, and the bereaved family in the post-1967 era and in the context of an increasingly divisive political scene and a volatile conflict situation. Given the fluidity of politics in the Middle East, the continued violence between Israelis and Palestinians, and the deadlock in peace negotiations, the attitude toward death for the country has remained at the center of the Israeli political discourse, yet its meaning is continuously reinterpreted and transformed.

In light of the multiplicity of voices regarding the patriotic ethos in an increasingly polarized Israeli society, it is important to note that this chapter focuses on those changes that have taken place within the national secular Hebrew culture that was constructed by Jews who settled in Palestine before the foundation of the state of Israel and their descendants, who are mostly secular and from European countries. This population constituted the mainstream of Israeli society that shaped its foundations and its national culture and took an earlier lead in the implementation of its secular ethos of patriotic sacrifice. The chapter therefore does not address the attitude toward patriotic sacrifice among religious Zionist groups who have emerged as a growing political force within Israeli society in the post-1967 era and whose patriotic ethos is deeply rooted in a religious framework; and it does not discuss other important groups within Israeli society, including Israel's Palestinian and Ultra-Orthodox Jewish citizens, the large majority of whom reject Israeli nationalist ideology or its secular ethos and do not participate in the military service. Similar studies on these groups' attitudes toward the ethos of sacrifice are clearly essential for arriving at a fuller view of the multiplicity of perspectives on these issues within Israeli society.

"With blood and fire Judea fell; with blood and fire Judea will rise!" is a verse from a famous poem by Yaᶜacov Cahan, written after the Kishinev pogrom of 1903. This verse assumed a life of its own as a Zionist slogan representing a new ethos of self-defense (Cahan 1948).[4] As a national movement, Zionism advocated Jews' historical move from exile to the ancient Jewish homeland, and saw the process of national rebirth as entailing inevitable sacrifices by individuals. Readiness to die for the homeland was thus perceived as an important characteristic shared by both ancient and modern Jewish compatriots. Jewish revolts against Rome during the first and the second centuries evolved into heroic national myths and served as an inspiration for the Zionist national revival.[5] As Cahan's verse articulated so clearly, blood—the symbol of both life and death—was perceived as a symbolic bridge[6] connecting the national struggles of these two eras, otherwise separated by centuries of life in exile.

The romantic view of national struggles for liberation was popular in Europe, and the embrace of socialist ideologies by the early Zionist settlers further contributed to the emphasis on collective over individual needs. Moreover, the glorification of sacrifice was embedded within a linear narrative leading to a vision of national redemption. Hebrew poets and writers of that period articulated the significance of sacrifice for national redemption: "My brethren, this land demands our blood," Avidgor Hameiri writes in 1927; and Yitzhak Lamdan expresses a similar idea: "In full jugs of youth, do we carry joyful blood and first clusters of life in baskets of love / Everything is an offering for the battle and a dedication to Masada" (Hameiri 1926–1927: 93; Lamdan 1971: 209–210).[7]

A heroic spirit and readiness for sacrifice constituted an important component of the image of the New Hebrew Man (see Almog 2000: 119–137; Elboim-Dror 1996; Firer 1985). As early as 1911, the publication of a memorial book for several pioneers who were killed in clashes with Arabs signaled the process of turning the dead into heroic symbols of patriotic sacrifice (Frankel 1986: 355–384). The historical battle of Tel Hai gave rise to the first Hebrew national myth of settlement and defense, and the words of the dying hero, Yosef Trumpeldor— "It is good to die for our country"—represented the essence of the ethos of patriotic sacrifice. Soon after the event, a well-known writer and public figure, Moshe Smilansky, highlighted the symbolic value of a new sacred place, sanctified by the blood of the fallen (Smilansky 1920: 1).[8] Trumpeldor's saying became an important educational slogan and the defense of Tel Hai contributed to the ethos of patriotic sacrifice that shaped the foundations for the commemoration of fallen soldiers in Israeli culture.[9]

The importance of patriotic sacrifice was transmitted through formal educational venues and political channels, and was also evident in children's literature and popular culture, more prominently from the late 1920s to the 1950s. A children's story tells of two lumps of soil that after observing Trumpeldor's extraordinary commitment to building the land were ready to sacrifice themselves by jumping into the revolving knife of the plow (Bergstein 1955). A children's song describes an attack on a bee community by a vicious wasp and hails the sacrifice of a small, heroic bee, who "died in order to save its people." Hebrew youth internalized this message. Yaᶜir, a young leader of an activist group and a poet, writes in 1932: "Our desire—to always live as free people; our dream—to die for our country" (Yaᶜir 1976 [1932]). And an Israeli man recalls as an adult the centrality of this ideal to him as a child of the 1950s: "You know what was . . . my biggest dream as a young man? That I die in the battle for the homeland, wearing a red [paratrooper's] beret. And this wasn't a nightmare, but an experience of self-fulfillment" (Rosen 1998: 62–63). A popular anecdote points out the excessive success of this educational trend during the 1950s and 1960s, recounting how schoolchildren would write letters to soldiers expressing their wish that the soldiers would die for the homeland. Another anecdote tells of a Palmach underground's commander who reprimanded his soldiers by declaring them unworthy of dying for the homeland.[10]

The breakout of an intense struggle following the United Nations' resolution in support of the creation of a Jewish state in Palestine in November 1947 gave a concrete expression to the "fire and blood vision" of national rebirth. With six thousand casualties—the majority of whom were between the ages of seventeen and twenty-five—the war marked a generational shift in those who carried the burden of defense from the founders of modern Israeli society to their sons, and contributed to the image of the Sabra (the Hebrew youth) as a fighter (Almog 2000: 119–137; Sivan 1991: 29–33, 120–125). That year, the poet Nathan Alterman published his famous poem, "The Silver Platter," in the daily paper *Davar*. The poem depicts a young man and woman who, while falling at the feet of a female figure representing the nation, declare: "We are the silver platter on which you were given the Jewish state." The poem addresses themes that are central to patriotic sacrifice: the act of giving underlying the sacrifice, the youth's full awareness and acceptance of their imminent death, and the nation's implied indebtedness to its fallen youth for this gift (Alterman 1947). The "silver platter" emerged as a common metaphor for patriotic sacrifice, and the poem became a canonic text in Israeli memorial ceremonies.[11] The sacrifice rhetoric also employed the family trope to convey intimacy in the new relationship between the fallen soldiers, their families, and the nation-state: the soldiers are referred to as "sons" of the nation, whereas their relatives become new members in the national community of "the bereaved family" [*mishpahat ha-shekhol*].[12]

The experience of the loss of sons raised the significance of the biblical story of the *Akeda*, "the binding of Isaac," as a paradigmatic text from the past that helps interpret the present. The biblical text of Genesis 22 describes God's test of Abraham's faith by presenting the demand to sacrifice his son Isaac, and Abraham's readiness to comply with this demand. In the biblical story, the actual sacrifice is diverted when Abraham hears the voice telling him to replace the bound Isaac with a ram at the moment he raises the knife on the boy. The *Akeda* has been a highly valued text in the Jewish tradition (it is recited in the synagogue on the high holiday of Rosh Ha'Shana) and generations of Jews have turned to it as a model of behavior in extreme situations of persecution and sacrifice.[13] Although Israeli society followed this traditional pattern of turning to the *Akeda* as a paradigmatic text, modern Hebrew culture secularized its traditional meaning by transforming religious martyrdom into readiness to die for the homeland. Yet in using the biblical text, the analogy between the past and the present is clearly incomplete: Whereas the biblical narrative provides Isaac with a miraculous rescue, the modern secular version offers no such relief as Israeli "sons" encounter their death in battle. In another departure from the biblical text, Isaac is no longer portrayed as passive but rather as a willing participant.[14] This modern Israeli version of the *Akeda* therefore highlights the cooperation between fathers and sons and the national solidarity around the ethos of patriotic sacrifice.

Since 1948, the *Akeda* has emerged as a key symbolic text of patriotic sacrifice in Israeli literature, art, theater, and film.[15] The mythical narrative made it possible to express pain and guilt toward fallen youth, and at the same time offered consolation in the broader framework of collective redemption: the biblical account of God's covenant with Abraham following the *Akeda* reaffirms the conception of individual sacrifice as leading to collective survival. This redemptive sequence thus reinforces the theme of death and rebirth. The poetic verse of the national Hebrew poet, Chaim Nachman Bialik, "In their death they commanded us to live," became another canonic phrase in mourning rhetoric, expressing the moral indebtedness by the community of the living to those who died and the mobilization of their deaths as a renewed commitment to collective survival (Bialik 1966: 79). The prominent theme of the "living-dead" soldiers in Hebrew war poetry and Israel's establishment of a direct temporal flow from its official "Memorial Day for Fallen Soldiers" to "Independence Day" similarly diffuse the finality of death.[16]

The intense memory work and the emergence of a wide range of memorial sites indicated the strong adherence to the ethos of patriotic sacrifice and the deep sense of indebtedness to those who died for the homeland. In addition to the establishment of an official Memorial Day for the Fallen Soldiers, Israeli society commemorated fallen soldiers by an extensive production of monuments, memorial books, songs, fiction, and poems, and through the practice of naming settlements, streets, parks, and forests after a collective group or individuals.[17] The cultural emphasis on moral indebtedness to the dead contributed to the portrayal of the nation, the fallen soldiers, and the bereaved families as a tight community that rallies around the ethos of patriotic sacrifice and cultivates the memory of the dead.

*   *   *

The Six-Day War of 1967 introduced another turning point in the development of the ethos of patriotic sacrifice in Israel. The extensive mobilization of soldiers on reserve duty and, even more so, the voluntary return of citizens who were abroad in order to take part in the battle, manifested a powerful commitment to the patriotic ethos. The sweeping victory that followed weeks of acute anxiety, and the territorial expansion as a result of the war led to national euphoria and generated a new sense of security. A new heroic lore emerged soon after the war, commemorating the eight hundred soldiers who died in it and lauding the behavior of military commanders and soldiers (Shamir 1996: 89–102).[18] Yet, along with the official and spontaneous creation of multiple commemorative rites that embraced the ethos of patriotic sacrifice, the war also generated first seeds of moral unrest. The publication of recorded conversations among kibbutz members who fought in the war did not challenge the ethos of patriotic sacrifice but revealed their moral anguish over the inhumane face of war and its impact on individuals (Shapira 1970; see Tsur 1976: 183).

Military clashes (primarily with Egypt along the Suez Tunnel) continued from 1967 to 1970 and brought a death toll of 721 persons, close to the total casualties in the "official" Six-Day War. Although these clashes were not officially recognized as a "war," Israeli popular discourse related to this continuing military engagement as the War of Attrition,[19] and news about those casualties and the 2,659 wounded marred some of the euphoria of the immediate post-1967 era. Nonetheless, it took the traumatic experience of the Yom Kippur War in 1973 to trigger a major political and ideological crisis. The unexpected attack and the anxiety over Israel's ability to overcome the enemies' forces, the duration of the war, and the high toll of 2,569 dead and about 7,000 wounded shook up Israeli society. In spite of Israel's ultimate military success, the Yom Kippur War generated an atmosphere of disillusionment and demoralization. Public outrage at what was seen as the military intelligence's and the government's failures to properly assess the situation and prepare for this war led to an official investigation that focused on these issues. This public response thus challenged the government's fulfillment of its obligation to protect citizens' lives and minimize their loss in the struggle for national survival. The difficulties encountered in this war and the number of wounded and dead generated an atmosphere of intense mourning and grief and increased awareness of the impact of the battle experience on individuals (Bilu and Wiztum 2000: 8, 14–16).

The Yom Kippur War led to the deepening of ideological, social, and political rifts within the society and a greater polarization of Israelis' positions about the conflict with the Palestinians and neighboring Arab countries. The traumatic war reinforced the feeling of besiegement and national isolation that gave rise to a new emphasis on historical continuity within the Jewish experience from exile to the homeland and to Israelis' growing identification with the Holocaust and its victims (Gertz 2000; Yadgar 2004: 54–79). But the war also led to new skepticism about earlier expectations that patriotic sacrifice would be limited to a transitory phase and would end with national rebirth. While the patriotic and the educational discourses continued to promote national symbols and myths of heroism, sacrifice, and survival, growing doubts addressed the situation of a repeating cycle of wars, leading the Right and the Left to conflicting interpretations of its resolution.

During the 1970s and 1980s, the early seeds of morbid humor and political satire that had emerged during the War of Attrition became more wide-spread.[20] Jokes and popular songs, works of fiction, satirical plays, and films offered counternarratives to the canonic national heroic lore and articulated a growing ambivalence toward the bloody reality and grim consequences of continuing wars. During this period, an anecdote that Trumpeldor did not utter his famous saying "It is good to die for our country" but uttered a juicy Russian curse became highly popular. In spite of historical evidence supporting the validity of his expression of readiness for patriotic sacrifice, the anecdote now appeared more credible to those who were critical of the gaps between the national rhetoric of patriotic sacrifice and the reality of the battlefield.[21]

Morbid humor was largely produced by the young generation facing the immediate threat of death in fulfilling their military duties. Examples of such expressions include the high school seniors' joke upon graduating that they will next meet on their school memorial plaque; the joking reference to the military cemetery "Saul's City" (Kiryat Shaul) as the "Youth's City" (Kiryat ha-Noar); and the gruesome reversal of the song verse, "there was a 'pile' of guys on the grass," that turns it to "there was a pile of grass on the youth." In a similar vein, the film Summer Blues (directed by Renan Schorr, 1987) depicts a group of high school seniors who, following the death of their friend in the army shortly after being drafted, put together a macabre show of song and dance to the patriotic saying "it is good to die for our country." During the War of Lebanon, Israeli television triggered a wave of shock, indignation, and disbelief following the broadcast of soldiers singing morbid lyrics about death and war injuries. The soldiers improvised these new sinister words to the melodies of naive folksongs or children's songs, which highlighted through contrast the morbidity of the lyrics. Similar expressions of a cynical attitude and black humor by soldiers during their military service or in rehabilitation wards can also be found in memoirs, fiction, and film.[22]

Political satire became a venue for targeting the absurdity of war and disillusionment with the continuing conflict. The work of Hanoch Levin, the most prominent playwright of political satire in the aftermath of the Six-Day War, expresses a highly irreverent attitude toward the glorification of war, heroism, and patriotic death. His cabaret piece, Victory Parade of the 11-Minute War, originally performed in 1968, was inspired by the Israeli General Gorodish-Gonen's victory speech in the Six-Day War. In this piece, the general addresses his soldiers, officers, and comrades-in-arms with great pathos and congratulates them for their astonishing victory. As he wishes to salute them, he realizes that he is standing in front of an empty field, and directs his salute to heaven (Levin 1987: 13).[23] In another piece, titled "The Fire and Blood Tango," Levin mocks Ya'acov Cahan's earlier glorification of sacrifice for national rebirth by describing the entire country engulfed by fire and blood (Levin 1987: 39).

The macabre humor can be seen as a form of indirect protest targeting the ethos of patriotic sacrifice: while it clearly has an aggressive edge, it falls short of open political confrontation. The deliberate use of debased language and shocking images stands in a sharp contrast to the lofty expressions and glorifying heroic images of the national lore. By dwelling on the immediate and grue-some consequences of the war with references to bodily dysfunctions, blood, and death, the humor challenges the distancing strategy employed by the patri-otic discourse. While these humorous texts allow the soldiers to express their anxiety about the war and diffuse some of their fears through laughter, they provoke intense anger and loud protest by those who consider these topics taboo and find this vulgar, absurd, or grotesque humor a repulsive form of sacrilege. Though such expressions were widely known among members of the youth movements and those in combat military service (i.e., youth who constituted · the core of the secular national Hebrew culture), when they became widely pub-licized by the television broadcast in 1982 or were performed on stage, they stirred up an intense public outcry for violating the sacred and glorified char-acter of patriotic sacrifice.

* * *

The growing awareness that the Israeli–Palestinian conflict continues to pre-sent a demand for sacrificing the sons triggered a renewed interest in the sym-bolic and moral meanings of the *Akeda*. The repeated use of the biblical story demonstrates the role of the myth as a symbolic bridge between the past and the present. In this dialogic process, the traditional text serves as a lens through which the current reality is examined while the present modifies the interpre-tation of the traditional text. As in the past, the *Akeda* is applied to the inter-pretation of collective traumas in which individual Jews sacrifice themselves for the group's survival. Yet increasingly, the biblical text serves as a venue to ar-ticulate doubts, guilt, pain, and anger about the continuing call for patriotic sacrifice. New interpretations of the *Akeda* therefore express diverse positions, ranging from painful acceptance to blunt criticism.

A poem titled "Heritage," written by the well-known Israeli poet of the "1948 generation," Haim Gouri, provides an example for an early reinterpreta-tion of the *Akeda*. The poem opens where the biblical narrative of Abraham's test ends, namely with the appearance of a ram. It goes on to describe the long life that Isaac enjoyed following that life-turning episode and concludes with the following verse:

> Isaac, as the story goes, was not sacrificed.
> He lived for many years, saw what pleasure had to offer,
> until his eyesight dimmed.
> But he bequeathed that hour to his offspring.
> They are born with a knife in their hearts. (Gouri 1981 [1961]: 565)

The poem thus suggests that the "binding of Isaac" is not a unique event in Jewish history but a recurring experience that is relived by every generation of Jews. Isaac becomes a collective representation of the Jewish people and the poem highlights his experience as key to the Jewish experience throughout the ages. With this interpretation, the poem defies the linear, teleological orientation of the biblical story that presents the *Akeda* as a singular occurrence with a redemptive ending and turns it into a cyclical recurrence. By implication, the poem undermines the redemptive orientation of the Zionist master commemorative narrative. Other texts, too, present a similar feeling of being entrapped within a cyclical recurrence of violence and express the fear that this situation makes sacrifice inevitable.[24]

The playwright Hanoch Levin draws on the *Akeda* narrative in several of his satirical pieces. In a short piece entitled *Isaac*, written in a pseudo-biblical style, he describes how Abraham begets his son and when Isaac is twenty years old, he goes to war against the Arabs and is killed in action. Abraham buries him and begets another Isaac, who grows up and when he reaches the age of twenty, he goes to war with the Arabs, is killed, and Abraham buries him. The cycle is repeated with no other change in the text except for Abraham's progressively older age. When Abraham reaches age one hundred, he decides to trick God and begets his own grandson, Jacob (Levin 1987: 149). The plot thus succeeds in getting out of the loop, and Abraham guarantees the continuity of his family line. By providing this absurd solution to Abraham's plight, Levin wishes to accentuate the absurdity of the continuing conflict that produces death in the name of survival. It is interesting to note, however, that a similar theme appears in other Israeli literary works.[25]

The continuing toll on young men's lives shifted the focus of the interpretation of the *Akeda* from fathers to sons, enhancing the identification with Isaac. Levin presents another version of the story, written in the form of a dialogue between Abraham and Isaac:

Abraham: My son, Isaac, do you know what I'm going to do to you now?
Isaac: Yes, Dad, you are going to slaughter me.
Abraham: This is God's command.
Isaac: I have no arguments, Dad, if you need to slaughter, do.
Abraham: I have to slaughter, I'm afraid there is no choice.
Isaac: I understand. You don't have to make it hard on yourself, simply rise and pull the knife on me.
Abraham: I do this only as God's messenger.
Isaac: Clearly as God's messenger, Dad. Rise as a messenger and pull your knife as a messenger on your only son whom you love.
Abraham: Great, Isaac, make it hard for your poor father, spoil his mood, as if it not enough for him as it is.
Isaac: Who makes it difficult, Dad, rise quietly and finish off your miserable son with one fatherly gesture.
Abraham: I know, it is easiest to blame me. Never mind, never mind, blame your lonely father.
Isaac: Who blames? You are only God's messenger, isn't it? And when God tells you to slaughter your son like a dog, you must run and slaughter.
Abraham: Great, great, this is what I deserve in my old age. Put all the blame on me if it suits you, on your old, broken father who, at his age, has to climb up a mountain with you, bind you to the altar, slaughter you and, after all this still needs to tell your Mom about all that. Do you think that I have nothing better to do at my age?

When Abraham is about to pull his knife on Isaac, his son tells him that he hears a voice. Abraham first denies hearing any voice but after Isaac reminds his father of his deafness, Abraham accepts Isaac's plea to replace him by the ram:

Isaac: Dad, I swear, I heard a voice from heaven.
Abraham [after a while]: Nu, if you heard, you heard. I, as you said, am a bit deaf.
Isaac: Sure, you know that on my part I was prepared [for the sacrifice], but a voice is a voice. (Levin 1987: 89–91)

Levin's Abraham is not the admirable, principled man of faith of the traditional myth but a pathetic, self-centered old man who focuses on his own difficulties in carrying out God's command and has no compassion for his son whose life he is about to take. Isaac's ironic voice presents a subversive reading of the *Akeda*. The conclusion of Levin's narrative leaves it ambiguous if Isaac indeed heard the voice or tricks Abraham into believing it so as to save his life (Baron 1998; Kartun-Blum 1995).

The new interpretive trend shifts Isaac's role from a "sacrifice" to a "victim." While these two concepts are encompassed within a single Hebrew term, *korban*, they convey different psychological, social, and moral implications for Isaac's role, and by extension, for the role of the fallen soldier.[26] Here, Isaac is no longer the young man who proves his own readiness for self-sacrifice along with his father, as the literature of the Independence War depicts. Instead, he is portrayed as a victim of his father's excessive eagerness to comply with God's demand to sacrifice his son. The portrayal of Isaac as a skeptical participant or a reluctant victim challenges the appropriateness of the *Akeda* as a symbolic representation of patriotic sacrifice since it contests the assumption of the inevitability of the sacrifice as well as the willingness of the sacrificed to die for the collective cause.

Even when the *Akeda* does not serve as an explicit frame of reference, it often serves as the subtext. This is evident in literary works that portray fathers as too eager to make a sacrifice or embrace the role of a bereaved parent. A Levin poem, "My Dear Father," is written as a monologue in which a fallen soldier addresses his own father from his grave:

My dear father, when you stand next to my grave,
Old and tired and very lonely,
And you see how they lower my body into the ground,
And you stay on top of me, my father,

Don't stand there so proud,
Don't hold up your head, my father,
We are left flesh to flesh
And this is the time to cry, my father.

Let your eyes then cry over my eyes,
And do not be silent for the sake of my honor,
Something that is more important than honor
Is laying at your feet now, my father.

And don't say that you made a sacrifice,
Because the one who sacrificed was me,
And don't use lofty words
Because I lie very low now, my father.

My dear father, when you stand next to my grave
Old and tired and very lonely,
And you see how they lower my body into the ground,
Ask for my forgiveness, my father. (Levin 1987: 89)

The performance of this poem triggered the public protest against Levin's satirical show *The Queen of the Bathtub,* and forced the Cameri Theater to discontinue it after nineteen performances. In 1970, such blunt criticism of the ethos of patriotic sacrifice, and worse—of a bereaved father who lost his son in battle—violated sacred values of Israeli society. Yet Levin was not alone in articulating a critical attitude toward fathers' readiness to sacrifice their sons.

Amos Oz's short story "By Way of the Wind," written as early as 1962, describes a father to whom the bereaved father's role provides a relief from his growing frustration with his son. The father, a kibbutz founder and leading figure in the Labor movement, is deeply disappointed in his son's character, but when the son volunteers with the paratroopers, he feels vindicated. During a parachuting display performed in a field near their kibbutz, the son is eager to impress the watchful crowd of kibbutz members, and violates the army's instructions. As a result, his parachute becomes entangled in electric cables and, as he is afraid to follow the suggestion to cut the straps in order to let himself loose, he remains bound to the cables. The father, embarrassed by his son's behavior, scolds and insults him, and the son eventually throws himself on the electrical cable and dies, still bound to his parachute. The narrator's ironic voice ends the story with the observation that "the status of a bereaved father wraps a halo of sacred agony," thus implying that the new status might compensate the father for the public humiliation he suffered from his son's behavior prior to his death (see Oz 1986 [1962]).

A. B. Yehoshua's novella *In the Beginning of Summer 1970* provides another example for this critical approach toward the embracement of the bereaved father role (Yehoshua 1974). Yehoshua describes a lonely, old, and beleaguered teacher who is alienated from his son and his colleagues at school, who receives the shocking news that his son has been killed in action. His new status as a bereaved father instantly transforms his colleagues' attitude and fills his life with a new meaning. The teacher imagines himself delivering a patriotic speech about death and bereavement:

Students, I don't want to overburden you with my sorrow, but I ask you to look at me, so that this [death] does not surprise you, because, here, in some way, I was prepared for his death, and this gave me my strength at this horrific moment. [30]

When summoned to identify his son's body, the father is shocked to find out that the dead man was misidentified. He is taken to a distant military camp where he finds his son alive and unaware of the confusion about his fate. The father, who had little contact with his son and hardly knows his daughter-in-law and young grandson, fails to connect with all three even when he meets them face-to-face under these stressful circumstances. His eagerness to assume the public role of a bereaved father is thus ironically juxtaposed with his role as an absent father.

The critical depiction of a bereaved father is an important theme in Yoram Kenyuk's 1981 novel, *The Last Jew* (1981). Wishing to establish a heroic image for his fallen son, the father embraces a fabricated biography that his son's friend produces in order to please the father. The friend describes heroic deeds that the son had never performed and assigns him to a more important battle than the one in which he encountered his death. He also credits the son with writing poetry, and even finds poems that he ascribes to the dead man. The father, an active participant in the bereaved parents' association, accepts this invented biography in spite of his wife's objections. Kenyuk extends his critique of the cult of the dead through the use of the grotesque. The son's friend begins to produce memorials for fallen soldiers based on this experience. Responding to bereaved families' demands to create elaborate memorials for fallen sons, he develops a lucrative "memory industry."[27]

These literary texts thus question the ethos of patriotic sacrifice by using the *Akeda* as a paradigmatic narrative of sacrifice made in the name of the collective good. This reinterpretation of the biblical text assumes a highly critical stance that targets its repeated use as representing the ethos of sacrifice in contemporary Israeli culture. The use of the *Akeda* in reference to the present, however, is not limited to the literary sphere, but has become part of popular and academic discourse. Thus, for example, an article on women's protests against the war and the continuing loss of lives characterizes the women's approach by their opposition to the *Akeda* myth; and bereaved parents refer to the myth in discussing their own grief (Mazali and Livne-Freudental 1998: 34–35; Tamir 1993: 225).

The continuing use of the *Akeda* demonstrates the vitality of a symbolic narrative that is open to diverse (and at times, contrasting) interpretations. Thus, the *Akeda* continues to serve as the embodiment of social solidarity and as a supreme expression of patriotic sacrifice and reinforces the society's commitment to remember those who died for the homeland. And at the same time, the *Akeda* also serves as a venue to express doubts, frustrations, and objections to the paradigm of sacrifice and its applicability to contemporary Israeli politics. With the deepening of social and political divisions within Israeli society, the protest against various aspects of patriotic sacrifice has increasingly become more direct and open, contributing to the further radicalization of the political scene.

* * *

For the first time, the Lebanon War (1982–1985) broke the national consensus that the war was essential for the nation's security and survival, a consensus that is a critical condition for the justification of patriotic sacrifice. The first Palestinian *intifada* that broke out in 1987 and the continuing Israeli military involvement in southern Lebanon deepened divisions between the Right and the Left in Israel: those who believed that the continuing control over the West Bank, Gaza, and Southern Lebanon guarantees for Israel's future security and that Israel has a right to control these lands, and those who advocated the pursuit of peace negotiations with the Palestinians and argued that a peace agreement justifies the price of territorial concessions.

In 1982, doubts about the goals of the extended invasion of Lebanon challenged two fundamental beliefs that are at the core of Israeli national culture: that Israel engages in wars out of *no choice* and that these wars represent a fight of *a few against many* (Gertz 2000: 1–26). The harsh criticism from the Left that this was a war of choice (*milhemet breira*) intensified following the massacre of Palestinians in the Sabra and Shatila refugee camps by Christian militias that had been collaborating with Israel. The public outcry led to mass demonstrations against the war and its impact on the civilian population in 1982 and 1983. Soldiers in uniform took part in this public debate and a selective conscientious objection to participating in this war (as opposed to serving in the army in general) grew to about 165 soldiers, primarily those on reserve duty. Most famous among these was the early case of an Israeli career officer, Eli Geva, who refused to lead his soldiers in a war he considered unjustified. His refusal attracted much public attention, and he was demoted and dismissed from the army (Linn 1996: 36–37, 73–78).

In the 1980s and 1990s, the Israeli Left was caught in a moral and an ideological dilemma, torn between its patriotic commitment and its opposition to the government's policies. On the one hand, many of its members abide by a strong patriotic tradition of responding to the call to arms regardless of one's political views and a code of personal loyalty to one's combat fellows founded on years of shared military experience (Hellman 1993).[28] On the other hand, participation in military operations that are governed by policies to which they are opposed requires these soldiers to risk their lives without accepting the goals for which they fight.

The proliferation of pro-peace organizations and protest movements in Israel from the late 1970s to the 1990s was undercut by organizational division and a lack of agreement on goals, agendas, and tactics. The centrist Peace Now, formed in 1978, advocated peace negotiations with the Palestinians and pursued civilian protests against the Lebanon War and other military actions, but expected its members to obey army rules when called to military service. The Four Mothers, which was founded in 1997 around the advocacy of a withdrawal from southern Lebanon, held a similar position. Their limited goal and the mass support it received led to the implementation of the withdrawal from Lebanon by Prime Minister Ehud Barak in May 2000. In contrast, the more radical movements *Yesh Gevul* [literally, there is a limit/border], formed a few months prior to the War of Lebanon, and Women in Black [*Nashim be-Shahor*] which became active in 1987, called to end the occupation of Palestinian territories and advocated the refusal to serve beyond the 1967 borders, even at the price of jail sentences. A relatively more recent movement, New Profile [*Profile Hadash*], rallied to legalize conscientious objection, supporting conscientious objectors' legal struggle in courts and those who received jail sentences (Bar-On 1985; Hellman 1993; Linn 1996).

The pro-peace protest movements thus represented a wide range of goals and pursued different tactics as they negotiated patriotic values and the call for sacrifice in this volatile political context. Groups such as Women in Black and The Four Mothers suffered from attacks by the Right and its members were confronted by hostile responses (Hellman and Rappoport 1997).[29] The highly charged atmosphere around these issues led to two politically motivated murders during pro-peace demonstrations: A Peace Now member, Emil Grunzweig, was killed in Jerusalem in 1983, and Israel's Prime Minister, Yitzhak Rabin, was murdered in Tel Aviv in 1995.

In a society where security is at the center of public awareness and the army has direct and indirect influence over political issues and careers (Kimmerling 1993), a protest on issues relating to security either from the Left or Right are easily perceived as subversive and dangerous. To avert accusations of lack of patriotism, protesters often try to display their right to protest by referring to their military rank, combat experience, or relation to a fallen soldier as a proof of their patriotic past.[30] In this context, women have a greater license to express their concern about the justification of the war and the call for patriotic sacrifice drawing on their roles as mothers and wives. This may account for the relatively high presence of women's groups within the protest movement. Yet the ideological and political divisions between the Right and the Left cut across gender lines. For example, the visibility of feminist Women in Black on the Left led to the establishment of an opposing women's group—Women in Green—that supports the Jewish settlements and the agenda of the Right.

Although it has attracted much public attention and has been on the rise since the outbreak of the second *intifada*, conscientious objection to military service on the Left is still relatively limited in scope among regular army recruits and reaches several hundreds among reserve soldiers. Israel's Supreme Court of Justice denied the right for "selective" objection (against military service beyond the green line) or exemption of military service on the basis of "universal" (general) conscientious objection to any military service (Gans 2004: 10–11, 22–23). Moreover, in recent years the army is more determined to persecute those who hold on to their objection to serve. Recently, the heated controversy about Sharon government's plan for withdrawal from Gaza and the dismantling of Jewish settlements has intensified the calls for conscientious objection on the Right and some of its leaders, including prominent rabbis, have made public their advocacy to refuse military orders to carry out this plan. Academic discussions and Israeli public discourse are currently engaged in analyzing and comparing the challenges that conscientious objection and civil disobedience on the Left and on the Right present to Israeli army, government, and legal system.[31]

* * *

The weakening of the patriotic sacrifice in the 1980s and early 1990s went hand in hand with enhanced awareness of the long-term impact of wars on individuals' lives. Such phenomena as battle shock and war traumas, wounded soldiers' and disabled veterans' ability to cope with their situations, and the experience of mourning and bereavement drew more public and professional attention. This trend reflects a significant shift from the earlier focus on the collective contribution of patriotic sacrifice in line with the collectivist ethos of the pre-state and early state periods. Although the scope of this article does not allow us to explore all these issues in detail, it is important to note that these topics are the subject of autobiographical writing, fiction, drama, film, and art, as well as of growing academic research (cf. Bilu and Wiztum 2000; Friedman 1993; Malkinson et al. 1993; Naveh 1993; Shamgar-Handelman 1986; Weiss 1997; Y. Zerubavel 2003). The following discussion addresses some of the issues related to the bereaved family's responses and the commemoration of the dead as part of the examination of the relations between the state and the families of fallen soldiers.

The patriotic ethos assumes a shared agreement on the value of patriotic sacrifice between bereaved families and the state, and the compatibility of collective and private memories related to fallen soldiers. The perception of harmonious relations based on an exchange between the bereaved families and the state follows this assumption: The state rewards the dead soldier's family members by granting them the official recognition of "a bereaved family," by taking care of their needs, and by sanctifying the fallen soldier's memory. On its part, the family accepts its role as a member of the national community of the bereaved and takes part in official commemorations of fallen soldiers, thereby displaying and reaffirming its acceptance of the value of patriotic sacrifice.

The greater scrutiny of the call for patriotic sacrifice led to significant transformations in the perception of the relations between the state and bereaved families. Public demand for greater accountability was not only directed to the government but also to the army, and led to families' insistence on information about the specific circumstances of their sons' deaths. Legal suits against the army, especially in cases of accidents, drew much publicity and indicate the ways in which the legal discourse has become an alternative channel competing with the patriotic discourse. Moreover, the recourse to legal action demonstrates that the bereaved families and the state may hold incompatible views of the soldier's death that lead to adversarial relations.

Ownership of the memory of the dead has emerged as another point of contention between bereaved families and state agencies: Who has the right to decide on the appropriate commemoration of fallen soldiers? Who has the authority to decide on how the memory of the dead is shaped? Within this context, the standardization of memory by the Defense Ministry became a contested issue. As the examination of private memorial books and school memorials for dead soldiers indicates (see Amit 1995),[32] commemorative traditions involve the emergence of shared patterns even if the individuals who create these memorials may not be aware of this phenomenon. Yet in the case of state-sponsored memorials, a policy of standardization is obligatory and deliberate, and stems from the democratic ideology that emphasizes citizens' equality. Furthermore, the standardization of fallen soldiers' memorials highlights the importance of the collective over the uniqueness of individuals and reaffirms the value of patriotic sacrifice.

Yet some bereaved parents opposed the standardization of memory in official commemoration of fallen soldiers—manifested in uniform funerals, uniform tombstones and inscriptions—which had been accepted as a given. They argued that these restrictions limited the expression of their memory of the dead. Their demand to participate in the determination of the script on their sons' tombstones resulted in lawsuits when the Ministry of Defense refused to grant room for the families' input. In 1995, the Supreme Court accepted a bereaved family's position, arguing that the official agencies' collectivist approach is archaic and paternalistic. The court required the Ministry of Defense to allow families some flexibility in determining the inscriptions on tombstones within the framework of its guidelines (Rubenstein 1997; see *Ha'aretz* 28 March 1995).

In a challenge to the conception of a national community that unites bereaved families and the nation in their shared experience of loss and joint commitment to commemorate the dead, recent works of Hebrew literature depict bereaved families' greater preoccupation with their private pain and memory work and their reluctance to take part in the state ceremonies that are public and impersonal in character (Rosenthal 2001: 59–80).[33] The tensions between collective and individual memories defy the assumption of compatible and harmonious relations between bereaved families and the state, which underlie the ethos of patriotic sacrifice.

Two recent novels by well-known women writers, published by mainstream Israeli publishers, stand out as powerful examples of this recent trend. Yehudit Hendel's *The Mountain of Losses* (1991) and Batya Gur's *Stone for a Stone* (1998) focus on bereaved families and explore their response to their sons' deaths during their military service. Gur's novel is a fictional account inspired by the case of a soldier who was killed in an accident during a "roulette" game held by his unit. The novel portrays the bereaved mother's desperate struggle to bring to court top officers in that military unit whom she sees as responsible for her son's unjustifiable death. The mother, an artist, also bitterly objects to the standardized inscription of patriotic rhetoric on her son's tombstone, which she sees as another manifestation of the army's attempts to cover up the real circumstances of her son's death: "It is all a lie. A big lie. And not even an accident. He was murdered and this will be written here now, as it ought to be. It will be written that he was murdered by his commanders, led like a lamb to the slaughter" (1998: 27). Her struggle with the state institutions and her demand that the high commanders will be prosecuted is nonetheless doomed to failure. During this process, she becomes increasingly isolated from her family and community, although she remains supported by other women in court. In an act of a private revolt against the state, she destroys the military tombstone on her son's grave and replaces it with her own sculpture with the inscription that the son "was led as a sheep to the slaughter by his commanders." The use of the Holocaust-related phrase "like sheep to the slaughter" in reference to a fallen soldier is highly subversive. It portrays him as a "victim" rather than a "sacrifice," and implies an analogy between him and the Jewish victims of World War II. When the court rules in favor of the army, the mother commits suicide on her son's grave, asserting her ultimate defiance of the state.

Yehudit Hendel's powerful novel portrays one day in bereaved parents' lives spent in the military cemetery where their son is buried. The novel describes the parents' internal and social worlds, consumed by their private grief and total devotion to memory work years following their son's death. The detailed portrayal of their visit to the military cemetery illuminates the bereaved families as a shadow community whose life is immersed in daily visits to their sons' graves. The bereaved families continue to care for their dead as a way of maintaining their ties with them: they cultivate small gardens around the graves, bring food and other items that the dead had liked, and worry if the dead can still feel the heat or the cold or might get worried if they notice that their visitor is sick.[34] In contrast to the conventional societal perception of cemeteries as the territory of death where time stands still, the parents feel that their lives in the outside world are meaningless and frozen, whereas they become alive in the cemetery where they reconnect with their dead sons. In this novel too, a bereaved mother who suffers from depression and growing isolation from her husband, friends, and the "bereaved family" community takes her own life.

These works and others address the continuing difficulties that the bereaved families experience in integrating their loss into their lives. As a recent study of bereaved parents indicates, "bereavement is a most, if not the most, key existential issue for the bereaved parent." And in contrast to their assumption of gradual acceptance of the loss and return to normal life, the researchers identify "a continuing and intense engagement in the experience of loss and in [their] obsessive involvement with their dead son" (Rubin and Dichterman 1993: 54; see also Bilu and Wiztum 2000: 11–14; Tamir 1993). Similarly, as I discuss elsewhere, literary works and films about war widows disclose their vulnerable position and the gaps between the ideology of patriotic sacrifice and their own experiences.[35] While the war widow's position as a part of the "bereaved family" bequeaths on her the symbolic status of a national symbol, she feels the pressure of public scrutiny and a judgmental attitude by those around her, and is likely to experience a decline in her social status.

Leah Aini's novel, *Sand Tide* (1992), is written in the form of the widow's interior monologue, which she addresses to her late husband. The young woman recounts with sensitivity and humor her pain and extreme isolation immediately after her husband's death, as well as her later experiences as she finds employment and makes new friends. Even though her behavior presents signs of accommodation to her new situation, the widow refuses to depart from her dead husband. Eventually she makes a bold move to the cemetery, motivated by her wish to live next to him. In so doing, she rebels against what she regards as the society's coercive policy of separating her from him. The police remove the widow from the cemetery and bring her to a mental clinic.

These novels are, obviously, works of fiction, yet they address topics that touch on sensitive social and psychological issues that are part of contemporary Israeli life and express them in more subtle and complex ways than public discourse may allow. In sharp contrast to the state's designation of a specific time and space for commemorating fallen soldiers, these works show bereaved families' continuous involvement with the dead and how the loss re-shapes their lives. Bereaved parents, war widows, bereaved siblings, and orphans that are portrayed in Israeli fiction and film also demonstrate the unsettling gaps between their official status as a symbolic extension of a fallen soldier, and the social and psychological difficulties they face. The literature exposes the shortcomings of the national rhetoric of patriotic sacrifice that fails to provide adequate tools to help these individuals process this trauma. More gravely, the literature shows that the bereaved family members might face the risk of becoming increasingly marginalized; their families may break down under the pressure of loss; and at times, loneliness and despair and refusal to accept death might drive them to extreme forms of behavior (Zerubavel 2003). Thus, in contrast to the ethos of patriotic sacrifice that emphasizes the contribution of "altruistic suicide" to social solidarity and is demonstrated by the family's relation with the state, these works of fiction highlight tensions and dissention around the experience of loss and the destructive long-term effects on the family and society that they generate.

* * *

This chapter has examined the ethos of patriotic sacrifice that was constructed in the pre-state period and the early years of the state of Israel. Through the analysis of literary texts and public discourse, it has also explored the changes that have been introduced to the interpretation of the patriotic pact from the 1960s to the late 1990s. During the formative years of nation building, the patriotic rhetoric of self-sacrifice was an important component in the development of a secular national Hebrew culture. In this historical context, the call for sacrifice was largely believed to be an inevitable part of a transitional phase leading to the formation of a Jewish state. Although the first decades following the establishment of the state indicated that violence continued, the victory in the Six-Day War of 1967 reinforced the belief in Israel's security and ability to survive. In spite of the gradual decline of the collectivist ethos in economic and social spheres, the military confrontations and wars reinforced the spirit of readiness to die for the country in the name of collective survival. The glorification of the fighting soldiers and the extensive commemoration of fallen soldiers strengthened this trend and the belief in the shared agreement about the inevitability of patriotic sacrifice and its value.

Early signs of skepticism regarding the cost of sacrifice appeared in the 1960s but became more noticeable in the post-1973 period. The growing political divisions in Israeli society during the 1980s and 1990s undermined earlier agreement on the fulfillment of the sacrificial act, targeting various aspects of the pact between the state and its citizens. The political debate on the justification of wars, the use of military force in the ongoing conflict with the Palestinians, and a growing insistence on families' right to know the particular circumstances of soldiers' deaths indicate a more skeptical approach to the definition of "patriotic sacrifice" as necessary and inevitable. The challenge of the state's control over the commemoration of fallen soldiers and the awareness of the long-term impact of war experiences, injuries, and loss on soldiers and bereaved families articulate the rise of a more individualistic ethos that questions the rewards for "altruistic suicide."

While the educational discourse continues to represent themes and texts that embody the spirit of patriotic sacrifice (Bar-Tal 1998; Furman 1999), popular discourse and artistic use of national myths, such as the *Akeda* and Trumpeldor's last words, challenge of the once hegemonic ethos. The subversive versions of Trumpeldor's patriotic saying, "It is good to die for our country," illustrate these changes. It has been turned from an affirmative statement into a question: "It is good to die for our country?"; it has been replaced by an affirmative statement representing an opposing view, "It is good to *live* for our country" or a *curse* in Russian that denies the dying person's sentiments toward patriotic sacrifice; it has served as a comment on the use of excessive force in the name of patriotism, "It is good to *club* [or: hit] for our country," and as an individualistic declaration, "It is good to die for *ourselves*."[36]

This chapter has focused on those expressions that reflect the weakening of patriotic sacrifice as a hegemonic ethos of Israeli society, yet it is important to note that patriotic sacrifice still plays a considerable role in Israeli national culture. Although evading military service has become more acceptable among high school graduates and the number of cases of conscientious objection has risen, these are limited phenomena within a broader trend of compliance with the call to arms and the risk of death for the nation. The prestige assigned to service in selective combat units has remained high among Israeli youth, and voluntary recruitment to them has not declined, even if the motivation may be grounded in more individualistic goals such as proving oneself and self-fulfillment (Cohen 1997; Hellman 1993; Levy 2001; Linn 1996; Shavit 2000; Stern 1990). Similarly, the great significance attached to the army and the ethos of patriotic sacrifice is evident in the protest movements' attempts to negotiate between their political views with patriotic values.

Yet, as this chapter shows, attitudes toward patriotic sacrifice are in flux and continue to respond to changes in Israeli public's perception of the Israeli-Palestinian conflict. Recent developments since the outbreak of the second *in-*

tifada in 2000 and the escalation of the conflict produced deep disillusionment from the prospect of peace negotiations and led to a stronger consensus about the justification of self-sacrifice as a means to guarantee collective survival. While these changes appear to have weakened the Left's opposition to government policies, the government's declared intention to evacuate Jewish settlements in Gaza might lead to a rise in conscientious objections to the call of military duty on the Right. Within this explosive situation, the intertwining of violence, nationalism, religion, and memory continues to shape and transform current attitudes toward patriotic sacrifice.

Notes

Please note that all translations of Hebrew texts are mine, unless otherwise noted. The bibliography provides the English translation of the Hebrew titles; transliteration is added in those cases where original titles may not be easily identified. All Hebrew sources are identified by [Hebrew] in the bibliography.

1. For the sociological definitions and analysis of sacrifice as a religious act, see Hubert and Mauss 1964: 1–13.
2. On the significance of soldiers' commemoration for the modern state, see Mosse 1990: 79–92. On Israeli memorials and military cemeteries, see Azaryahu 1996, and Handelman 2004: 147–160.
3. On the theory of gifts as a form of exchange, see Mauss 1967.
4. The early Jewish organizations of self-defense in Palestine, Bar-Giora and Ha-Shomer, adopted this verse as their slogan. See, Heilprin 1977: 242 and Shapira 1992: 105–113. Cahan's verse is also carved on stones at Ha-Shomer's historic cemetery.
5. For the analysis of three major heroic myths—Masada, the Bar Kokhba revolt, and Tel Hai—see Y. Zerubavel 1995, Bitan 1996, and Shapira 1992: 125–141. Although they were dissenting views to this trend, they were marginalized within the predominant emphasis on heroism and self-sacrifice. See Gordon 1952: 401–408; Gorny 1966.
6. On the symbolic bridge between Antiquity and the Zionist revival, see Y. Zerubavel 1995: 13–36. For a broader discussion of the construction of continuity between the past and the present, see E. Zerubavel 2003: 37–54. One of the most fascinating manifestations of the construction of a symbolic continuity between the ancient and the modern struggles for national liberation are the military burials that the State of Israel provided to bones identified as "ancient Jewish warriors," similar to those given to its fallen soldiers. For a fuller discussion of such a funeral for the Bar Kokhba fighters, see Aronoff 1986: 105–130, and Y. Zerubavel 1995: 129–130, 185–191.
7. Note that Lamdan uses here Masada as a collective representation of *Zion*, the ancient Jewish homeland, and does not refer specifically to the events of 66–74 C.E. reported by Josephus.

8. For similar expressions of the value of blood as a form of the sanctification of the land, see Y. Zerubavel 1995: 43–47; Shapira 1992: 110–111, 130–131, 147–149.

9. On the theme of self-sacrifice and its prominence in stories, poems, songs, plays, and rituals performed in the annual commemorations of Tel Hai, see Y. Zerubavel 1995: 86–95. On the impact of the Tel Hai Day commemorations on memorializations of Israeli fallen soldiers, see Ben-Amos and Bet-El 1999.

10. The anecdote on the Palmach commander is recounted in Netiva Ben-Yehuda's memoirs of her experience in the Palmach underground (1981: 127).

11. See Dan Miron's discussion of the poem in Miron 1992: 63–87. For a critique of his interpretation, see Hirschfeld 1992. See also Lomsky-Feder 2004.

12. For the concept "the bereaved family," see Witztum and Malkinson 1993: 243–245. On the role of bereaved families in the commemoration of the dead, see also Azaryahu 1995: 123–132; Sivan 1991: 119–230. The name of the organization of the bereaved families, Yad Labanim (The Memorial for the Sons), ignores other relations with the dead such as spouses and children.

13. See Spiegel 1979 for a fascinating study of the transformation of the *Akeda* throughout the ages. Spiegel's analysis suggests earlier subversive interpretations of the biblical text.

14. See Milman 1991: 56–62 for a discussion of the changing presentation of Isaac's role.

15. For a recent anthology of Hebrew poetry on the *Akeda*, see Ben-Gurion 2002. For further discussion, see Kartun-Blum 1995, 1999: 17–65; Ofir 1979; Steiner 1975.

16. This connection is clearly not unique to Israeli national ideology. See Mosse 1990: 70–78 and Bellah 1970: 68–86. On this theme in Israeli literature, see Y. Zerubavel 1995: 91–95 and Hever 2001: 50. On the symbolism of following Israel's Memorial Day by Independence Day, see Azaryahu 1995: 55–56; Handelman 2004: 101–142.

17. On the multiplicity of memory sites related to the War of Independence, see Azaryahu 1995; Shamir 1996: 41–84; Sivan 1991: 119–230.

18. It is not surprising, therefore, that the largest military parade took place on Independence Day in 1968. See Azaryahu 1999: 103.

19. These figures and the figures below are quoted in Schiff and Haber 1976. The War of Attrition was only recently recognized as one of the State of Israel's official wars.

20. It should be noted that the rise of morbid humor at a time of war is not unique to Israeli culture. This phenomenon is also known as "black humor" or "gallows humor." See Obrdlik 1942; Davidson 1972: 482; Dundes 1987; Sloan 1974: 22, 49, 65, 68. Macabre humor was also known among the Palmach youth of the 1940s, as is evident in Ben-Yehuda 1981, and my recorded interview with M. Z. (1978, cassette no. 53).

21. The version about Trumpeldor's Russian curse expresses a deeply set belief that he could not have possibly uttered such a patriotic statement while dying and hence this must be a fabricated story. For fuller discussion of this case, see Y. Zerubavel 1994: 105–123.

22. On the soldiers' lyrics, see *Ha'aretz*, 28 December 1982 and 29 December 1982; Michael 1982; Shenhar 1989. For examples of wounded soldiers'

macabre humor, see Ben-Amotz 1973; Ha'elyon 1973; and the film *Repeat Dive*, directed by Shimon Dotan, 1982.

23. The play was originally performed in 1970.

24. For a more elaborate discussion of these interpretations of the *Akeda*, see Ofir 1979: 63–64.

25. In Moshe Shamir's *He Went in the Fields* (1972 [1948]), the father's first response upon receiving the news that his son was killed in action is to ensure that the son's girlfriend does not carry out her plan to have an abortion. In the movie version by the same title (directed by Yosef Milo, 1967), the last episode shows the grandfather greeting his soldier-grandson in the exact same manner he used to greet his son. This episode and the fact that the son is called after his dead father demonstrate the continuity of memory within the family. In A. B. Yehoshua's novel, *Mr. Mani* (1990), the father ensures the continuity within his family line after his son is killed by Arabs by impregnating his son's wife.

26. Thus, in a poem by Yitzhak Laor, "This Idiot, Isaac" (1985), the speaker reproaches Isaac for his excessive obedience to Abraham and suggests an alternative course of action, "[to] lock up his father, his only one, Abraham, in a prison, in an asylum, in the basement of the house so as not to be slaughtered." To reinforce this point, the speaker warns Isaac not to trust Abraham's fatherly instincts: "Isaac, Isaac, remember what your father did to Yismael, your brother." This deliberate inversion of the *Akeda* presents the relations between Abraham and Isaac as adversarial and offers Isaac an alternative mode of action in the form of rebellion against his father. See Baron 1998: 21–22; Feldman 1998.

27. *The Last Jew* is a highly intricate novel with multiple subplots that show the recurrence of patterns in Jewish history. The subplot about the memory industry in this novel was used as the basis for an Israeli film, *The Vulture*, directed by Yeki Yoshe, 1981. In the present context, it is interesting to note that Kenyuk's critique is not limited to the case of Israeli society, and it suggests analogies with German and American parents who lost their children. For further analysis of this novel, see Y. Zerubavel 2002.

28. The conformity to the patriotic ethos in spite of one's participation in civic protests is satirized in the film *Late Summer Blues*, directed by Renan Schorr, 1987.

29. In spite of the greater appeal of The Four Mothers' narrow agenda, this organization too was subject to condemnation and ridicule. See, for example, *Nekuda* 211: 53 and 220: 63 (1998). On the political murders during peace demonstrations, see Feige 2002: 168–169, 204–218; and Peri 2000.

30. Among famous examples of this strategy are the open "officers' letter" to the prime minister in 1978 and a letter of reserve soldiers to the prime minister in October 1996. The publication of the "combatants' letter," signed by fifty-one reserve officers and combat soldiers who returned from their duty in the Gaza Strip in January 2002 led to the establishment of the movement "Courage to Refuse" which, according to website www.seruv.org consists of 628 signatures, half of whom have received jail sentences (as of 26 October 2004). Similarly, the "pilots' letter" of September 2003 is another example of selective conscientious objection to participate in the bombardment of civilian Palestinian population.

31. Since Fall 2004, Israeli media has frequently addressed this issue. See also the recent exchange on this subject in the issue of *Alpayim* magazine, an important intellectual forum. See Gans 2004; Sagi and Shapira 2004.

32. On the depersonalization of state commemorations for fallen soldiers, see Ben-Amos and Bet-El 1999; Lomsky-Feder 2004; Weiss 1997: 92–95.

33. Weiss (1997: 95–97) describes art exhibits that articulate an oppositionist stance toward memorial ceremonies. See also Schwartz 2000 and Y. Zerubavel 2003. For further psychological research on the bereaved, see Tamir 1993; Rubin and Katz-Dichterman 1993.

34. See Hannah Naveh's excellent essay on this novel as articulating a female discourse of bereavement, which is more private and nurturing and stands in opposition to the male military discourse on heroism, patriotic sacrifice, and loss (Naveh 1998).

35. For a more elaborate discussion of the literary representation of war widows, see Friedman 1993; Y. Zerubavel 2003.

36. In the original Hebrew, the deliberate distortions of Trumpeldor's saying preserve either its original structure or sound, or both. See Dani Kerman's cartoon of the Tel Hai monument (first published in *Dvar Hashavua* [1979]; reprinted in Y. Zerubavel 1995: figure 17), which transforms the saying into an open question. For the use of "It is good to live for our country," see Ben-Porat et al. 1974: 293. Linn (1996: 142) refers to a 1989 play entitled "It is good to club for our country" ["Tov nabut be'ad artsenu"] in the context of the Israeli response to the first Palestinian *intifada*. Finally, "It is good to die for ourselves" was inscribed on the shirt of Aviv Gefen, a famous Israeli singer who did not serve in the army, described by Nahum Barnea (1996).

References

Aini, Lea. 1992. *Sand Tide [Ge'ut Ha-Khol]*. Tel Aviv: Hakibbutz Hameuchad. [Hebrew]

Almog, Oz. 2000. *The Sabra: The Creation of the New Jew*. Berkeley: University of California Press.

Alterman, Natan. 1947. The Silver Platter. *Davar,* 19 December. [Hebrew]

Amit, Noa. 1995. Patterns of Commemoration and Their Link to Cultural Models: The Case of Memorial Books for Fallen Soldiers. M.A thesis, Tel Aviv University. [Hebrew]

Aronoff, Myron, ed. 1986. *The Frailty of Authority*. New Brunswick: Transaction.

Azaryahu, Maoz. 1999. The Independence Day Military Parade: A Political History of a Patriotic Ritual. In *The Military and Militarism in Israeli Society,* ed. Edna Lomsky-Feder and Eyal Ben-Ari, pp. 89–116. Albany: SUNY Press.

———. 1996. Mount Herzl: The Creation of Israel's National Cemetery. *Israel Studies* 1 (2): 46–74.

———. 1995. *State Cults*. Sde Boker: Ben Gurion University of the Negev Press. [Hebrew]

Barnea, Nahum. 1996. The Brave Soldier Gefen. *Yediot Ahronot,* 18 October. [Hebrew]

Baron, Erella. 1998. The Deceptions of a Voice from Heaven: The Theme of the Akeda in Hanoch Levin's Protest Theater. *Bikoret u-Farshanut* 33: 5–31. [Hebrew]

Bar-On, Mordechai. 1985. *Peace Now: The Portrait of a Movement.* Tel Aviv: Hakibbutz Hameuchad. [Hebrew]

Bar-Tal, Daniel. 1998. The Rocky Road toward Peace: Beliefs on Conflict in Israeli Textbooks, *Journal of Peace Research* 35 (6): 723–742.

———. 1993. Patriotism as Fundamental Beliefs of Group Members. *Politics and the Individual* 3 (2): 45–62.

Bellah, R. N. 1970. *Beyond Belief: Essays on Religion in a Post Traditional World.* New York: Harper & Row.

Ben-Amos, Avner, and Ilana Bet-El. 1999. Holocaust Day and Memorial Day in Israeli Schools: Ceremonies, Education, and History. *Israel Studies* 4 (1): 258–284.

Ben-Amotz, Dan. 1973. *I Don't Give a Damn [Lo Sam Zayin].* Tel Aviv: Bitan. [Hebrew]

Ben-Gurion, Arie, ed. 2002. *Lay Not Thine Hand upon the Lad.* Tel Aviv: Keter. [Hebrew]

Ben-Porat, Yeshaʾayahu et al. 1974. *The Oversight [Ha-Mehdal].* Tel Aviv: Special Edition. [Hebrew]

Ben-Yehuda, Netiva. 1981. *1948—Between Calendars.* Jerusalem: Keter. [Hebrew]

Bergstein, Fania. 1955. The Lumps of the Galilee Soil [*Rigvei Ha-Galil*]. In *Red Beads,* pp. 164–170. Tel Aviv: Hakibbutz Hameuchad. [Hebrew]

Bialik, Haim Nachman. 1966. If You Desired to Know [Im Yesh Et Nafshekha La-Daʿat]. In *Poems [Shirim]*, p. 79. Tel Aviv: Dvir. [Hebrew]

Bilu, Yoram, and Eliezer Wiztum. 2000. War-Related Loss and Suffering in Israeli Society: A Historical Perspective. *Israel Studies* 5 (2): 8–16.

Bitan, Dan. 1996. "Blooming Power": Myths of Active Heroism in the Beginning of Zionism. In *Myth and Memory: Transfigurations of Israeli Consciousness,* ed. David Ohana and Robert S. Wistrich, pp. 169–188. Jerusalem: Van Leer. [Hebrew]

Cahan, Yaʿacov. 1948. The Song of the Biryonim. In *Collected Works of Yaʿacov Cahan.* Tel Aviv: Hotsaʾat Vaʿad Ha-Yovel. [Hebrew]

Cohen, Stuart. 1997. Toward a New Portrait of the (New) Israeli Soldier. *Israel Affairs* 3 (3–4): 77–117

Davidson, Efraim. 1972. *Our Humor: An Anthology of Humor and Satire in Hebrew Literature from Its Beginning to Date.* Hulon: Biblos. [Hebrew]

Dundes, Alan. 1987. *Cracking Jokes: Studies of Sick Humor Cycles and Stereotypes.* Berkeley: Ten Speed Press.

Durkheim, Emile. 1951. *Suicide: A Study in Sociology.* New York: Free Press.

Elboim-Dror, Rachel. 1996. He Is Coming, the New Hebrew Is Arriving from Amongst Us: The Hebrew Youth Culture of the First Waves of Immigration. *Alpayim* 12: 104–135. [Hebrew]

Feige, Michael. 2002. *One Space, Two Spaces: Gush Emunim, Peace Now, and the Construction of Israeli Space.* Jerusalem: Magnes. [Hebrew]

Feldman, Yael. 1998. Isaac or Oedipus? Jewish Tradition and the Israeli Aqeda. *Biblical Studies/Cultural Studies, Journal for the Study of Old Testament* 226: 159–189.

Firer, Ruth. 1985. *The Agents of Zionist Education.* Haifa: Haifa University Press. [Hebrew]

Frankel, Jonathan. 1986. The "Yizkor" Book of 1911: A Note on National Myths in the Second Aliya. In *Religion, Ideology, and Nationalism in Europe and America:*

Essays Presented in Honor of Yehoshua Arieli, pp. 355–384. Jerusalem: Zalman Shazar Center for Jewish History.

Friedman, Regine Mihal. 1993. Between Silence and Abjection: The Film Medium and the Israeli War Widow. *Filmhistoria* 3 (1–2): 79–89.

Furman, Mirta. 1999. Army and War: Collection Narratives of Early Childhood in Contemporary Israel. In *The Military and Militarism in Israeli Society*, ed. Edna Lomsky-Feder and Eyal Ben-Ari, pp. 141–168. Albany: SUNY Press.

Gans, Chaim. 2004. Right and Left: Ideological Disobedience in Israel. *Alpayim* 27: 9–45.

Gertz, Nurith. 2000. *Captive of a Dream: Myths in Israeli Culture.* London: Valentine Mitchell.

Gordon, A.D. 1952. *Collected Works: The Nation and Labor.* Jerusalem: The Zionist Library. [Hebrew]

Gorny, Yosef. 1966. The Romantic Element in the Ideology of the Second Aliya. *Assufot* 10: 55–75. [Hebrew]

Gouri, Haim. 1981 [1961]. Heritage. In *The Penguin Book of Hebrew Verse*, ed. and trans. T. Carmi, p. 565. New York: Penguin.

Gur, Batya. 1998. *Stone for a Stone.* Tel Aviv: Am Oved. [Hebrew]

Ha'elyon, Yaʿakov. 1973. *A Doll's Leg.* Tel Aviv: Am Oved. [Hebrew]

Hameiri, Avigdor. 1926–1927. Blood Sacrifice. *ha-Noar Ve-Ha-Aret* 1: 93. [Hebrew]

Handelman, Don. 2004. *Nationalism and the Israeli State.* Oxford: Berg.

Heilprin, Yisrael, ed. 1977 [1941]. *The Book of Heroism: A Historical Literary Anthology.* Vol. 3. Tel Aviv: Am Oved. [Hebrew]

Hellman, Sara. 1993. Refusal to Participate in the War as an Attempt to Redefine Citizenship. Ph.D. dissertation, the Hebrew University of Jerusalem. [Hebrew]

Hellman, Sara, and Tamar Rappoport. 1997. These Are Ashkenazi Women, Alone, Arabs' Whores, Don't Believe in God, and Don't Love the Land of Israel: "Women in Black" and the Challenge of Social Order. *Teoria U-Vikoret* 10: 175–192. [Hebrew]

Hendel, Yehudit. 1991. *The Mountain of Losses* [*Har Ha-Toʾim*]. Tel Aviv: Hakibbutz Hameuchad.

Hever, Hannan. 2001. *Suddenly the Sight of War: Nationality and Violence in Hebrew Poetry of the 1940s.* Tel Aviv: Hakibbutz Hameuchad. [Hebrew]

Hirschfeld, Ariel. 1992. In the Place Where Miron Is Silent. *Ha'aretz*, 3 July. [Hebrew]

Hubert, Henri, and Marcel Mauss. 1964 [1898]. *Sacrifice: Its Nature and Function.* Chicago: University of Chicago Press.

Kartun-Blum, Ruth. 1995. Isaac Rebound: The *Aqedah* as a Paradigm in Modern Hebrew Poetry. *Israel Affairs* 1 (Spring): 185–202.

———. 1999. *Profane Scriptures: Reflections on the Dialogue with the Bible in Modern Hebrew Poetry.* Cincinnati: Hebrew Union College Press.

Kenyuk, Yoram. 1981. *The Last Jew.* Tel Aviv: Hakibbutz Hameuchad. [Hebrew]

Kimmerling, Baruch. 1993. Militarism in Israeli Society. *Teoria U-Vikoret* 4: 123–140. [Hebrew]

Lamdan, Yitzhak. 1971. Masada. In *Isaac Lamdan*, ed. and trans. Leon Yudkin, pp. 209–210. Ithaca: Cornell University Press.

Laor, Yitzhak. 1985. This Idiot, Isaac. In *Only the Body Remembers.* Tel Aviv: Adam. [Hebrew]

Levin, Hanoch. 1987. *What Does the Bird Care.* Tel Aviv: Siman Kriah & Hakibbutz Hameuchad. [Hebrew]

Levy, Orna Sasson. 2001. Excitement and Control: Naturalizing Military Service in the
    Narratives of Israel: Combat Soldiers. Paper presented at the annual meeting
    of the Association for Israel Studies, Washington, D.C.
Linn, Ruth. 1996. *Conscience at War: The Israeli Soldier as a Moral Critic.* Albany:
    SUNY Press.
Lomsky-Feder, Edna. 2004. The Memorial Ceremony in Israeli Schools: Between State
    and Civil Society. *British Journal of Sociology of Education.* 25 (3): 291–305.
Malkinson, Ruth, Simon Rubin, and Eliezer Witztum, eds. 1993. *Loss and Bereavement
    in Jewish Society in Israel.* Jerusalem: Ministry of Defense Press. [Hebrew]
Mauss, Marcel. 1967. *The Gift.* New York: Norton.
Mazali, Rela, and Rachel Livne-Freudental. 1998. In the Mother's Name: Mothers and
    Wives, Who Reject the *Akeda* Myth, Are Searching for Their Place on the
    Israeli Protest Map. *Mi-Tsad Sheni* 11: 34–35. [Hebrew]
Michael, B. 1982. From the Songs of the Land of Cyprus. *Ha'aretz,* 31 December.
    [Hebrew]
Milman, Yosef. 1991. Remember What Your Father Did: The *Akeda*—the Founda-
    tions of Its Meaning in the Biblical Narrative and its Transformation in
    Contemporary Protest Poetry. In *The Akeda and the Reproach* [*Ha-Akeda
    Ve-Ha-Tokheha*], ed. Zvi Levi, pp. 53–72. Jerusalem: Magnes. [Hebrew]
Miron, Dan. 1992. *Facing the Silent Brother: Essays on the Poetry of the War of Indepen-
    dence.* Jerusalem: Keter. [Hebrew]
Mosse, George L. 1990. *Fallen Soldiers: Reshaping the Memory of the World Wars.*
    Oxford: Oxford University Press.
Naveh, Hannah. 1998. On Loss, Bereavement, and Mourning in the Israeli Experience.
    Alpayim 16: 85–120. [Hebrew]
———. 1993. *Captives of Mourning: Perspective of Mourning in Hebrew Literature.*
    Tel Aviv: Hakibbutz Hameuchad. [Hebrew]
Obrdlik, Antonin J. 1942. Gallows Humor: A Sociological Phenomenon. *American Jour-
    nal of Sociology* 47: 709–716.
Ofir, Yosef. 1979. The Theme of the Akeda in Israeli War Poetry. *Maʿalot* 11 (1): 2–7;
    11 (2): 6–11. [Hebrew]
Oz, Amos. 1986 [1962]. By Way of the Wind [Derekh Ha-Ruʾah]. In *Where the Jackals
    Howl,* pp. 43–63. Tel Aviv: Am Oved. [Hebrew]
Peri, Yoram, ed. 2000. *The Assassination of Yitzhak Rabin.* Stanford: Stanford Univer-
    sity Press.
Rosen, Rami. 1998. We Dreamed to Die for the Country. *Ha'aretz, Weekend Magazine,*
    13 March: 62–63. [Hebrew]
Rosenthal, Rubik. 2001. *Is Bereavement Dead?* Tel Aviv: Keter. [Hebrew]
Rubenstein, Elyakim. 1997. On the Fundamental Law: Human Dignity and Freedom
    and the Ministry of Defense. *Iyunei Mishpat* 21: 21–61. [Hebrew]
Rubin, Simon, and Dvorah Katz-Dichterman. 1993. The Responses of Parents to a
    Son's Death in War. In *Loss and Bereavement in Jewish Society in Israel,* ed.
    Ruth Malkinson, Simon Rubin, and Eliezer Witztum, pp. 51–70. Jerusalem:
    Ministry of Defense Press. [Hebrew]
Sagi, Avi, and Ron Shapira. 2004. Civil Disobedience and Conscientious Objection.
    Alpayim 27: 46–71.
Schiff, Zeev, and Eitan Haber, eds. 1976. *Israel Army and Defense: A Dictionary.*
    Tel Aviv: Zmora, Bitan, Modan. [Hebrew]

Schwartz, Yigal. 2000. Lost Words. *Ha'aretz Weekend Magazine,* 25 February: 10. [Hebrew]

Shamgar-Handelman, Lea. 1986. *Israeli War Widows: Beyond the Glory of Heroism.* South Hadley, Mass.: Bergin & Garvey.

Shamir, Ilana. 1996. *Commemoration and Remembrance* [*Hantsaha Ve-Zikaron*]. Tel Aviv: Am Oved. [Hebrew]

Shamir, Moshe. 1972 [1948]. *He Went in the Fields.* Tel Aviv: Am Oved. [Hebrew]

Shapira, Anita. 1992. *Land and Power* [Herev Ha-Yona]. Tel Aviv: Am Oved. [Hebrew]

Shapira, Avraham, ed. 1970. *The Seventh Day: Soldiers' Talk about the Six-Day War.* New York: Scribner.

Shavit, Uri. 2000. Compulsory Recruitment—No Longer So. *Ha'aretz Weekend Supplement,* 26 May: 18–22. [Hebrew]

Shenhar, Aliza. 1989. To Be There: Protest Songs by Soldiers in the War of Lebanon. *Hetz* 1 (April): 34–43. [Hebrew]

Sivan, Emanuel. 1991. *The 1948 Generation: Myth, Portrait, Memory.* Tel Aviv: Ma'arkhot. [Hebrew]

Sloan, Jacob, ed. 1974. *Notes from the Warsaw Ghetto: The Journal of Emmanuel Ringelblum.* New York: Schocken.

Smilansky, Moshe. 1920. A Sacred Place. *Ha'aretz,* 14 March: 1. [Hebrew]

Spiegel, Shalom. 1979. *The Last Trial.* New York: Behrman House.

Steiner, Moshe. 1975. Between the *Akeda* and the Heroic Struggle. *Ha-Umma* 45: 409–420. [Hebrew]

Stern, Ron. 1990. A Radical Change in the Motivation for Military Service. *Ma'arkhot* 360: 28–35. [Hebrew]

Tamir, Gilam. 1993. Long-Term Adjustment among War Bereaved Israeli Parents. In *Loss and Bereavement in Jewish Society in Israel,* ed. Ruth Malkinson, Simon Rubin, and Eliezer Witztum, pp. 213–230. Jerusalem: Ministry of Defense Press. [Hebrew]

Tsur, Muki. 1976. *Doing It the Hard Way* [Lelo Kutonet Passim]. Tel Aviv: Am Oved. [Hebrew]

Weiss, Meira. 1997. Bereavement, Commemoration, and Collective Identity in Contemporary Israeli Society. *Anthropological Quarterly* 70 (2): 91–101.

Witztum, Eliezer, and Ruth Malkinson. 1993. Bereavement and Commemoration in Israel: The Dual Face of the National Myth. In *Loss and Bereavement in Jewish Society in Israel,* ed. Ruth Malkinson, Simon Rubin and Eliezer Witztum, pp. 231–258. Jerusalem: Ministry of Defense Press. [Hebrew]

Yadgar, Yaacov. 2004. *Our Story: The National Narrative in the Israeli Press.* Haifa: Haifa University Press. [Hebrew]

Ya'ir [Avraham Stern]. 1976 [1932]. The Unknown Soldiers. *In My Blood You Will Live.* Ya'ir Publications. [Hebrew]

Yehoshua, A. B. 1990. *Mr. Mani.* Tel Aviv: Hakibbutz Hameuchad.

———. 1974. *In the Beginning of Summer 1970.* Tel Aviv: Schocken. [Hebrew]

Zerubavel, Eviatar. 2003. *Time Maps: Collective Memory and the Social Shape of the Past.* Chicago: University of Chicago Press.

Zerubavel, Yael. 2003. Female Images in a State of War: Ideology, Crisis, and the Politics of Gender in Israel. In *Landscaping the Human Garden: 20th Century Population Management in a Comparative Framework,* ed. Amir Weiner, pp. 236–257. Stanford: Stanford University Press.

———. 2002. The Mythological Sabra and the Jewish Past: Trauma, Memory, and Contested Identities. *Israel Studies* 7 (2): 115–144.

———. 1995. *Recovered Roots: Collective Memory and the Making of Israeli National Tradition.* Chicago: Chicago University Press.

———. 1994. The Historical, the Legendary, and the Incredible: Invented Tradition and Collective Memory in Israel. In *Commemorations: The Politics of National Identity,* ed. John R. Gillis, pp. 105–123. Princeton: Princeton University Press.

Part Two.   *Resolution and Reconciliation*

4   Commemoration under Fire: Palestinian Responses to the 1956 Kafr Qasim Massacre

Shira Robinson

In late November 1957, the Hebrew and state-sponsored Arabic press in Israel printed a series of articles describing an extravagant "ceremony of reconcilia-tion" held in the small and impoverished Palestinian border village of Kafr Qasim. Over four hundred distinguished guests attended the event, including cabinet ministers, Knesset members from the ruling MAPAI party (*Mifleget Poʿalei Erets Yisrael*), military government representatives, national trade union officials, and "notables" from neighboring Arab villages. The idea behind the *sulha*—so named by its government-appointed organizers after the Bedouin custom in which two tribes make peace over a ceremonial meal of bread and salt—was to heal the remaining wounds from the 29 October 1956 Israeli border patrol massacre of forty-eight Palestinian Arab citizens, all but four of whom were residents of Kafr Qasim.[1] The day of the ceremony, 20 November, marked exactly one year and three weeks since the first day of the Sinai War and the fateful evening when village day laborers returning home were lined up and summarily shot for unknowingly "violating" a curfew that had been announced only thirty minutes before.

Behind the fanfare of the ceremony—comprised of speeches calling for vil-lagers to move beyond the tragedy for the sake of coexistence, promises of gen-erous government reparations to the wounded and the families of the victims, and a sumptuous full course meal—lurked a heavy air of intimidation, anger, and pain. In contrast to the reports of much of the mainstream media, the Arabic-language newspapers *al-Ittihad* and *al-Mirsad,* sponsored by the non-Zionist Communist Party, MAKI (*ha-Miflaga ha-Communistit ha-Yisraelit*), and the left-Zionist MAPAM Party (*Mifleget ha-Poʿalim ha-Meʾuhedet*) respec-tively, denounced the so-called *sulha* as a fraud. They attacked the MAPAI gov-ernment for using pomp and circumstance to conceal the grossly inadequate financial compensation being provided to the victims, as well as for the im-mense pressure exacted by military authorities to force male representatives of the injured families to attend the ceremony and thereby validate the officially imposed "truce." MAKI, MAPAM, and other left-wing Jewish and Arab circles also accused the authorities of trying to wash their hands of the "affair" by using the *sulha* as a pretext for canceling the ongoing trial of eleven border patrol guards accused of carrying out the massacre (*al-Mirsad,* 21 November 1957; *al-Ittihad,* 15 and 22 November 1957). The *sulha* was, in effect, a dramatic effort by the state to impose its own memory of the crime.

In the years following the 1948 war, the conflict over collective memory-making was lost on neither Jewish Israeli leaders nor their Palestinian citizen-subjects. Not only were the memories of flight and expulsion, family separation, and land loss still fresh, but beyond these recollections lay the oppressive reality of military rule. From August 1948 through December 1966, a formal military administration governed the daily lives of the country's remaining Palestinian Arab population, restricting their movement, expression, and employment, and largely isolating them from Jewish Israeli society. The evolving practices of surveillance and discipline that Palestinians had to confront in this regime served only to reinforce their wartime losses and to remind them that their presence was unwelcome in the new state.[2]

The massacre in Kafr Qasim took place at the height of military rule and brought these tensions to the fore, sparking a critical historical process marked by an escalating cycle of state violence and grassroots memorial activity. With each anniversary, the repressive measures adopted by the authorities to prevent the popular memorialization of the slain revealed the nascent state's attempt to erase the independent expression—and even the public visibility—of its Arab residents. The government's initial cover-up of the crime and the fierce struggle that emerged over its memory ultimately helped to transform the act of commemoration into a central site of resistance to military rule.

This essay moves beyond the crime to examine the decade of physical and discursive clashes that erupted as a result of countrywide Palestinian efforts to commemorate its victims. I argue that the key to understanding the ongoing potency of the massacre's memory today lies as much in its deeply contested aftermath as it does in the event itself. On the historiographic level, I trace how the massacre and the responses it generated established a precedent for organized protest against civil inequality and heightened the stakes of asserting a distinctly (but not monolithic) Palestinian memory, history, and identity in Israel. More broadly, I highlight the relationship between state suppression of memory and the formation of grassroots resistance around it.

"Mow Them Down!"

The massacre in Kafr Qasim took place in the early evening of 29 October, just as Israel, in collusion with France and Great Britain, was preparing to attack Egypt's Sinai Peninsula.[3] That morning, Colonel Yiskhar Shadmi, brigade commander of Israel's Central District, was instructed to take all precautionary measures to maintain quiet on the Jordanian border. To carry out this order, he requested special permission to move up the start of the evening curfew from 10 P.M. to 5 P.M. in the seven southern Triangle villages under his jurisdiction, including Kafr Qasim. Shadmi then gathered the border patrol battalion commanders who had been placed under his authority and instructed them to "shoot to kill" anyone found outside his or her home after the curfew, including women and children. In response to a question regarding those workers returning after 5 P.M. who were unaware of the curfew, he offered only the thinly veiled phrase in Arabic, "Allah yirhamu [May God have mercy on him]."[4] These orders and clarifications were passed on down the chain of command.

That afternoon, at 4:30 P.M., a young sergeant visited the home of Kafr Qasim's 74-year-old *mukhtar* to inform him of the curfew change. Wadiᶜ Muhamed Sarsur pleaded that he would not have enough time to spread the word to the four hundred villagers working in the quarries, olive groves, and fields located not only adjacent to the village but also as far away as Lod, Jaffa, and Ramat Gan.[5] When these entreaties proved fruitless, the *mukhtar* and several relatives visiting him at the time left to spread the word. By 4:55 P.M., not a single person was outside. Soon thereafter, Sarsur began to hear shooting, which continued, according to the watch of his grandson, until 7 P.M. (Military Court Session 11/5/57; Qahwaji 1972: 158–162).[6]

The majority of the murders took place at the entrance of the only road leading to the village, on its western edge.[7] The border patrol unit stationed there used rifles and machine guns to carry out nine waves of killings, ranging from small attacks on a few men returning on bike, foot, or donkey, to larger assaults upon groups of up to twenty men and women arriving in trucks. It seems clear that soldiers took the "shoot to kill" order quite seriously, for in each operation they reportedly checked to ensure that no wounded remained and to fire repeatedly at those who appeared to be alive (Tubi 1956). The testimony of ᶜAbd Allah Samir Bdeir, who arrived with the first group of workers, offers a vivid image of the manner in which the soldiers followed their orders:

> Roughly five minutes before 5 P.M., I arrived at the entrance of the village . . . along with three other workers—on bikes. We came across a unit of border patrol guards in a car—about twelve with an officer at their head. The workers said, "*Shalom,* officer." The officer asked them [in Hebrew], "Are you happy?" They answered, "Yes." The guards got out of the car and ordered the workers to stand. The officer ordered, "Mow them down! [*Tiktsor otam!*]" When the guards began to shoot, I lay on the ground and rolled over onto the road, at which point I screamed even though I wasn't injured. I stopped screaming and pretended to be dead. The guards continued to shoot the other workers who had fallen. Then the officer said, "Enough! They're dead already. It's a shame to waste the bullets." (Tubi 1956)[8]

In the course of two hours, border patrol guards murdered nineteen men, six women, ten teenage boys (ages 14–17), six girls (ages 12–15) and seven young boys (ages 8 to 13). In almost every killing wave at least one person survived with injuries and a small number escaped unharmed (Kafr Qasim Local Council [KQLC] 1996: 5).[9] Late that night, while the curfew was still in effect, the army drove in between thirty and forty residents from the nearby village of Jaljuliya, provided them with hoes, and ordered them merely to dig as deeply and as quickly as possible. While they did not yet know it, these men were standing in the middle of the village cemetery and digging the graves of the slain (Bdayr 1998; Ibrahim Sarsur, Rabiʿ 2002).

Contested Memories Today

In the eyes of most Israeli Jews, the massacre in Kafr Qasim represents little more than a tragic blip on the screen of the state's historic treatment of its Arab minority—a crime that was committed by an unusually barbaric group comprised largely of uneducated, Moroccan immigrants and (other) "Arab haters" who did not reflect the general population of citizen-soldiers, or the ethos and conduct of the army (Kordov 1959; Linenberg 1972).[10] As traditional Israeli and Zionist accounts point out, the convicted commander and soldiers were duly sentenced to prison within a range of eight to seventeen years, the government paid damages to the families of the injured and the slain, and the army enshrined the military court's ruling that soldiers were obliged to refuse to obey any command they deemed to be a "manifestly illegal order."[11] In short, the majority of Israeli Jewish society believed (and continues to maintain) that the political and military establishment reacted swiftly, responsibly, and justly to the crime.[12]

For most Palestinian Arab citizens of Israel, who in 1956 comprised 11 percent of the population, the massacre represented the inevitable (if most brutal) outcome of eight years of what was commonly labeled Israel's "policies of national oppression" against them. Along with military rule and the deprivation of their civil rights, these policies were expressed in the ongoing confiscation of their land, their consistent portrayal in official discourse as a fifth column, and the cultivation of racist attitudes against them in Jewish schools. Above all, the murders in Kafr Qasim sparked widespread fear that few social, political, or legal safeguards were in place to prevent the repetition of a similar assault—a sentiment that won partial confirmation as a result of the government's heavy-handed responses to the crime. These included its seven-week media gag on the "incidents"; its refusal to hold a public trial despite Arab and Jewish demands to do so; its pardoning of the convicted soldiers and the appointment of the responsible commanders to high government posts; its failure to compensate fully the wounded and bereaved families; and its imposition of the *sulha*.[13] The state's ongoing refusal to acknowledge formal responsibility for the massacre continues to aggravate all of these wounds today.[14]

In recent years, the gap between these accounts has slowly begun to narrow, as the release of previously classified military documents has revealed critical information regarding the military prelude to the crime (Rosenthal 1991).[15] This has not ended the debate over whether the massacre was planned, however. Many Palestinians—Kafr Qasim residents in particular—continue to draw connections between the killings of 1956 and the expulsions of 1948—a link that few Israeli Jews have thus far accepted.[16]

Until more documents are declassified, there is no way of creating a more complete picture of what happened. Even then, we may never know the "truth." In any event, the long term impact of the massacre on village residents and other Palestinians seems more important for understanding its significance. Indeed, even the most sophisticated analyses of the military prelude tend to undermine the historic agency of Arab citizens by depicting them as passive objects of state practices (Masalha 1997: 21–30). By shifting our focus to the diverse ways in which they responded to the massacre, we privilege the actions of the people who were affected by it and can begin to address the social history of this community on its own terms. This is not simply a call to provide a forum for the voices of a neglected historical group, although that would be a worthy (if difficult) project of its own. Nor is it an exclusive and misleading search for "moments of overt resistance" in order to understand the driving motors of Palestinian history (O'Hanlon 1988). Rather, I am arguing that the history of the massacre's aftermath is critical to understanding social and political transformations within the Arab community as well as to changing minority–state relations through the early 1970s.

Indeed, the following account reveals a very different picture of pre-1967 Israel from that portrayed in contemporary scholarship and popular discourse. By contextualizing the massacre within the broader social mechanics of military rule, it contests the official narrative that treats the event as a historic exception. Instead, I underscore the climate of violence that has buttressed the state's structural discrimination against its Palestinian citizens since 1948 and at the same time challenge prevalent historiographic claims regarding the "acquiescence" of the Arab minority before the 1967 war.[17]

Commemoration: Between Mourning and Resistance

The history of Kafr Qasim's memorialization is rooted in two sets of contested memories and representations of the massacre, neither of which has been addressed in the existing scholarship.[18] One is that between village residents of Kafr Qasim and other Palestinians, particularly the urban intelligentsia and Communist political elite. For the first three years, local memorials consisted of private gatherings of the bereaved families at the mosque and a silent procession to the cemetery, which slowly developed into more politicized, village-wide commemorations. By contrast, the national response was characterized by unprecedented mobilization, expressed in the formation of local committees, memorial meetings, and strikes. The second, starker divide is that which surfaced between the Israeli state and the Palestinian population as a whole. Here the memorial power of the massacre developed dialectically with the authorities' attempts both to cover up the crime and to obstruct any commemorative act that might be linked to the articulation of an alternative political order.

The past fifteen years have witnessed increasing academic interest in the relationship between collective memory and identity formation. Some scholars have focused on the ways in which ruling elites selectively inscribe memory in monuments, museums, and other material objects in order to impose a particular construction of national history and identity (Gillis 1994: 5). Others have identified the commemorative ceremony itself as the key to lasting "social memory" (Connerton 1989). Israeli academics, for their part, have been among the most enthusiastic participants in these discussions. It is thus of enormous significance that few have been willing to address in explicit terms the confrontation between Palestinian Arab and Jewish Israeli memories.[19] A recent essay collection illustrates how even Israeli Jews who seek to write critically about memory in Israel rarely speak directly about Palestinians, whether the latter reside within or outside the state's pre-1967 borders (Ben-Ari and Bilu 1997).[20] In this collection, Don Handelman and Lea Shamgar-Handelman's article on the memorialization of national death is a case in point. Departing from the premise that Israeli state territory is a contested space, they argue that Israeli Jews—like other national groups—endow their territory with particular meaning "to constitute landscapes that . . . are unified by their claims of ownership and belonging." The placement and commemoration of national death, they continue, is central to asserting these claims. While the authors provide numerous examples of memorial sites to substantiate their thesis, they elide the critical point: *who* is contesting Jewish Israeli claims to the land, what is the nature of those claims, and how are they contested? (Handelman and Shamgar-Handelman 1997: 86).

The history of Kafr Qasim compels us to address precisely these questions. If, as the authors assert, the body of Jewish Israeli sacrifice constitutes one of the central and most visible claims of unity of Zionist presence on Israeli territory, where can we locate the presence of Palestinian national death and alternative claims to that space? Because the prevailing asymmetry of power has prevented the erection of monuments or memorial sites dedicated to fallen Arab soldiers, citizens, or villages in public spaces, we need to look elsewhere for sites of counterclaims to space.[21] In the case of the massacre, which produced the first mass memorialization of Palestinian death in Israel, we must draw our attention to the memorial processions, meetings, and demonstrations that were held throughout Arab villages and towns for the first decade following the crime. These commemorative gatherings, often involving hundreds of moving (and often vocal) bodies in both public and private spaces, were deemed threatening enough to Jewish claims to space that military authorities immediately sought to suppress them by force. Although activists may not have initially planned these gatherings simply as a means of enacting an Arab presence in Jewish Israeli space, the state immediately perceived them as such and Palestinians in turn became increasingly aware of the high stakes of their memorial work.

Unveiling the "Conspiracy of Silence"

News of the atrocity in Kafr Qasim leaked out almost immediately, but it took almost two months and an enormous lobbying campaign waged by

Communist Party Knesset members and various public circles before Prime Minister Ben Gurion agreed to lift the media blackout he had imposed.[22] Nonetheless, his aim was to conclude the affair as quickly as possible and to clear the reputation of the army, which had just pulled off what the press was celebrating as a stunning victory against Egypt. As far as he was publicly concerned, the massacre was a tragic accident—the outcome of ambiguous military orders, ill coordination among the border patrol, and a group of savage, "abnormal" soldiers.[23] Thus on 6 November he issued an obscure statement regarding the "injury" of a number of villagers on the Jordanian border and announced the government's intention to try the accused soldiers and pay a small advance to the victim's families until the closed inquiry commission he established determined the total damages to be awarded (*NER,* November–December 1956: 36).[24]

It was not until mid-November that the first details indicating the gravity of the slaughter surfaced, thanks to the circulation in the Knesset of testimonies that a young MAPAM party secretary had recorded illegally from the hospitalized wounded (Dori 1998).[25] Still, even as partially censored accounts began to appear in the press and further details emerged from private channels, Jewish and Arab MAKI representatives who attempted to raise the issue formally met only hostility and erasure (*al-Ittihad,* 27 November 1956; ʿ*Al ha-Mishmar,* 15 November 1956).[26] The level of outrage and rumors within certain public circles finally reached its breaking point with *Davar*'s 7 December publication of a special poem by Natan Alterman—a MAPAI supporter and close friend of Ben Gurion—that denounced the cover-up of the crime.[27]

Recognizing the futility of the media gag, the prime minister issued his second and final statement on the matter in a parliamentary address on 12 December. Declaring that "there is no people in the world which holds life dearer than the Jewish people," he went on to provide a deeply ambivalent definition of the status of the Arab citizens of the state:

> Not only is there to be one law for the stranger and the citizen, but the stranger living among us is to be treated with love. The Arabs of Israel are not strangers, but citizens with fundamentally equal rights. In regard to human life, however, the civil status of any man makes no difference. The lives of all men are sacred. (*NER* 1956: 35)

It is not surprising that in 1956, the prime minister of Israel was unable to articulate precisely how or where the Palestinian Arab minority fit into the nation's social, cultural, and political landscape. Indeed, the military's conduct toward Arab citizens consistently demonstrated its failure to distinguish between the different juridical statuses of the Palestinians with whom it came into contact—particularly those living closest to the borders who were often caught in the cycle of refugee "infiltration" and Israeli military reprisals. This explains why, as philosopher Yigal Elam has noted, "The order [to kill Arab curfewbreakers] was not of a kind that did not conform to the spirit of the times" (Elam 1990: 61; see also Morris 1993).

The Initial Aftermath: November 1956 through March 1957

The weeks and months following the massacre, and particularly Ben Gurion's announcement on 12 December, produced an array of reactions in Arab communities throughout Israel. For residents of urban centers and scores of other villages in the Galilee and Little Triangle, this period witnessed the transformation of a relatively unknown border village into the motive force of unprecedented grassroots protest against military rule.[28] For the mourning residents of Kafr Qasim, however, virtually the only thing that mattered was figuring out how to move on, financially as well as emotionally.

Inside the village, residents were cut off from the outside and lived in a state of shock, grief, fear, rage, and (for some) hunger for months. In their small community of only two thousand people, most of whom belonged to one of six extended families, almost everyone lost a relative. Meanwhile, the army imposed a cordon around the village for at least three months, denying entrance to journalists, friends, and other members of the public who came to pay their condolences (*NER* 1956: 20; *al-Ittihad* 4 January 1957).

Palestinians outside Kafr Qasim also received the news of the massacre with a mixture of horror and fear, but their ability to take action was shaped by their distance from the event itself.[29] By early January these sentiments were transformed into mass mobilization. If Arab citizens tended to view the massacre, the official gag order on the press, and the government's decision to try the accused behind closed doors as further confirmation of their unwanted presence in Israel, they also believed that it was their right and obligation to assert that presence and to defend their promised rights as equal citizens. As a result, the following weeks and months spawned a spontaneous letter-writing campaign to the government, informational meetings in Palestinian population centers such as Acre, Nazareth, and Haifa, and a general strike.

As expected, MAKI presented the most radical analysis of the massacre, accusing the government of hiding behind the trope of the "manifestly illegal order" to conceal what had been a premeditated murder ordered by the highest ranks of the state (*al-Ittihad,* 18 December 1956; Habibi 1976: 7–9). Not everyone in the Arab community was prepared to level this accusation. Nevertheless, a broad consensus emerged among students, lawyers, village municipal leaders, and others who joined the chorus of opposition that the fundamental roots of the massacre were the ongoing military administration and the accompanying Jewish attitudes of mistrust and chauvinism toward the Arab population. Demands for a public trial and concrete measures in order to prevent the repetition of a similar assault thus intensified in the wake of Ben Gurion's equivocal Knesset speech and continued well after the *in camera* trial began. The torrent of letters and petitions that flowed into the government during this period marked an important development: their authors were constructing a nascent Arab discourse of rights and entitlement that the state would eventually have to account for, even if only in rhetoric.[30]

The first signs of a decentralized, grassroots protest movement appeared in late December, as further details of the slaughter reached the population, widespread calls for a public trial and a parliamentary investigation met with silence, and reports of the government's intimidation of Kafr Qasim's residents emerged. The process of mobilization began when a socially diverse group of men from around the country convened. They met at the Haifa home of Elias Kusa, a prominent, independent attorney, and issued a call for a general strike on 6 January, the date scheduled for the opening of the military trial.[31]

In the days that followed, planning meetings were held in Nazareth, Haifa, and the villages of the Galilee and Little Triangle, accompanied by growing reports of police subterfuge and harassment, the tightening of travel restrictions, and the ongoing military closure of Kafr Qasim. Further momentum gathered with celebratory calls to action in *al-Ittihad*, which promised "a memorable day in the history of struggle against the policies of national oppression that led to the Kafr Qasim slaughter." The day would succeed, the editors declared, despite the authorities' campaign to sabotage the strike (*al-Ittihad*, 4 January 1957).

The first mass expressions of opposition to the Kafr Qasim massacre and the policies that led to it transformed town and village streets of the Galilee and Little Triangle into virtual battlegrounds between security forces and Palestinian workers, peasants, merchants, and students. Despite the relatively modest itinerary for the day—a two-hour work stoppage, mourning prayers, and public meetings—military government authorities did everything they could to undermine the memorial activities. As armed police bands roamed city and village streets to intimidate the population and hunt down local organizers, other units, intelligence agents, and Arab informers paid home "visits" and pressured inhabitants to break the strike. In several cases, authorities entered shops and cafes, threatening to revoke the owners' licenses if they participated; in others, police ordered already striking merchants to re-open their stores (*al-Ittihad*, 8 January 1957).[32]

The fiercest battle took place in Acre, where a dramatic three-day dispute between strike organizers and the MAPAI-backed Islamic Committee culminated in the closing of the al-Jazzar mosque and the seizure of the city by hundreds of security forces aiming to prevent outside delegations from attending the prayer sessions and open meeting scheduled there. Despite these efforts, at least forty men managed to pass through a thick police barricade to enter the Dallalin Café, which organizers had selected as an alternative meeting site. There, following the recitation of the *fatiha* (opening chapter of the Quran) over the souls of the victims, they spoke in turn about the details of the massacre as well as problems faced by Arab citizens in employment, land, and civil rights (*al-Ittihad*, 8 January 1957). It is important to emphasize that although MAKI activists were widely involved in the memorial events, they did so alongside a small but growing grassroots force that—thanks to the aggressive tactics of the police—

was quickly beginning to appreciate the enormous mobilizing potential of memorial work.[33]

At the end of the day, strike organizers were able to note some impressive gains, including the scores of protest letters cabled from Palestinian villages and towns throughout the country, and their success in mobilizing hundreds of Arab citizens around memorial events.[34] The only serious fallout was the one-month banishment order issued to nine residents of the Little Triangle, which Ben Gurion announced was their punishment for attempting "to exploit the tragic incident for the purpose of racial incitement" (Knesset Minutes, 9 January 1957: 715).[35] In a furious speech to the legislature, Knesset member Tawfiq Tubi connected the illegality of these orders, which authorized the arrest of the nine without charge, to the state's refusal to allow Arab citizens to express their feelings in response to the massacre. Ben Gurion, for his part, denied receiving any letters from the Arab public. The country had already denounced the incident, he replied, and Tubi had no right to speak for the Arab community since there were "other parties" representing it.[36] In fact, it is very unlikely that the prime minister was unaware of these cables. Here was a moment—like many others that preceded and followed it—where the partial failure of force to silence independent Arab expression led to an unbalanced war of words and concluded with the official suppression of an alternative historical memory.

What happened in Kafr Qasim itself during the celebrated strike? Apart from a one-line note in *al-Ittihad*'s otherwise detailed report that residents struck "completely," we have no historical record of their experience.[37] Beyond the pain and fear that enveloped the village, the bereaved were focused on surviving. As local councils, political parties, and activists around the country continued to press their demands for an open trial throughout the winter and spring, families of the wounded and killed were relying on the charity of neighbors in order to make ends meet. By January, the government had still failed to distribute any damages, including the advance payment promised by Ben Gurion (*Al ha-Mishmar*, 21 January 1957; *al-Ittihad*, 15 and 25 January 1957). For the rest of the year the village remained effectively under siege and was all but severed from the stepped-up opposition campaign waged by sections of the Palestinian community outside (*al-Ittihad*, 26 February, 15 March, and 9 April 1957).

Compensation, Commemoration . . . "Celebration"

On the surface, the commemoration of the massacre's first anniversary and the *sulha* appear as though they were independent events. It makes more sense, however, to view them as the culmination of a protracted legal battle that began soon after the early crisis over compensation and ended with the state's attempt, by means of the *sulha*, to "terminate" the entire "Kafr Qasim affair" on its own terms. Both events were the product of Ben Gurion's desire to pay as small a financial and political price as possible for the crime.

The scandal over the unpaid damages began in June, with the results of the Zohar Commission of Inquiry nowhere in sight.[38] Still unable to return to work and distrusting the commission's intention to act in their best interests, eight of the thirteen wounded survivors began to work with Jewish attorneys to press for the establishment of an interministerial committee to determine the proper damage claims (ʿAl ha-Mishmar, 18 November 1957; Davar, 18 November 1957). Meanwhile, unbeknownst to the lawyers, a group of five local Arab and Jewish "mediators" working on behalf of the military government began paying a series of visits to the injured and the families of the victims. Led by Petah Tikva Mayor Pinhas Rashish, who was also an employer of many village residents, the group used various illegal means to coerce the families into accepting a privately arranged damages settlement on the condition that they cancel their claims against the state.[39] By the time the attorneys discovered the efforts of the newly formed "Public Committee," the group had obtained the signatures of the families and immediately thereafter received the prime minister's endorsement.[40]

It was in the shadow of this feverish, undercover legal maneuvering that the people of Kafr Qasim marked the massacre's first anniversary. Although the bereaved wished to hold their memorial service in private, the authorities had different plans. Due to the events of the year, the media attention around the trial, and the government's desire for a speedy resolution of the damages settlement, they sought to find the right balance between appearing sensitive to public opinion and ensuring a quiet and controlled ceremony. Thus they quietly waged a pro-government, anti-MAKI media campaign and worked with the village MAPAI branch to arrange a suitable list of guests (al-Yawm, 27 October 1957).

On the morning of 29 October, Arab and Jewish well-wishers who came to pay their respects had to obtain clearance at three police barricades in order to enter the village. Only strict MAPAI loyalists, border patrol and military government officials, non-MAKI journalists, and a few delegations from nearby Arab communities were permitted entry. There, guests found the village shrouded in two layers: civil and military police surrounded village entrances, while black ribbons covered the rest—schools, shops, and the entire road from the western entrance to the central site of the crime (al-Ittihad, 1 November 1957; al-Mirsad, 31 October 1957; ha-Boker, 30 October 1957).

For the most part, the carefully prepared list of speakers and intimidating presence of military government authorities enabled commemoration organizers to maintain tight control over the tone and content of the ceremony (al-Ittihad, 1 November 1957). On a few occasions, however, mourning villagers managed (intentionally or not) to disrupt the organizers' presentation of the event as a demonstration of the government's goodwill. In the courtyard of the mosque, Husni Wadiʿ Sarsur, local MAPAI leader and son of the mukhtar, headed off a series of speakers, all of whom who expressed their condolences and praised the authorities' response to the incident (al-Yawm, 30 October 1957).[41] One participant later informed al-Ittihad that

When . . . Sarsur stood and called for people to forget the massacre and announced that the government promised to pave the road to the village and connect us to the water grid as compensation for the blood that was spilt, loud grumbling began to occur among the villagers. . . . They began to cut him off, taking these words as an insult to the memory of their slain. (*al-Ittihad*, 1 November 1957)[42]

The remarks of Elias Agassi, head of the Histadrut's Arab Department, met a similar response from mourners when he offensively referred to the massacre as a "casualty of misunderstanding" between Jews and Arabs, and moralized that the villagers should be grateful for Israel's strong democracy, as demonstrated by the trial and the right of citizens to express their outrage.[43] Following the speeches, organizers reportedly failed to prevent mourners from making their way to the cemetery. The same participant testified that

> The entire village gathered there to the side of the graves crying and weeping. When Agassi arrived . . . where the mourning prayers were being held, the worshippers screamed in his face, demanding that he leave the area and saying, "Leave us, Agassi. [How dare] you kill a man and walk in his funeral!" (*al-Ittihad*, 1 November 1957)

Just one week after the crowd of unwelcome visitors left residents of the besieged village to themselves, news of the Public Committee and its final recommendations was leaked to the media, and Kafr Qasim again returned to the media spotlight and heightened government surveillance. To conclude the affair "in a celebratory manner" (Segev, *Ha'aretz*, 10 November 1957), the committee announced its plan to hold a special ceremony along the model of the *sulha* (*Ha'aretz*, 22 November 1957). The decision to appropriate this indigenous Bedouin ceremony—used historically as a means for communities to resolve their internal disputes without the heavy hand of state intervention—was deliberate. In contrast to the ongoing trial, the *sulha* could gloss over the imbalance of power between subjects of the military government and the state, and reproduce an image of Palestinians as ancient tribesmen who either rejected or did not understand modern judicial procedures.

The "truce" imposed on the people of Kafr Qasim can be seen as the product of Ben Gurion's desire to wash the hands of the military government, the MAPAI party, and the border patrol all at once. First, by applying the regulations of social security, which covered work accidents, rather than those designed to compensate for injuries or death resulting from an act of war, the state robbed the villagers financially and evaded its responsibility for the crime (*'Al ha-Mishmar*, 18 and 19 November 1957; *Jerusalem Post*, 18 November 1957). Coupled with the financial incentive of deploying a third party to "negotiate" between the village and the government was an even greater political incentive. By presenting the *sulha* in Kafr Qasim as a reconciliation between two warring parties, the government could situate the massacre within a contrived history of symmetrical violence between Arabs and Jews.[44] More significantly, it is difficult not to draw connections between the *sulha* and the trial, which at that point was far from over. The fact that the authorities attempted to bring the accused murderers themselves to the ceremony—the only aspect of the entire affair that villagers successfully opposed—lends support to the local council's argument today that the *sulha* was necessary to lighten the weight of the court verdict and clear the path for the soldiers' early release. If the victims could pardon the perpetrators, the council asserts, it would be that much easier for the government to do the same (KQLC 1996: 37; *Ha'aretz*, 21 November 1957).

The actual *sulha* was carried out in much the same way as the first anniversary ceremony, only it required more preparation, a greater enforcement of discipline, and a more elaborately choreographed performance.[45] For their own part, villagers participated in the charade solely out of fear and the absence of a viable alternative. Their practical decision notwithstanding, for them and for most Palestinians in Israel who personally remember the event or learned about it from others, the *sulha* remains an indelible stain on Israel's historical record, an assault on the dignity of the victims and the Arab community as a whole. While the state, with the help of the mainstream Hebrew-language media, may have publicly succeeded that day in dramatizing its hegemony and imposing its own memory of the massacre, it did so only through the use of force and the imagery of exoticism—a fact which few villagers have forgotten (*Ha'aretz*, 22 November 1957; *la-Merhav*, 22 November 1957; *Jerusalem Post*, 21 November 1957).[46] The event is part of the crime that Palestinians commemorate today (Darwish 1996; Glicksberg and Bdayr 1997; KQLC 1996, 1997; Kafr Qasim official website 2005).

Policing Memories, Remembering Police: The First National Anniversary Strike

While the military government succeeded, overall, in enforcing the discipline and submission of the residents of Kafr Qasim during the first anniversary of the massacre and the fabricated ceremony of reconciliation, it encountered much more serious opposition from the broader Arab community. In October 1957, the national strike and day of mourning witnessed a previously unseen eruption of open protest against military rule and national discrimination, bringing more than a thousand Arab citizens into the streets and several hundred others to public meetings (*al-Ittihad*, 26 October and 1 November 1957). The unprecedented turnout was due in part to the successful organizing efforts of MAKI activists, who established a national commemoration day coordination committee, but probably also to the outrage caused by a series of landmine explosions and army shooting exercises that took place that year in or near several Arab villages (Habibi 1976: 62).[47] Although these incidents resulted in the death of twenty-two children and the injury of eight others, the state failed to investigate them seriously—a reaction that many perceived as further proof of contempt for Arab life (*al-Ittihad*, 28 October 1957).[48]

Although the scheduled events for the October commemoration closely resembled that which took place in January, they were distinguished by a heightened level of discursive and physical confrontations between protesters on the one hand and the police and military government on the other. *Al-Ittihad*'s pre-anniversary announcements combined strident denunciations of the authorities' renewed intimidation campaign with rallying cries to defy it. In a notable rhetorical shift, editors modified the familiar call against the "policies of national oppression," announcing the people's intention to "express their vengeance against the continuation of the *policies of Kafr Qasim*" (*al-Ittihad*, 11 October 1957; emphasis added). In addition to its bolder tone, the MAKI leadership was more cognizant of the stakes over commemoration, no doubt in part due to its experience in January. Even before the anniversary, they self-consciously asserted, "The government wanted us to forget the slaughtered people but . . . this [memorial activity] . . . the popular meetings . . . [and] the general strike have frustrated [its] wishes" (*al-Ittihad*, 25 October 1957).

Physical clashes also reached new heights. In defiance of police squads who from the approach of dawn reportedly roamed city and village streets and threatened merchants and community leaders, several thousand workers, students, peasants, and merchants joined strikes and memorial meetings around the country. The authorities responded not only by forcibly dispersing and arresting demonstrators but also by taking more drastic steps to prevent the visible and vocal protest of Arab citizens—confiscating microphones to be used at demonstrations, spreading threatening rumors of travel bans to Jerusalem on Christmas, and forcing villagers to erase memorial slogans on the walls outside their homes (*al-Ittihad*, 1 November 1957; *Ha'aretz*, 30 October 1957).

Recognizing the magnitude of the 1957 strike serves as an important corrective to the existing historiography on Israel's Arab citizens, which widely records the clashes that erupted during the 1958 May Day celebrations in Nazareth as the first expression of open opposition to military rule. Because those clashes erupted in the wake of two Pan-Arab victories in Iraq and Syria, respectively, many scholars (including those representing the official Israeli perspective) have incorrectly attributed them to "foreign incitement" rather than to part of an internally generated opposition movement (Stendel 1996: 96–98; Schwarz 1959: 16–18).[49] The broad participation in the 1957 strike also corrects the mistaken impression that the Popular Front—the first alliance of communist and non-Communist Arab nationalists in Israel—was born solely out of the committees that formed in response to the May Day arrests the following year (Beinin 1990: 202).

In short, the first anniversary strike to commemorate the Kafr Qasim massacre compels us to give greater consideration to the long-term and contradictory processes of Palestinian resistance rather than to an episodic or event-based understanding of their history. Although the strike was undoubtedly prompted by a specific event, it was one that recalled other atrocities from 1948 and beyond, and one that went on to shape early expressions and forms of opposition. By appreciating the role of the 1957 strike, we see that resistance to military rule and the construction and suppression of Palestinian memory in Israel was not based on a single incident or limited to a certain group. Rather, it developed over a long period of time and often in uneven ways. The annual, countrywide activities commemorating the Kafr Qasim massacre and the clashes that erupted around them played a critical role in these processes, endowing Arab citizens with lasting memories of confrontation with the state and creating a tradition of civil protest that they could draw upon in their future struggle for equality.

Local Struggle/National Struggle: Recollections of the Memorial Movement

The subject of the massacre in those days was the private property of the village itself. In the early years . . . it did not matter to us what was happening outside, beyond the borders of the village itself. It was a private pain. . . . With time, through our opening up toward society, we saw that it was necessary for us to pass on the pain and to place it in the hearts of the others. . . . This belief pushed us to call on parties to come to the village [to commemorate] with us every year.

—Ibrahim Sarsur, chair, Kafr Qasim Local Council (1998)

The protests and commemorations . . . were not limited to the village itself, because it was not only a special event for Kafr Qasim. Rather, this was something that pertained to public opinion at large, and to all Arabs . . . The first strike of the Arab people surrounding the problem related to their situation in Israel was on the first anniversary of the massacre. It was a general strike, upheld by the majority of the people.

—Tawfiq Tubi, former Knesset Member, MAKI (1998)

Depending on whether they are from Kafr Qasim or outside it, Palestinians in Israel offer somewhat different, and at times conflicting, historical narratives of the impact of the massacre and its aftermath. In some cases these discrepancies reflect their dissimilar experiences; in other cases they reflect the attempt by outside activists, primarily leaders of the Communist Party, to construct a particular vision of the past in order to position themselves as the authentic—or in Gramscian terms, organic—leaders, of the Arab population (Gramsci 1971: 5–16; 204–210). Indeed, the contours of the memorial movements within and outside Kafr Qasim shifted considerably through the late 1960s.

In their historical reconstruction of the memorial movement, most village activists recall that the practice of commemoration was centered in Kafr Qasim itself. Due partly to lack of interest and even more to fear of reprisal, they insist that it took well over a decade for the ceremony to evolve into its current, political form, one that incorporates the outside community. Even those who were active early on recall that while memorial meetings took place in other villages and towns, it was only in Kafr Qasim that they observed annual strikes. On the whole, their stories are personal and local, rooted in the pain that consumed the bereaved families and in villagers' incremental successes as well as failures in defying the threats of the military government and its local collaborators to walk in what is now the annual commemorative procession (ʿAmr 1998; Bdayr 1998; ʿAli Salim Sarsur 1998).

By contrast, Communist Party activists have consistently emphasized the *national* movement they led in opposition to the massacre, celebrating in particular the two strikes of 1957; the dozens of party members who went to prison through 1966 in the battle over the right to commemorate; and the annual activities sponsored by local chapters of MAKI's Kafr Qasim Anniversary Day Committee (*al-Ittihad*, 1 November 1966). For a decade, the committee led memorial gatherings around the country, dispatched solidarity delegations to Kafr Qasim the day before the anniversary, and cabled public messages of condolence to the village (MAKI Central Committee 1997: 78–79).

What these contested memories reveal is that for many years the massacre produced different meanings and experiences for different people, all of which were shaped by their personal connection to the crime, place of residence, level of political engagement and mobility, socioeconomic status, and access to information. The authorities' annual military closure of Kafr Qasim, which continued through the tenth anniversary, helped to construct these disjointed experiences in critical ways.[50]

One way to explicate the shifting impacts of the massacre over the first decade and to begin to reconcile the national and local narratives is by juxtaposing oral accounts of villagers against *al-Ittihad*'s annual coverage of the anniversary.[51] Among the most significant differences between the two memorial movements was the pace of change. On the national front, each anniversary provided activists and intellectuals with a new opportunity to reflect on elements of continuity and change since 1956 in local, regional, and international politics, to reassert the Arab community's united response to the crime, and to draw additional political lessons from it. In the early years, *al-Ittihad* offered extensive coverage of memorial activities and arrest campaigns of organizers around the country but little or nothing about what was happening in Kafr Qasim itself. This state of affairs stemmed from the inability of correspondents to enter the village on the anniversary and from the lack of political activity there, apart from the local strike. During those years, families and friends would gather for intimate ceremonies at the mosque and then walk to place flowers on the tombstones of the slain. As one activist recalled, villagers were simply too scared to do anything more (ʿAmr 1998).[52]

The absence of explicit, coordinated political action in Kafr Qasim for the first three years after the massacre contrasted with a relatively high level of activity throughout the rest of the country. As Palestinians gradually became less fearful of openly expressing their opposition to military rule, the meanings ascribed to the massacre widened. Commemoration became an effective tool with which activists could mobilize the Arab community to protest subsequent acts of state violence, neglect, and discrimination. In this way, the form and focus of commemorations changed from year to year.

In 1959, for example, the massacre's anniversary coincided with the Knesset's electoral campaign. The editors of *al-Ittihad*' solemnly recalled the "[Sinai] ag-

gression and the tragedy," and for the first time drew explicit connections between Kafr Qasim and other Israeli massacres of Palestinians in Deir Yasin,
Qibya, Gaza, Nahalin, Gaza, and Rafah (27 October 1959).[53] Like the rest of the
media, however, their main interest was in the elections, and for the first time
the massacre became the object of explicit political competition. Most parties
vying for Arab votes felt compelled to address it, by praising their own response,
denouncing others for their inaction, or claiming that no other party could prevent it from happening again.

Editorials, memorial announcements, open meetings, demonstrations, and
slogans around each anniversary of the massacre offer a glimpse into the cycle
of violence and conflict that has shaped the historical relationship between Israel and its Arab citizens. In 1961, for example, the anniversary fell just one
month after the shooting death by Israeli soldiers of five unarmed Palestinian
youth attempting to cross the border into Egypt. The incident received wide
attention in the Arabic press and among the Israeli left, and brought home for
many Palestinians the blurry line between Israel's violent retaliation policies
against refugees on the borders and its treatment of Arab citizens inside. The
public mourning of the victims and the response to their murder drew upon
the legacy of Kafr Qasim's commemoration, involving police threats against
funeral and memorial services, protest cables to the government, and more
(al-Ittihad, 24 and 29 October 1961).[54] The next anniversary marked another
attack on Arab citizens, this time on workers in Rishon Letsion (al-Ittihad,
29 October 1962).[55]

Some years witnessed more activity and confrontation with the authorities
than others. In 1964, Palestinians held large memorial meetings and demonstrations to protest the founding of Carmiel, a new Jewish settlement established
on the confiscated land of three Galilee villages. Many viewed the government's
decision to hold the settlement's grand inauguration ceremony on 29 October,
the anniversary of the massacre, as particularly indicative of the state's contempt for the Arab community (al-Ittihad, 23 October 1964).[56] In a now familiar pattern, a heightened level of mobilization met with increased harassment
by the police, who arrested meeting organizers, conducted home raids, and imposed sieges on villages and towns where strikes and silent demonstrations were
held (al-Ittihad, 27 and 30 October 1964; la-Merhav, 30 October 1964).[57]

Kafr Qasim itself witnessed nothing on the level of open meetings, demonstrations, or street clashes with police in this period, although it was during the
early 1960s that the tradition of today's commemoration ceremony—involving
a procession from the massacre site to the cemetery, sign-holding, poetry read-
ings and political speeches—was born. Notably, the introduction of each of
these elements entailed the courageous decision of organizers, who were acutely
aware of the risks they could incur as a result of their actions. In 1960, villagers
held their first memorial procession, and in 1961, fifteen-year-old ʿOmar ʿAmr
and his friends spent the equivalent of three days work in the fields to rent a
megaphone in order to read an announcement to participants. They continued
this practice every year, despite the objections of the shuyukh (elders) and re-

peated arrests by local military authorities. As more residents began to join the processions over time, the authorities turned to additional forms of harassment, such as threatening to revoke the work permits of anyone seen participating, pressuring local council members to cancel the ceremony, and arresting village activists one or two nights before the anniversary, releasing them just a few hours after the morning procession (Bdayr 1998; ʿAli Salim Sarsur 1998; ʿAmr 1998; ʿAl ha-Mishmar, 6 November 1960).[58]

One aspect of the local memorial movement of which al-Ittihad's annual coverage enables us to capture a small glimpse is the gradual process by which young people in Kafr Qasim became increasingly politicized and began to draw explicit connections between the local memorial struggle and political concerns facing the larger Arab community. Although the paper reported little on the actual commemorations inside, the voices of village residents began to appear sporadically in the form of anonymous letters, conversations with village youth, and a few detailed descriptions of ceremonies (al-Ittihad, 28 October 1960, 31 October 1961, 3 November 1963; 25 October 1963).[59] One such letter appeared in 1962, in a bold and angry missive signed under the pseudonym of Tariq Ibn Zayyad, who condemned the organizers of the sulha as traitors and threatened fellow villagers who tried to stop the procession from taking place:

> Those who specialize every year in suppressing our voices through threats and intimidation will not be able to cover up the crime and to make it forgotten, because it is stirring in the hearts of thousands of citizens . . . As for those who cooperate to prevent us from organizing the procession to visit the graves of the martyrs, read the fatiha over their souls . . . and . . . let the tears flow for the beloved and relatives, they will come to know how they will be overthrown. (al-Ittihad, 30 October 1962)[60]

These letters and articles appeared to serve several interests at once. First, their authors clearly sought to win support for their activities by reaching out to the part of the Arab population that they recognized to be the most sympathetic to their struggle. The texts also targeted fellow villagers—both to condemn resident collaborators and to empower others to join the procession. Finally, they also served the interests of al-Ittihad's editors by enabling them to represent the voices of an imagined community that had in fact never been active in the Communist Party. The act of publishing these voices thus allowed the newspaper to portray Kafr Qasim as part of the broader national struggle, with MAKI at its helm. Although it is uncertain whether these texts had any impact on people's decisions to participate in the ceremony, the ability of at least some villagers to speak directly to a countrywide audience marks a significant shift insofar as it represents part of the process by which the internal and external memorial movements came together.[61]

The multiple responses to the Kafr Qasim massacre among village residents, the Israeli state, and the Palestinian population at large underscore the need to rewrite the dominant Israeli narrative of the crime and to explore memory as a "category of practice" (Abu El-Haj 2006; Rogers and Brubaker 2000). The decade of clashes over the act of commemoration and the failure of more recent Israeli scholarship to address this aspect of the country's past illustrate the ongoing refusal of Israeli political culture to make room for Palestinian (or any non-Zionist) memories.[62] Here, as in other contested histories, memory is not merely the aftermath of the conflict but its very embodiment (see also Novick 2000).

The historical struggle over Kafr Qasim's commemoration also underscores how the very conditions that led to the massacre were structural—not exceptional—in the history of Israel's treatment of its Palestinian Arab minority under military rule. Specifically, the state's repressive response in the aftermath of the crime shows how the attitudes and established mode of behavior toward the Arab population continued to produce a climate of violence that underwent little, if any, substantive change through the mid-1960s. Although scholars have been correct to identify the subtler, more discursive ways that ruling groups mobilize collective memory to maintain social control, I have highlighted the violence to which states have resorted to achieve the same ends.

What the massacre did change was the courage of many Palestinians to openly protest the continuation of military rule. It did so by planting the seeds of an unprecedented grassroots campaign that connected the active memorialization of the victims to heightened demands for equality. This opposition campaign did not end in 1957, but rather continued through the end of military rule and shaped relations between Arab citizens and the state in critical ways. As I emphasize above, the commemoration movement was neither homogenous nor internally coherent. Its uneven development and contested history illustrate that organized resistance rarely begins among the most vulnerable and terrorized, who may often have different (or more limited) interests than their leadership. Finally, while the massacre itself became a permanent fixture in the collective memory of Palestinians in Israel (and to a lesser extent of those outside it), the active project of remembering the event was never fixed in time or place; rather, it developed—and continues to evolve—according to shifting relations between Arabs and Jews in Israel and changing matrices of the Arab-Israeli conflict more broadly.[63]

Forty-nine years later, the Israeli government has yet to launch an independent parliamentary investigation or to accept full responsibility for the massacre. The trope of exceptionality continues to dominate popular and academic discourse surrounding the crime.[64] And yet, the second Palestinian uprising that erupted in September 2000 and Israel's complete reoccupation of the West Bank and Gaza Strip since February 2002 has recalled the legacy of Kafr Qasim in new ways. Notably, since the al-Aqsa Intifada began, the famous 1957 military court ruling on the obligation of soldiers to disobey an "illegal order" above which hangs a "black flag" has become a rallying cry among *both* critics of the Occupation and opponents of any plan to end it (Jacobson 2004).[65] Of more immediate consequence for Palestinians citizens and Jewish antiracism activists within Israel is the ongoing failure of the Justice Ministry to prosecute any of the police officers found responsible for the shooting death of twelve citizens and the injury of hundreds of others during countrywide Arab protests against discrimination in October 2000 (Dalal 2003).[66] There is a clear relationship between the "October Events," the enormous wounds they (re)opened, and the ongoing historiographic silence around the 1956 massacre.[67] The growing social and political alienation of Palestinians in Israel, the rise of police brutality against them, and heightened Jewish support for their expulsion, are all symptomatic of the cumulative effect of the suppressed memories of violence that have haunted Israeli society since 1948 (Blecher 2002; Yiftachel 2002).

For most residents of Kafr Qasim, the memory of the massacre remains alive. Until the state acknowledges its responsibility for the crime, discloses all documents pertaining to its prelude and aftermath, issues a formal apology, and includes the full story of the massacre in the curriculum of both Arab and Jewish schools, villagers will continue to commemorate the tragedy as a form of political protest. In fact their demands go much further than this, as the fortieth anniversary memorial book attests:

> Reconciliation cannot be bought with lambs or liras because the souls of our martyrs are not for bargaining. If the intention is to reach a settlement of reconciliation, this requires two parties, not one. Our hand is stretched out, but any basis for peace must include the recognition of the right of Palestinians to establish a state in the West Bank and Gaza Strip, with Jerusalem as its capital. . . . Kafr Qasim is recorded in its import and blood of martyrs as an additional chapter in the Palestinian struggle. The *sulha* will come with just peace and with complete freedom inside Israel. (KQLC 1996: 38)

Notes

Special thanks to the people in Kafr Qasim, Jaljulia, Tel Aviv, and Haifa, who took the time to revisit their memories with me in the summers of 1998 and 2002.

1. Three of the four were workers from Tayyiba, Jaljuliyya, and Kafr Bara, respectively, who happened to be driving or returning home with the residents of Kafr Qasim that day. The fourth was an eleven-year-old boy from Tayyiba who was shot and killed when he went out to buy cigarettes for his father.

2. See, especially, Kemp (2004) on Israel's early "interlocking of 'security needs' and 'population management.'"

3. This summary draws primarily from Habibi 1976, published on the twentieth anniversary of the massacre. Habibi bases much of his account on the published verdict of the military court.

4. Anton Shammas once noted the "paradoxical fact that Israeli army jargon, which is largely based on spoken Arabic, has done much to deepen the gulf between Arabs and Jews" (Shammas 1983).

5. After 1948, the only work available to most Palestinian peasants was day labor in the fields, orchards, and quarries owned by Israeli Jews. In many cases

they continued to work on land they had previously owned or farmed but which the Israelis confiscated during or after the war.

6. I thank journalist Ruvik Rosenthal for sharing his copy of the military court trial records with me.

7. Curiously, the deaths of these forty-three were the only deaths investigated in the trial; the other five cases were dropped, and those responsible were not questioned (Habibi 1976: 73–74).

8. Thirty years later, Ofer recalled without remorse that his unit had merely "followed orders" on the day of the massacre, just as he had done in other "incidents no less horrific," and as the Germans had done during the Holocaust (Karpel 1986).

9. According to Tubi (1956), most of the thirteen survivors lived due to extraordinary circumstances, such as by feigning death or hiding under a tree all night.

10. Only a few of the accused officers were in fact Moroccan or of "Mizrahi" background. Mainstream liberal Ashkenazi discourse in Israel has tended historically to attribute anti-Arab racism and brutality to Arab Jews, thereby deflecting attention from the participation of European Jews (who have always constituted the majority of the Israeli elite) in the structures that enable and reproduce discriminatory practices toward Palestinians. See also, Rabinowitz 1997.

11. The judges convicted the accused on the basis of their unquestioned obedience to a "manifestly illegal order" (in this case, shooting innocent civilians). One factor that evidently led to the ruling was the impression left by the files of at least ten other previously classified cases submitted by the prosecution in which soldiers involved in the murder of Arab civilians claimed that they were merely "following orders" (Lavie and Gorali 2003). But due to the ruling's vague formulation, it became little more than a trope invoked to reinforce the image of the Israeli army's "purity of arms" (Elam 1990: 59). See also Bilsky (2002). It is worth noting that in the forty-seven years since the trial, no military court has ever accepted the "illegal order" concept as the legitimate defense of a soldier accused of disobeying an order.

12. Elam provides the sharpest critique of this reaction: "The entire legal affair . . . is illustrated as a ritualistic process through which the state and the entire society purified itself of a minor infraction which was attributed to it" (Elam 1990: 58–59). Ozacky-Lazar similarly concludes that "in the eyes of most Jews [Kafr Qasim] is a forgotten affair . . . remembered more as an internal debate about the limits of obeying military orders and the legality of those orders" (Ozacky-Lazar 1996a: 44). English-language surveys purporting to cover the general history of "Israeli Arabs" echo this sentiment. They generally ignore the *sulha,* the question of compensation, and the memorial campaign (Peretz 1958; Schwarz 1959; Cohen 1965; Stendel 1996).

13. Although the top three officers convicted were sentenced for between fifteen and seventeen years each, they were all released after fourteen months and had their military ranks reinstated (Karpel 1986; Habibi 1976: 75–78). Shadmi was the leading military figure found responsible for the massacre. In a separate trial, the court convicted him of an administrative error (for extending a curfew without permission from the military governor) and symbolically fined him one *grush*—the equivalent of a penny at that time.

14. In 1997, Moshe Katsav, then the minister responsible for Arab Affairs, visited Kafr Qasim on commemoration day and expressed the government's condolences for the tragedy. He was the highest state official ever to visit the village on the massacre's anniversary, though he missed the ceremony itself. Many Palestinians were outraged by what they viewed as this weak offering, while others saw the visit as a moderate step forward (Algazy 1997).

15. In 1991, Ruvik Rosenthal obtained access to the military trial transcript and exposed a previously unknown plan, named Operation Mole, which formed the backdrop to the killings. Rosenthal concluded that, although the operation's ambiguous orders contributed to the massacre by creating the conditions for the mass flight of Arab citizens from the Little Triangle region, the massacre itself was not planned.

16. Kafr Qasim lies at the southern edge of the Triangle, and many Palestinians maintain that the army intentionally planned a massacre there because, similar to what happened after the 1948 massacre in Deir Yasin, it would immediately send a wave of panic northward and lead, through the domino effect, to the flight of the population to Jordan. To substantiate this claim, villagers point to the fact that on the day of the massacre, soldiers blocked all but the eastern edge of the village, thus permitting only one direction in which to escape (KQLC 1996). Some also believe that the army deliberately chose Kafr Qasim as the site of the crime in order to avenge the village's successful defense against Jewish forces in 1948, a victory that saved numerous villages to its north from destruction: Sarsur, interview.

17. Most surveys of Israeli Arabs tend to lack historical dimension, focusing on the population's loyalty to the state, its participation in the formal political process, and its "modernizing" potential. Ian Lustick (1980) investigates the official policies designed to maintain the community's marginalized status, but he ignores the ways in which Arab citizens have resisted this status. My own analysis departs not only from this older scholarship, including that of Lustick, but also from more recent claims that the massacre produced no "meaningful changes" in state–minority relations (for example, Ozacky-Lazar 1996b).

18. The available sources limit the following discussion largely to formal political activity, a focus that inevitably silences other forms of commemoration that took place.

19. The near absence of Palestinians in more than ten years of publication of Tel Aviv University's prominent journal, *History and Memory*, is a noted example. On the other hand, the appearance of three new works since the original version of this article was completed may indicate the seeds of a new openness in the Israeli academy (Ben-Ze'ev 2002; Benvenisti 2000; Meget 2000).

20. The two exceptions in this collection are Tamar Katriel on the pioneer museum and Dan Rabinowitz on Upper Nazareth.

21. Here I am referring to public spaces shared by Jews and Arabs. In recent years, several commemorative monuments and plaques have been built in Palestinian locales, including Shafa ʿAmru, ʿIlabun, ʿIlut, Sandala, and Sakhnin (ʿAwawdah 2001). Kafr Qasim also now has two monuments dedicated to the victims of the massacre.

22. *Al-Ittihad* editors and others frequently used the term *conspiracy of silence* (for example, *al-Ittihad,* 27 October 1959).

23. "How can people from among us do such a thing?" Ben Gurion asked fellow members of the cabinet on 11 November 1956. "It is horrifying. . . . We have a wonderful army, but apparently there are incidents and circumstances in which people lose their minds" (*Ha'aretz,* 28 March 2001; see also Ozacky-Lazar 1996a: 42).

24. The Zohar Commission protocols remain classified.

25. Latif Dori first had to sneak past the heavily guarded entrance to the hospital, which was also housing the soldiers wounded in Egypt. Until then, no one knew the condition of the survivors because Kafr Qasim remained under a tight cordon and no villagers had obtained a permit to visit them (ᶜAmr 1998).

26. On 13 November, the speaker of the Knesset revoked Esther Vilenska's right to speak and ordered her words "Kafr Qasim incident" stricken from the record. One week later Knesset Member Tawfiq Tubi met a similar fate (Tubi 1998).

27. Natan Alterman, "Thum ha-meshulash" (Triangle Zone), *Davar,* 7 December 1956.

28. The "Little Triangle" forms the narrow Israeli-held strip of the larger district circumscribed by the three West Bank cities of Nablus, Tulkarm, and Jenin. During the Arab Revolt from 1936 to 1939 this district was the center of rebel activity and became known by the British as the "Triangle of Terror" (Swedenburg 1995: xxxii).

29. See the police intelligence reports regarding the popular fear that spread through the city of Nazareth, located in the Israel State Archives (ISA L 53/24 [1957]—"Strike in Territories of Military Government"; L 53/25 [1954– 1956]—"Minorities: General, Jezreel District").

30. These letters are divided between the Kafr Qasim Municipal Archive (KQMA) and the files of the Interior Ministry, Minorities Division in the ISA. In the KQMA, see, for example, Arab Students of Hebrew University to Speaker of the Knesset et. al., 5 January 1957; IGUD association cable to Ben Gurion, n.d.). In the ISA, see, especially, the correspondence between Yani K. Yani, Kafr Yasif local council chair, and Minister Israel Bar-Yehuda (ISA, G 2215/22 [1957]—"Security: Central District"). See also *al-Ittihad,* 18 December 1956. Although this paper trail drew upon an emerging tradition of written protests to the authorities that began in 1948, the post-massacre letters mark a significant shift because of their volume and assertive language.

31. "Announcement to Arab Citizens," 4 January 1957 (ISA, G 2215/22).

32. Correspondents offered detailed coverage of strikes in Nazareth, Acre, Haifa, Shafa ᶜAmru, Ramle, and the villages of Rama, ᶜArraba, Sakhnin, Sulam, Shafa ᶜAmru, Tayyiba, Tira, Tamra, Kafr Yasif, and Umm al-Fahm.

33. ISA, G 2215/22. (On police surveillance, see ISA, L 174/7 [1951–1961]—"Arab Acre"; L 80/6 [1957]—"Prevailing Moods.")

34. These numbers must be appreciated in light of the almost total reliance of the Arab population on the military government and other MAPAI-dominated institutions for employment, health, and other social services during this time.

35. Temporary exile and house arrest were frequently imposed to discipline Arab

citizens who expressed opposition to military rule (Jiryis 1976; Kanafani 1968; Ighbariya 1988).

36. These were MAPAM, which could not mount serious public opposition due to its partnership in the ruling coalition, and MAPAI's "Arab lists."

37. None of the village residents I interviewed recalled this day.

38. In fact, Zohar had already sent Ben Gurion their final report on 11 November 1956, which recommended the establishment of a special medical committee to address the damages question. A year later, however, the prime minister's office claimed never to have received it. Ben Gurion likely feared that adopting Zohar's recommendation would reinforce the responsibility of the state (Zohar to Ben Gurion, 16 November 1957, ISA, G 5593/4674).

39. Petah Tikva lies eight kilometers west of Kafr Qasim and is the closest Jewish town to it. By the mid-1950s the town's Histadrut office employed a high proportion of village workers. The Committee's other members included two other prominent (Jewish) MAPAI members on the town council and two Palestinian Arabs from nearby villages known to Kafr Qasim residents as government collaborators (Ibrahim Sarsur 1998; ʿAli Salim Sarsur 1998). It is unclear whether this "deal" was to include the cancellation of all judicial as well as financial claims, but it was widely rumored later that the government sought to use this as a back channel to terminate the trial (Davar, 18 November 1957; ʿAl ha-Mishmar, 18 November 1957). The consent forms summarizing the committee's findings were in Hebrew, which most of the families at that time could not read, adding to their vulnerability (al-Mirsad, 31 October 1957; Ha'aretz, 10 November 1957; ʿAl ha-Mishmar, 18 November 1957).

40. The state's participation in the Public Committee's activities is beyond dispute. Military Government officials attended its final meeting and played a direct role in pressuring families to agree to its findings by threatening to deny them work and travel permits, and in at least one case, to deport them (Ibrahim Sarsur 1998). Ben Gurion himself blocked the formation of the proposed interministerial committee in early November when he refused to send a Defense Ministry representative to participate (Davar 19 November 1957; ʿAl ha-Mishmar, 19 November 1957).

41. See also, "Report of the District Commander of Minorities in Ramle," October 1957 (ISA, G 2215/22: doc. 70).

42. See Scott (1990: 154–156) on the act of grumbling as a relatively safe expression of subaltern dissent.

43. Agassi was born in Baghdad in 1909 and was fluent in Arabic and familiar with Arab cultural mores. In other contexts he was considered to be "always respectful of Arab [citizens]" (Lockman 1996: 197–198).

44. Recalling the massacre of Jews near Jerusalem in 1929, ceremony master of ceremonies A. Shapira declared, "Violence between the Jews and Arabs of this country did not start at Kafr Qasim, and violence breeds violence" (Jerusalem Post, 22 November 1957).

45. See the elegant, bilingual invitation in ISA, G 2215/22.

46. The coverage of the Jerusalem Post captures the kind of discourse employed to convince the public of the authenticity of the ceremony and the reconciliation that it had achieved: "The men sat down to eat, and the youth and children of the village gathered around the guests, laughing and joking and stop-

ping every now and then to drink from the newly installed water taps, which are more prominent in everyone's mind by now than last year's tragedy." Although the ceremony "seem[ed] cruel, with its roasted meats and dishes of fruit set before the relatives of the dead," the reporter tried to assure her readers, it was necessary for the healing process, "just as a festering ulcer must be cut out to save a limb" (*Jerusalem Post,* 22 November 1957).

47. From 1956–1958, residents of several villages discovered additional bombs in schools, playgrounds, and churches (Jiryis 1976: 155).

48. See also, attorney Hana Naqqara's correspondence with Interior Minister Israel Bar-Yehuda (October–November 1956, ISA, G 2215/22, doc. 60).

49. Stendel served as deputy to the prime minister's advisor on Arab Affairs in the 1960s.

50. It is impossible to overstate the impact of this physical separation imposed on the Arab population, particularly on villagers. The fact that they were terrorized is in large part why they turned inward.

51. Because of MAKI's leading role in the equality struggle, we can also glean much from *al-Ittihad*'s array of meeting announcements, editorials, signed columns, and anonymous letters about how Arab citizens came to position themselves and the crime within a broader trajectory of Palestinian history.

52. ʿOmar ʿAmr was fifteen years old at the time of the massacre and became a leading activist in the local memorial movement. ʿAdil Bdayr (1998) offered the same explanation.

53. Those massacres took place, respectively, in April 1948, October 1953, March 1954, August 1955 (Khan Yunis), November 1956 (Gaza), and November 1956.

54. More than one thousand people joined the funeral procession there, despite reported police harassment, and several hundred returned—defying police and MAPAI party warnings—to attend the traditional memorial service held forty days later. In Nazareth, high school students suspended their studies for five minutes in memory of the boys, and Arab citizens in other regions sent cables demanding a parliamentary investigation. That year, the Kafr Qasim anniversary meeting in Haifa commemorated both tragedies.

55. See Imil Tuma, "From Kafr Qasim to Rishon Letsion," in which he compares Israeli attacks on the Syrian border to the intensification of oppression against Arab citizens. "The roots of hostility against workers in Rishon, and before this in Nazareth, are the same as the roots of Kafr Qasim. . . . The Rishon attack reminds us that the struggle is not over."

56. The committee called for a strike at Sajur and silent demonstrations at the entrances to Dayr al-Asad and Biʿna, the three villages whose land was confiscated to build the new settlement. Notably, none of the signatories were from Kafr Qasim itself.

57. Over the years, students and teachers in several villages were dismissed or punished for participating in commemorative strikes (al-Haj 1995: 125; *al-Ittihad,* 8 November 1958).

58. In 1967 (*after* the end of military rule), ʿAmr was arrested in the middle of the night and temporarily exiled to Haifa a few days before the anniversary.

59. On 28 October 1960, several young men told *al-Ittihad,* "You will still find many people who are scared of you [MAKI] and . . . some of the others," but

expressed their outrage that Dahan had been released and then hired as the advisor on Arab affairs in Ramle: "He's in charge of security. The murder of our people [was seen] in the interests of security!"

60. Tariq Ibn Zayyad is known in Arab Islamic history for conquering Gibraltar in the eighth century.

61. Poetry was somewhat more successful in bridging these two movements. It is difficult to find a Palestinian poet who has *not* written about the massacre, and their texts became a standard feature of ceremonies around the country. Many poets were themselves imprisoned for "infiltrating" Kafr Qasim on the day of the anniversary, and the authorities went to great lengths to censor their work in the press. It is possible to argue that the effect of their attempt to suppress memorial poetry only bolstered the conviction of memorial participants to recite it (Boullata and Ghossein 1979: 32; Disuqi 1959, 1970; *al-Ittihad,* 23 October 1964).

62. One exception must be noted here. Two years after the completion of this research, journalist Ruvik Rosenthal published a critical essay collection on the massacre and its impact. Notwithstanding the value of the book in its own right, it is important to note that it focuses overwhelmingly on the massacre's impact on Israeli Jewish society (reproducing a previous imbalance) and only briefly touches upon the contested aftermath explored above (Rosenthal 2000).

63. In one controversial incident of "forgetting" in 1998, nationally acclaimed soccer star Walid Bdayr told a reporter who asked about his slain grandfather, "This matter belongs to the past; we don't speak about it at home." Both Bdayr's remark and the widespread attention it received in the Hebrew press was consistent with the historic efforts of the authorities to rid Arab sports fields of Palestinian nationalist sentiment (Sorek 2000).

64. In October 1999, in the midst of an acrimonious national debate over the introduction of new history textbooks, Education Minister Yossi Sarid urged civics teachers to mark the massacre annually in order to teach Jewish school children to distinguish between a legal and an illegal order. Framing Kafr Qasim as a shameful but exceptional moment in Israeli military history, his recommendation omitted both the wider context in which the massacre took place as well as its contested aftermath (Greenberg, *New York Times,* 7 October 1999; Hockstader, *Washington Post,* 31 October 1999; Rotem, *Ha'aretz,* 27 October 1999; Sarid, *Jerusalem Post,* 11 January 2000). Despite its modest aims, the proposal aroused fierce opposition and was never systematically implemented. To this day, the story of the massacre is not included in the required curriculum for the high school matriculation exams.

65. See, for example, the debate between two air force pilots on whether the "black flag" flies over the Israeli army's operations in the territories or the call to refuse to execute these operations (Shohat 2002; Goren 2002). Other Israeli Jews invoked the metaphor following the High Court's rejection of popular petitions to halt Israel's extrajudicial assassinations of Palestinians in the Occupied Territories (Levy 2002). By contrast, one pro-settler group of academics issued a press release in April 2004 declaring that the prime minister's Gaza disengagement plan "raises the black flag of illegality alongside the white flag of surrender" (Professors for a Strong Israel 2004). Palestinians also invoked the metaphor. See the comparison drawn at the 2001 commemora-

tion ceremony by Sami Issa, local council chair in Kafr Qasim, between the illegality of the army's orders in his village in 1956 and the illegality of its orders in the Occupied Territories in 2001 (Nir 2001).

66. The police also shot and killed a Gaza resident who was working in Israel at the time.

67. This relationship is not only figurative. Just six weeks after the demonstrations and their bloody ending, Palestinian attorney Ayman ʿAwda threatened to resign from a coalition established by the Mayor of Haifa after the latter denounced him for boycotting a dinner with Minister of Science, Sport, and Culture two weeks before. The dinner had fallen on 29 October, on the anniversary of the Kafr Qasim massacre, and ʿAwda decried the decision by the government to choose this date to "make the *sulha* with the Arab public" (Galili and Nir 2000).

References

Abu El-Haj, Nadia. 2006. Archaeology, Nationhood, and Settlement. In *Memory and Violence in the Middle East and North Africa*, ed. Ussama Makdisi and Paul Silverstein, ch. 9. Bloomington: Indiana University Press.

Algazy, Yosef. 1997. Katsav ba le-hitnatsel ba-Kfar Qasim (Katsav Comes to Apologize in Kafr Qasim). *Ha'aretz*, 30 October.

ʿAmr, ʿOmar 1998. Interview with author. Kafr Qasim, 6 and 7 September.

ʿAwawdah, Wadiʿ. 2001. *Dhakira la tamut:* shuhud ʿayan fatahu qulubihim wa-hajarat dhakiratihim li-yarwu ma jara lahum f'al 1948—ʿam al-nakba (Memory Does Not Die: Eyewitnesses Open Their Hearts and Memories to Tell the Story of What Happened to Them in 1948—Year of the Catastrophe). Haifa: al-Jalil l'al-Tibaʿa w'al-Tajlid.

Bdayr, ʿAdil. 1998. Interview with author. Kafr Qasim, 7 September.

Beinin, Joel. 1990. *Was the Red Flag Flying There? Marxist Politics and the Arab-Israeli Conflict, 1948–1965*. Berkeley and Los Angeles: University of California Press.

Ben-Ari, Eyal, and Yoram Bilu, eds. 1997. *Grasping Land: Space and Place in Contemporary Israeli Discourse and Experience*. Albany: SUNY Press.

Benvenisti, Meron. 2000. *Sacred Landscape: The Buried History of the Holy Land since 1948*. Berkeley and Los Angeles: University of California Press.

Ben-Ze'ev, Efrat. 2002. The Palestinian Village of Ijzim during the 1948 War. *History and Anthropology* 13 (1): 13–30.

Bilsky, Leora. 2002. Kufr Qassem: Between Ordinary Politics and Transformative Politics. *Adalah's Law Review* 3: 69–78.

Blecher, Robert. 2002. Living on the Edge: The Threat of "Transfer" in Israel and Palestine. *Middle East Report* 225: 22–29.

Boullata, Kamal, and Mirène Ghossein, eds. 1979. *The World of Rashid Hussein: A Palestinian Poet in Exile*. Detroit: Association of Arab-American University Graduates.

Brubaker, Rogers, and Frederick Cooper. 2000. Beyond "Identity." *Theory and Society* 29: 1–47.

Central Committee of the Israeli Communist Party (MAKI). 1997. *Kafr Qasim:*

al-majzara w'al-ʿibra (Kafr Qasim: The Massacre and the Lesson). Tel Aviv-Jaffa.

Cohen, Abner. 1965. *Arab Border Villages in Israel.* Manchester: Manchester University Press.

Connerton, Paul. 1989. *How Societies Remember.* Cambridge: Cambridge University Press.

Dalal, Marwan. 2003. *Law and Politics before the Or Commission of Inquiry.* Shafaʿamr: Adalah—The Legal Center for Arab Minority Rights in Israel.

Darwish, Shaykh ʿAbdallah Nimr. 1966. *Fiʾl-dhikra al-sanawi al-acbaʾur l-majzarat Kafr Qasim: risalat al-shuhada li-kul al-ʿuqala* (On the Fortieth Anniversary of the Kafr Qasim Massacre: Message of the Martyrs to All Those Who Are Sensible). Kafr Qasim: The Islamic Movement in Israel.

Disuqi, Mahmud Mustafa. 1970. *Dhikrayat wa-nar* (Memories and Fire). Tel Aviv: ha-Dafus he-hadash.

——. 1959. *Maʿa al-ahrar* (With Freedom). Tel Aviv: ha-Dafus he-Hadash.

Dori, Latif. 1998. Interview with author. Tel Aviv, 8 September.

Elam, Yigal. 1990. *Memalei ha-pekudot* (The Executioners). Jerusalem: Keter Publishing House.

Galili, Lili, and Ori Nir. 2000. From King Faisal Square to Golan Bridge Street. *Ha'aretz,* 19 November.

Gillis, John R. ed. 1994. *Commemorations: The Politics of National Identity.* Princeton: Princeton University Press.

Glicksberg, Naftali (dir.) and ʿAdil Bdayr (prod). 1997. *al-Dhikra al-arba ʿin l-majzarat Kafr Qasim: al-film al-wathaʾiqi li-majzarat Kafr Qasim* (The Fortieth Anniversary of the Kafr Qasim Massacre: The Documentary Film of the Kafr Qasim Massacre). Kafr Qawim: KQLC.

Goren, Ran, and Benny Barbash. 2002. Right of Reply/It's a War Crime (reply to Yigal Shohat). *Ha'aretz,* 8 February.

Government of the State of Israel. 1956–1957. *Divrei ha-Knesset* (Knesset Minutes). Jerusalem.

Gramsci, Antonio. 1971. *Selections from the Prison Notebooks of Antonio Gramsci.* Ed. and trans. Quintin Hoare and Geoffrey Nowell Smith. New York: International Publishers.

Ha'aretz. 2001. When Ben Gurion Told the Cabinet about the Kfar Kassem Massacre. 28 March.

Habibi, Imil. 1976. *Kafr Qasim, al-majzara—al-siyasa* (Kafr Qasim: The Massacre—The Politics). Haifa: Arabesque.

al-Haj, Majid. 1995. *Education, Empowerment, and Control: The Case of the Arabs in Israel.* Albany: SUNY Press.

Handelman, Don, and Leah Shamgar-Handelman. 1997. The Presence of Absence: The Memorialization of National Death in Israel. In *Grasping Land: Space and Place in Contemporary Israeli Discourse and Experience,* ed. Eyal Ben-Ari and Yoram Bilu, pp. 85–128. Albany: SUNY Press.

Ighbariya, Taysir. 1988. *ʿArayn al-thuwar: Umm al-Fahm 1935–1965* (Lion's Den of the Rebels: Umm al-Fahm, 1935–1965). Haifa: Taysir Ighbariya.

Israel State Archives. Records of the Interior Ministry, Minorities Department. RG 56: G 2213; G 2215/22.

——. Records of the Israel Police. RG 79: L 53/24; L 53/25; L 174/7; L 80/6.

——. Records of the Prime Minister's Bureau. RG 43: G 5593/4674.

Jacobson, Alexander. 2004. The Black Flag. *Ha'aretz,* 5 August.

Jiryis, Sabri. 1976 [1969]. *The Arabs in Israel.* Trans. Inea Bushnaq. New York: Monthly Review Press.

Kafr Qasim Local Council (KQLC). 1997. Video of the Fortieth Anniversary Commemoration Ceremony.

———. 1996. *al-Dhikra al-arbaᶜun l-majzarat kafr qasim: al-majzara ᶜala haqiqatiha* (The Fortieth Anniversary of the Kafr Qasim Massacre). Kafr Qasim: KQLC.

Kafr Qasim Municipal Archive. 1956–1957. Selected papers.

Kafr Qasim Official website. n.d. Photo Gallery of the Massacre: "solha1.jpg" and "solha2.jpg." http://www.kufur-kassem.com/arabic/arabic.htm. Accessed 1 March 2005.

Kanafani, Ghassan. 1968. *Adab al-muqawama fi filastin al-muhtalla, 1948–1966* (Resistance Literature in Occupied Palestine, 1948–1966). Beirut: Dar al-Adab.

Karpel, Daliah. 1986. Ken, anahnu mi oto ha-kfar (Yes, We Are from the Same Village). *Ha-ᶜIr,* 10 October.

Kemp, Adriana. 2004. "Dangerous Populations": State Territoriality and the Constitution of National Minorities. In *Boundaries and Belonging: States and Societies in the Struggle to Shape Local Identities,* ed. Joel Migdal, pp. 73–98. Cambridge: Cambridge University Press.

Kordov, Moshe. 1959. *11 kumtot yerakot ba-din: parshat kfar qasim* (Eleven Green Berets on Trial). Tel Aviv: A. Narkas.

Lavie, Aviv, and Moshe Gorali. 2003. I Saw Fit to Remove Her from the World. *Ha'aretz,* 29 October.

Levy, Gideon. 2002. Black Flag Hangs over the Supreme Court. *Ha'aretz,* 3 February.

Linenberg, Ron. 1972. Parshat Kfar Qasim be-raʾi ha-ᶜitonut ha-yisraelit (The Kafr Qasim Affair in the View of the Israeli Press). *Medina, Memshal, ve-Yahasim Beinleᶜumiyim* 2 (1): 48–64.

Lockman, Zachary. 1996. *Comrades and Enemies: Arab and Jewish Workers in Palestine, 1906–1948.* Berkeley and Los Angeles: University of California Press.

Lustick, Ian. 1980. *Arabs in the Jewish State: Israel's Control of a National Minority.* Austin: University of Texas Press 1980.

Masalha, Nur. 1997. *A Land without a People: Israel, Transfer, and the Palestinians, 1949–1996.* London: Faber and Faber.

Meget, Ilam. 2000. *Birᶜam: kehilat zikaron meguyesset* (Birᶜam: A Community of Mobilized Memory). Menashe, Israel: Givat Haviva Institute for Peace.

Morris, Benny. 1993. *Israel's Border Wars, 1949–1956: Arab Infiltration, Israeli Retaliation, and the Countdown to the Suez War.* Oxford: Clarendon Press.

NER (Newspaper of the Ihud Association). 1956. Documentary Material on Kfar Kassim. *NER* 8 (2–3): 20–36.

Nir, Ori. 2001. The Palestinianization of Bereavement. *Ha'aretz,* 2 November.

Novick, Peter. 2000. *The Holocaust in American Life.* Boston: Mariner Books.

O'Hanlon, Rosalind. 1988. Recovering the Subject: Subaltern Studies and Histories of Resistance in Colonial South Asia. *Modern Asian Studies* 22 (1): 213–222.

Ozacky-Lazar, Sarah. 1996a. Hitgabshut yahasei ha-gomlin bein yehudim le-ᶜaravim be-medinat yisrael: ha-ᶜasur ha-rishon, 1948–1958 (The Crystallization of Mutual Relations between Arabs and Jews in the State of Israel: The First Decade, 1948–1958). Ph.D. dissertation, Department of Middle East History, University of Haifa.

———. 1996b. Mezima be-october: mivtsa sinai ve-parshat kafr qasim ba-ᶜeini ha-ᶜaravim be-yisrael. (October Conspiracy: Operation Sinai and the Kafr Qasim Affair in the View of the Arabs in Israel). Paper presented at the University of Haifa, November.

Peretz, Don. 1958. *Israel and the Palestine Arabs.* Washington, D.C.: Middle East Institute.

Professors for a Strong Israel. 2004. Re: Black Flag, White Flag. Statement to the Press, 4 April. Electronic document, http://professors.org.il/releases/01apr04.htm. Accessed 1 October 2004.

Qahwaji, Habib. 1972. *al-ᶜArab fi dhill al-ihtilal al-israʾili mundhu 1948* (The Arabs in the Shadow of Israeli Occupation since 1948). Beirut: PLO Research Center.

Rabiᶜ, Mustafa. 2002. Interview with author. Jaljuliya, 8 June.

Rabinowitz, Dan. 1997. *Overlooking Nazareth: the Ethnography of Exclusion in Galilee.* Cambridge: Cambridge University Press.

Rosenthal, Rubik. 2000. Kfar Kassem: iruᶜim ve-mitos (Kafr Qasim: Events and Myth). Ed. Rubik Rosenthal. Tel Aviv: ha-Kibbutz ha-Meuchad.

———. 1998. Interview with author. Tel Aviv, 13 September.

———. 1991. Mivtsa ha-farferet (Operation Mole). *Musaf Hadashot,* 25 October.

———. Selected papers copied from the Kafr Qasim trial, copied from the Archive of the Israel Defense Force, Givatayyim.

Sarsur, ᶜAli Salim. 1998. Interview with author. Kafr Qasim, 6 September.

Sarsur, Ibrahim. 1998. Interview with author. Kafr Qasim, 6 September.

Schwarz, Walter. 1959. *The Arabs in Israel.* London: Faber and Faber.

Scott, James C. 1990. *Domination and the Arts of Resistance: The Hidden Transcript.* New Haven: Yale University Press.

Shammas, Anton. 1983. Diary. In *Every Sixth Israeli,* ed. Alouph Hareven, pp. 30–44. Jerusalem: Van Leer Institute.

Segev, Shmuel. 1957. The Race for Kafr Qasim. *Ha'aretz,* 10 November.

Shohat, Yigal. 2002. Red Line, Green Line, Black Flag. *Ha'aretz,* 18 January.

Sorek, Tamir. 2003. Palestinian Nationalism Has Left the Field: A Shortened History of Arab Soccer in Israel. *International Journal of Middle East Studies* 35 (3): 417–437.

Stendel, Ori. 1996. *The Arabs in Israel.* London: Sussex Academy Press, 1996.

Swedenburg, Ted. 1995. *Memories of Revolt: The 1936–1939 Rebellion and the Palestinian National Past.* Minneapolis: University of Minnesota Press.

Tubi, Tawfiq. 1998. Interview with author. Haifa, 17 September.

———. 1956. Memorandum to the Knesset. 23 December. Untitled, archived material, Givat Haviva Research and Documentation Center, Jewish-Arab Series: section 35, box 6.

Yiftachel, Oren. 2002. The Shrinking Space of Citizenship: Ethnopolitics in Israel. *Middle East Report* 223: 38–42.

5 The Making and Unmaking of Memories: The Case of a Multi-Confessional Village in Lebanon

Anja Peleikis

> It is not easy to open wounds, it's very painful, but if you don't want them to fester you must open them and cleanse them and then pour balm onto them.
>
> —Desmund Tutu, Chairman South Africa Commission on Truth and Reconciliation

"We live in a time when memory has entered public discourse to an unprecedented degree," assert Antze and Lambek (1996: vii). This holds particularly true for the case of Lebanon. Fifteen years after civil war, Lebanese society remains torn between the politics of remembering and forgetting. While many politicians and influential personalities have adopted a strategy of deliberately ignoring recent war memories in their public practice and discourse, critical voices refer to the danger of forgetting, claiming that any form of national reconciliation demands a reworking of the past. In this chapter, I examine the Lebanese politics of memory at a local level. Analyzing the discourses and practices of local politicians and the memory work of villagers in the course of their everyday life, I want to demonstrate how selective recollections of the past are used to create and (re)define local and confessional hierarchies and identities, and how this influences the (im)possibilities of reconciliation practices and peaceful coexistence.

Memories of Confessional Coexistence in Prewar Times

The Village[1] under study is situated in the extreme south of the prefecture (*muhafaza*) of Mount Lebanon, in the Shuf district (*qada²*) of the Iqlim al-Kharrub region. Built on several different hills, the Village proudly boasts three clearly visible places of worship, a mosque, a Greek Catholic church, and a Maronite church. For centuries Shiʿites, Greek Catholics, and Maronites have lived next to and with each other. Confessional (sectarian) identity was not always the main divide within this locality. It is, however, today, despite the local and national public emphasis on interconfessional cooperation and reconciliation following the country's long civil war that severely affected the Village. The fact remains that in 1998 the population of the Village amounted to roughly 2,000 individuals, over 90 percent of whom were Shi'ites, although the population registration records indicated a population of over 9,000, the majority of whom were recorded as Christian.[2]

Many elderly villagers interviewed expressed nostalgia for a lost, pre–civil war, world. They strongly emphasized past days when "We were all the same. We all dressed the same way. We all did the same things. We lived like brothers and sisters." Yet shared local identity was not a given simply because of the fact that Christians and Muslims used to live in one place. On the contrary, social relations across confessional borders had to be confirmed, created, and reproduced again and again through the diverse everyday practice of neighborhood relations, mutual assistance in agriculture, and attendance at religious rituals of the confessional "Other." Nevertheless, the older inhabitants do mourn the fact that a diverse social landscape of local interaction and practice embedded in the complexities of confessional, family, and clientelistic social alliances collapsed, and was utterly changed, as a result of war and the concomitant processes of modernization and globalization. While nostalgic references to multiconfessional coexistence in the Village ignore the fact that people were anything but "all the same," they do evoke a past in which religious lines were not drawn in as sharp and sectarian a manner.

People explained, for example, that belonging to a specific village quarter made up an important part of their local identity that was confirmed by neighborhood affiliations and often transcended confessional differences. Many old villagers still have vivid memories of their childhood when children of the same village quarter (*hara*) formed groups of girls and boys who spent their free time together exploring nature around the village, having fights, and holding competitions with children from another *hara*. The children from *hara tahta*, the center of the village, made up a group of Christians and Muslims. This rivalry between children of different village quarters was also reproduced politically among adults. The notable Greek Catholic family from *hara tahta* competed against the notable Greek Catholic family from *hara fawqa* for leadership of the village. Both had loyal followers from all three confessions. Thus, many patron and client relations were transconfessionally organized, and discourses of loyalty mediated the relations between them. These local notables had, in turn, different patrons on a regional level in Mount Lebanon (Peleikis 2001: 408).

In addition, local identity was constructed through mutual assistance in agriculture. The majority of the Christian and Muslim inhabitants were farmers who, following the agricultural rhythm of the year, cultivated olives, wheat, and fruit. The hilly countryside required that people cooperate in the development and maintenance of terraces and the irrigation of the fields, so that villagers from various confessional backgrounds were dependent on each other for survival. Such cooperation was reinforced because residents belonged to specific neighborhoods that, in turn, played important roles in maintaining transconfessional relationships and producing local identity. People recalled how neighbors often helped each other when economic or social problems arose, and female neighbors, in particular, created distinctly gendered transconfessional social spaces. Many women, for instance, revealed how they walked to the well together to fetch water, and at times stayed there all day to wash clothes and their children. At the well, these women would exchange daily news and village gossip, contributing, they now insisted, to the making of a local identity through their daily practices and interactions.

A common local identity was also underscored by the practice of attending and respecting each other's life-cycle rituals of birth, marriage, and death. Some of the villagers who were interviewed vividly remembered that on such occasions they habitually exchanged visits and gifts, thereby expressing transconfessional social relationships and a sharing local identity. Elderly villagers patiently explained to me that the entire village was invited to marriage festivities, with a flower given to every house as an "invitation card." On the wedding day, Christian and Muslim neighbors accompanied the bride from her father's house to the house of the groom, and in the case of a Christian couple, everyone participated in the marriage ceremony at the church. Later, the villagers celebrated the wedding, sharing food and drink, and performing the *dabka* (a traditional Lebanese village dance). It was common practice, the elderly inhabitants emphasized, that all villagers attended funeral ceremonies either at the church or in the *Husayniyya* (a Shiʿite assembly hall where mourning rituals for the deceased take place). During religious feast days, people generally paid homage to the rituals of "the Other" by attending the ceremonies or exchanging presents.

These recollections emphasize not that confessional difference was insignificant or absent but the opposite: religious difference existed and was reproduced through family and marital relations, albeit as but one identity marker jostling for position among other competing identities such as those produced by patron–client relationships, family networks, and neighborhood associations. These were often mobilized according to specific needs and in certain contexts, and largely prevented emergence of enduring religious divisions from the reality of religious differences. It was the civil war, however, together with the urban and international migration that it fostered, that at once politicized and redefined confessional difference at a local level.

Disparate Memories

It was a Sunday, I can remember it well. We woke up very early from the bombing. There were many, many cars on the road then. We left around six o'clock. The representatives of the Lebanese Forces told us that we were to leave. I left with my mother and my sister by the road to Jezzine as the coastal road to Beirut was too dangerous. We stayed overnight in a Christian school in Marjayoun. The next morning the Israelis took us in buses from Marjayoun to Haifa. From there Israeli boats took us to Beirut, to the harbour of Jouniye.

The day of 25 April 1985, remembered now as *yawm al-tahjir,* the day of expulsion, is evidently inscribed in individual as well as the collective memory of the Village's Christian population. Most of the people who spent that particular morning in the Village and were forced to flee can still relate the story of the last few hours or minutes before they left their houses. Following Maurice Halbwachs, who stated that memory is rarely private as it links an individual to the group, to events involving other people, and to a group consciousness (1980 [1950]), it is clear that the memory of the expulsion, with its attendant shared narrative of flight from the home and life in exile, has contributed profoundly to the construction of a highly confessionalized shared group identity. This identity depends on a contrast with those Villagers who did not have to flee and thus, by definition, do not share the traumatic memories of 25 April 1985. Because the expulsion took place along confessional lines and, as a consequence, separated the local population spatially, people from different confessional backgrounds have very different memories of this traumatic day in the history of the Village. I would argue that this spatial separation and total rupture of communication between people of the same Village, who were once involved in producing a shared local identity through daily communication and practices, led to the development of separated confessionalized local identities.[3]

Thus for many Village Shiʿites, 25 April 1985 stands out as a "remembrance day of liberation." Many of them had suffered under the presence of the Maronite-dominated militia, the Lebanese Forces,[4] who entered the Shuf mountains following the Israeli invasion in 1982 and notoriously set up camp near the Village. Between 1982 and 1985 many of the Village Shiʿites, especially political activists, and their families had to flee to Saida and Beirut to escape the persecution of the Lebanese Forces. A seventy-five-year-old Shiʿite man who remained in the Village throughout the three years described his experiences as follows:

After the beginning of the civil war we still lived peacefully in the village. In the first years after 1976 Christians and Muslims in the village helped each other, for example by donating blood to each other. When the Israelis invaded the country, everything changed. The Lebanese Forces came and set up a camp near the Village. They mobilized many of the young Christian men, who then started working for them and wore their uniform. In those three years they destroyed the village where we had lived in relative peace for the previous ten years of war. The young Christians in Lebanese Forces uniforms came to our house twenty times. We did not belong to anyone. Once they came and said: "You have weapons!" But we had none. They searched the whole house and threatened us with their guns. They took me and my son to their camp for several days and interrogated us. It was horrible. But only some of the Village Christian youth behaved like this. Not all of them!

Many villagers described how the local population of various confessional, family, and political backgrounds remained in the village until 1982. When government structures collapsed in the initial years after the outbreak of war in 1975, they were replaced by a local committee *(lajna sha°biyya)*. Most members of this committee were left-wing, pro-Palestinian villagers who came from various confessions and family backgrounds. When Israel invaded Lebanon in 1982, however, this committee was dissolved, marking for many villagers the final breakdown of local coexistence. On the heels of the Israeli invasion, the Lebanese Forces under Samir Geagea expended great efforts to seize both inter-confessionally mixed as well as mostly Christian villages in this area that had previously been under Palestinian control. However, the Lebanese Forces were unable to maintain control of this "conquered" zone; consequently, their rule ended in a debacle in 1985, leading to the flight of the Christian population.[5] Despite the fact that the Shi°ites referred to what the Christians called "the day of expulsion" as "the day of liberation," many did not welcome the departure of the local Christian population, although all were relieved that the rule of the Lebanese Forces had come to an end. This turn of events allowed at least those Shi°ites who had fled before to return to their Village without fear of persecution.

Between 1985 and 1991, the Village was officially under the control of the Druze militia, the Progessive Socialist Party (PSP) that had come down from the Shuf mountains after the withdrawal of the Israeli and Lebanese Forces. The PSP was present in the Village in the form of a civil administration *(idara madaniyya)* to whom the Shi°ite population had to pay taxes. The *idara* also organized the distribution of abandoned houses and land to Shi°ite Village families as well as to Shi°ite refugees who arrived there after 1985 from South Lebanon. The PSP militia profited financially from this practice, as people had to pay taxes for "new properties" and land. Local Shi°ites often took great pains to defend the belongings of their Christian neighbors. Abu Ussama, an old Shi°ite man related the following:

> When the people tried to take over my neighbor's house, I did everything to prevent it. I told my son to live in the house. Not one single knife, fork, or spoon was missing. When the war was over I gave the key of the house back to my neighbor.

This case remained an exception, however, since most abandoned houses were plundered—often by militias coming in from outside. Village refugees recall that most people left without anything, hoping to return as soon as possible. But the enforced absence lasted far longer than anyone had expected—most people did not see their Village again for more than ten years. The more prosperous families with apartments in the city were lucky in that they could move to their homes in Beirut. Others found refuge with relatives or friends. The rest had to seek refuge in schools, monasteries, or former hotels. A few people from the Village, already living in Beirut, organized a relief campaign for villagers in need. They found apartments, distributed clothes and furniture, registered the children in schools, provided the sick with medicine, and organized burials for

those who had died. The abrupt transition, predictably, was not easy, as the refugee struggled to reorganize their lives in new and largely unfamiliar surroundings. A sixty-year-old woman interviewed described her difficulty in integrating
into their "new homes" in the following manner:

> We stayed with many other Christian refugees from the South in a large building,
> a former hotel, in a village in Kesrouan (a Christian dominated area in Mount
> Lebanon). Mainly, we did not mix much with the local population, but stayed
> together with the other refugees. It was difficult for my husband to find a job and
> sometimes for my children in school. The village population always regarded us as
> outsiders, as displaced.

As they organized their lives in new surroundings, the Villagers had no contact
with their former Shi'ite neighbors who had remained in the Village. During
the war, in fact, it was easier for Christians in East Beirut to contact their migrant relatives and friends abroad than to get in touch with their Shi'ite neighbors in West Beirut or the Village a few kilometers away (see Khalaf 1993: 143).
A new phase was reached in the division of the country, namely a "division into
quasi sectarian cantons" (Picard 1996: 127), that paved the way for the "terri-
torialization of identities" (Khalaf 1993: 89). According to Khalaf, almost half
the villages and towns had been made up of inhabitants of more than one confession before the war (1993: 103). This demographic perspective changed dramatically in the course of the war. Whereas the proportion of Christians living
in the southern regions of Mount Lebanon (to which the village under study
belongs) was 55 percent in 1975, it had shrunk to roughly 5 percent by the late
1980s due to massive displacement (Khalaf 1993: 103).

The upshot in the case of the Village was clear. As the Village itself became
predominantly Shi'ite as a result of the war, Christian refugee Villagers starkly
elaborated and then mobilized a confessional identity, and concomitantly marginalized any memory they may have had of transconfessional local Village
practices before the expulsions of 1985. They did so precisely at the time that
they no longer had any personal contact with the Shi'ites of the Village and as
they struggled to adapt to their new lives as displaced persons in unfamiliar surroundings, where most people felt either superior to and/or were suspicious of
Muslims—and in any case, where most of the inhabitants had never enjoyed the
proximity to Muslims that the refugee Villagers had experienced. In this process
of adaptation to cloistered confessional communities, the religious "Other"—
the Muslim—was increasingly constructed as an anonymous enemy, devoid of
history and context, by refugees who themselves struggled with their very real
and very specific fate as victims of historical displacement and expulsion.

Places of Memory in Postwar Times

The Document of National Accord (the Ta'if Agreement) signed by the
Lebanese members of parliament in Ta'if, Saudi Arabia in 1989 ended the war
officially and laid the foundations of the "Second Lebanese Republic." The right

of return for the displaced was written into the Peace Accord, establishing a legal basis for the government policy of returning refugees to their original residence localities (Ménassa 1995: 140). The Ministry of the Displaced was founded in 1992 with the aim of developing and implementing policies of return and financially supporting restoration and reconstruction of public buildings and facilities, and of sanctuaries and private houses (Ministry of the Displaced 1998). In this context, a program designed to facilitate the "Reintegration and Socioeconomic Rehabilitation of the Displaced" was launched by the Ministry in 1994 in cooperation with the UNDP. It included financial donations as well as social projects intended to encourage reconciliation processes between returnees and local residents. In their 1998 report, the Ministry states that by the end of 1997, "29 reconciliations" had taken place in villages that were once the scene of bloody confrontations and massacres. In the forefront of these official reconciliation meetings, contacts between the displaced and residents were organized to make "coming together" possible. Three of these so-called reconciliations were followed by "home return festivals" under the auspices of the President of the Republic and several State officials (Ministry of the Displaced 1998: 25). Nevertheless, the return of the displaced has been an extremely difficult and sensitive issue, especially in communities that experienced extreme confessional fighting and massacres. The state-sponsored ceremonies were intended to be a first step, and to lay the groundwork for a new interconfessional politics at the local level. But what was needed even more were reconciliation practices and the restoration of everyday relationships, something that seldom occurred in the aftermath of these "official reconciliation events." In many cases, the displaced people were slow to re-enter their villages of origin; for most of the refugees, in fact, return has thus far been limited and partial.

The very idea of reconciliation—what it means and how it might be implemented effectively—has been the subject of much debate. In the case of South Africa, for example, Kenneth Christie writes that it often appears to reflect a spiritual or religious dimension; "in short, a healing method for a society that needs to be healed (Christie 2000: 147)." According to him, reconciliation in the form of the restoration of relationships and the redistribution of resources—namely "economic reconciliation"—should be part of the country's much broader reconstruction and transformation process (Christie 2000: 147).

In the case of Lebanon, it becomes obvious that the economic situation of those displaced effectively limits a renewed "coming together." Most of the people who fled the village under study in 1985 do not want or are not able to return to their village permanently. Some had worked in Beirut before the war, others found work there during and after the war and their children now attended school there, and thus they were reasonably integrated in the Christian communities they have lived in since 1985. Many simply could not afford to return to the village that did not offer them enough opportunities for work. Most of those who did return were indeed either retired or poor farmers hoping for a better income there than in other parts of Mount Lebanon where they had worked as low-paid agricultural laborers. Many people, however, wanted to retake possession of their village houses and properties, so that the initial years after the civil war were marked by negotiations to induce the Shiʿites to move out of the houses they had occupied following the displacement of 1985. The "Ministry of the Displaced" became actively involved in the process of handing over properties to the Christian owners after the war and providing financial aid for the reconstruction process.

In subsequent years, many Christian families did begin to renovate their houses and return more often to the village, mostly on weekends and sometimes during the summer. Gradually, they became involved in reappropriating their locality materially and symbolically. They expressed themselves in the rebuilding of their private houses, as well as in their construction of religious places such as churches and graveyards, and in their initiation of religious ceremonies. Following Nora, I would argue that churches and graveyards have become *"lieux de memoire,"* places of memory, while the familiar landscapes of living memory, the *"milieux de memoire,"* have disappeared (Nora 1998: 11). Similarly, Aleida Assmann defines places of memory as dispersed fragments of a lost and destroyed life-world (Assmann 1999: 309). As a result of the civil war, Christian presence in everyday life in the Village has all but vanished. Despite the state-sponsored mandate for reconciliation, the newly renovated homes—empty of pre–civil war furniture and artifacts—silently but powerfully underscored the sharp and in a sense irreversible rupture with prewar times.

In the absence of irretrievably lost material relics, the Christians of the Village concentrated on renovating their churches and openly celebrating religious holidays. The Feast of the Assumption of the Blessed Virgin Mary on 15 August is an important Christian religious celebration. In 2000, the day was marked by a procession from the Maronite to the Greek Catholic Church. Priests from both confessions headed the procession, followed by a group of adults and children carrying candles and singing. This religious procession was very much part of the local life before the war. Older Christian and Muslim Villagers can remember how Shiʿites often walked in the procession and carried candles. Similarly, it was common for Christians to pay their respects and attend commemoration ceremonies for Imam Husayn at the *Husayniyya* during the ten days of *ʿAshuraʾ* (day of mourning sacred to the Shiʿites that commemorates the seventh-century martyrdom of Husayn). By 2000, however, the ritual of 15 August had itself become a *lieu de memoire,* a reminder of times past that bore little relevance to current daily life in the Village. While Christians sought to affirm and legitimize their presence in the Village by walking through it, no Shiʿites were seen near the procession, let alone walking in it. On the contrary, many Shiʿites were disgruntled, and one among them remarked that "They want to show they are back in the Village. They want to make clear that they dominate the Village. But in fact they only come at the weekends and are not interested in the Village."

The Shiʿite villager who expressed this sentiment did not completely reject the return of the Christian population but contended that Christians only came on weekends and lived in what had become effectively confessionalized space. Despite trying to reclaim the Village by rebuilding churches, by enacting religious rituals, and by reconstructing houses, it was East Beirut and the Christian-dominated areas of Mount Lebanon that had become the main residence area for the Village's erstwhile Christian population. Years of forced displacement had led to a radical change in their relationship to their home locality. On the one hand—as described above—they mobilized confessionalized identities that both unmade memories of multi-confessional local practice and promised integration into the new localities. On the other hand, the insecurity of displacement has made it all the more important for the refugees to claim a secure and fixed origin, and it is in nostalgia for the idealized Village that they are able to construct an emotional landscape of home. As Dietmar Dath has put it, "Homes are 'origin stories' constructed as *retrospective* signposts within visual space, acoustic space, and even tactile space. They are *made for coming from*" (Dietmar Dath cit. in Morse 1999: 68).

Although in the above sense, nostalgia, as Patricia Seed has written, "springs from capitulation, resigning oneself to the irretrievable loss of familiar objects and well-liked faces, the bonds of friendship, shared learning, and languages" (Seed 1999: 91), it can also be viewed differently. Nostalgia can be seen as a form of politicized memory that blends a longing for the past and its evocation in present social reality to create a specific strategy of empowerment and re-anchoring in the village. Thus, for example, while a confessionalized identity that consistently overlooked transconfessional prewar local practice has taken root among refugees, a countervailing but no less politicized form of memory has also become evident in a wave of local nostalgia that has found expression in local Village politics. The municipality members elected in 1998 as part of the first local elections held since the end of the civil war have been eager to turn a page on the past and to ignore wartime memories. Like the refugees, but with entirely different effect, they have sought to mobilize nostalgia to construct a heroic and unifying narrative of the days before war. In their publications, in the local Village journal, on the official Village website, and in oral discourse, municipality members draw from a distant past to reveal what they believe is the great history of the Village. "New archaeological discoveries prove," the official website declares, "that the Village has existed since 50 BC. A Byzantine temple nearby is proof that the Village and its surroundings have left their mark on history."[6]

Antiquity, of course, evokes millennial stability, deeprootedness, and continuity, but it also provides a discourse of timelessness that allows local leaders to construct new decontextualized memories. The municipality's website, for example, extols the "unique view of the sunset, the peaceful hills and valleys of the Village, the taste of bread soaked in fresh olive oil, green nature well preserved."[7] Local leaders, in other words, paint local life in idyllic colors where places and artifacts such as olive oil presses, mills, and fountains are embraced and described as folklore items and are optimistically marketed as tourist sites.

In the light of this approach to memory, the civil war takes on the semblance of "dark chaotic" times, a short and almost inconsequential interval better left unremarked.

This memory work must be understood in the context of the social actors involved in this redefinition. Most members of the municipality are thirty- to fifty-year-old men and women (thirteen men and two women) hailing largely from a local elite background. Most have never lived in the Village. As children they probably spent the weekends there and as adults they migrated abroad. In contrast to most of the elderly inhabitants who have actual memories of daily local interaction and practices, of conflicts and political struggles, and finally of war, displacement, and violence, the municipality memories of the Village relate to childhood weekend trips, colored by the stories of their parents. These memories developed a life of their own in the course of migration. More and more, the village of these transnational migrants has turned into an emotional landscape, a place of happy childhood memories, of continuity and rootedness in a world of high mobility.

These localized memories, which are at the same time products of national and global embeddedness, accompanied these people when they re-entered the village at the end of the civil war when they were involved in local politics. Here, any semblance of civil war, of destruction and uprootedness, simply does not fit into their nostalgic view of romantic local life, which they combine with their future projections of a modern, democratic local community in a global world. I believe this combination of nostalgia and global ideas, at first a seeming contradiction, actually reflects the multiple identities and simultaneous locations within the local, national, and global contexts of the municipality members. This is expressed in their projects of reconstructing places of the past and at the same time fostering the construction of new "modern" sites, as for example, a huge football stadium. In my view, local politicians have become agents of nostalgia for the sake of future-oriented local development policy.

In this future-oriented approach, recent wartime memories are totally silenced. Village buildings that could trigger unheroic memories of the civil war are left untouched. Such buildings are not demolished because local officials are probably afraid that the act of destruction might rekindle old struggles and conflicts. Buildings such as the local Culture Club (*al-rabita al-thaqafiyya*), a place of transconfessional political debates and struggles between local elites and nonprivileged youth in the 1960s and early 1970s, have been left untouched. When a group of younger Villagers demanded the reopening of the Culture Club, the municipality refused. "Trouble will arise again," explained the mayor, who at the same time was involved in the opening of a new "Culture Club" under a different name (*al-maktaba al-baladiyya*), in which the municipality could hold what it calls "unpolitical events" such as exhibitions on "pre-historic and more recent archaeological items" found in the surrounding area of the Village.

The municipality's attempt to reconstruct a new inclusive memory is predicated on preventing divergent and potentially acrimonious public discussions of the recent past. For community leaders, this redefined local memory—based on ideas of a reinvented heroic past and imagined future—must serve as a basis for the emergence of new, "modern," and "democratic" village interaction and practice. The new sports stadium and a new library were created to link the youth living in the city with the youth in the Village. At the opening speech in 2000 for the library, for example, the mayor stressed that this new site should be for the entire youth of the Village. It is doubtful, however, that under the given circumstances of "institutional forgetting" any new transconfessional local public sphere and identity can emerge beyond mere words and handshakes. In everyday village life, transconfessional social interaction and practice is practically nonexistent. Mistrust, anger, and prejudices prevail under the surface of a public discourse that claims "we are all children of the village."

When villagers remember in everyday life, they do so in their socially separate confessionalized local spaces. Whereas some remember the difficult escape or the humiliation as displaced persons, others remember the Israeli invasion in particular and the suffering under the Lebanese Forces. But seldom does one find exchange and communication of civil war memories across confessional lines that might lead beyond fractured memories. Despite the fact that civil war memories are silenced in public discourse and official practice, they often return with a vengeance and express the depth of division within this multi-confessional community: When a Greek Catholic man from the Village, a former Lebanese Forces activist, died in Beirut in May 2000, his body was brought back to the Village for the funeral. Members of his family expected their Shiʿite neighbors to be at the funeral as it had been a tradition in pre-war times for the entire village to attend a funeral. But the Shiʿite neighbors could not forget what this man had been responsible for and categorically refused to attend the funeral. The incident led to strong words between these families of different confessions, and demonstrated once more how dominant and important the recent past is for the feelings and agency of many villagers—the officialpublic silence regarding the civil war notwithstanding. Tellingly, the municipality that had been trying hard to create confessional harmony was unable to meet collectively (that is, with both its Christian and Shiʿite members) to defuse the crisis. When they tried to intervene, the barely repressed bitter memories of the civil war immediately and dramatically rose to the surface. There was simply no agreement on how to interpret the war, where to assign blame, and how to relate the recent past to the present. Any further discussion of the issue threatened to paralyze the municipality, and it seemed as if any discussion of the civil war at all was simply too dangerous a topic to contemplate.

It became clear, in short, that there was no basis for the emergence of new local public sphere in which diverse political, family, and confessional groups, particularly the younger generation who only got to know each other after the war, could at least meet and exchange memories, and perhaps create a viable local identity in the process. Aware of this problem, a few of the motivated Village youth took the initiative of bringing young people from all parts of the community together. When the municipality opened the new library, this group of Village youth organized film events on the weekends. They tried to directly recall officially "silenced memories" by screening films about the civil war. Their explicit goal was to encourage younger Christians and Muslims living in the village or in Beirut to use the new library as a place to get to know one another, and even more, to relate to one another's experiences and memories. Like the municipality members, they wanted to create a viable new local identity. These young students, however, mobilized in a manner quite different from that of their local leaders, using significant "places of memory" such as the Culture Club as a main point of reference. Contrary to local leaders who considered the struggle for the Club in the 1960s and 1970s (and the debates it witnessed) to have been a forerunner of the civil war that led to anarchy and chaos, these young activists saw the 1960s and early 1970s as a time when underprivileged groups began to question the local and national order of things dominated by the elites. For them, the Culture Club was a "revolutionary place" where under-represented, underprivileged Christian and Muslim youth fought together for the leadership against the elites who had run the Club since its initiation.

Similar to the youth of that time, these young people dreamed of questioning the power of the local elites and hoped to overcome a dominant "culture of sectarianism" (Makdisi 2000). But despite their efforts at promoting a dynamic and new interconfessional identity that could transcend religious divisions, very few young people came to watch the films in the Village. Indeed some of the young Christians who watched them one weekend were only inspired to meet separately the following weekend in their "confessionalized home spaces" to watch videos with their fellow Christians. The organizers felt utterly let down in the face of such lack of support from local government and the villagers themselves, and many of them have resigned in the face of the new elites epitomizing the politics of the past. Their activities confirmed yet again that in this postwar locality there are no shared transconfessional public spaces where people—young or old—have the chance to meet, remember, and, of course, to learn from their memories by creating visions for the future.

Memory for the Future?

In the meantime, local politicians, many of whom have local elite family backgrounds, reinforce their power by adopting and embodying a national policy of "silenced memory." Although the members of the municipality are local politicians, most of them live in Beirut and are linked through forms of family alliances or patron–client relations to the national political scene. Their local reconstruction projects show clear similarities to national reconstruction policies. On a national level, this politics finds expression in the massive postwar reconstruction of Beirut's city center (see Makdisi 1997). The Company for the Development and Reconstruction of Beirut's Central District, better known as Solidere, expropriated the land at the city center and bulldozed most of the buildings damaged during the war to create space for their vision: "Beirut: Ancient City of the Future."[8] This clean empty space has thus become a (re-)construction site for an envisioned future, a future that wants to resemble a chosen past. Urban planners and architects have reinvented the past by referring to ancient heritage, which then has been taken out of its lived continuum and been newly frozen into the stone structure of postmodern architecture. According to Genberg and Hanssen, this kind of memory politics inscribed in urban planning discloses a form of therapy and pedagogy. It tries to transform an unheroic, traumatic war-lived memory into a heroic salubrious one based on the aesthetic appeal of the ancient past (Genberg and Hanssen 2001: 237–238). This attempt to resurrect "the happy days before the war" and anchor them in a deep-rooted Lebanese "ancient history" seems to erase the lived memories of war. It consequently reflects a dominant discourse in Lebanese postwar society that aims at "turning the page," and wants to "forget the past" and start anew.

Various authors admittedly have actually emphasized the need for collective forgetfulness and stress the dangers of focusing on the past.[9] The violations that have been lived through can obsess a country, and analyzing the past can drain the dynamic energy so desperately needed for working for a new order. The focus on past violations runs the risk of being counterproductive so that instead of healing, it can actually cause fresh wounds and cleavages in an already deeply divided society. Elias Khoury, Lebanese novelist, literary critic, and editor of the weekly cultural supplement to the leading Lebanese daily *An-Nahar*, sees forgetting as a human necessity:

> People have to forget. If I do not forget my friends who died in the civil war I cannot live, I cannot drink and eat. . . . The question is what to forget and what to remember. It can be an ideological choice. (Cited in Mejcher 2001: 139)

Similarly, Amal Makaram, one of the organizers of the conference titled Memory for the Future, which was held in Beirut on 30–31 March 2001, pointed out in her opening lecture the necessity of "turning the page." Yet in her view, this cannot be done without reading this page critically; she asserts that "Reading the page" and finding out what happened to the dead, the missing and the kidnapped, listening to stories of mothers who lost their daughters and sons, wives who lost their husbands and husbands who lost their wives, as well as listening to the war experiences of children, should be a first step in breaking the silence and addressing Lebanon's past; a first step in demanding responsibility and justice.[10] In asserting this point of view, Makaram echoes the warning of Richard Werbner, who noted that unheard and unaddressed memories and traumatic experiences bear the danger of being "buried." According to Werbner, "buried memories" produce unfinished narratives: "[P]opular history in which the past is perceived to be unfinished, festering in the present—these are narratives which motivate people to call again and again for a public resolution to their predicament" (Werbner 1998: 8). Subjected to "buried" (or silenced) memory, people often do not so much forget as recognize—and then all the more forcefully—that they have not been allowed to remember. Situations in which people feel compelled to unbury their memories and reject their past submission are potentially explosive (Werbner 1998: 9).

Having studied diverse postconflict societies, researchers and activists have called for memory projects at all levels of society to prevent a development of this kind.[11] They believe that "atrocities refuse to be buried" and that remembering and telling the truth about terrible events are the prerequisites for restoring social order and healing individual victims (Herman 1997:1). According to Richard Goldstone, postconflict societies generally have three options in the aftermath of gross violations of human rights: to either forget the past and grant the perpetrators a blanket amnesty; to prosecute the perpetrators or at least the leaders; or, as a third option, to establish truth commissions before which victims are given the opportunity of publicly testifying about their experiences (2000: ix).

The Lebanese government decided on the first option. A general amnesty for "crimes of the war" was declared in 1991 under President Elias Hrawi. This decision made it impossible to prosecute notorious war criminals and led to the Lebanese postwar reality that those responsible for the massacres and gross violations of human rights are now sitting in the cabinet and in high government positions. Yet in Lebanon and elsewhere, granting a blanket amnesty to the perpetrators of massive crimes is an unacceptable solution for many people. As Goldstone has noted in the case of South Africa,

> Forgiveness by the criminals themselves of their own crimes is a certain recipe for future hate and violence. Such impunity is an unambiguous message to all would-be war criminals, that they could go about their own dirty work secure in the knowledge that they will not be called to account. (Goldstone 2000: x)

The third option of establishing truth commissions has rapidly gained currency around the world and has gained increasing attention in recent years. According to Priscilla Hayner, a researcher on truth commissions worldwide, this interest in tackling the past by collecting testimony from victims and witnesses is, in part, a reflection of the limited success in the judicial approach to accountability (Hayner 2000: 34). It reflects the obvious need for very distinct measures to recognize past wrongs and to confront, punish, or reform the individuals and institutions responsible for violations. Hayner points out four identifying features that characterize so-called truth commissions (Hayner 2000: 35). First of all, a truth commission focuses on the past. Secondly, it does not investigate a single event but the record of abuse over a period of time. Thirdly, a truth commission is a temporary body, whose work generally concludes with the submission of a report. And finally, a truth commission is officially sanctioned by the government (and/or by the opposition where relevant) to investigate the past. Official sanction gives the commission more power and more access to information, as well as protection to undertake investigations; it is more likely that its conclusions and recommendations will be given serious consideration (Hayner 2000: 35). In some cases, truth commissions have been set up by the United Nations (as in the case of El Salvador) or by various NGOs (as in

Rwanda). They are usually established by the latter when governments have refused to investigate past atrocities.

Since many Lebanese postwar political figures in and out of government were active participants and protagonists in the war, they have no present-day interest in tackling Lebanon's violent past, let alone in accepting personal responsibility. Yet critical voices demand that any kind of Truth and Reconciliation Commission in Lebanon be a civil society initiative, uniting courageous and credible persons from all parts of Lebanese society. These voices believe in the enormous significance of such a critical reworking of the past. As Waddad Halawani, representative of the Committee of Parents of the Kidnapped and Disappeared in Lebanon, pleaded, "If we do not work on our past, it is as if war has not ended yet."[12]

The South African "Truth and Reconciliation Commission" is, of course, an outstanding example of how such a commission could work. Paul Haupt, Director of Perpetrator Studies at the Cape Town Institute for Justice and Reconciliation, who came to Lebanon for the Memory for the Future Conference, spoke of the South African experience. He explained that the South African Truth and Reconciliation Commission was founded on the belief that telling the truth about past violations of human rights, viewed from different perspectives, facilitates the process of understanding a divided past, whilst public acknowledgement of untold suffering and injustice helps to restore the dignity of victims and allows perpetrators to come to terms with their own past (Haupt: 2001: 5). This assertion by Haupt confirms the assessment made by other researchers of postconflict societies who have repeatedly stated that official public exposure of what happened is an important form of justice that can bring significant solace to victims. Julie Mertus, who studied war crime tribunals in Rwanda and the former Yugoslavia, believes that victims need to hear their stories told aloud and to see others listening to their stories. They need a full public account of what happened—an account in which they see their own memories, an account that exposes the "Truths":

> These Truths have taken on a life of their own. They are so thick with history, power and fear that the actual truth does not matter any more. Allowing competing Truths to float through the air in the same space, unjudged and unquestioned, can be a revolutionary act. The Truths may always exist. But the telling can narrow the gap between Truths, creating a common bridge towards something else— towards an existence beyond these Truths. (Mertus 2000: 159)

Analyzing the South African Commission, several authors stated that its most important effect was to provide a space—however imperfect—for remembrance, and a way of developing shared memories. In the words of Paul Haupt:

> I submit that it is this imperfection that is perhaps the greatest strength of the work of the TRC. It has not established a single, comfortable truth of the past, it has not ever established all the truth of the past but it has facilitated vibrant and engaging dialogue about a collective memory that had never been spoken. (2001: 9)

The memories of those who participated in the TRC represent for Haupt a national narrative of untold suffering and injustices. Through a shared collective memory that encompasses suffering and multiple truths, a redefined national identity could emerge. Nevertheless, there are still major problems to face, as Kenneth Christie mentions:

> Of course, there are icebergs of resentment, some big enough to sink the Titanic we might imagine! The point is that if we are to have any hope for the future, mechanisms like the TRC offer us a chance to help thaw the icebergs and get on with forging shared values and attributes, allowing us to remember and not forget, but of course, to learn from memory. (2000: 187)

"Thawing the icebergs of resentment" appears to be a challenging and difficult task on facing postwar Lebanon, as local and national politicians strongly espouse the politics of forgetting (and of letting bygones be bygones). The Village setting explored in this chapter provides a vivid example of how in Lebanon these contested narratives of untold suffering and injustice reside in living memory, still awaiting narration. The task of giving space to diverse, multiple, and contesting memories remains. Only by completing this process can war memories be incorporated into a nation's collective identity. As Halawani puts it so eloquently, "We have to remember the past, not because we want to stay in the past, but to recognize the past so that we will be able to develop a new future." [13]

Notes

This essay is based on a research project funded by the German Research Council (DFG), which formed part of the group project "Locality and the State" at the Centre for Modern Oriental Studies, Berlin (Germany). Research in the village under study was carried out for several months between 1998 and 2001. I am thankful to the anonymous resources for their helpful comments on an earlier draft of the paper. Special thanks go to Paul Silverstein and Ussama Makdisi for their patience and careful revision of this chapter.

1. I will refer to the village under study as the *Village* with a capital *V*. The processes and actions that took place in this community are representative for many other localities. When I talk of *the Christians, the Muslims,* and the *Greek Catholics* in the Village, I am aware that these categories are also social constructions that are not static but underlay dynamic change and redefinition (see especially Makdisi 2000 and Peleikis 2001). It is important to draw a line between religious and confessional identities in the Lebanese context. Whereas a religious identity expresses a person's beliefs and practices, a confessional identity is first and foremost a political one. Here religious heritage, symbols, and habitus are used to legitimize differences that find their institutional expression in the Lebanese political system of confessionalism.
2. Interview with mayor of the Village, Beirut, 4 September 1998.
3. For a detailed description and analysis of this process, see Peleikis 2001.

4. A Christian militia formed by Bashir Gemayel. See Hanf 1993: 192f.
5. Picard (1996: 127) points out that the word "'Debacle', however, is too weak a word to describe what the local Christian population had to suffer by way of reprisals for the adventure of the Lebanese Forces, the massacres and hasty flight of several tens of thousands of newly homeless people."
6. From the Village website set up by the local municipality http://www.joun.leb.net. [*Editor's note:* The website is no longer functional.]
7. This description is taken from the Village website. http://www.joun.leb.net. [*Editor's note:* the website is no longer functional.]
8. "Beirut: Ancient City of the Future" is a motto used in Solidere's promotional literature (see el-Dahdah 1998: 68).
9. See Ernest Gellner's statement, cited in Khalaf (1998: 131).
10. Amal Makarem, personal communication, Beirut, 4 August 2001.
11. See for example Mertus 2000, Hayner 2001.
12. Waddad Halawani, personal communication, Beirut, 4 August 2001.
13. Personal communication, Beirut, 4 August 2001.

References

Antze, Paul, and Michael Lambek, eds. 1996. *Tense Past: Cultural Essays in Trauma and Memory.* New York: Routledge.

Assmann, Aleida. 1999. *Erinnerungsräume. Formen und Wandlungen des kulturellen Gedächtnisses.* Munich: C. H. Beck.

Christie, Kenneth. 2000. *The South African Truth Commission.* New York: St. Martin's Press.

el-Dahdah, Farès. 1998. On Solidere's Motto: "Beirut: Ancient City of the Future." In *Projecting Beirut: Episodes in the Construction and Reconstruction of a Modern City,* ed. Peter Rowe and Hashim Sarkis, pp. 68–77. Munich, London, and New York: Prestel.

Genberg, Daniel, and Jens-Peter Hanssen. 2001. Beirut in Memoriam: A Kaleidoscopic Space out of Focus. In *Crisis and Memory in Islamic Societies: Proceedings of the Third Summer Academy of the Working Group Modernity and Islam Held at the Orient Institute of the German Oriental Society in Beirut,* ed. Angelika Neuwirth and Andreas Pflitsch, pp. 231–262. Beirut and Würzburg: Ergon, 2001.

Goldstone, Richard. 2000. Foreword. In *Looking Back, Reaching Forward: Reflections on the Truth and Reconciliation Commission of South Africa,* ed. Charles Villa-Cicencio and Wilhem Verwoerd, pp. viii–xiii. London: Zed Books

Halbwachs, Maurice. 1980 [1950]. *The Collective Memory.* Trans. F. and V. Ditter. New York: Harper.

Hanf, Theodor. 1993. *Coexistence in Wartime Lebanon: Decline of a State and Rise of a Nation.* London: The Centre for Lebanese Studies in association with I. B. Tauris.

Haupt, Paul. 2001. Between Memory and Hope: The Role of Memory in the South African TRC Process. Unpublished manuscript given at the Seminar "Memory for the Future," Beirut, 30–31 March.

Hayner, Priscilla. 2001. *Unspeakable Truths: Confronting State Terror and Atrocity.* London: Routledge.

——. 2000. Same Species, Different Animal: How South Africa Compares to Truth Commissions Worldwide. In *Looking Back, Reaching Forward: Reflections on the Truth and Reconciliation Commission of South Africa,* ed. Charles Villa-Cicencio and Wilhelm Verwoerd, pp. 32–41. London: Zed Books.

Herman, Judith. 1997. *Trauma and Recovery: The Aftermath of Violence—From Domestic Abuse to Political Terror.* New York: Basic Books.

Khalaf, Samir. 1998. Contested Space and the Forging of New Cultural Identities. In *Projecting Beirut: Episodes in the Construction and Reconstruction of a Modern City,* ed. Peter Rowe and Hashim Sarkis, pp. 140–164. Munich: Prestel.

——. 1993. *Beirut Reclaimed: Reflections on Urban Design and the Restoration of Civility.* Beirut: Dar an-Nahar.

Makdisi, Saree. 1997. Reconstructing History in Central Beirut. *Middle East Report* 203: 23–25.

Makdisi, Ussama. 2000. *The Culture of Sectarianism: Community, History, and Violence in Nineteenth-Century Ottoman Lebanon.* Berkeley: University of California Press.

Mejcher, Sonja. 2001. *Geschichten über Geschichten: Erinnerung im Romanwerk von Ilyas Huri.* Wiesbaden: Reichert Verlag.

Ménassa, Béchara. 1995. *Constitution libanaise. Textes et commentaires et accord de Taef.* Beirut: Les Editions l'Orient.

Mertus, Julie. 2000. Truth in a Box: The Limits of Justice through Juridical Mechanisms. In *The Politics of Memory: Truth, Healing & Social Justice,* ed. Ifi Amadiume and Abdullahi An-Na'im, pp. 142–161. London: Zed Books.

Ministry of the Displaced. 1998. *The Achievements and the Requirements for the Completions and Consolidation of the Home Return of the Displaced: From November 1st, 1992 to December 31st, 1997.* Beirut: Ministry of the Displaced.

Morse, Margaret. 1999. Home: Smell, Taste, Posture, Gleam. In *Home, Exile, Homeland: Film, Media, and the Politics of Place,* ed. Hamid Naficy, pp. 63–74. New York: Routledge.

Nora, Pierre. 1998 [1984]. *Zwischen Geschichte und Gedächtnis.* Frankfurt am Main: Fischer.

Peleikis, Anja. 2001. Shifting Identities, Reconstructing Boundaries. The Case of a Multi-confessional Locality in Post-war Lebanon. *Die Welt des Islams. International Journal for the Study of Modern Islam* 41 (3): 400–429.

Picard, Elizabeth. 1996. *Lebanon: A Shattered Country.* New York and London: Holmes & Meier.

Seed, Patricia. 1999. The Key to the House. In *Home, Exile, Homeland: Film, Media, and the Politics of Place,* ed. Hamid Naficy, pp. 85–94. New York: Routledge.

Werbner, Richard. 1998. Beyond Oblivion: Confronting Memory Crisis. In *Memory and the Postcolony: African Anthropology and the Critique of Power,* ed. Richard Werbner, pp. 1–17. London: Zed Books.

6 The Algerian War in French Memory: Vengeful Memory's Violence

Benjamin Stora

(TRANSLATED BY PAUL A. SILVERSTEIN)

With each successive generation, children of immigrants are becoming more fully integrated into contemporary French society. However, entire segments of the French public continue to reject foreigners and French people of foreign origin, a fact testified to by the continued support for the ongoing xenophobic rhetoric of France's extreme right parties headed by Jean-Marie Le Pen and Bruno Mégret.[1] Nearly forty years after Algeria attained independence in 1962, the repetition of colonial historical situations seems to be more and more prevalent in the lived reality of contemporary France. This process has allowed the Algerian War to entrench itself in an internal French debate over a number of issues deriving from the war, including the veteran status of former French soldiers in Algeria, the revolt of children of Harkis, and *pied-noir* demands for reparations.[2] Such a contemporary displacement to France of values and feelings elaborated during the 132 years of French Algeria requires further analysis.

The genealogical relationship between the Muslim presence in France and a stubborn colonial memory inherited from a South lost to decolonization plays an important role in Front National (FN) politics and propaganda. The specter of a French Algeria continues to haunt the nostalgic memory of the extreme right. For several years, the FN has invoked actors from the Algerian War more frequently than those from Vichy.[3] Or perhaps, popular anti-Arabo–Islamic sentiment, coupled with an older antisemitic obsession, provides Front National discourse with a powerful historical and singular weight.

In his notion of an "eternal France," Le Pen invents a history rooted in an anti-Islamic myth: "We have been able to avoid the fatal consequences of Islamic invasion. This required the sacrifice of hundreds of thousands of Europeans who perished bearing arms; they refused to live under the *dhimmis,* the legal status accorded by the Qu'ran for infidels. Thanks to them, our bronze church bells still ring" (Le Pen 1990). The French nation, seen as a monolithic entity, is praised for its struggle against an external (and internal) enemy, considered to be first and foremost the Islam incarnated by Arabs residing in France. A training brochure for Front National militants states that, "We can affirm the same thing just as vigorously in a language accepted by the general public. Maybe we should say, 'We must organize the return of Third World immigrants to their homelands', instead of, 'Let's throw those dirty Arabs (*bougnoules*) into the sea!'"[4]

Above all, "immigrants" are men of the South, from the Maghreb and, in particular, Algeria. Behind the Front National's denunciation of a "Jewish conspiracy" resides an anti-Muslim obsession: "The nature of immigration has changed. On our soil, we are witnessing the clash of two fundamentally different cultures. Islam, which already represents France's second major religion, forbids assimilation and threatens our own identity, our Western and Christian civilization" (Le Pen 1985: 218). In a meeting held during the 1988 presidential elections, Le Pen exclaimed: "As long as we live, France will never become an Islamic republic!" (*Le Monde* 19 April 1988).

A French "Confederacy" (*Un "sudisme" à la française*)[5]

Southern men, such as soldiers, *pied-noirs,* OAS officers, and activists, have a particular image of French Algeria.[6] By referring to specific moments in American history (namely the arrival of European colonists, the eradication of native peoples, slavery, economic booms, the pioneering spirit, and Manifest Destiny), they still believe that the colonial social model remains more valid than ever. They claim their struggle for the cause of a French Algeria will never cease. They have transported and installed in France a "Confederate" (*sudiste*) tradition that the French historian Jean-Michel Lacroix, evoking the early years of the United States, describes in these terms:

> The Indian question provided a false alternative. The only choice it offered was between assimilation and expulsion. The first solution, which required Indians to cede territory, implied that they become civilized and assimilate into Americans. The second solution signaled that if Indians wanted to protect their identity, they had to move off their land so coveted by pioneers. . . . In an 1812 speech [James] Madison encouraged Indians to Americanize, inviting his "little red children" to copy Whites. (1996: 152–153)

Throughout the long conquest of Algeria during the nineteenth century, the French colonizer encouraged the colonized to fit into the mold the former had created for the latter. Because access to education was carefully monitored, the few colonized who managed to climb the professional ladder were necessarily proud of their accomplishment. Successfully assimilated, they could contemplate the "collective prostration" that they overcame after shedding their native culture, considered by the French to be "barbaric." In an 1891 report, a French legislator preached the virtues of assimilationist instruction for those natives not considered to be entirely backwards: "A barbaric race, already equipped with a half civilization, a more or less standard social level, solid mores anchored in social tradition, and a firmly entrenched religion, can hardly be forced to submit to the same laws as those governing a neighboring race still in the stage of savagery. We need to find other ways to win them over" (Burdeau 1892: 141).

Assimilation or eviction, such a schema is far distinct from American models of "hybridity" or the "melting pot"—but the former ideology was established before the American Civil War and the abolition of slavery. In the years that followed, black and white Americans were theoretically and legally granted equal access to social advancement. It soon became clear, however, that legal civil rights brought little actual freedom in the South, with America's northern and southern halves reconciling under new antiblack policies. Discrimination entered all facets of public life and was subsequently legitimized by the Supreme Court in 1896. Segregated housing, employment, and military units spread to the North as Southern blacks migrated in search of work. This gave rise to black neighborhoods/ghettos like Harlem. Progressively, American blacks, in spite of their high degree of assimilation, effectively became the objects of an internal, nonterritorial colonization within their own country. The development of this insupportable situation in a country that proudly called itself "the world's greatest democracy," with the transfer of a "Confederate" situation of segregation to the North, notably resonates both in twentieth-century colonial Algeria and, subsequently, in France of the 1990s.

The concept of Confederacy (*sudisme*), as opposed to South African apartheid, is a more apt model for examining the treatment of Algerian immigrants (and their French-born children) in France. Evoking colonization and its hierarchical social organization, the notion of an Algerian Confederacy also recalls decolonization's bitterness, resentment, wounded memories, and hidden desires for revenge.

A "Confederate" imaginary—akin to that held today by the "poor whites" (*petits blancs*) of the United States—grew and calcified at the heart of French of society. It includes its own references, myths, emblematic figures, and a civil war: the Algerian War. In 1991, Jacques Roseau, the director of a major association for repatriated French Algerians, sat down with the producers of the television series *The Algerian Years* (*Les années algériennes*). Interviewed just two years before his assassination, Roseau explained, "French Algerians are a youthful people who hailed from the entire Mediterranean region in addition to metropolitan France. They came to Algeria to create a new country often under very difficult conditions . . . They're a young people like the Americans."[7]

French Algeria, a Half-Formed America
(*L'Algérie française, une Amérique à mi-chemin*)

After the Algerian War, supporters of the OAS produced a number of texts in which themes outlining a French "Confederacy" were in clear evidence. Barely twenty-five years after the war, a work titled *OAS* appeared with a preface written by Pierre Sergent, a former OAS soldier and current member of the National Front, that revisited the principal themes upheld by partisans of a French Algeria. First, Algeria was portrayed as a "new frontier" for France, a half-formed America with wide (open?) spaces to conquer and exploit. "For France, Algeria is a pioneering frontier with vast riches, a space to master, a land of adventure. It was essentially France's dream to have a faraway South, its personal *American West* whose cities bristling with skyscrapers would one day evoke California rather than the Auvergne!" (Gauchon and Buisson 1987: 14). At first a land of wonder, a territory of unexpected encounters, a place of unbelievable discovery that obviated the need to travel to faraway America, Algeria was transformed by the colonizing impulse into a universe of riches.

Nineteenth-century military, travel, and journalistic narratives played an important role in the construction of a myth of Algeria as a southern El Dorado, a new promised land. However, from other narratives we now know that, instead of such luminous landscapes and proud nomads, Algeria was principally a land of half-starved Muslims and bloodthirsty European adventurers.[8]

Into this imagined Algerian wilderness a new race of pioneers was portrayed as advancing with great courage (and difficulties):

> These *"pied-noirs,"* this *American* people, we could almost say, were born in a veritable *melting-pot* where all the populations of the western Mediterranean were mixed together, where survivors of failed French revolutions were united with other victims of territorial upheavals. Little by little, a unique culture arose from this mixture, with its own lifestyle, dialect, and even cuisine! "An annoying and arrogant people," complained some observers occasionally. These *pied-noirs* exhibited common traits of what Marie Elbe calls "an adolescent race," a youthful people who takes great pride in having domesticated a territory. (Gauchon and Buisson 1987: 12)[9]

An entire literature emerged calqued—unselfconsciously—on the model of the American South, replete with clichés of ghost towns, crimes of passion, and heightened but repressed sexuality. Algeria became an emblematic region that embodied the solitude of passion, where the almost tangible, scorching midsummer heat weighed like a predestination.

Problems arise when an "adolescent" people settles in a country already undeniably populated. Regardless, the duty of the conqueror (after crushing and subjugating the indigenous population) is to provide protection and the benefits of a civilizing mission. In an 1886 report on native schools in Constantine, the school inspector Gustave Benoist stated, "Our natives are children, grown children. We must speak to their eyes and capture their imagination in order to tap into their minds and stimulate them. . . . Geography should be taught outdoors; that is where our *little savages* will learn how to orient themselves" (Benoist 1886: 138–139; emphasis added).

A "terrible" reality shone through Republican generosity: these grown children/ little savages had a long route to travel before reaching civilization's distant shores. In the triumphant years of conquest, partisans of colonial ideology only evoked indigenous peoples to show how much they owed and how much they were devoted to France. Colonial discourse paid no attention to the anterior and present conditions of Algerian Muslims, as it saw no place for them in the "New Algeria." The South was a realm of distinct communities whose members never crossed paths, despite sharing the ravages of poverty; indeed, the European Algerian standard of living was considerably lower than that of residents of metropolitan France.[10] In this immense, "vacant" land where the law of segregation (*la loi de l'exclusion*) reigned supreme, a certain fraternity between men proved possible on the condition that each remained in his social and communitarian place. The Algerian South was not a homogeneous space, but rather a patchwork of distinct communities. With its strong interpersonal bonds, this colonial Algeria resembled "Medieval society with its social contract of group protection and safeguarding of traditions. These conditions were revivified by insecurity and terrorism, that has forced the vassal to seek refuge under a suzerain" (Gauchon and Buisson 1987: 14).

French Algeria thus became in the colonialist mind a country of vast dimensions and great plains, filled with exhausted European adventurers and hostile (if subjugated) natives, of heroic military charges—a society attached to a glorious rural past opposed to a distant, industrialized North. These elements transformed the Algerian War into a nostalgic western filmed in Technicolor. It was a rough-and-tumble South with its own lost innocence, covered wagons, and "Mormons" smitten with the land, "acted out" by heroes straight out of a John Ford or Howard Hawks film. Was it simply a coincidence when, in 1998, Daniel Simonpieri, the National Front mayor of Marignane, appeared at a town carnival dressed as a Confederate officer? (*Le Canard Enchaîné*, 3 June 1998).[11]

The Algerian War and the Birth of the "Confederacy" ("*Sudisme*")

The Algerian War played a pivotal (and bloody) role in the emergence and construction of a durable "Confederate" ("*sudiste*") narrative. Supporters of French Algeria were haunted by the possibility of secession. After General De Gaulle's famous speech of 16 September 1959, which for the first time evoked the possibility of Algerian self-determination, the Veterans Authority (*Anciens combattants*) "objected to the idea that secession could be granted to states (*départements*) constitutionally part of the [French] Republic." Likewise, the May 13th Popular Movement (a predecessor of the OAS), "rose up with shame and indignation against the proposal of *secession,* a veritable insult to our fallen comrades" (*Le Monde*, 18 September 1959). From a Franco-Algerian conflict, the Algerian War was transformed into a French civil war, fought in the hearts of French Algerians; in their avowed desires for revenge against metropolitan France, the distant North; in their unavowed remorse for having been abandoned by France; in the fear and hatred in which Algerians and *pied-noirs,* adversaries and partisans of French Algeria, clashed.

In 1987, supporters of French Algeria wrote as follows:

This was our war of secession, comparable to the one fought in the United States between the traditional South and the industrialized North. The reader will remember what was at stake, and will perhaps understand the anguish, naiveté, and even excesses experienced by the *Confederates* (*sudistes*). The most powerful *Confederates,* like lords during an idealized Middle Ages, respected their contractual obligations to protect the less fortunate, while the latter, in turn, shifted from despondency to wild and desperate rebellion, driving them "to suicide by revolt," as Marie Elbe has noted. . . . Those who see in the 1960s schism a vast conflict between a Confederate (*sudiste*) Algeria and the industrial Unionism (*nordisme*) of metropolitan France would not be mistaken. What remained from the French imperial mystique—the spiritual residue of a certain colonial tradition—could coexist neither with modern technological imperatives (*la civilisation technicienne*) nor with the interpersonal relations such a technocratic society demanded. (Gauchon and Buisson 1987: 15)

The Algerian War was linked to a history of colonial wars of conquest through which the South was forcibly conjoined to metropolitan France. The army brought with it a notion of "civilization," a new set of values, and a singular model of evolution with which to define the natives' future. Inevitably, the French army found itself on the front lines of the Algerian War, attempting to suture the rifts between North and South, between the two sides of the Mediterranean. However, the army's resolve and identity proved tenuous on the eve of combat. Shortly after the trials of World War II, the French army was deployed in the Far East where it experienced a new shock, that of decolonization. From 1947 to 1954, the military infiltrated Indochina, engaging guerrilla forces it was ill-prepared to fight. Soon, however, it felt left behind, if not forgotten, by the politicians and public opinion of a Fourth Republic France preoccupied with postwar reconstruction. Indeed, the overseas armies became newsworthy only when President Pierre Mendès-France proposed to withdraw support for the Indochinese conflict. Forgotten, the French army was soon defeated at Diên Biên Phu on 7 May 1954, thus ending a colonial drama that the French public never accepted as its own. Alone in mourning for the loss of Indochina, the same overseas army was subsequently sent to Algeria where, beginning in November 1954, it began an "operation to maintain order," an innocuous title for the military intervention that remained in place throughout the war.

After the experience of Indochina, the military elite—captains, colonels, and generals—decided never to surrender, never to resign itself to a new defeat. Attempting to think like the enemy, the military understood the Algerian fighters as not simply patriots fighting a conventional war, but also as ideological soldiers waging a new form of revolutionary warfare. In ideological terms, they opposed the spiritual values of the Christian Occident to Marxist materialism and Islamic fanaticism. General Raoul Salan underscored this representation during his 1962 trial for his attempted putsch in Algeria in April 1961:

I make no excuses for my refusal to see a French province's destiny put to a vote and then see it sold off, scorning our most sacred of duties. I make no excuses for having defended *Mediterranean France*[12] and by extension the free world, even if the free world was blind or indifferent to our efforts. I make no excuses for fighting the spread of Communism to within one hour of Marseille, bringing Paris within reach of its short-range missiles. I make no excuses for having defended the wealth that our young pioneers brought from the Sahara to France thereby ensuring our petroleum supplies.

Populist, anticapitalist, and antiestablishment, the French revolutionary right has historically favored a "New Order."[13] Supporters of the OAS (with those emerging from Vichy) carried out their struggle in 1980s France:

> The OAS is not just a subversive group in the typical sense of the term. In addition to opposing Republican laws, the OAS wishes to overthrow a culture of social conformity born from the workings of the economic system. It does this at the risk of being an object of reproach in the majority's eyes. It is despised in a society of ease whose only religion is bulimic, consumerist well-being. In contrast, these "samurais" devote themselves to stoic sacrifice. Loathed in a French society that has become more and more conservative in relation to its increasing stability and prosperity, [the OAS values] audacity, courage, and adventure more than ever. (Gauchon and Buisson 1987: 15)

Confederate Nationalism under a Republican Mask

If colonial history has been transmitted to French society essentially via reference to the "Algerian model," it is because Algeria had been considered the "jewel" of French imperial crown because of its high land value (after the forced removal of Muslims), its large colonial population (more than one million people), and its administrative attachment to France for more than a century (thus establishing a "French Algeria"). Colonial Algeria was composed of three French districts (*départements*), marking a juridical difference from a distant colony like Senegal or a protectorate like Tunisia. In the words of *pied-noir* author Gabriel Audisio, "Algeria became our only overseas territory that we succeeded in making part of France."

Since the end of the nineteenth century, Algeria was no longer governed by the Ministry of the Colonies but by the Ministry of the Interior. Republican assimilationist ideology was born out of the Third Republic's attempt to homogenize the French national legal body through standardized education (national schoolbooks backed by state representatives known derogatorily as "black hussars"), the separation of church and state, linguistic and cultural standardization, and the expansion of a centralized government. The Third Republic transplanted these principles of cultural assimilation and political integration— treated as universal Republican values—to the colonies. This "export" of Republican ideology occurred simultaneously with the economic expansion of French nationalism at the end of the nineteenth century, and such neouniversalist principles were quickly applied to Algeria, considered to be an integral part of France since 1848. On the one hand, Republican assimilationist discourse attempted to erase diversity and unite individuals as equal citizens. On the other, it had operated as segregationalist in its reification of gender and ethnic differences.

"French Algeria" appeared as a slogan—an ideological rallying point—promulgated by the European minority in colonial Algeria. Algeria was considered to be a unique colony, with a legal system that differed from that established in other parts of the Empire. In the early twentieth century, legislator Arthur Girault explained that

> This special treatment may seem arbitrary at first glance. However, the colonial problem in Barbary is so particular that its laws and its future were unique. . . . Algeria is inhabited by diverse native populations who hate each other and have no concept of nationality. . . . Among these diverse and divided men, religion is becoming a stronger and stronger link. Islam is spreading. (Girault 1907: 3–5, 71, 77)

In opposition to other manifestations of assimilationism in colonial Algeria, the Republic underscored how Islam epitomized the natives' irreducible difference and distance from "Western civilization." Emile Larcher, a law professor in Algiers, wrote,

> It is foolish to impose metropolitan organization and legislation on a colony that differs from a French department in almost every way, shape or form from its native races to its climate. . . . If assimilation implies the application of institutions from the mother land in the colonies, we must be very careful not to confuse it with its caricature—a craze for uniformity. (1903: 16–17)

Forcing heterogeneous populations into a monolithic state apparatus, the colonial government created a divided law for Algerian Muslim subjects and French citizens. The result was neither wholly French nor Algerian. It created a particular legal system predicated on the notion of a timeless, essential difference between French and indigenous populations.

This false Republican model can lend itself to a particular form of racism; the occupation of a territory and subjugation of its residents was rationalized in the name of a civilizing mission seeking to eliminate the essential difference between subjects and citizens. In order to remain on a territory invaded by the conqueror, the "Other" was forced to acquire trappings of civilization and attempt to resemble the already civilized occupier. The benefit of civilization was deployed as a favor bestowed upon the native: not physically exterminated, the latter was granted the possibility of acquiring the colonizer's superior culture.

Until the mid-twentieth century, French nationalism hid behind the mask of Republican universalism. The struggles of decolonialization of the 1950s and 1960s unmasked this deception. The Algerian War represented a clash between two types of nationalism deployed respectively by the French and Algerian sides: one "universal and secular," the other "communitarian and religious." During the war, such nationalist ideologies could be distinguished more clearly. Those leaders on the French Left who preached Republican universalism essentially recycled nineteenth-century French nationalism; they simply redefined the nation in universalist terms. By contrast, supporters of a French Algeria, reunited in the OAS, recruited exclusively from the ranks of the extreme right in France.

The end of the Algerian War marked the origin of a new worldview that would take root several years later in France. This nationalist model relied on the concept of pristine cultures that are different from the West and whose domestication is futile. In order to avoid internal culture wars, it maintained as preferable the construction of a barrier designed to keep different peoples in their respective places. Such barriers had already been established in the South, in colonial Algeria. However, after Algerian independence, new barriers were seen as necessary, particularly in the North. The Algerian War by no means implemented a policy of physical extermination of segments of the Algerian population. The war functioned, above all, as an opportunity to present two "solutions" to what was understood as a problematic confrontation between Islamic and Republican ideals: assimilation or segregation. The war introduced large segments of the French public to the existence of a putative ethno-racial fracture in which Algerian Muslims were viewed as inassimilable because of their essential otherness. Previously dominated by antisemitism (anti-Judaism), classical French racism thus added another dimension: anti-Arab racism. Such anti-Arab sentiment was transplanted to France in large part by a segment of the population that had once inhabited "the South."

Memories of the South as a "French Algeria"

France's colonial memory, still largely repressed, weighs heavily on the nation's cultural and political scene. Of all the buried memories of colonial Africa, colonial Asia, and colonial North Africa, French Algeria fills the collective imagination with the most "traces" (*signaux*). The loss (or "abandonment," from the perspective of supporters of French Algeria) of this immense territory —long considered an integral part of France—wounded French national pride. This loss marked a crisis for French republican ideology insofar as it had to acknowledge the "amputation" of a part of the supposedly indivisible French nation. To the dismay of colonialist nationalism, memories of the "Algerian years" further manifested themselves due to the presence and *physical evidence* (*la puissance physique*) of the war's actors on French soil. These groups included one million *pied-noirs* and their children, 1.5 million soldiers who had fought or lived in Algeria for as many as two or three years, one million Algerian immigrants and their children (the "Beurs"), and tens of thousands of Harkis.

By the time of the millennium, between four and five million people in France had a "living" memory (*mémoire "à vif"*) of Algeria. As it becomes more and more distant, the Algerian War has become lodged in French memory as a foundational historical moment. In this respect, it is important to understand how different memories of the war establish and utilize a Southern imaginary. In the struggle between *pied-noir* "memories" (*souvenirs*) and those of Algerian immigrant youth emerges a structure of confrontation reminiscent of colonial times.

Pied-Noirs, Memories of Exile

After 1962, the memory of French Algeria was essentially transmitted through notions of a "lost homeland." In the pain of upheaval from their native land, a majority of *pied-noirs* who massively (nearly one million between 1962 and 1964) fled Algeria took with them memories that painted Algeria as a type of El Dorado or lost city of Atlantis. The writer Jean Brune, a fellow disciple with Albert Camus of the Lycée d'Alger, correctly insisted on the "rights of men not to be driven away from their childhood memories." In his 1999 work *Les étés perdus* (*Lost Summers*), Jean Pélégri takes the reader on a tour of his childhood land, the Mitidja, the source of his life and inspiration. In the works of Emmanuel Roblès, Jean-Luc Allouche,[14] and Alain Vircondelet,[15] there exists a similar emotion, a painful, embodied memory of exile.

Other *pied-noir* writers produced works that foreground happy memories while erasing colonial inequities. In France, this narrative of a distant South is primarily expressed in very intimate and immediate terms. Memories are embellished by a warm and sunny story of a lost Eden, a paradise destroyed by war (Hureau 1987). In this vein, female European authors began writing melancholy memoirs, beginning in 1962. In part, these memoirs recall the segregated nature of Algerian society and how the fault lines were imprinted in the geographical distribution of communities across the urban landscape. Describing Sétif as a multi-ethnic exception to the rule, the ethnographer Joëlle Bahloul writes, "In Sétif, houses were inhabited by multi-ethnic domestic groups—mainly Jewish and Muslim families. *It was rare for Jewish families to share intimate domestic space with Christian families.* In other, even rarer instances, Christian and Muslim families shared living space (Bahloul 1992: 25, emphasis added).

During the Algerian War, these community-based social divisions crossed the Mediterranean and took root in and around metropolitan French factories. The heroine of Claire Etcherelli's *Elise ou la vraie vie* [Elise or the True Life] recalls,

A long time ago I discovered the deep-seated hostility workers had towards each other. The French didn't like the Algerians or any foreigners for that matter. They accused them of stealing their jobs and then of not knowing how to do them. Shared pain, shared sweat, shared demands were all just "window dressing" according to Lucien. Slogans. It was everyone for himself. Most people brought their grudges and suspicions to work. You couldn't hate the Arabs on the outside and call for worker solidarity on the job. Things got out of hand sometimes. Everybody hid behind their race or nationality when they went on the attack or the defensive. ... Algerians lived together in closed neighborhoods, shantytowns, or seedy hotels. (1967: 166–167)

Female Europeans born in Algeria—*pied-noires*—as well as Muslim and Jewish women have narrated the war in their own fashion. They have written either to illuminate their community's sentiments or to revive senses experienced during the colonial period. Michèle Villanueva, for instance, evokes the divided universes expressed in the Oran European community's "fear of the Other." Villanueva recalls, "Even as a child or teenager, I could never understand this divided world, this source of latent, unspeakable malaise. The Arabs, who we speak the least about, really lived separately in the Ras-el-Aïn ravine" (1992: 12). This sublime memoir details the fears and obstacles that hindered intercommunity contacts. Conversely, Algerian women likewise relate their fears of the European Other. Assia Djebar explains in one novel, "For me, French homes emitted a strange odor, reflected a secret light. My eyes were transfixed by the Other's shore. During my childhood, just before the war that would end in independence, I never entered a French household. I didn't visit a single French classmate's house" (1985: 34). Beyond the walls of each of these memories exists a landscape of multiple Algerias. Superimposed, they never meet.

"Beurs," Traces of War, Civic Memories

In opposition to a *pied-noir* community recreated in exile, there exists another memory of Algeria and the war of national liberation. It flourished in French society, particularly during the 1980s, among the children of North African immigrants. The first wave of North African immigrants—mainly Algerians—arrived on French soil between 1920 and 1930. France's immigrant population rose sharply in 1945 and again in 1963–1964. By 1974, when France's borders were officially sealed off, one million North Africans resided in the metropole (cf. Stora 1992).

The Algerian war of independence left an indelible mark on the memories of immigrant families in France. What relationship do second-generation immigrants—for the most part French citizens—have with a war fought between 1954 and 1962? Members of this age group seem to oscillate between two poles. On the one hand, the second generation appears indifferent toward the war; they wish to escape from the heroic portrayal of a conflict that, while fought long ago, still haunts their parents' generation. On the other hand, they have maintained an affective tie to the war that serves as a "resource," an alternate source of identity, for them living in the heart of French society. Their literary works, published in France between 1975 and 1990, reveal an ongoing ambivalence and discomfort toward the war among the second generation.

Second-generation literature appears to come to terms with the internal flux and contradictions, if not fragmentation, of the personal projects of its authors. Drifting memories between here (France) and there (Algeria), plus incomplete knowledge of the details of the war and subsequent exile, undermine the writers' explicit concerns. The real event—the conflict—comes off, in the end, as almost "unbelievable." Nonetheless, it is always present through a set of recurring themes: migrations of the protagonist, exilic displacements, the quest for a father figure, and portrayals of the tragic night of 17 October 1961, when Algerian protesters were massacred by Parisian police. The 1980s marked a turning point when second-generation Algerian youth entered the public arena to fight for the recognition of their civic rights. At that moment, bitter, vitriolic texts became the norm. Yet between the tormented lines and rebellious passions roamed the ghosts of battered memories.

At the beginning of the 1980s, France discovered that "second-generation" youth were on a quest for their identity some twenty years after Algerian independence. Brahim is one of them. Shortly after emigrating from his native Kabylia—a region bloodied during the war—little Brahim loses his smile when he sees his brother murdered in the Latin Quarter on 17 October 1961. In *Sourire de Brahim* (Brahim's Smile; 1985), Nacer Kettane writes, "The banks of the Seine were littered with corpses. Blood flowed under the Pont Mirabeau. Drowned, shot, and tortured men. You, eternal witnesses of this butchery. You, suspended breaths of life that shall replenish the memory of generations in search of their identity." Mohamed Kenzi, in *La Menthe sauvage* (Wild Mint; 1984), mixes tender childhood memories with the sounds of war: departure for France to join his father; the strangeness of Paris; Nanterre, the "no-man's land" (*la "zone"*) of shantytowns and the echoes of war within the nascent immigrant community. The novel exhibits a balanced mixture of introspection and openness to French consumer society, a mother's fatalistic resignation to the repetition of ancestral rituals, and a traditional family in crisis stemming from the clash between paternal authority and questioning children. It is all there in gestation, visible twenty years after the conflict ended.

Themes of the relations between children, fathers, and the war are likewise found in *Le Harki de Meriem* (Meriem's Harki 1989), in which Mehdi Charef tells the story of Saliha and Sélim. Their family was forced to leave Algeria with the French army in 1962 because Azzedine, their father, was a Harki. The novel describes the milieu of Muslim soldiers fighting on the side of the French forces during the conflict, almost testifying on behalf of them as it details the many reasons they ended up enlisting in the French army. After 1962, the Harkis are generally rejected. Only the Algerian grandmother seems to understand that the bonds of blood are stronger than the fractures of history. After racists in Reims murder Sélim, his mother returns to their native village to guard the family plot. The novel designates neither victims nor guilty parties in war's barbary, rather portraying only figures who struggle with their own demons.

The pressure of memory hardly let up in the 1990s. In *Vivre me tue* (Living Is Killing Me; 1997), we discover that Paul Smaïl's grandfather, Ahmed, died in French uniform, while his uncle Mehdi was murdered in Paris in October 1961. His father worked for the French railways. Paul, a young "Beur," subsequently attempts to be a model of integration. As a child in the Parisian immigrant neighborhood of Barbès, and a night watchman at a cheap hotel in the nearby red-light district of Pigalle, this amateur boxer feels the punch of racism. Smaïl's stories are striking for their harsh, violent portrayals, if not occasional tenderness.

In what the media had dubbed the Beur Movement, the children of Algerian immigration composed a new vision and memory of colonial history. They accomplished this most notably in 1983 and 1984 with large-scale protest marches against racism and civic inequality. After a long dormant period, memory had re-awoken. This return of memory brought with it demands of reparations, justice, and equality. The bicultural Beurs demanded to be accepted as full-fledged French citizens while simultaneously demonstrating respect for Algerian traditions and for their parents who had fought for Algerian independence. The demand for equal citizenship did not break the lines of filiation and genealogy that linked the Beurs to the struggles of their fathers and grandfathers, partisans of an independent Algeria. In the process, a multi-vocal memory was created.

Since arriving in the *metropole,* a number of "European" Algerians have had a tendency to reconstruct a memory around social or community-based hierarchy. They commonly invoke Islam as a barrier to integration in France, thus marking an implicit continuity with a colonial social structure that relied on ethnic, not national, criteria. In striking contrast, the Beurs demanded full citizenship—something never accorded their relatives during the colonial era. Children of Algerian immigrants refuse communitarian insularity. They desire to leave the social and cultural ghetto for mainstream society. This resonates in 1980s discourse with an embrace of civic equality and a rejection of the reproduction of a colonial situation, of a hierarchical society based on communitarianism.

By contrast, the "European" memory employed a discourse that reproduced the hierarchical ethnic and spatial living conditions of colonial Algeria. Firmly entrenched on French soil, repatriated "European" Algerians constituted a loud echo chamber in which the extreme right's exclusionary slogans reverberated. This is exemplified even twenty years later in the words of a resident of Noyon in the Oise region. Interviewed days after France captured the World Cup of soccer in 1998, he remarked to a journalist, "This is the first time I've seen so much joy in Noyon. . . . Just as quick as it came it'll go away. People will go back to their neighborhoods and their labels. We stay among own kind. That's the way it is" (*Libération* 20 July 1998).

These two types of memories of the South—colonization and French Algeria—are the property of two statistically important, and nearly numerically equal, French communities. Together, European Algerians, Algerian immigrants, and Beurs represent several million people who retain some memory of Algeria. Adding veterans and Harkis, it is clear to see the great extent to which shockwaves of the Algerian war continue to rattle contemporary French society. It is from the well of wounded memories that the extreme right drinks.

Memories of Revenge: The Extreme Right's Grand Return

The spirit of the OAS lives on in the extreme right thanks in large part to waves of amnesty from war crimes granted by the successive governments of the Fifth Republic (cf. Stora 1998: 211–218). Since Algerian independence, amnesties have allowed the war to be forgotten. On 22 March 1962, two amnesty provisions were included in the Evian Accords that officially ended the war:

In order to facilitate the self-determination of the Algerian people . . . Those shall receive amnesty who have committed infractions that aided or abetted the Algerian insurrection before 20 March 1962. Those shall receive amnesty who have committed infractions during the maintenance of order against the Algerian insurrection before 20 March 1962.

The law of 17 June 1966 granted amnesty to those who committed "infractions against state security during the events in Algeria." This law, which concerned the insurrection against the legal government, granted amnesty to members of the OAS as well as to those who fought against it. The law of 31 July 1968 granted full legal amnesty for those infractions perpetrated in relationship to the events in Algeria, including those "committed by soldiers serving in Algeria at the time." The former leaders of the OAS were all freed after the "events" of May 1968, including Raoul Salan, Jacques Soustelle, Georges Bidault, Antoine Argoud,[16] Gilles Buscia,[17] Pierre Sergent, Jean-Jacques Susini, and Jean-Marie Curutchet.[18] Elected President of the Republic in 1974, Valéry Giscard d'Estaing—a supporter of French Algeria after 1956—took other measures besides amnesty. Most notably, he called for reparations for repatriated European Algerians. In addition, the law of 16 July 1974 overturned all criminal sentences handed out during or after the Algerian War.

The 1970s witnessed an increase in attacks against Algerian immigrants and organizations. The bombing of the Algerian consulate in Marseille on 14 December 1973 was followed by waves of bomb attacks in Paris, Lyon, and Roubaix in July 1975. An organization called Delta—drawing its name from the symbol used by OAS militias—took responsibility for the 2 December 1977 assassination of Laïd Sebaï, the chairman of the Algerian government's *Amicale des Algériens en France*. In 1977, the journalist René Backmann estimated that at least seventy Algerians were assassinated in France between December 1971 and December 1977. This was a dark period in which politicians and mainstream society refused to talk about Algerian murders. Fausto Giudice aptly posed the question:

> What are Arabicides? Racist crimes? Ethnic clashes? Crimes of civil war? Revenge killings? Arab bashing? Manhunts? They are a bit of everything. But more than that, beyond the endless repetition—the banalization—of gestures, speeches, silences, and attitudes, [Arabicide] is a uniquely French type of crime for which our penal system has no provisions. Arabicide has become a social model. (1992: 11)

After the election of socialist President François Mitterrand, the return of the extreme right to the French political and ideological scene coincided with a resurgent debate on the consequences of the Algerian War. On 29 September 1982, Prime Minister Pierre Mauroy presented a legislative proposal "concerning the regulation of specific consequences stemming from events in North Africa." Mitterrand himself had declared a few days earlier, "It is the nation's duty to pardon."

However, such a pardon is exactly what Pierre Joxe and a large number of socialists in the National Assembly (such as Lionel Jospin and Michel Rocard) refused to do. Mauroy's proposal, eventually passed under extraordinary circumstances, actually went a great deal further than previous amnesty legislation. The proposal provided "professional retraining" for policemen and administrators who had lost their civil service jobs between 1961 and 1963. Most importantly, it placed in the army reserves eight generals who had commanded paratrooper divisions during the attempted putsch of April 1961.

The socialist government, however, did not stop at granting amnesty. It jumpstarted the careers of executives, officers, and generals who had been convicted or reprimanded for having participated in subversive actions against the republic. Paratroopers were welcomed back into the French army in November 1982. Such policies provoked a raging debate, in which some argued that the mistakes and ghosts that haunted French memories of the war should simply be forgotten. Others questioned if reintegrating subversive elements into the army actually amounted to supporting OAS activism, encouraging a political agenda that had been silenced since the end of the war in 1962.

The resulting "compromise" largely succeeded in repressing past conflicts, seeking to erase once and for all the memory of the Algerian War. However, the repressed memories did not vanish, and through the repetition and the multiplication of symptoms, the conflict manifested itself in unorthodox ways. Amnesty, which attempted to mask and to forgive, actually set the stage for other conflicts and regressions.

The levying of sanctions against those responsible for atrocities committed during the Algerian war prevented France from draining the abscess of the war's memory. The lines between what "*is*" and "is not" a crime were erased and the responsible parties remained nameless. France resigned never to do what the Americans did during and after Vietnam: bring their own war criminals to justice. Indeed, the November 1982 law, justified by massive pardons, only abetted the OAS's nostalgia. Leaders of the extreme right, mustering only 0.8 percent of the vote during the presidential election of 1981, re-entered the French political arena. The tortures, crimes, and racial discriminations perpetrated during the Algerian War were forgiven. However, ongoing and particular memories of the war lived on in mainstream society.

A reconstructed and embellished colonial memory found itself transformed into a *pied-noir* memory of "revenge." If the Algerians really wanted independence, what were they doing in France? How did they dare demand civil equality? "Revenge" thinkers literally advocated a "return" to Algeria by pointing out the intolerance European Algerians faced at the end of the war. As Joseph Ortiz averred,

> Immigrants have absolutely no rights in France because, after all, what rights were granted to the people who constructed their country generation after generation? What was their feeling towards European Algerians and French Muslims? It was either the suitcase or the casket. Civilized people like ourselves would never use such slogans. But when you're talking about the future of thousands of French families, one shouldn't hesitate from using solutions completely devoid of excessive sentimentality. (Cited in Rollat 1985: 213)

This exclusionary memory was steadily transformed into a *secret* memory of revenge (*mémoire de revanche* inavouée). In this schema, colonial France brought "civilization" to "tribes" whose presence in the Hexagon threatens the integrity of French culture. Eugène Ibagnez, an extremist of the USDIFRA—an organization representing the union of Algerian exiles (*repliés*)—explained, "Marseille and its surroundings have their own Casbah and shantytowns where the underworld rules. We've had enough. Because they resist integration and choose to remain foreigners, Algerians will always be hated by us Roumis. Is being shocked by all these North African shops racist? Is it normal to tolerate all these individuals who bankrupt the state?" (cited in Temime 1991: 175). Denouncing the "colonization of France," Le Pen's rival for control of the National Front, Bruno Mégret, took up the same themes at the Marignane secessionist congress in January 1999.

In the case of Algerian immigrants, the formerly colonized—portrayed in racist discourse as veritable metropolitan intruders—are attacked for colonizing "civilized" territory. Those forced into political or economic exile, those long thought to be "docile subordinates" under the colonial system, now find themselves portrayed as triumphant "colonizers" in a certain French collective imaginary. This discourse of revenge, which does not acknowledge the historical break of decolonization, puts colonial era racism back into circulation. Its classic stereotypes of "the good Arab" who is docile and content and "the fanatical Arab" who has a political or social agenda, has gained currency once again. North Africans, and Algerians in particular, have become even more the objects of repulsion, as they recall with their presence on French soil the last war France fought (and lost), a conflict that remains a deep and open national wound.

From Resentment to "Reprisals"

Since the 1980s, issues of the Algerian War, immigration, and socioeconomic exclusion have been intertwined. Behind the classical theme of foreign invasion that returns with each new economic crisis (as was the case during France's interwar period), stands the "Arab." In French racist imagery, the foreign vampire who sucks the blood of "eternal France" no longer has the face of the "golden calf-worshiping" Jew. For a few years now, this "Other," this problematic intruder, is the Muslim "fanatic." In their introduction to a special issue on immigration of the *Nouvel Observateur* in 1984, Jacques Julliard and Anne Fohr wrote,

Let's admit it. Two months ago we sent out a questionnaire on immigrants in France, and here we are today with an enormous dossier on Arabs. Arabs dominate our entire survey. Marx said about the nineteenth-century proletariat that there was always someone in his company more proletarian than himself—his wife. Well, the foreigner residing in today's France has someone more foreign than himself—the Arab.

There is a conflict that obsesses at the heart of the immigration "problem." Behind the "immigrant" there is the "Arab"; behind the "Arab," the "North African"; behind the "North African," the "Algerian." North African immigrants are viewed as unassimilable into French society because they are viewed as profoundly different from other immigrants (such as those from the interwar period; cf. Gervereau et al. 1998). Such a perceived difference is explained by Islam. Accordingly, this population is represented as holding a belief system that excludes it from the mainstream values of French society. Questions raised during the colonial period resurface behind what is known as the "immigration problem." Are the tenets of Islam compatible with the French Republic? Should immigrants be granted the right to vote? Should they be restricted to a separate "second electoral college" as was the case in Algeria in 1947? Should France put into place a process of assimilation that requires immigrants to abandon their religious "personal status" in order to achieve citizenship?[19] Or, rather, should citizenship accept a diversity of communities? Borrowing from a colonial lexicon, French immigration discourse has progressively slid during the 1990s from a focus on "immigrants" to "Muslims," thus recapitulating a colonial dichotomy between "Algerian Muslims" and France.

The philosopher Cornélius Castoriadis explained in the documentary television series *Les Années algériennes* that, "There is a knife between the Algerians and the French. This knife is an imaginary projection of France's violent and sexual phantasms about North Africans—specifically Algerians." This knife is further associated with another sort of racism, namely colonial racism. It feeds off the defeat of 1962. The French invaders of Algeria in 1830 and their colonial successors interpreted their victory as a sign of their superiority. It became logical for them to occupy a territory and to subjugate its population, as all such actions contributed to "civilizing" Algeria. Residing on his native yet conquered soil, the "Other" was seen as owing it to himself to acquire the trappings of civilization. Civilization was a gift bestowed upon the native; it granted him access to superior knowledge.

France, Recognition

For many years, the Algerian War did not officially exist in France. The state only recognized it as "operations aimed at maintaining order." In 1973 and 1974, when "Algerian veterans" obtained benefits provided to other war veterans, people still hardly talked of the war as a "conflict." Despite the prosaic words of Jean-Pierre Chevènement (1975), the future Minister of Defense— "The Algerian War has left a crack in the spirit of its combatants. We must widen it"—nothing has changed since the 1960s. On 18 September 1996, while receiving members of the United Front of North African Veterans at the presidential palace, the former lieutenant-turned-president Jacques Chirac stated that the time had come to replace "maintenance of order" with the *mot juste:* "war." He was preaching to the choir.

On 21 October 1997, while responding to a legislator's question about the role the former Paris police chief Maurice Papon played in the 17 October 1961 massacre of Algerian protesters, Prime Minister Jospin enunciated those taboo words: "Algerian War." At that moment, he also announced that the 17 October 1961 archives would be opened to researchers. This decision represents an important change that allows researchers to answer many unresolved questions about the event. On 5 May 1999, Jospin went even further, announcing that the government "decided to facilitate access to public archives relevant to these events in conformity with the procedures established by law." "The Prime Minister," the communiqué specified, "has asked ministers responsible for these archives to grant passes to persons seeking access to them."

On 10 June 1999, the National Assembly debated a proposal of legal semantics to change "operations to maintain order in North Africa" to "Algerian War" in all legislative and legal texts. Since November 1954, the Algerian War had been officially termed "an operation to maintain order," and later a "peacekeeping" mission. For close to a half century, heads of state, ministers in charge of repatriated European Algerians, and laws concerning military pensions avoided a word explicitly obfuscated in the official propaganda of leaders of the era. Moreover, the government avoided making payments to veterans who had fought "over there." However, in everyday conversations, newspapers, history books,[20] and high school final examination questions, people talked about the war, about its several hundred thousand casualties, among whom were twenty-four thousand French conscripts killed in the countryside and cities of Algeria.

Legislators who had fought in Algeria were reticent to speak about the battles, rapes, and tortures of the war, but, communists and Gaullists alike, they supported the lexical change in the name of their fallen brothers. Unanimously, 117 legislators passed the socialist bill to replace "operations to maintain order" with "Algerian War" in the French Republic's documents. From this point on, the Algerian War was no longer a "war with no name." But, across the Mediterranean, this ruling left Algerians perplexed.

At another level, the substitution of "Algerian War" for "maintenance of order" will have consequences for history teachers and researchers. One consequence was that after 1962, France had effectively ignored its former adversaries —the National Liberation Front (FLN), its armed branch (ALN), and the Algerian civilians more generally. It had also ignored information saying that its officers had committed war crimes in France's name. In short, France had concealed the truth about the repressive acts it had committed: eight thousand villages destroyed, one million Algerians deported, hundreds of thousands incarcerated, Algerian civilians murdered and tortured daily. This chapter of the war has finally been opened. High-ranking officers guilty of war crimes can finally be brought to justice. A taboo has vanished. And this despite General de Gaulle's proposition (later backed by Mitterrand) to readmit generals Salan, Challe, Jouhaud, and Zeller—all former OAS members—back into the French Army.[21]

Taboos disappear, but already dissenting voices are making themselves heard in France. Many fear that the use of the term *war* trivializes the unique place of the Algerian conflict in history. After hearing of the new official appellation for the war, an "Algerian veteran" did not hesitate to write,

More than "war," I think "maintenance of order" and everything it brings to mind—the interrogations, reprisals, raped Muslims—is a better description of the procedures we deployed. I am afraid that the term "war," because of its semantic open-endedness, will enable France to camouflage its systematic and dishonorable campaign in Algeria. (Menuet 1999)

The risk remains that "normalizing" the war will end up legitimizing its excesses (*bavures*). The recourse to "war" as a moral exception ultimately frees the actors of the Algerian drama from all responsibility for the imposition of the colonial system at the origin of the conflict. It clears the consciences of those who may feel guilt for the acts they committed. However, calling it *war* could also be interpreted as the end of amnesia and the stabilization of memories, indispensable conditions for ending the repression of past actions committed during this difficult time. It might also lead the way to an end of the "French Confederacy."

An End to the "French Confederacy"

Labeling the events of October 1961 a massacre, opening archives, and the Papon Trial[22] marked the beginning of France's recognition of the Algerian War. Likewise, in Algeria memories are resurfacing that examine colonial realities. Algeria and France are beginning to examine their suffering faces in the mirror. The movement from memory to the writing of history permits those who have been traumatized the courage to examine their past, to stop mythologizing, to stop prevaricating. It helps them to simply understand.

While the electoral popularity of the extreme right seems to be fading, a May 1999 survey, conducted by CSA Opinion and published in *La Tribune de l'Immigration,* revealed that anti-immigrant sentiment has spread beyond the extreme right. A total of 36 percent of the French respondents claimed they were not racist at all; 28 percent acknowledged some racism; 24 percent indicated being not very racist; and 10 percent simply admitted to being racist.[23] Moreover, a large majority indicated a preference to see the government crack down on immigration flows. While this survey conveyed France's willingness to discuss the "integration of immigrants," it also demonstrated a collective fixation on North Africans. North Africans were considered to be the primary victims of racism (76 percent of respondents), ahead of young citizens of North African origin (65 percent), with Sub-Saharan Africans, Gypsies, and Jews considered less at risk. One out of ten French respondents admitted to disliking North Africans, while only 7 percent of those surveyed saw them in a sympathetic light.

How should one interpret this ambivalence between the waning popularity of the extreme right and an ongoing set of fantasies about North Africans tied to colonial history? It is important to examine the ambivalent transfer of colonial history. For years, hostile attitudes toward North African immigrants have been apparent. Over time, other, more complex attitudes have developed. At the millennium, new generations of French people are living in a culture of humdrum hybridity. National identity is not constructed in opposition to a distant, "barbaric" South. Instead, it is constructed by the addition—the absorption—of outside cultures. It is becoming more and more difficult to view the "Southern man" as a person to be feared. Over the span of a number of years—from Algerian independence in 1962 to the millennium—Algerian memories that were transmitted contributed to the repetition of the conflict. These violent memories revealed vengeful attitudes and underscored the presence of dangerous desires. The stakes are different for today's memory of the Algerian conflict that the children and grandchildren of Algerian immigrants safeguard. The latter explicitly reject assimilation and invoke a multiplicity of cultural belonging that they claim to be reconcilable with the Republic. Their struggles dovetail with a global transformation of democratic societies toward an avowal of pluralism.[24] Declaring themselves for civil rights and against segregation, they cry out for social reform in the name of republican values. In so doing, they aim to carry out the ideals of the Republican pact: equal opportunity for all citizens regardless of origin. A French multi-culturalism (not to be confused with communitarianism) emerges, founded on a legal basis in which individual and collective rights prosper. However, the expansion of political rights remains insufficient.

Across the Mediterranean, "Northern" segregation has taken on a more insidious form. As was the case in the United States, which was confronted with the "black question" in the 1960s and 1970s, France's "immigrant problem" has jumped from the political to the social arena. More and more second generation immigrants—who disavow the appellation Beurs—demand that political gains must be accompanied by economic improvements in the domains of work, housing, and education.

Understanding the transmission of memories of Algerian history is essential for grasping the current predicament that French society faces. This transmission may represent resistance to changes affecting France, a memory that relies heavily on the model of *French* Algeria: belief in a strong state, a heightened French "ethnic" nationalism, the importance of "colonial missions," racial and religious hierarchies, segregation of communities, a corporatist social organization, and so on. On the contrary, the transmission could lead to a recognition of postwar French sociological or cultural realities, halting the repetition of war imaginaries and shattering prejudices that are often reduced to the level of stereotype. If the latter possibility proves true, one may witness the beginning of a peaceful memorialization of the colonial past where different narratives meet, mix, and even remain in opposition. It could result in clearheaded recognitions freed from excitation and hatred.

Notes

1. *Editor's note:* Le Pen's party, the Front National (FN), and Mégret's breakaway Mouvement National have received electoral scores of over ten percent in

French national elections since the early 1990s. In the mid-1990s, the FN won three mayoral races in second-tier cities in the south of France. In the 2002 first round of the presidential elections, Le Pen won 16 percent of the popular vote, advancing to the second round ahead of the socialist candidate Lionel Jospin.

2.   On the subject of memory of the Algerian War, see Stora 1998. [*Editor's note:* Since the war was officially categorized as a "police action," veterans of Algeria were originally denied *ancien combattant* status and the benefits that accrue to it. Harkis (or "repatriated French Muslims") were Algerian subjects who participated in the French war effort and subsequently "repatriated" to France after the war. *Pied-noirs* were European settlers in Algeria with access to French citizenship who likewise "returned" to France at the end of the war. *Pied-noir* (literally, "black-feet") refers to their birth on African soil.]

3.   *Editor's note:* Vichy refers to the Nazi occupation of France from 1940 to 1944, when former French war hero Maréchal Pétain set up a semiautonomous collaborationist government in southern France with its capital in the spa town of Vichy. The Vichy government enacted many policies of religious and social conservatism that dovetailed with the propaganda of extreme right French political movements, including Charles Maurras' Action Française, the ideological ancestor of the FN. The Vichy government further institutionalized antisemitism and abetted the Nazi deportation of French Jews to concentration and death camps.

4.   *Les Principes du programme,* brochure for the Institut de formation du Front national, 20 February 1989.

5.   *Editor's note:* In this section and throughout the rest of the text, the author uses *sudisme* as an analogical device to refer to two separate moments of French colonialism in Algeria and their parallels in American history. In the first moment, *sudisme* refers to an ideology of Manifest Destiny, by which French colonialists arrogated the right to appropriate Algerian territory on the basis of its underutilization by indigenous populations. This relationship of conquest parallels western expansion in U.S. history and the relationship between white settlers and Native Americans. In the second moment, *sudisme* references more precisely a "Confederate" relation whereby French "southerners" in Algeria distinguished themselves from metropolitan "northerners," and effectively engaged in a civil war to maintain their rule in the colonies. The racialized dynamic of segregation between such "Confederates" and Muslim Algerians parallels that between American Southern whites and blacks in the immediate aftermath of slavery.

6.   *Editor's note:* The OAS, or Organization of the Secret Army, was a breakaway group of French army officers in Algeria who opposed the French government's negotiations with the Algerian National Liberation Front for Algerian independence. Headed by General Raoul Salan, they attempted multiple assassinations of President Charles de Gaulle and, in April 1961, seized power in Algiers during a putsch that lasted four days.

7.   Jacques Roseau, speaking in the first episode of the television documentary, *Les années algériennes,* entitled "Love and Hate," first aired in September 1991 on France 2.

8.   See the military narratives collected in Lucas and Vatin 1975. In *Tartarin de Tarascon* (1890), another traveler, Alphonse Daudet, presents Algeria under a

different, more somber light—he highlights an inefficient administration, depraved caliphs, and colonists addicted to rape and alcohol.

9. During the nineteenth century, an abundant literature explained colonization as the resurrection of a Latin culture during a "dark era of Islam." (See the work of Louis Bertrand and/or Ernest Mercier. Both provide a genealogy of the Algerian *melting pot*.)

10. In 1954, only 35 percent of French Algerians had a standard of living higher than the average standard of living in the metropole; 25 percent had an equal standard of living; 72 percent earned 15–20 percent less, even though the cost of living in Algeria was not lower than in France.

11. In September 1998 during its annual Bleu-Blanc-Rouge party, the National Front hosted a delegation from the Council of Conservative Citizens, an association from the U.S. South, a Klu Klux Klan–type organization that was waging an active anti-Clinton campaign.

12. This speech can be compared to the early days of the military conquest of Algeria, which Eric Savarese (1998: 198) describes as "The progressive conquest of Algeria. Sanctioned by the French victory over the Emir, it permitted the establishment of a *Second France* under the African sun."

13. Ze'ev Sternhell (1998) has shown the presence of fascist ideas in France since the end of the nineteenth century. He contests the commonly held notion that the French Revolution allowed France to otherwise escape fascist tendencies that were ultimately imported by the Nazis.

14. In *Les jours innocents* [*Days of Innocence*] (1984), the author journeys from Constantine to Paris via Jerusalem. It is a tale of travels and detours, of ordinary exile expressing the joys and dangers of being simultaneously similar and different from others.

15. In *Alger l'amour* [*Algiers My Love*] (1982), Vircondelet returns to his childhood home and the family burial plot. In this work of mourning a lost land emerges tragic images of the Algerian War.

16. Former Chief of Staff for General Massu, Argoud was head of OAS operations in France. He was kidnapped by French intelligence agents on 25 February 1963.

17. Born in Bizerte in 1938, Buscia was an Algerian paratrooper who joined the OAS in 1961, headed operations in Corsica, and then directed OAS Métro. He was linked to assassination attempts against President Charles de Gaulle and Prime Minister Georges Pompidou. He is the author of *Au nom de l'OAS, requiem pour une cause perdue* [In the Name of the OAS: Requiem for a Lost Cause] (1981).

18. Former network chief of the "Actions et Renseignements" (Actions and Intelligence) wing of the OAS, Curutchet described the preparations for the 1960 and 1961 French putsches in his work *Je veux la tourmente* [I Crave the Tempest] (1973).

19. *Editor's Note:* In colonial Algeria, citizenship was restricted to Algerian Muslims who had given up their "personal status" of Islam, who had apostatized themselves and declared their loyalty to the French Republic.

20. Nearly 2,500 words were devoted to the subject of the Algerian War. On this question, see Stora 1997.

21. See the editorial by Hassan Zerrouky in the Algerian newspaper *Le Matin* (June 1999).

22. *Editor's note:* In October 1997, Maurice Papon was brought up on criminal charges for his participation in the deportation of French Jews to death camps during his tenure as Interior Minister under the Vichy regime. While the trial did not officially concern his subsequent role in the October 1961 massacres, the media and popular demonstrations made the connection evident.

23. Survey published in the Moroccan newspaper *Al-Bayane* on 1 June 1999.

24. In 1992, a high court injunction set into motion the famous case of the Islamic headscarf. This case gave secularism (*laïcité*) a pluralist character and allowed for the public expression of religious choice previously relegated to the private sphere. [*Editor's note:* In January 2004, new legislation was passed overriding the 1992 decision and banning the *hijab* from French public schools. This amounted to a reversion to assimilationist understandings of *laïcité.*]

References

Allouche, Jean-Luc. 1984. *Les jours innocents*. Paris: Lieu Commun.

Bahloul, Joëlle. 1992. *La maison de mémoire. Ethnologie d'une demure judéo-arabe en Algérie, 1937–1961*. Paris: Métaillé.

Benoist, Gustave. 1886. *De l'instruction et de l'éducation dans la province de Constantine*. Paris: Hachette.

Burdeau, Antoine. 1892. *L'Algérie en 1891*. Paris: Hachette.

Buscia, Gilles. 1981. *Au nom de l'OAS, requiem pour une cause perdue*. Nice: Lefeuvre.

Charef, Mehdi. 1989. *Le Harki de Meriem*. Paris: Mercure de France.

Chevènement, Jean-Pierre. 1975. *Le vieux, la crise, le neuf*. Paris: Flammarion.

Curutchet, Jean-Marie. 1973. *Je veux la tourmente*. Paris: Laffont.

Daudet, Alphonse. 1890. *Tartarin de Tarascon*. Paris: Flammarion.

Djebar, Assia. 1985. *L'amour, la fantasia*. Paris: Lattès.

Etcherelli, Claire. 1967. *Elise ou la vraie vie*. Paris: Gallimard.

Gauchon, Pascal, and Patrick Buisson. 1987. *OAS, les plus beaux textes de l'Algérie française*. Bièvres (France): Editions JPN.

Gervereau, Laurent, Pierre Milza, and Emile Temime. 1998. *Histoire de l'immigration en France au XX siècle*. Paris: BDIC Somogy.

Girault, Arthur. 1907. *Principes de colonization et de législation sociale*. Paris: Sirey.

Giudice, Fausto. 1992. *Arabicides, une chronique française, 1970–1991*. Paris: La Découverte.

Hureau, Joëlle. 1987. *La mémoire des pieds-noirs*. Paris: Orban.

Kenzi, Mohamed. 1984. *La menthe sauvage*. Lutry (Switzerland): J.-M. Bouchain.

Kettane, Nacer. 1985. *Sourire de Brahim*. Paris: Denoël.

Lacroix, Jean-Michel. 1996. *Histoire des Etats-Unis*. Paris: Presses Universitaires de France.

Larcher, Emile. 1903. *Traité élémentaire de législation algérienne*. Paris: A. Rousseau.

Le Pen, Jean-Marie. 1990. Editorial. *L'identité* (March–April).

———. 1985. *La France est de retour*. Paris: Carrère.

Lucas, Philippe and Jean-Claude Vatin. 1975. *L'Algérie des anthropologues*. Paris: Maspero.

Menuet, Michel. 1999. Editorial. *Le Monde*. 18–19 July 1999.

Pélégri, Jean. 1999. *Les étés perdues*. Paris: Seuil.

Rollat, Alain. 1985. *Les hommes de l'extrême droite: Le Pen, Marie, Ortiz et les autres*. Paris: Calmann-Lévy.

Savarese, Eric. 1998. *L'ordre colonial et sa légitimation en France métropolitaine*. Paris: Harmattan.

Smaïl, Paul. 1997. *Vivre me tue*. Paris: Balland.

Sternhell, Ze'ev. 1998. *La Droite révolutionnaire*. Paris: Gallimard.

Stora, Benjamin. 1998. *La gangrène et l'oubli*. Paris: La Découverte.

———. 1997. *Dictionnaire des livres de la guerre d'Algérie*. Paris: Harmattan.

———. 1992. *Ils venaient d'Algérie. L'immigration algérienne en France, 1912–1992*. Paris: Fayard.

Temime, Emile, ed. 1991. *Migrance, histoire des migrations à Marseille*. Vol. 4. Aix-en-Provence: Edisud.

Villanueva, Michèle. 1992. *L'Echarde, chronique d'une mémoire d'Algérie*. Paris: Maurice Nadeau.

Vircondelet, Alain. 1982. *Alger l'amour*. Paris: Presse de la Renaissance.

Part Three.   *Archaeology of Memory*

7 Can the Subaltern Remember? A Pessimistic View of the Victims of Zionism

Gabriel Piterberg

IN MEMORY OF EDWARD W. SAID

The chapter is concerned with two instances of violence and their interplay with memory. The first is a reading of documentation produced by the agencies of the nascent Israeli bureaucracy that played an important role in creating the horrifically effective abstraction known as "the refugee problem," a "problem" created during and after the 1948 war. Concretely, I read some textual production of the Israeli establishment's Arabists and Orientalists in the context of the expulsions of the 1948 war and its aftermath, and the attendant enterprise of rendering the refugees memory-less objects and the land impossible to remember as Arab. The second instance is an interpretation of a relatively recent Israeli documentary, which deals with the settlement Yemeni Jews in Kineret (on the southwestern shore of Lake Galilee) and their expulsion by the later, East European, settlers of the Second *Aliya*.[1] The events occurred in the 1910s and 1920s, but memory still lingers.

The argument I wish to sustain deals with each of the cases separately and then relates one to the other. From the mainstream Israeli vantage point, the physical and discursive "Zionization" of Palestine was on the whole successful. From a Palestinian perspective, it made the land, landscape, and geography virtually irrecoverable memory in concrete ways. Dialectically, however, this success has given birth to what is embodied in the discourse of the *Nakba* (Catastrophe), which is an indomitable countermemory to the Israeli Independence, an attempt to resist erasure. In this respect, however, the chapter's focus is more the history of erasure than the history of the attempts to resist it. The memory of the Yemeni Jews, I show, has also been subjected to a dialectical process, albeit of a different nature. In order to obtain what is presumed to be a legitimate memory, they have had to claim a retroactive recognition as Zionist pioneers (*halutzim*). In other words, the memory the surviving Yemenis, their offspring, and sympathizers have forged and embraced, is the one that those who had expelled them from Kineret constructed.

The attempt to relate to one another these two instances of violence and memory may offer an interesting perspective on the nature of the Israel as a case of a state that is the product of European settlers' nationalism. The conclusion, it will be suggested, is that in such a case, in order to be able to challenge the inherently exclusionary nature of the state and make it more universally inclusive, subalterns must somehow gain distance from it without being completely absent. What remains otherwise, as the critical attempt of the Yemeni Jews to remember and be remembered will illustrate, is to be accepted by the hegemonic state without really challenging the hegemony itself.

The ideological context of the discussion that will unfold is the Zionist foundational myth that underlies Israeli politics and culture even today. It consists of three components: the negation of exile (*shelilat ha-galut*), the return to the land of Israel (*ha-shiva le-Eretz Yisrael*), and the return to history (*ha-shiva la-historia*). Because these components are inextricably intertwined, I stress the way they relate to each other. There are no neutral definitions, of course, and the one offered here is rather basic but from a clearly critical perspective.[2]

The Zionist story of "how we have gotten to where we are and where we should go henceforth," known in scholarly parlance as master-narrative, is founded upon the negation of exile. This myth establishes continuity between an ancient past in which Jewish national sovereignty over the land of Israel existed, and a present that is the renewal of that past in the shape of the Zionist colonization of and settlement in Palestine. Separating the ancient past from its reincarnation in the present is a sort of interim period (a rather long one, it might be noted): the period of exile.

The negation of the period of exile, albeit in various ways and varied degrees of rigidity, is shared by all Zionists and is founded upon their uncontestable presupposition: from time immemorial the Jews have constituted a territorial nation. It follows that a non-territorial existence of Jews must somehow be abnormal, incomplete, and inauthentic. Exile as a historically experienced period in and of itself is devoid of significance. Although it might give birth to important cultural achievements, exile could not, by definition, have been a wholesome and authentic realization of the nation's *Geist*. Jews as individuals and Jewish communities, according to the negation of exile, had a partial and, most significantly, transitory existence. They were waiting to be redeemed and "ascend" (make *aliya*) to the land of Israel, the only site on which the nation's destiny could fully materialize. Within this mythical framework, for exilic Jews to be in an existentially ephemeral state of mind, meant that they were potential or proto-Zionists: their existence was always accompanied by an immanent urge "to return" to the land of Israel.

The second component of the foundational myth, the return to the land of Israel, complements the first and is central to our discussion. With increasing intensity after the irrevocable rejection of the Uganda Plan in 1905, Zionist institutions, and later the state of Israel, have invested tremendous efforts in "reclaiming" what they consider the site to which they return both materially and ideologically. If the negation of exile depicted non-territorial Jewish existence as partial, inauthentic, and abnormal, the return to the land of Israel would rectify and remedy all this. In Zionist terminology, the myth of return promised to deliver the normalization of the Jews individually and collectively. However, normalization through territorial sovereignty would be attained only by returning to a particular site: the land of Israel according to the biblical story, and its elaboration in Protestant culture in the eighteenth and nineteenth centuries.

The site designated for the re-enactment of Exodus, the land of Israel, was also constructed as empty. The claim that Zionist leaders and settlers had assumed that Palestine was literally empty, that they were ignorant of the Arab presence there, or that they ignored it is a misconception that still prevails in some quarters. The emptiness of the land is, it cannot be overemphasized, a construction of nationalist–colonial ideology. It has two main characteristics. The first is that together with the Jewish nation, the land of Israel too was in exile as long as there had not been Jewish sovereignty over it. The land being in exile should also not be understood literally: it means that it too did not have a meaningful and authentic history, that it too was awaiting redemption. That is why the return to the land of Israel is so clearly a concomitant of the negation of exile. Their combination culminates in a twofold negation: (1) of the historical experience of Jews in exile and, (2) of the historical experience of Palestine without Jewish sovereignty. That is also why the well-known Zionist slogan, "a land without a people to a people without a land," is so uniquely quintessential.

The emptiness of the land on the one hand and the recognition that it was inhabited by natives on the other were "harmonized" by forging a typically colonial hierarchy with regard to the historical custody over that land. This hierarchy was, again, seen to derive from the Bible (by putatively secular nationalists). It accorded the settling Jews—by virtue of the fact that they were returning—such exclusive privileges as ownership and historical rights, and at the same time rendered the Palestinian Arabs part of the natural environment. In modern masculine Hebrew culture, to know a woman in the biblical sense and to possess her, and the knowledge and possession of the land, became almost interchangeable.[3] Put differently, as far as the land of Israel was concerned, the Zionist settlers became sovereign subjects who acted, and the native Palestinians became objects who were acted upon.

In a way the return to history is another formulation with different accents of the previous two components. According to the return to history, Jews as a collective had been outside of history, within which all European nations had been all along, because they had been in exile. In this sense, Zionism fundamentally embraced and reiterated the Christian view of Judaism as it was secularized by the Enlightenment's concept of modern historical consciousness. Only nations that dwell in the soil of their homeland, gain sovereignty, and are therefore responsible for their own destiny and can shape it, have history by this logic. The return of the Jewish nation to the land of Israel by negating its docile and passive existence in exile would not only result in normalization, but would also engender its return to the history of civilized nations.

Retroactive Transfer

The present discussion is indebted to an excellent study by Haya Bombaji-Sasportas (Bombaji-Sasportas 2000).[4] Inspired by critical approaches to colonial knowledge, Bombaji-Sasportas interprets the ways in which the Israeli bureaucratic and academic textual production and practices played a significant role in the construction of the expelled Palestinians as an abstract problem—by incessantly classifying and categorizing them (as a "humanitarian issue," as "friendly versus hostile," as "urban versus rural," and other analogous categories) —and ultimately in their objectification and dispossession. Continuing this line of thought, I illustrate the workings of the attempt to make sure that Arab Palestine, at least the part of it that came under Israeli sovereignty after 1948, was something that at best could be remembered by absence and at worst could not be remembered at all.

It is appropriate to commence with comments on the emptying of what would become the state of Israel from the majority of its Palestinian population and, concretely, on the debate of whether or not there had been an Israeli master plan to perpetrate a comprehensive transfer of the Palestinian Arabs.[5] The debate's implicit assumption must be brought to the fore: expulsions not emanating from a master plan are morally superior to expulsions that constitute a systematic execution of a master plan, for each case evinces a qualitatively different depth of intentions. There is, first, in this obsessive search for a master plan a problematic privileging of the perspective of the perpetrators and a disregard for the perspective of the victims. Although the existence of an explicit Israeli intention—or lack thereof—to cleanse Palestine from Arab presence is an important question, from the point of view of the Palestinian victims the result is what matters most. For those Palestinians who lost their homes, property, rights, and identity, it matters less how this occurred: as a result of an officially conceived master plan of massive transfer; the initiative of military commanders on the spot and local bureaucrats, who implicitly understood that this was the intention of the political leadership; as a result of atmosphere and ideology that rendered massive transfers desirable; or any combination of the above. What matters to them most is, presumably, the fact of being refugees and dispossessed. More generally, only the victor can afford the luxury of purgatory rituals that purify bad conscience. The victim is forced to face the results.

Second, the possibility of massive transfer (whether strategically conceived or improvised and haphazard) was inherent in the evolution and nature of the Zionist colonization of Palestine prior to the unfolding of the 1948 war. To begin with, the state of mind underpinned by the foundational myth of the return to the land of Israel was amenable to such a course of action. Then there was the actual consideration of the notion of transfer long before 1948; and from the late 1930s, after the report of the Peel Commission, transfer became more than an abstract idea (Masalha 1992, 1999). As Ze'ev Sternhell correctly observes, Zionism was, among other things, a typical case of Central and East European organic nationalism (Sternhell 1998: 3–47). This kind of nationalism was especially feral in its insistence on ethnic homogeneity. Bearing in mind the fact that the possibility of a bi-national state was resoundingly rejected by the Zionist movement as well as the decisions it adopted in the 1940s, when one looks at the demography of the 1947 Partition Plan one must conclude that the establishment of as exclusively as possible a Jewish state and the transfer of the Palestinians were two sides of the same coin. No one has put it more succinctly and prophetically than Hannah Arendt in 1945:

> The Atlantic City Resolution [October 1944] goes even a step further than the Biltmore Program (1942), in which the Jewish minority had granted minority rights to the Arab majority. This time the Arabs were simply not mentioned, which obviously leaves them the choice between voluntary emigration and second-class citizenship. (Arendt 1945 [1978]: 131)

Third, the excessive emphasis upon the explicit and intentional transfer scheme is not only morally questionable but also factually misleading. What in hindsight might be deemed the most meaningful explicit decision taken by an Israeli government—as distinguished from individual officials and bureaucratic agencies—regarding the Palestinian–Zionist dispute was not systematically to expel all Palestinians. Rather, the crucial decision was *to prevent them from returning* to their homes at all costs, regardless of the circumstances in which they had "left," and no matter how clearly their "departure" intended to be temporary and tentative.[6]

This should not be taken be mean that there were no massive expulsions, such as the infamous Operation Danny (10–14 July 1948) that resulted in the Lydda massacre and the transfer of the entire population of the cities of Ramlah and Lydda (10 miles southeast of Tel Aviv) to Jordan (Morris 1991: 272–283). The point is that the conscious and explicit decision was, amidst an unfolding Palestinian collapse, to make sure that this collapse was irreversible. The temporary cabinet became heedful of this with the fall of Haifa in April 1948. By June of that year, the foreign minister and darling of Israeli moderates until today, Moshe Sharett (then Shertock), articulated it as a policy in no uncertain terms:

> To my mind this is the most surprising thing: the emptying of the country by the Arab community. In the history of the land of Israel this is more surprising than the establishment of the Hebrew State itself . . . This has happened amidst a war that the Arab nation declared against us, because the Arabs fled of their own accord—and their departure is one of those revolutionary changes after which history does not revert to its previous course, as we see from the outcome of the war between Greece and Turkey. We should be willing to pay for land. This does not mean that we should buy holdings from each and every [Arab]. We shall receive assets and land, which can be used to help settle Arabs in other countries. But they do not return. And this is our policy: they do not return. (Morris 1991: 43)

Owing to their particular ways of thought and expression, bureaucrats sometimes come up with chillingly succinct and apt terms. Yosef Weitz, the most relentless proponent of transfer (Morris 1986) and director of the Jewish National Fund's Land Department, serves as an outstanding example. As early as 28 May 1948, in an in entry in his diary on a meeting with Sharett, Weitz created a narrative with a single bureaucratic term: retroactive transfer (*transfer be-di'avad*).[7] Weitz, who at that point also headed a semiofficial transfer committee of three members, asked Sharett whether he thought an orderly action should be taken to make the occasion of the Arabs "leaving" the country an irreversible fact, and defined the result of such an action a "retroactive transfer." According to Weitz, Sharett replied in the affirmative.

Weitz's term underlay the nonpublic discourse of Israeli officials and politicians. From the collapse of Arab Haifa in April 1948 as a possible marker, and with increasing intensity and ferociousness during the fall of that year, the Israeli part of Palestine was becoming Arabless without there having been a an explicit master plan to transfer the occupied population. The ways in which this "Arablessness" initially came into being varied from the fleeing of the wealthy, through the temporary movement of civilians away from areas where heavy fighting was expected, and encouragement of such movement by the Israeli army by means of violence, terror and propaganda, to full-fledged expulsions.[8] What is amply documented and demonstrable is precisely this intentional policy of "retroactive transfer"; it is, moreover, this policy that was systematized, bureaucratized, and legalized in the 1950s with far-reaching consequences for both Palestinians and Jews within and without Israel, and for the nature of the Israeli state. Even today, what fundamentally underpins the nature of the state is the return of Jews and the nonreturn of Arabs. If this return–nonreturn dynamic disappeared, the state would lose its hegemonic identity. A rhyme attributed to Mahmoud Darwish captures this dynamic very precisely: "*La ya'ud ila al-Yahud* (No one returns but the Jew)."[9]

Erasure

Physically, during the 1948 war, the work of implementing the policy of no return consisted in the demolition of occupied villages and, to some extent, urban neighborhoods, the settlement of Jews in places rendered Arab-free, and the confiscation of land and property. This policy was completed and made systematic and legal in the 1950s, and it affected both the refugees outside Israel and those Palestinians whom the state defined as citizens and some as present absentees (this category will be discussed later; Morris 1991: 213–265 and Bombaji-Sasportas 2000: 113–121). The physical erasure of Arab existence in order to realize the policy of no return was also discursive. The producers of this component comprised a group of officials, who, in one or another way, had gained what was considered authoritative knowledge and expertise on "the Arab question." The knowledge that gave authority to their views and memoranda was Orientalist, and it was acquired in two main ways. One was through various activities among and interactions with Arabs in the pre-state period in the spheres of diplomacy (in the foreign policy department of the Jewish

Agency) or intelligence (in the intelligence unit of the Haganah, the SHAY [Hebrew: *Sherut Yediʿot;* English: *Information Service*]). The people thus "trained" knew mostly spoken Arabic, took pride in being field experts, and were known as Arabists (*Arabistim*). The other way through which this knowledge was gained was with formal higher education in European universities, mostly German ones, and/or at the Hebrew University. These more highly educated officials knew written Arabic (*fusha*), assumed that they had a wider and deeper perspective than their field counterparts, and were known as Orientalists (*mizrahanim*). When the state was established, most of them could be found in the intelligence community, in the research and Middle East departments of the Foreign Office, or as advisors on "Arab affairs" to the prime minister (Bombaji-Sasportas 2000: 17–22; Beinin 1995: 179–201; Eyal 1993: 39–55).

The subjectivity of the Palestinian refugees was undermined in variegated ways, one of which was to define their plight as humanitarian and then to tie it inextricably to an overall resolution of the Arab-Israeli conflict, with the hope and knowledge that such a resolution was not forthcoming. Bombaji-Sasportas correctly observes that this early Israeli strategy was instrumental in the objectification of the refugees, and that the construction of this Gordian knot has been accepted as a given state of affairs by Israeli scholarship, both the establishment-oriented and the critical (Bombaji-Sasportas 2000: 31–33). From a different perspective, Asher Goren of the Israeli Foreign Office also noted this. In a memo that summarized the various positions on the refugees (27 September 1948), he reiterates the purportedly objective connection between the Arab–Israeli conflict as a whole and the Palestinian refugees, and concludes by saying that "The compromise-seekers [among Arab statesmen] want return [of the refugees to their homes]. The warmongers object it. The will of the refugees is unknown nor does anyone ask them."[10]

The transfer committee formulated for the first time what would later become the official Israeli narrative of the "refugee problem." This semiofficial body was headed by Weitz, and it submitted its first report in November 1948.[11] The committee's main function was not to establish a narrative, of course, but to oversee the execution of the policy of nonreturn by, first of all, the systematic demolition and erasure of Palestinian villages and urban neighborhoods, and then by the systematic seizure of land and property owned by Palestinians. The report was a massive project that contained detailed information on the Palestinians and the activities of the committee. The textual purpose was to lead to the inevitable conclusion, underlain by the guise of narrative objectivity and authority, that the Palestinian refugees would not be allowed to return to their homes, and that the only solution would consequently be their resettlement in Arab countries. In hindsight, this report may be seen as a sort of Ur-text of the Israeli discourse—academic, political, and bureaucratic—on the "refugee problem" at least until the publication of Benny Morris's work beginning in the late 1980s.

This narrative was what the state officially presented for propaganda and foreign policy purposes. The untruthfulness of this narrative is evident; it might also be plausible to suggest that the contemporaries who shaped it knew that it was fraudulent.[12] According to this narrative, the Palestinians themselves, their leadership as well as that of the Arab states, bear sole responsibility for the creation of the "refugee problem." Arab and Palestinian leaders, the Mufti of Jerusalem Hajj Amin al-Husayni most notably, had advised the Palestinians temporarily to leave their homes, return with the victorious Arab armies and claim not only their own property but also that of the defeated Jews. It was therefore the responsibility of the Arab states to see that the refugees were resettled in their countries. This resettlement was justified by the historical responsibility for the displacement, as well as the "scientific fact" that Arab societies were the only appropriate space for the refugees, since the nature of Palestine had been transformed, and by the fact that Israel was now preoccupied with the absorption of Jewish refugees who had had to flee from those Arab countries.[13]

To understand how the policy and discourse of nonreturn tried to eradicate Palestinian memory, it is best to examine concrete cases and documents. One is Tel Aviv University. Zvi Yavetz is professor emeritus of Roman history, one of the founders of that university, especially of its faculty of humanities and school of history, and has been one of the university's most influential associates for three decades. In a recent article, Yavetz reminisces about the foundation of Tel Aviv University, the negotiations with academics, politicians, and bureaucrats, and the role he played in this procedure. In passing, he mentions that at one point a decision was taken to move the nascent university from its provisional lodgings at the heart of Tel Aviv to Shaykh Muʾnis (Yavetz 1995: 101–129).

In the deliberations of early May 1948 that followed the fall of Haifa, Golda Meir (then Myerson) too mentioned Shaykh Muʾnis. Speaking at the Central Committee of MAPAI (the hegemonic labor party), she wished to launch a thorough discussion on the "Arab question," and, concretely, on what to do with locations such as Haifa that had become substantially Arabless. In presenting her views, she incidentally introduced a meaningful distinction that would become prevalent among officials, politicians, and army officers, between "hostile" and "friendly" villages, and correspondingly, whether and how to apply the policy of nonreturn. Implying that the distinction she drew ought to entail different Israeli attitudes, Meir said:

> What do we do with the villages that were deserted . . . without a battle by [Arab] friends? Are we willing to preserve these villages so that their inhabitants may return, or do we wish to erase any trace [*limhok kol zekher*] that there [ever] was a village in a given place? (Morris 1991: 185)

She further stated that it was unthinkable to treat villagers who had fled because they did not want to fight the Yishuv (the said meeting took place on 11 May, four days before the declaration of the state), "like Shaykh Muʾnis," in the way that "hostile villages" had been treated (Morris 1991: 185), strongly suggesting that the policy of "retroactive transfer" was already being implemented. The inhabitants of Shaykh Muʾnis did not gain much from being classified as "friendly." Until late March 1948 the leaders of this large village north of Tel Aviv prevented Arab irregulars from entering the community, and even loosely collaborated with the Hagana. Then, however, the Irgun abducted five of the village's notables. Shaykh Muʾnis was consequently deserted en masse (30 March 1948), and the town literally disappeared. This incident was confirmed three months later by an IDF intelligence source (Morris 1991: 165). Golda Meir's seemingly poignant question in early May, on what was to be done with a friendly village like Shaykh Muʾnis, was asked with the full knowledge that it had ceased to exist at the end of March, and is a typical example of soul-searching à la Labor Zionism: crocodile tears shed over a fait accompli.

Back to Professor Emeritus Yavetz and Tel Aviv University. Ex-Shaykh Muʾnis became part of an affluent neighborhood at the northern end of Tel Aviv, named Ramat Aviv. In the 1960s, Tel Aviv University was built on precisely the site where Shaykh Muʾnis had been less than twenty years earlier. Yavetz, a well-known leftist (in the Israeli context) and 1948 veteran, does not utter a word about what Shaykh Muʾnis had been before it became Tel Aviv University. From 30 March 1948, Shaykh Muʾnis simply could not be remembered, for it was literally not there; since the 1960s, the absence of Shaykh Muʾnis has been Tel Aviv University.

There is one twisted, colonial exception. As the university grew larger and wealthier, a luxurious VIP club was built in the 1990s called the Green House. The architecture is the particular Orientalist Israeli version of an "Arab house," and the site is a hill where the house of the *mukhtar* of Shaykh Muʾnis had once been. The information on the past of the site, and who owned it, may be found in the menu of the Green House.

More generally, the Israeli officials were cognizant of the significance of memory and the need to erase it. Shamai Kahane composed one of the most striking documents in this respect. Kahane was a high-ranking official in the foreign office. In 1953–1954 he was the personal and diplomatic secretary to the minister of foreign affairs (Sharett). Kahane was considered a foremost authority on "the refugee problem," and was a pivotal figure in the creation of the huge body of knowledge housed in the foreign office on the Palestinian refugees, known as "Operation Refugee File."[14] The attempt to eradicate Palestinian memory was systematized in the first few years after the 1948 war. Kahane was then a senior official at the research unit of the foreign office's Middle East department. His initial suggestion was put forth in a letter he addressed to the acting director of the Middle East department, Ziamah Divon, on 7 March 1951. Here is the text of the letter:[15]

PROPAGANDA AMONG THE REFUGEES IN ORDER TO SOBER THEM FROM ILLUSIONS OF RETURN TO ISRAEL

You should be efficiently assisted by propaganda of photos that would very tangibly illustrate to them [the refugees] that they have nowhere to return. The refugees fancifully imagine that their homes, furniture and belongings are intact, and they only need to return and reclaim them. Their eyes must be opened to see that their homes have been demolished, their property has been lost, and Jews who are not at all willing to give them up have seized their places. All this can be conveyed in an indirect way that would not provoke feelings of vengeance unnecessarily, but would show reality as it is, however bitter and cruel.

Ways of infiltrating such material: a brochure or a series of articles accompanied by photos published in Israel or abroad, in a limited circulation that would not make waves in the non-Arab world, but would find its way to Arab journalists who by prearrangement would bring the pertinent materials within it to the notice of the refugees. Another way: to print the photos with appropriate headings (the headings are what matters!) in a brochure that was supposedly published in one of the Arab countries. The photographic material should draw a contrast between Arab villages in the past and how they look today, after the war and the settlement of Jews in the abandoned sites. These photos ought to prove that the Jewish settlers found everything in ruins and have put a great deal of work into restoring the deserted villages, that they tie their future to these places, look after them and are not at all willing to give them up.

There is a certain risk in this proposal, but I think that its benefits would be greater than any damage it could do, and we should consider very carefully how to carry it out efficiently.

The significance of Kahane's letter is not limited to propaganda. It is a faithful illustration of the state of mind of the Israeli establishment, to the extent that it strove to transform the consciousness and memory of its victims. The letter was a preamble to a thorough report on every imaginable aspect of "the refugee problem" that Kahane prepared in 1951.[16] The immediate context of the report was the activity of the UN Appeasement Committee during that year and the conference it sponsored in Paris. The report reiterated the by-now familiar Israeli narrative and policy. Its remarkable feature regarding power and memory is twofold: (1) the swiftness of the inculcation of the retroactive transfer narrative, to the extent that Palestine's Arab heritage seems retroactively transient; and (2) the rhetoric of this discourse, whereby the undesirability of Palestinian return comes through as an objectively detached state of affairs, not an ideological position and a predicament created by the state itself.

Trying to refute the notion of repatriation, Kahane not only points to the familiar culprit for the creation of "the refugee problem," but he also pretends to be concerned with the well-being of refugees. By doing this, Kahane illustrates how Arabless—as well as unmemorable—Palestine had become in his mind. He comments that "nationally, the growth of an Arab minority will hinder the development of the state of Israel as a national homogeneous state."[17] In an outburst of seeming altruism, Kahane further observes that repatriation is an impractical solution from the refugees' own perspective:

If the refugees had returned to Israel they would have found themselves in a country whose economic, social and political structures differed from those of the country they left behind. The cities and most of the deserted Arab villages have since been settled by Jews who are leaving their ineradicable imprint on them . . . If the refugees had come back to the realities that have developed in Israel, they would have certainly found it difficult to adjust to them. Urban professionals, merchants and officials would have had to wage a desperate battle for survival in a national economy within which all the key positions are held by Jews. Peasants would have been unable, in most cases, to return to their lands.[18]

In terms of simple chronology, the point just made on the swiftness of the events becomes even more remarkable, if it is borne in mind that Kahane was actually reaffirming the content, if less the form, of an earlier report, of 16 March 1949. That report too was written to address the international activity that issued from UN Resolution 194. According the Morris (1991: 340) and Bombaji-Sasportas (2000: 148), its authors seem to have been Michael Komey, director of the department for the British Commonwealth affairs in the foreign office, and Zalman Lifshitz, ex-member of the transfer committee and advisor to the prime minister on land issues.[19] This early report, composed in English, was entitled "The Arab Refugee Problem."[20] Although in terms of information and stance the report is not substantially different from Kahane's, it has a significant rhetorical addition. As with the later report, this, too, underscores the impossibility of Palestinian "repatriation" by an objective, detached, reality-has-changed rhetoric. It adds, however, a tragic emplotment. In this tragic narrative, the predicament of the refugees is latently conveyed as if it were the result of a natural disaster, whose outcome is sad but inevitable and irrevocable. And, of course, it is as if the perpetrator, the state for which the document speaks, and the authors themselves, are outside of what they convey to be mere description (note the use of the passive voice and the impersonal constructions). The ability to acquire the state of mind of the perfectly detached observer this early (March 1949), even for political expediency, is quite striking:

> During the war and the Arab exodus, the basis of their [the refugees'] economic life crumbled away. Moveable property which was not taken away with them has disappeared. Livestock has been slaughtered or sold. Thousands of town and village dwellings have been destroyed in the course of the fighting, or in order to deny their use to enemy forces, regular or irregular; and of those which remain habitable, most are serving as temporary homes for [Jewish] immigrants . . . But even if repatriation were economically feasible, is it politically desirable? Would it make sense to recreate that dual society, which has bedevilled Palestine for so long, until it led eventually to open war? Under the happiest of circumstances, a complex and uncertain situation is created where a single state must be shared by two or more people who differ in race, religion, language and culture.[21]

Present Absentees

Thus far I have used Weitz's chillingly precise term, *retroactive transfer,* as the narrative that tells the story of the Israeli attempt to transform Palestine into an "unreturnable" and unmemorable geography for the "external" refugees during the 1948 war and the first few years of statehood. I now turn to use another such term, which is both administrative and legal, in a similar way for the "internal" refugees: *present absentees* (*nokhehim nifkadim*). The distinction between "external" and "internal" refugees raises a problem of which I am well aware. As Sasportas-Bombaji amply and freshly demonstrates, "external" and "internal" make up but one discursive category among many constructed by the Israeli political and bureaucratic establishment to control, objectify, and ultimately dispossess the refugees.[22] I use them here to show the history of their construction, not to sustain their objective existence.

In general, the history of the term *present absentees* is the history of the dispossession and displacement of those Palestinians who found themselves in the period 1948–1952 within the state of Israel (the estimated number is 160,000). It is also the history of the implicit apartheid features of the state of Israel until today: the interplay between the overt and formal inclusion of the Palestinian citizens within the state, and their tacit and structural exclusion from the same state whose citizens they formally are. It is this dialectic of being formally present but in many crucial ways absent that, like the previous notion of retroactive transfer, makes the legal–administrative definition of present absentees so chillingly accurate.

There is an identifiable context within which the Israeli Palestinian "internal" refugees were forced collectively to remember themselves and their land as present absentees. This historical context was the state-orchestrated campaign to loot the land and property of the "internal" refugees and its concomitant, the legalization of this state plundering in the early 1950s. The category of "absentees" was originally a legal term that identified those refugees who had been "absent" from their homes but "present" within the boundaries of the state as defined in the 1949 Armistice Agreements. The vast majority of the Palestinians thus defined were not allowed to return to their homes and/or reclaim their property and/or seek compensation. The legal category was necessary for the main law that underlay the state practice of loot, namely, the Law of Absentees' Property promulgated in 1950. Essentially, the Law of Absentees' Property was a formalization of a huge land transaction that the state had done with itself. A thinly disguised entity called "the Custodian" was authorized to sell absentees' land defined in Clause 1(b) of that Law to the Development Agency, a governmental body created specifically for this purpose. This agency then sold the lands thus plundered to the Jewish National Fund. At the end of the chain, these lands were privately leased to Jews only (hence the devious procedural significance of the JNF), and gradually became de facto private property and de jure state owned.[23]

If the Law of Absentees' Property defined in legal terms what an absentee was, the fully dialectical predicament, the status of present absentees, was coined in a more literary way by yet another high-ranking official from the foreign office, Alexander Dotan. In the early 1950s, he was in the department of international institutions in the foreign office. When UNWNRA had finished its activities in Israel in the early summer of 1952 and passed responsibility for the "internal" refugees to the Israeli government, Dotan was appointed as the coordinator of the interministerial policies regarding this issue, and as chair of the advisory committee on refugees (July 1952). After some research, Dotan wrote a series of memoranda in November 1952 intended to fill gaps in the knowledge on the refugees, and to suggest solutions for "the refugee problem." The first document (of 9 November 1952) was specifically concerned with the Palestinian refugees within the state of Israel, those who had not been allowed to return to their homes and many of whom dwelt in other Palestinian villages and towns. Dotan identified and defined these people—for the first time it would seem—as "present absentees."[24]

One striking feature in this document is again literary: the tragic emplotment, the seeming empathy, and the objective rhetoric of the author that is reminiscent of the observing, ostensibly detached anthropologist. Dotan's portrayal of how the present absentee remembers through absence is cast as Realism:

> The fundamental problem of the refugee, who is wholly dependent on government policy, is land. The current position is that a refugee will often live in a village in Galilee, adjacent to his deserted lands and village, as if at an observation post. The distance is usually just a few kilometres and, in most cases, the refugees would have been able to cultivate their land from their present place of residence, if they had been allowed to do so, even without returning to the deserted and destroyed village. From his place of observation and present shelter the refugee follows what is happening on his land. He hopes and yearns to return to it, but he sees the new [Jewish] immigrants who are trying to strike roots in the land, or those who have farmed it out from the Custodian, or the way the orchards are gradually deteriorating because no one looks after them. The refugee desires to return to his land, if only to some of it when it is mostly already settled by Jews, and he therefore usually seeks to lease it from the Custodian, something that is denied to him.[25]

Dotan was adamant that, politically and culturally, condemning these Palestinians to forever being present absentees was impossible as a policy. His conclusion, however, was not to grant the right of return and real citizenship at least to the "internal" refugees or the Palestinian Israelis in general. As can be readily seen from the essence of the foundational myths, *return* and *Arabs* or *Palestinians* constituted—still constitute—an unthinkable combination of words within the confines of the Zionist-Israeli discourse. What Dotan had in mind was a comprehensive policy of the assimilation (*hitbolelut*)[26] of the Palestinians into the Jewish–Israeli society and state through the obliteration of their memory, identity, and culture. The starting point of his second memorandum (12 November 1952) was that the problem and solution of the present absentees and the Arab minority as a whole were inseparable. The title, correspondingly, is "Final Solution[27] to the Refugee Problem in Israel and a New Policy toward the Arab Minority."[28]

Critical of the attitude and policies of the state, Dotan warns that they might engender a feeling among the Israeli Palestinians that they are "a persecuted national minority that identifies with the Arab nation."[29] He proposes a new strategy, "which should, on the one hand, aspire to integrate the Arabs into the state by . . . opening to them the gates of assimilation and, on the other hand, this new policy should fiercely combat those who are unwilling or unable to adapt to the [Jewish] state . . . It may be rightly asked what the prospects are that the Arabs would assimilate. This can be answered only through experience, but if one wished to draw a lesson from history one could say that assimilation has been a very common feature in the Middle East since time immemorial."[30]

Indicative of this type of nationalist–colonial consciousness is the way in which Dotan envisaged the *"hitbolelut"* of the Palestinians, the irreversible obliteration of their collective identity:

> The realization of such a new policy requires a comprehensive onslaught upon the Arab minority by both the state and the Jewish public in the country, and it seems that an important instrument of it might be the formation of a secular Jewish cultural mission. The mission would act as the emissary of the Jewish people and Israeli progress in the Arab village. Under no circumstances should party politics be allowed within or through it. This mission would establish special training seminars for Jewish counselors to operate in Arab villages, on the lines of our counselors in the *ma'abarot* [transition camps for Jewish immigrants] or in the new settlements, and like *the missions to the Indian villages in Mexico*. These counselors would infiltrate the villages together with the refugees, who would begin to settle them, and would accompany the refugees from the first day of their installation . . . Missions of two to three male and female counselors for every twenty to thirty villages should suffice to effect agrarian changes within them. Such a mission would reside in a village; teach Hebrew; offer agricultural instruction, medical assistance and welfare; supply social guidance; act as natural mediator between the village and the authorities and the Hebrew community; and keep a security check on everything that happens in and around the village. Such a mission could acquire influence on all village matters and fundamentally alter them within a few years.[31]

Dotan's proposal incurred the wrath of Ben Gurion's powerful and ruthless advisor on Arab affairs, Joshua Palmon, who favored the continuation of oppressive military government in the hope that this would enhance the "retroactive transfer" among the "internal" refugees as well. But Dotan counterargued and proceeded undeterred. His next report, dated 23 November 1952, further developed the idea of Arab assimilation. He added urgency to his idea by mentioning that the pressure on Israel to grant the Arabs "cultural autonomy" may mount. There could hardly be a more tangible example of the conscious attempt to erase Arab Palestine as a memorable geography than the final brick of Dotan's assimilation edifice. He writes to the foreign minister:

> An important tool for us is accelerated reconstruction of ancient geographical names and Hebraicization [*shi'abur*] of Arabic toponyms. In this respect the most important task is to disseminate the practical use of the new names, a process that has run into difficulties among Jews too. In Jaffa the name "Jibaliyya" is still current, although "Giv'at Aliya" is gradually disinheriting it. By contrast, a Hebrew name has not been found yet for "Ajami," and some new immigrants still incorrectly call the Arab neighbourhood within it the "Ghetto" or "Arab Ghetto." It is possible, by being strictly formal and with adequate indoctrination, to make the Arab inhabitants of "Rami" [in the Upper Galilee] get used to calling their village, in speech and writing, "Ha-Rama" (Ramat Naftali), or to make the inhabitants of "Majd al-Krum" [also in the Upper Galilee] become used to calling their village "Beit ha-Kerem." From the inhabitants of what the Arabs called "Shafa 'Amru"

[near Haifa], I have already heard the [Hebraicized] name "Shefarᶜam." (Laor 1995: 132)

"An Unpromised Land"[32]

At the beginning of the twentieth century, some Jewish families from Yemen, led by Rabbi Israel Saʾiri, immigrated to Palestine. In 1912, they settled by the swamp lands of Kineret (Lake Galilee) and lived in the Motor House and its vicinity (the location is the southwestern corner of the lake). In 1913, that land was given, by contract, to a group of settlers from what would later be mythologized as the pioneers (*halutzim*) of the Second *Aliya*. They were to establish the agricultural cooperative of Kineret (*Kevutzat Kineret*); this settlement, too, would acquire a mythical status in the Zionist pantheon of the colonization of Palestine. For a decade the two groups—the Yemenis and East Europeans—lived separately but in relative harmony. In the latter part of the 1920s, the east Europeans deemed the scarcity of water and arable land acute. They applied pressure on the Zionist settling institutions to transfer the Yemenis elsewhere, and to hand over their water allocation and land. In 1930, eighteen years after they had arrived in the Kineret area, the Yemenis were transferred to Rehovot (southeast of Tel Aviv), where they founded the neighborhood of Marmorek. Sitting on the trucks that took them from Kineret to Rehovot, the Yemenis could witness in real time how erasure transformed remembering into forgetting: the comrades of Kevutzat Kineret wasted no time and immediately began to plough the Yemenis' allotments, lest memories lingered.

The documentary *An Unpromised Land* is a powerful, hard-to-watch illustration of colonial–nationalist consciousness and practice. It may also be seen as a proleptic reminder of what would facilitate the expulsion of the Palestinians in 1948 and thereafter, the project of deleting their memories and existence in what became Israel, and the historiography that has sustained and justified this. Since the chief concern of this essay is a critical reading of the hegemonic discourse, my analysis of the documentary film concentrates on the representatives of this discourse. It must be emphasized, however, that the film gives ample voice to the victims and their memories: the old Yemenis who were expelled from Kineret, and their offspring and sympathizers.

Another point should be made clear. In addition to the emotions and memories of the event's protagonists (i.e., those who expelled and those who were expelled), the significance of remembering this event stems from the ideological and cultural magnitude of the site. Kevutzat Kineret, its Second *Aliya* founders, its museum and cemetery, and its environment (Lake Galilee, River Jordan, and palm trees) constitute one of the most venerated shrines of Zionist/Israeli nationalism.[33]

Focusing on the representatives of the hegemonic discourse, I wish now to interpret the texts offered by the film at three levels. The first is a voice from the period when the expulsion took place through a "primary source." The second comprises the voices of Kevutzat Kineret's founders interviewed at the time the film was made, and of members of Kineret's second generation. The third deals with the voices of professional Zionist historiography.

At the first level, the most powerful text is an archival document: a letter addressed in 1929 by Shlomo Kinarti and Benzion Israeli, both revered pioneers, to the Agricultural Center. The letter is read in the film in a narrator's voice:

> There is one thing we shall by no means give up [:] in the plot we have designated for plantation, bananas must be planted this spring. This is the only thing we can do this year to ease the material difficulty and [thwart] the danger of extinction and annihilation. We have had enough of being in confrontation with the whole world, with the Zionist Executive . . . with nature . . . with the Yemenis. We shall not have another plot for planting bananas in the next few years except for this Yemenis' land, and it has to be at our disposal. The importance of this plantation for us needs no elaboration.

What stands out in this forceful document is the distinction between historical subjects (the writers and their addressees), who act upon the world, and objects (the Yemenis), who are acted upon. Demanding to appropriate the Yemenis' land (and implicitly cause their transfer), Kinarti and Israeli presented it as a zero-sum-game: either they got that land or Kevutzat Kineret would perish. But what about the perishing of the Yemenis' settlement (or, for that matter, of many a dozen Arab villages)? The question could not, and cannot, be asked because it was/is unthinkable. Also illuminating is the unselfconscious classification of the obstacles to Kineret's success and prosperity: one category consists in human agents (the Zionist Executive and other institutions); the other is nature, of which the Yemenis are part and parcel.

At the second level there is, first, the voice of the aforementioned Kinarti, now an old man reflecting on the expulsion episode. Two of the texts are especially pertinent. One is near the end of the film, when Kinarti is asked whether he has any regrets about the expulsion he perpetrated. In a decided tone, Kinarti replies that had the same situation recurred he would have acted precisely as he had, because "this [the expulsion] was the Yemenis' salvation" and because "one does not have regrets about a good thing." The other is undiluted, romantic Orientalism: "Personally, I had a really sentimental attitude to the Yemenis. I saw in them an ethnic group, exotic as they say, and I saw in them the real Jews, that's how I imagined. Their language—for they speak in the Yemeni accent—I always thought that maybe this is the language our forefathers used to speak two thousand years ago."

Then, still at the second level, there are the offspring of Kineret's founders, present members of the Kevutza. Aharonik is not just another member. He is the son of the aforementioned Benzion and Haya Israeli. His is the voice of triumphant authority: there is only one absolute truth, which can be found only in the documents of the sort cited above. The location of this authority is unmistakable: "*I have protocols that show* . . . " is Aharonik's favorite rhetoric. His is also the authority to interpret the Yemenis' feelings and how they ought to remember, in a way that is reminiscent—albeit in a cruder fashion—of the British officials and politicians, who, after 1882, appointed themselves to speak in the name and on behalf of Egypt's history (see Said's *Orientalism*). The film shows two old Yemenis who wander around Kineret and its cemetery, occasionally shedding a few tears. Aharonik is reproachful at first: "I think that there is no room for this [feeling of] insult and all these frustrations." He then grants the Yemenis that their tears are "authentic." They are not, however, shed because of "frustration," but "simply because their relatives were buried here in dozens." "It is a matter of nostalgia, a matter of memories," he remarks with an aura of therapeutic authority.

Edna Friedler is another "daughter of Kineret." Her voice illustrates how methodically and fundamentally memories of existence can be eradicated. Filmed on the site where the Yemenis resided, she tells us, in effect, how easily a human site can be rendered part of nature or agriculture. Again, the site could have been an ex-Arab village and the speaker, say, a guide from the Nature Preservation Authority:

> This plot—it was called the Yemenis' Plot. What this Yemenis' Plot is I don't know, I didn't know [as a child]; until this day I don't know unless I read and take special interest . . . There used to be here a kind of thick palm tree, huge, and this was the site of the Yemenis' Plot. I don't even remember what had been here, why it is called the Yemenis' Plot. I've never seen a Yemeni here, and no, as a child it never occurred to me to ask. Maybe, if I had dug in Kineret's history, in the archive, then perhaps it is told or something. But I didn't bother and I know nothing about it.

The last voice at the second level is a dissenting one. Amiram Idleman, whose outward appearance is awkward, seems to be the odd one out. It is evident from the film that once he had heard about the expulsion of the Yemenis and what followed, his activities were highly instrumental in causing the whole affair to resurface. At the same time, his voice anticipates an observation I shall offer below: Idleman's protest is that the Yemenis did not get what they had earned, that is, a *halutzim* (pioneers') memory in the Zionist narrative. He wants, in effect, one and the same memory for the Yemenis and those who expelled them:

> What is being done here is erasure from history. No one can [i.e., has the right to] erase someone else from history. I, as a son of Kineret, had never heard this story until I coincidentally came across it. And I felt that enough had been erased, that pioneers . . . had been erased; they had been erased from history. Who are we to erase them from history? . . . Does anyone here have exclusive possession of history?

The third level is made up of the voices of the professional guardians of state memory and Zionist historiography. An official tour guide offers the first contribution. His text concisely exemplifies colonial nationalism's propensity for getting chronology utterly wrong. He is filmed at the end of a session with visitors to Kineret. Apparently, at the time for questions a Yemeni woman (whose parents, it transpires, were expelled from Kineret), Bat-Sheva Margalit-Weinberg, can no longer restrain herself and explodes: the tour guide is from the kibbutz, she says; this much is evident from his distorted presentation that completely ignores the Yemenis' perspective and feelings. The tour guide then passionately interrupts and says to Bat-Sheva: "But tell me, in the [19]50s, wasn't there a problem when new immigrants [*olim hadashim*] were brought and transferred from one place to another, and today [early 1990s] isn't there a problem with new immigrants?"

For the guide, in whose consciousness Israeli Zionism is so deeply ingrained, there are sovereign historical subjects—the Zionist East European elite—and objects upon which the elite acts: swamps, Palestinians, wastelands, new immigrants, and so on and so forth. It is this consciousness, rather than ignorance or worse, that makes possible the chronologically absurd analogy between the Yemenis, who had settled in Kineret a year *before* the East Europeans, and the new immigrants. The analogy is also made possible, of course, by the fact that both the Yemenis and most of the new immigrants of the 1950s are "Orientals" and therefore natives, who can be objectified, dispossessed, and expelled. The point is highly instructive. What creates the chronologically absurd hierarchy of relation to the land is the foundational myth of the return to the land of Israel; and the sovereign subjects who are enacting the return are the European settlers. The rest—Palestinian Arabs and Oriental Jews—are natives at varying degrees of "native-ness."

The final, highly significant, voice is that of the professional Zionist historian. It is put forth by Professor Anita Shapira, one of the foremost, most gifted articulators of laborite Israeli ideology. Her work and public appearances have earned for her the affectionate title of "the Princess of Zionism." She has one monologue in the film:

> We must not judge people of one period by the norms of people from another period because it is very easy to reach the conclusion that they were intolerable, but they were not intolerable. Within their value system they acted rightly. And they were not guided, for instance, by ethnic motivations. I am confident that, similarly, if a group from Neturey Karta [a radically anti-Zionist sect of Orthodox Jews] had settled there, Orthodox Jews or even just religious Jews, or even members from a *moshava*—non-socialists, and let us come even closer, suppose that there had been there settlers from the [Zionist] labor movement but with slightly different ideals, which had not been congruous with Kineret's social texture, would Benzion Israeli have hesitated to treat them as he treated the Yemenis? I have no doubt that he wouldn't have [hesitated].

Two comments should be made on Shapira's disturbing apologetics. The first is that justification through contextual relativism of what should at most be explained seems to have become a preferred ideological mechanism with Zionist historians (for instance: that the transfer of whole populations on an ethnic/national basis was not considered unreasonable, or evil, in the first half of the twentieth century). Why Shapira and many of her colleagues are oblivious to the ethical danger of this relativism, by which historical actions cannot be judged because they were perpetrated within their contextual value systems, is a rather depressing question. The fact that the East European settlers would have indiscriminately expelled anyone and everyone, and that they would have done so in accordance with their contextual value system, suffices to render what they actually did tolerable. Not a whole lot of sensitivity is needed to remember that six decades ago Jews, Gypsies, homosexuals, and many others were indiscriminately exterminated because they were not deemed congruous with a certain social texture according to a certain contextual value system. The conspicuous absence of this rather basic sensitivity among many a Zionist historian stems from the fact that theirs is a historical consciousness of victorious sovereigns.

The second comment is on the particular sort of justifying context Shapira has in mind. This context is exclusively that of the East European founders of Kevutzat Kineret: they have a vantage point, they have a value system, considerations, and intentions. The Yemenis are typically absent from this omnipotent context: they happened to be there as coincidental, eligible candidates for transfer. They are objects, part of nature, and as such possess neither agency nor history, just like the expelled and dispossessed Palestinians. Shapira's objectification of the Yemenis is not only fundamental, but is also emblematic of most—there are exceptions—Israeli scholars who are politically and socially identified with what is known as the Peace Camp. Within this centrism, atrocities inflicted upon "others" do not matter because they are consequential for the victims (and hence there is no simple, human compassion for them), but because they are consequential for "us," "our image of ourselves," and "how we are seen by our equals in Europe and America." "We" should therefore explain away these actions and put them in their "proper" context. The swiftness with which even a critical discussion of such atrocities becomes a therapeutic session for "us" is quite remarkable.

Conclusion

The problem that begs consideration now is the interplay between two pairs: of violence/memory and inclusion/exclusion. The similarities in the discursive objectification of, pertinently, the Palestinian Israelis and the "Oriental" Israelis are quite striking. No less striking, however, are the ultimate goals of the policies of the Israeli state and its construction of a hegemonic memory. In the case of the Palestinians, the goal, through displacement and denial, has been fundamentally exclusive vis-à-vis a state and a collective that have been defined as exclusively Jewish. In the case of the "Orientals," also through displacement and denial, the goal was ultimately inclusive.

The significance of this is manifold. To focus on the act of remembering, its interplay with the dynamics of inclusion/exclusion produces an interestingly paradoxical result. The Yemenis, however much their eventual inclusion has been problematic, cannot remember outside the discursive confines of the hegemonic memory constructed by the state. In the interpretation of the documentary *An Unpromised Land,* I identified "representatives of the hegemonic discourse" as the subject matter of my analysis. It should now be stated that this phrase is in a way misleading, for the entire film, however purposefully critical, is nonetheless dominated by that hegemonic discourse. The clearest indication of this domination is, typically, a presupposition that is never questioned—by the filmmakers, by those who expelled/were expelled, by the younger generation, or by the historians. That is so not because there is a conspiracy not to question the presupposition, but because the hegemonic discourse renders the questioning unthinkable: granted that the scarcity of water and land had become acute, why was/is it automatic and obvious that the Yemenis, who had settled first in Kineret, had to be transferred and not the East Europeans?

The other indication is the voice of the protesting Yemenis and those sympathetic to their misfortunes (see especially Amiram Idleman's text presented earlier). To be sure, they are all bitter, loaded with painful memories and doubtful as to whether the expulsion was necessary and justifiable. More pertinent to the politics of colonial–nationalist memory, identity, and historiography, however, is what the victims, their relatives and supporters, and the filmmakers wish to gain. And what they wish to gain is a stake in the Zionist narrative of the colonization of Palestine. The purpose, in other words, is that the Yemenis be admitted to the hegemonic Israeli memory as *halutzim* (pioneers). Although the reason for this is obvious, the fact remains that the sympathetic purpose is not to be liberated from the perpetrators of the expulsion but to join them.

I obviously do not wish to suggest that the exclusion of the Palestinian Israelis from the Israeli state and collective has been advantageous or that their lot has been better than that of the "Oriental" Israelis. This exclusion, however, has made it possible for them to remember not only independently from the state-constructed memory but also in opposition to it. Numerous texts, ceremonies, and other articulations of these subversive and dissenting ways of remembering come to mind, among them Mahmoud Darwish's poetry, the prose of Emile Habiby and Antoun Shammas, the annual commemoration of the Land Day (*Yawm al-Ard*, 30 March 1976 and thereafter), and many more. None has been more politically meaningful and effective, however, than the increasingly common remembrance of 1948 as *Nakba* (Catastrophe), in opposition to the Jewish Israeli Independence. No other trope of memory has so successfully conveyed the fact that Palestine/Israel is still binational.

Pessimism is unavoidable, however, and the move from memory to current politics shows that the exclusionary force of the settlers' nation-state has prevailed. It has been successful in co-opting the Mizrahi Jews and in preventing a potential alliance of the nonwhite subalterns. With the exception of groups of progressive intellectuals, the history of potentially mass movements of Mizrahi opposition to the hegemony of the state is a depressing affair. The explosion in the early 1970s of a truly radical working-class movement, the Israeli Black Panthers, which emanated from the poor neighborhoods of Jerusalem such as Musrara and Qatamon (whose Palestinian inhabitants had been expelled in 1948) was quelled by the state, and the next wave wound up with Shas, a reactionary and racist party that, far from considering the Palestinians possible allies, joined in their oppression wholeheartedly.

Finally, the defiant and assertive mood of remembering 1948 as *Nakba* notwithstanding, the traumatic aspect of the memory of 1948 as transfer has not vanished. The massacre of thirteen Palestinian Israelis by the police in October of 2000 is a recent reminder. In his powerful *Present Absentees* (1992), David Grossman was astonished and upset when he realized the depth of this memory. Dr. Nazir Yunis, a distinguished surgeon in a central Israeli hospital, intimated that "There is no [Israeli] Arab who doesn't envision how he will be transferred [note the typical Israeli habit in Yunis's Hebrew of giving Hebrew morphology to foreign words—*eikh yetransferu oto*], and I am not innocent of this fear." Grossman was initially outraged by the fact that Yunis could deem transfer possible and, especially, that he thought people like Grossman would let this happen. After a while, however, Grossman candidly pondered: "Today, in retrospect, I am no longer convinced that the anger I expressed to Dr. Nazir Yunis, when he told me about his transfer-fear, was not a bit excessive and was meant to hide (from myself) the fact that, somewhere deep inside, I knew that his fear was not unfounded" (Grossman 1992: 247–248). Far away from the Middle East in sunny California, in increasingly frequent moments of dark pessimism, I share Grossman's sincere confession and Nazir Yunis's fear.

Notes

1. A wave of laborite and socialist Zionist immigrants to Palestine in the period 1904–1914. Because this group supplied the political Israeli elite, Ben-Gurion most notably, it acquired mythical proportions and exhibiting affiliation with it was politically advantageous.
2. Assisted by: Evron 1986; Myers 1995; Piterberg 1996; Raz-Krakotzkin 1993, 1994; Laor 1994; Barnai 1995; Silberstein 2000.
3. I cannot present an interpretation of Israeli culture here. Laor's critical work (1995) is the best, most sensitive and insightful attempt heretofore to show how the literary establishment has been coopted and mobilized by the state to write the hegemonic memory and delete the memories of the subaltern, the Palestinian first and foremost. See especially pp. 76–105 ("The Sex Life of the Security Forces: On Amos Oz"), and pp. 115–171 ("We Write Thee Oh Homeland").
4. I am deeply grateful to the author for giving me permission to make use of her work, and for making available to me several documents from the Israeli State Archives.
5. The literature on this question is substantial. For notable examples see: Abu-Lughod 1971; Said and Hitchens 1988; Morris 1986, 1987, 1990; Elam 1990; Masalha 1992, 1999; Rogan and Shlaim 2001.
6. Bombaji-Sasportas shares this observation (2000: 54). Morris notices of course the significance of the prevention policy but nonetheless ascribes much importance to whether there was a premeditated policy of transfer (Morris 1991: 148–265).
7. Several scholars notice this term as Weitz coined it. Elam (1990: 39), however, seems to be more aware than others of the narrative-framework offered by it,

and uses *transfer be-diʿavad* as the title of his chapter on this issue in Elam 1990: 31–52.

8. See especially Morris's attempt systematically to classify each and every case on which he could gather information, in Morris 1987 and 1991, in the Maps Appendix and the invaluable index to these maps.

9. Private communication from Itzhak Laor, to whom I am grateful.

10. Israeli State Archives/Foreign Office/Corpus of the Minister and Director General 19-2444, Vol. II, p. 6 (henceforth SA/FO/CMDG).

11. SA/FO/CMDG, 3/2445. This particular file contains documents of the period August–November 1948, including the report of the Transfer Committee. The committee was thus named by Weitz. See also Morris 1986.

12. The latter suggestion is supported by the comparison between this official narrative and the internal, nonpublic discourse that is discussed in this paper. To this one might add retrospective admissions by such high-ranking officials from that period as Yaacov Shimoni, who called it in 1989 "the fraudulent version" (cited by Elam 1990: 48–49, n.17).

13. On the foundational significance of the Transfer Committee and its November 1948 report, see also Bombaji-Sasportas 2000: 55–61, 115–121.

14. For more details on Shamai Kahane, see in Sasportas-Bombaji 2000: 100, 119, 163–168.

15. SA/FO/CMDG 8/2402.

16. SA/FO/CMDG 18/2406.

17. Ibid.

18. Ibid.

19. On the identification of the authors, see Morris 1991: 340, and Bombaji-Sasportas 2000: 148.

20. SA/FO/CMDG 19/2444, Vol. II.

21. Ibid., pp. 4–5.

22. See especially her discussions on "The construction of a body of knowledge and the framing of the refugees as a scientific object" (Bombaji-Sasportas 2000: 44–66), and "The categorization of the refugees," (Bombaji-Sasportas 2000: 67–99).

23. The text of this law is rather long and is accessible in any official collection of the Israeli Parliament's legislation. For critical comments on the law, see Korn 1997: 91–96, and Segev 1984: 93–95.

24. SA/FO/CMDG A/2/2445 (a-948 II).

25. Ibid., p. 4.

26. It is noteworthy that Dotan deliberately uses the term that is so pivotal in the self-justification, even the raison d'être, of the Zionist movement: to prevent the disappearance of the Jewish people through assimilation in the Diaspora.

27. For an official of a state whose justification comprised the Bible and the Holocaust, the use of this particular term is rather striking.

28. SA/FO/CMDG 2/2445 A (a-948 II).

29. Ibid., p. 2.

30. Ibid.

31. Ibid.

32. This is the English title of an Israeli documentary shown on Israeli television (among other venues). The Hebrew title is *A Bowing Palm-Tree* (*Dekel Shefal*

Tzameret), 1992, produced by Amit Brauer, directed by Ayelet Heller, scripted by Rivka Yogev and Ayelet Heller, edited by Rivka Yogev.

33.   It is a case that would neatly fit into both Benedict Anderson's and Pierre Nora's writings on nationalist memory and historical consciousness. See the two chapters Benedict Anderson added to the 1991 edition of *Imagined Communities*, "Census, Map, Museum," and "Memory and Forgetting," and Nora 1989.

References

Abu-Lughod, Ibrahim, ed. 1971. *The Transformation of Palestine: Essays on the Origin and Development of the Arab-Israeli Conflict*. Evanston: Northwestern University Press.

Anderson, Benedict. 1991. *Imagined Communities: Reflections on the Origin and Spread of Nationalism*. London: Verso.

Arendt, Hannah. 1945 [1978]. Zionism Reconsidered. In Hannah Arendt, *The Jew as Pariah: Jewish Identity and Politics in the Modern Age*, ed. Ron Feldman, pp. 131–163. New York: Grove Press.

Barnai, Yaacov. 1995. *Trends in the Study of the Land of Israel, 634–1881*. Jerusalem: Magnes. [Hebrew]

Beinin, Joel. 1995. "Know Thy Enemy, Know Thy Ally." In *Arabs and Jews during the British Mandate*, ed. Ilan Pappé. Givat Habiba: Center for Peace Publications. [Hebrew]

Bombaji-Sasportas, Haya. 2000. Whose Voice Is Heard/Whose Voice Is Silenced: The Construction of the "Palestinian Refugee Problem" in the Israeli Establishment, 1948–1952. M.A. thesis, Ben-Gurion University of the Negev. [Hebrew]

Brauer, Amit, Ayelet Heller, and Rivka Yogev. 1992. *An Un-promised Land (A Bowing Palm-Tree)* [Hebrew documentary film].

Elam, Yigal. 1990. *The Executioners*. Jerusalem: Keter. [Hebrew]

Evron, Boas. 1986. *National Reckoning*. Tel Aviv: Dvir. [Hebrew]

Eyal, Gil. 1993. Between East and West: The Discourse on "The Arab Village" in Israel. *Theory and Criticism* 3: 39–55. [Hebrew]

Grossman, David. 1992. *Present Absentees*. Tel Aviv: Ha-Kibbutz Ha-Meuchad. [Hebrew]

Korn, Alina. 1997. The Arab Minority in Israel during the Military Government (1948–1966). Ph.D. dissertation, Hebrew University of Jerusalem. [Hebrew]

Laor, Yizhak. 1995. *Narratives without Natives*. Tel Aviv: Ha-Kibbutz Ha-Meuchad. [Hebrew]

Masalha, Nur. 1999. A Critique on Benny Morris. In *The Israel/Palestine Question*, ed. Ilan Pappe, pp. 211–220. London: Routledge.

———. 1992. *Expulsion of the Palestinians: The Concept of "Transfer" in Zionist Political Thought, 1882–1948*. Washington, D.C.: Institute for Palestine Studies.

Morris, Benny. 1991. *The Birth of the Palestinian Refugee Problem, 1947–1949*. [Hebrew]

———. 1990. *1948 and After: Israel and the Palestinians*. Oxford: Clarendon Press.

———. 1987. *The Birth of the Palestinian Refugee Problem, 1947–1949*. Cambridge: Cambridge University Press.

———. 1986. Yosef Weitz and the Transfer Committees. *Middle East Studies* 22: 522–561.

Myers, David N. 1995. *Re-inventing the Jewish Past: European Jewish Intellectuals and the Zionist Return to History*. New York: Oxford University Press.

Nora, Pierre. 1989. Between Memory and History: Les Lieux de Memoire. *Representations* 26: 7–25.

Piterberg, Gabriel. 1996. Domestic Orientalism: The Representations of "Oriental" Jews in Zionist/Israeli Historiography. *British Journal of Middle Eastern Studies* 23: 125–145.

Raz-Krakotzkin, Amnon. 1994. Exile within Sovereignty (Part 2). *Theory and Criticism* 4: 113–132. [Hebrew]

———. 1993. Exile within Sovereignty (Part 1). *Theory and Criticism* 4: 23–56. [Hebrew]

Rogan, Eugene, and Avi Shlaim, eds. 2001. *The War on Palestine: Rewriting the History of 1948*. Cambridge: Cambridge University Press.

Said, Edward, and Christopher Hitchens. 1988. *Blaming the Victims: Spurious Scholarship and the Palestinian Question*. New York: Verso.

Segev, Tom. 1984. *1949: The First Israelis*. Jerusalem: Domino. [Hebrew]

Silberstein, Laurence J. 2000. *The Post-Zionism Debates: Knowledge and Power in Israeli Culture*. New York: Routledge.

Sternhell, Zedev. 1998. *The Founding Myths of Israeli Nationalism, Socialism, and the Making of the Jewish State*. Princeton: Princeton University Press.

Yavetz, Zvi. 1995. On the First Days of Tel Aviv University: Memories. *Alpayim* 11: 101–129. [Hebrew]

8   Beirut, a City without History?

Saree Makdisi

The Republic of Lebanon gained its independence in 1943; its history came to a sudden end in 1946. For, according to government education policy, there is no history of Lebanon after 1946, the year in which the official unified history curriculum draws to a close.[1] As a result, students in Lebanese schools that adhere to the state curriculum are taught all about the Phoenicians and the Romans, the Greeks and the Persians, and the various stages of Turkish rule. But about the events, the tragedies, and the triumphs of independent Lebanon they are not told a thing—least of all about the long Lebanese war that began in 1975 and came to a kind of end in 1990, a war that left almost two hundred thousand dead, hundreds of thousands more wounded both physically and psychologically, and a country in ruins. It is true that shortly after the end of the war, the new government mandated the creation of a new history textbook that would bring Lebanese students up to date. Historians supposed to represent the country's various sectarian factions were appointed to work together on the writing of the history book, as though to settle differences in writing that they had been unable to settle on the battlefield.

After several rounds of negotiation and compromise (which threatened to make this the shortest history book ever written, since only those accounts on which all the factions agreed would be included, giving each faction a kind of veto power over the whole project), the first of the new history textbooks, for grades 3 through 6, was delivered to schools in 2001. However, it was promptly recalled by the Ministry of Education, since, even after all the compromise, one of the factions still took issue with the book's treatment of one particular episode in the country's past—namely, the description of the Arab conquest in 636 A.D. as just that: a *conquest*. The textbooks for grades 7 through 9, which were already in production, were never delivered to schools either. Three years later, rumors were again circulating in Beirut that a "new new" official history textbook would soon be made available (see Wettig 2004).

The replacement text has yet to appear, and in the meantime Lebanon remains a country without an official history—that is, a country officially without history—and especially without a history of the war whose aftereffects linger on in our own discordant time. If the general amnesty on war crimes was supposed to enable the writing of the history of the war, the fact that the history has yet to appear thus suggests that the war itself—crimes and all—may not really be over, that its causes and preconditions remain quite fully intact and ready to go into another round. One Lebanese historian noted recently, for example, that the persistence of sectarianism in all aspects of Lebanese social, cultural, and political life gives the lie to the government's repeated proclamations that the war has ended unequivocally. "In my opinion," he writes,

> the most important thing we can do now is to open the way for critical and honest vision based on the acknowledgment of the vicissitudes and pitfalls of this history which persist in spite of the government's claim that the war has ended, in spite of its general amnesty on war criminals from all sects, in spite of its announcement of a unified history textbook, in spite of its reconstruction of the ruined center of Beirut under the slogan "Beirut: An Ancient City for the Future." (U. Makdisi 2001: 49)

A process of historical acknowledgment along terms such as these—one for which South Africa's Truth and Reconciliation Committee is perhaps the appropriate model—has yet to take shape on a large scale. The turbulence following the assassination of former prime minister Rafik Hariri (and several other people) in early 2005 also seemed to serve as a reminder of how easily the country could slide back into civil war. The very fact that many of the key figures in the current political struggle have names harking back to the days of the war does not bode well for the future, even if they have changed sides several times in the past. Indeed, hearing news of Gemayels, Jumblatts, Aouns, and others at it again, against a backdrop of anonymous car bombings, does little to inspire confidence that Lebanon has moved on from where it was in 1975 or 1976 or 1989.

This sense of historical confusion is not limited to the official pronouncements and publications of the Lebanese government, for there is everywhere a widespread denial of the country's recent past. For this reason, a visitor to contemporary Beirut who wishes to buy a postcard to send to friends or relatives will have a great deal of difficulty finding a card other than one of those first printed before the long civil war of 1975–1990. It is virtually impossible to find a postcard showing Beirut in its current state. Instead, one can find dozens of cards showing the city in its former glory, presenting, for example, images of Martyrs' Square bustling with cars and people in the 1950s, of the gleaming Phoenicia Hotel in its heyday in the 1960s, or of the crowded streets of the commercial center in the years before the war. Virtually every bookstore, corner stationery, and magazine stall in Beirut faithfully maintains its rotary stand of prewar postcards; sometimes the stand will be set to one side, or banished to the inner regions of the shop, or allowed to gather dust and cobwebs; but almost always it will be there.

In these postcards, reprinted in the thousands long since 1975, Beirut has been frozen in time. In most cards, one can see streams of cars that are dominated by the rounded Mercedes sedans that crowded the streets of the city at the time; one card shows Beirut International Airport as it stood just before nine o'clock in the morning one sunny day in the summer of 1952 or 1962 or 1972. With the widely disseminated postcard of Riad al-Solh Square, one can be rather more precise in the dating: there is the cinema marquee announcing the Costa-Gavras film *Z*, starring Yves Montand and Irene Papas, which was released in 1969. One does not, however, find among such cards an image of Beirut in 1976 or 1982 or 1990—or for that matter 2005. In the story these cards tell, time might just as well have stopped at the beginning of the long Lebanese war in 1975. Indeed they express the general reluctance (surely not limited to Beirut's postcard distributors and newspaper vendors) not simply to remember the war, but to think about it, to consider it carefully, to learn its lessons.

Utterly irreconcilable with the present-day reality of Beirut, these images of an unrecoverable time in Beirut's past express neither nostalgia nor amnesia. They are prosthetic devices, and, just as a prosthetic limb does not actually restore a lost arm or leg but rather replaces it, these images do not so much rekindle collective memories of those lost times and places as take their place. They do not, in other words, serve either to recall those times and places to memory, or to mourn their loss through a kind of collective and self-imposed amnesia. Rather, they serve as substitutes for the practice both of memory and of forgetting, and in so doing they fill in the gap left by the trauma of the war. If the Lebanese choose not to remember—and in so doing to process—the trauma of the war, and if they can no longer clearly remember the days before the war fragmented and then swept the remnants of a bygone Lebanon away, at least they have the postcard images—and all kinds of other images as well—there to do that work for them.

The cards, then, are not really postcards at all. After all, for the twenty or thirty years that these postcards have been circulating through the newsstands and bookstores of Beirut, there were hardly any tourists there to buy them—and even if there had been, there was for much of the time no functioning postal system to deliver the cards to near or distant destinations. The postcards function inertly, just by being there, and by enduring long after the eradication of the physical reality to which they once corresponded. In the face of the discordant asynchrony of contemporary life, the cards seem to relieve Beirutis of the obligation either to remember or to forget; in so doing, the appeal of their presence is that they offer to free Beirutis from the burden of history itself.

Let me try to be more precise about the status of history, and particularly of history writing, in Beirut. In substituting an image of the past for the proximate history they so resolutely evade, the postcards eradicate also the possibility of history, acknowledging the force only of a present or *the* present. "During the war," writes Jean Said Makdisi in the 1999 Afterword to her *Beirut Fragments: A War Memoir*,

> our eyes were always fixed on what we were sure would be the halcyon days of the future after it ended. Let the war end, we thought, and all would be well. We would emerge from the abyss into the light. Historical quarrels and divisions would mutate into a harmonious and productive unity based on justice. In this vision of the future, I think, we felt somehow that the best of the past would be preserved, the worst purged by our travails. We had paid a heavy price for the evils of the past, and we deserved a better future. But the future is now, and it is a hard reality,

shorn of these illusions. There was to be no reward, after all, for the suffering. (J. Makdisi 1999: 256-257)

When they are thought of at all, the memories of the war remain raw and undigested. Other than those confirmed dead, thousands were kidnapped and disappeared without a trace; their families have been unrelieved by a mourning that never took place. There is no monument to the war in Lebanon, no public recognition, no public memorial commemorating the legions of the dead. The most obvious candidate for such a monument would surely have been the bullet-riddled statue of the "martyrs" of another war (Lebanon's struggle for independence) in Beirut's Martyrs' Square. But the statue was whisked away by the company responsible for the reconstruction of central Beirut, and, when it was replaced—more than a decade after the reconstruction program got underway —it was quietly returned to more or less its original location, only without commentary, without an inscription, without even a passing reference to its origins or to its iconic role in the civil war as a marker of the center of the city that had become a marker of the line of division within the city: the symbolic focal point of the entire war. In the meantime, Martyrs' Square itself has been leveled, and where it once stood a new Virgin Megastore and the skeleton of a brand-new mosque are under construction—its unusually compelling loudspeakers are already up and running—and are competing for the attention of passersby, few of whom are likely to remember the martyrs for much longer. "Somewhere along the way," writes Makdisi, "a decision was made to forget the past and to move on. . . . What was past was past, and what was lost was lost. A general amnesty was declared to wash away the sins of the past. A clean start, it was said, was the right course of action to take, and we were to turn a new page. But there has been no redemption; oblivion and amnesia are not redemption" (J. Makdisi 1999: 258).

Oblivion and amnesia are, indeed, not redemption. What has gripped Beirut since the end of the war, however, is not exactly amnesia in the proper, clinical sense of that term. Especially following a case of trauma, amnesia is the result of the unconscious overriding the conscious attempt or desire to remember; it is a sign of the unconscious intervening to protect consciousness from itself and from its memories of the trauma. But the loss that grips Beirut is hardly the work of an unconscious defense mechanism. For the general reluctance to engage systematically with the war, to embark on a collective historical project to digest and process the memories and images, to salvage a history from all those fragments and moments—and hence to project a future based on the hope of the war's genuine end—is partly a matter of public policy and partly a matter of a widespread popular will to deny. In contemporary Beirut, time itself has not quite stopped, but certainly the discordant, uneven, unfinished, rough present looms larger than either an increasingly remote past or the prospect of a brighter future, both of which seem to be fading away, leaving Beirut stranded, cut off from the past and the future. "The past," writes Lebanese novelist Rashid al-Daif, "flows towards the present, and the future too. The present is both the future and the past of the whole of time" (al-Daif 1995: 12). And, increasingly, a flat and depthless present is all that seems to be available: when there is not much sense of the past, and little prospect of the future, as discrete entities, past and future become extensions of a present from which there seems to be no escape.

Clearly, this is not just a matter of images, and certainly not just a matter of those postcard images on their own—which are, rather, symptomatic of a more general problem. Increasingly, however (and this is especially relevant to the generations born during and after the war and nurtured on the image-forms of contemporary visual culture), images, or really heaps of images unconnected to each other and to an overarching narrative of redemption or reconciliation, may eventually come to supplant other forms of memory, and eventually other forms of history itself. As such narratives start to fade away, history will increasingly take the form of unnarrated images. The Beirut postcards speak, then, of the dangers inherent in imagining a *present* frozen in time, and of a history that tends to imagine the past only as a present to answer our own present. This sense of the past as present may explain the proliferation of large picture histories of Beirut and of Lebanon that have appeared in recent years, carrying with them and conveying to the public imagination more and more images, and fewer and fewer narratives, with which to connect these images to each other and to anything else.

Let me give two other examples of this uncanny combination of imagistic plenitude and narratalogical or historical scarcity. The first is an organization called the Arab Image Foundation (FAI), which is based in Beirut and is, despite its name, overwhelmingly Lebanese in membership and orientation. The FAI's primary objective is "to locate and negotiate access to existing public and private photographic collections," and "to acquire, restore and inventory all kinds of photographs produced by residents of the Middle East and North Africa between 1860 and 1960, including portraits, landscapes, art, commercial, industrial, snapshot, medical and police images."[2] It claims—though it is difficult to judge the veracity of the claim—to have already amassed more than 20,000 prints and negatives and it has furnished materials for a number of exhibitions at galleries in Lebanon and Europe (most recently the October 2004 Hashem el Madani exhibit at the Photographers Gallery in London). The foundation has also published collections of its photographs in volumes such as *Mapping Sitting: On Portraiture and Photography,* which is based on a 2002 exhibit at the Palais des Beaux-Arts in Brussels, and which includes hundreds of photographs organized—if that is the correct term—according to style and genre.

Like the show to which it corresponds, *Mapping Sitting* in effect promises its audience something like a visual history of Lebanon and Palestine from the 1920s through the 1960s; that is, a claim to capture in visual form that period's underlying social and economic transformations, which, as the volume's editors point out, included evolutions in the social division of labor and corresponding mutations in "the established conventions of iconic representation" (Bassil et al. 2002). While this is undoubtedly an intriguing project—and the volume's images are often arresting—the most intriguing issue it raises is actually the question of how or whether such a history of transformation and modernization can be captured and conveyed in purely visual form, or whether on the contrary these images, however fascinating they may be, offer in fact not even the rudiments of such a history—its raw materials—but rather a *substitute* for it. The danger here, in other words, is that image fetishism (surely the postmodern analogue of an earlier era's commodity fetishism), in taking the place of narrative, makes the task or even the possibility of historical understanding, let alone reconciliation, that much more remote. In being frozen in visual form, history threatens to become an aesthetic object, a commodity, a spectacle, a fetish, rather than a narrative, a process, or a struggle.

The question of how or whether history can be adequately captured in visual form is also raised by the work of the Lebanese video artist Walid Raad, who is closely associated with the FAI (he is one of its founding members). Many of Raad's projects present to their audience what appear to be long-lost visual archives from the Lebanese civil war.[3] One, for example, is a series of video interviews with a Lebanese man who is supposed to have been held captive in the same room as each of the Western hostages held in Lebanon in the 1980s, but who has—until now—slipped out of all the official accounts of the hostage-taking. Two of the most suggestive of Raad's projects claim to be the work of Fadl Fakhoury, a fictitious Lebanese historian invented by Raad himself. One of these is a set of notebooks with photographs of racing horses and bookmakers' notes that are supposed to have been taken by the most prominent wartime historians, who are alleged to have met every week during the war at Beirut's racetrack to gamble on the horses; the other is a dossier of notes and photographs of cars that are supposed to match exactly all the makes and models and colors of vehicles used as car bombs during the war in Lebanon. Given enough time, Raad and his colleagues at the FAI could presumably furnish a comprehensive counter-(or really *alter-*) history of the war. What this work is meant to raise, obviously, is not so much the matter of how genuine history itself is narrated and documented, but rather the question of what constitutes genuine history in the first place. Thus, if Raad's meticulously annotated photographs, videos, notebooks and dossiers all turn out to be elaborate self-parodying hoaxes (though this is never actually confessed by the work itself, for nowhere does it concede that all of this "history" is in fact invented), what they push us to consider is the fraught nature of locating and identifying the materials, the building blocks, of "real" history. And the question of how we are supposed to recognize the real when we actually do encounter it is particularly pressing when it comes to visual forms. For not only does an immense collection of images threaten to displace reality rather than express it, but the aesthetic category of the image (or even aesthetic pleasure as such) threatens also to stand in for what was supposed to have been the painful act of remembrance. The risk that this kind of work expresses, in other words, is the possibility that its photographs and images might generate a kind of alter-history, such that "genuine" history itself is effaced through a process of not merely fetishism but of aestheticized numbness.

There are, of course, several more-or-less "genuine" histories of modern

Lebanon and of the Lebanese war, written by various individuals, either independently or with the implicit or explicit backing of one or another formerly warring faction. And many memoirs as well as several fictional and nonfictional accounts of the war have been published, in Arabic as well as English and French. But in the face of the prevailing difficulty in coming to terms with the past—whether as a result of forgetfulness, official amnesia, or a persistent sense of trauma—such writings face formidable obstacles in trying to present a consistent narrative. Perhaps inevitably, the more simplistic ones try to drive home one particular point of view, whereas the more complex ones spend much of their time contemplating the difficulty or even the impossibility of the task they face in trying to narrate and represent the unnarratable and unrepresentable. The best ones try to find a way to adapt to their own sense of formlessness and narratological anarchy by constantly inventing new forms, new narratives, or new structures; it is these that I will focus on in this, the second part of my essay.

It is no coincidence that one of the accounts of the war is called quite simply *Beirut Fragments*, the fragments of the title referring simultaneously to the fragments of shell casings (or shrapnel), the fragments of a shattered city, the fragments of a forsaken past, and the fragments constituting the book itself. The author of that book asks in the opening pages of her war memoir:

> How can I write about Beirut? . . . I tried to force the experience into a comprehensible shape. I searched for a form to fit it into, for some implement to help me impose my need for order on the chaos around me, and I found instead that the chaos imposed itself on me. . . . Forms defaulted one by one as I held them up for trial against a crumbling reality. I wanted something uniform to hold it all, for I am one person—am I not?—and my need for unity and exactness grew in proportion as the country about me fell further and further apart. (J. Makdisi 1999: 19, 22)

None of the stable forms appropriate to prewar reality can stand up to and contain the vertiginous realities of wartime: the prewar ideological containers, hegemonic narratives, symbolic structures—indeed the very vessels of subjectivity itself—all fail in the attempt to narrate the circumstances of wartime and its aftermath. It is not impossible to narrate the war, the past, the future, or the present, but such a narrative will demand new forms, new structures, and new devices. *Beirut Fragments* expresses this striving for new forms; even as you hold it in your hands, it repeatedly mutates, shedding old forms and adopting new ones as it goes along, and not just as it goes along, but as it goes backward and forward in rapid succession, and sometimes all at once. The difficulty here is not simply to come up with new forms to represent an ever-shifting reality, but to try to invent a new way of thinking the movement, the ebb and flow, of time and of history itself. If the stability of the passage from past to present to future has been undermined, what is needed is a new way of engaging with, and thinking through, the nature of time.

In his novels, Rashid al-Daif has suggested that rethinking time involves centrally rethinking the relations between past, present, and future. "Talking about the future is a kind of prophecy," says the narrator of one of al-Daif's novels, "and I am the last person to be concerned with prophecies. On the other hand, I am certain that talking about the past is just as difficult as talking about the future" (al-Daif 1995:12). Talking about the past in this way requires literally the powers of a prophet, for piecing together the fragments of a shattered past proves the identical challenge to that of anticipating the possibilities of many alternative futures. Just as one can determine one of any number of possible futures by one's performance in the present, so too can one retrieve one of any number of possible pasts according to one's performance in the present, which is why the present in al-Daif's novels seems so often to stretch out and embrace many possible pasts, and many possible futures, all at once. Here the past is not something that is fixed and done for once and for all: the past is a terrain that shifts kaleidescopically, and keeps shifting, according to one's performance of the present. Time here is, in short, a time of simultaneity and synchrony rather than a time of progress and redemption; it is, to be precise, a time of—to use Ernst Bloch's famous phrase—the simultaneity of the nonsimultaneous, that characteristic feature of a situation of incomplete modernization (see Bloch 1977).

Several of al-Daif's novels are narrated by characters who are already dead. For example, his 1986 novel *Fusha mustahdafa bayn al-nuʿas wa al-nawm* (which means "a targeted space between drowsiness and sleep," though it has been translated into English and published under the more prosaic title *Passage to Dusk*) begins with the story of the narrator's murder on the doorstep of his apartment in Beirut; unsurprisingly, that story starts to break down even as it is being told, with the narrator admitting to what he calls "a serious flaw" in his own testimony; the novel then rewinds and begins again with the identical setup, still on the doorstep of his apartment, only the narrator is not killed this time (see al-Daif 1986). The novel alternates back and forth between these two and many other possible narratives, none of which finally triumphs over the others. Progress in time is not at issue here: there are many pasts and many futures, and together they unevenly and heterogeneously constitute many presents. The reader is left to sift through the possibilities.

Al-Daif's sixth novel, *Azizi al-Sayyid Kawabata,* or *Dear Mr Kawabata* (published in 1995), begins with a similar constitution and de-constitution of the present and of memory. Walking down the street, the narrator surreally confronts an other who is himself; again he is narrating after his own murder (narrators who are dead are a common feature in postwar Lebanese fiction). After this, al-Daif's narrator suggests what it takes for the past or the memory of a past to exist at all:

> It is said, Mr Kawabata, that at the moment when a man dies, his whole life flashes before his eyes like a film and he recalls everything that has happened to him from his birth to his last moment. I can assure you that nothing like this happened to me. When I died several times in the moments after I had been wounded in the neck and shoulder, in every part of my body, I did not remember anything at all. No memories of any sort whatever passed in front of my eyes. Nothing, not even

the world after death, could distract me from the pain I was feeling. (al-Daif 1995: 3)

Like *Beirut Fragments*, al-Daif's other novels, the work of Elias Khoury, Huda Barakat, and others, *Azizi al-Sayyid Kawabata* is largely concerned with the vicissitudes of narrative, of temporality, and of their relationship to memory and to history itself in a time of pain. In the case of postwar Lebanese writing, history and pain are inextricable from one another; moreover, the loss of one is inseparable from the loss of the other. The loss of historical memory, the collective amnesia gripping Lebanon, thus expresses a sense of numbness where there really ought to be a sense of pain. Self-recognition is itself a painful experience: a moment in which one recalls one's pain and feels it all over again with renewed intensity. Memory, self-recognition, and the narration of pain are here inseparable. A problem of identity or self-recognition is automatically a problem of narration and memory engulfed by pain. What drives all these books, however, is not merely a meditation on the difficulty, or even the impossibility, of presenting a straightforward narrative of chronological or diachronic continuity, but rather a restless series of experimentations with alternative forms and structures of narrative, of remembering, of temporality and of subjectivity and identity.

If straightforward chronological narratives—above all the narrative of progress and redemption, not to mention that other narrative called *modernization* —do not work, then other forms of narrative and of chronology must be invented. If one stable narrative voice, adequate to all circumstances, seems to fail, then multiple voices will take over instead, which is why we see the stable narrative self of *Azizi al-Sayyid Kawabata* breaking down in the opening lines of the novel. "I am one person—am I not?" asks the author of *Beirut Fragments* as she searches for a form adequate to the task of narrating her memoir, but the hesitation in the question itself already suggests its own answer: "No, you are not." One person, one identity, whose oneness is stabilized—guaranteed self-recognition—would be able to produce one stable and straightforward narrative. The multiplicity of narratives, the presence of many selves or many identities, and the iteration of sequences and of alternative pasts and futures: these are not a matter of historical despair but rather of an almost utopian moment of hope. Manuel Vázquez Montalbán is right to warn that, "in the final stages of the contest between the old and the new, the inevitable often slips through unnoticed" (see Montalbán 2002). What such experimentations as al-Daif's preserve is the possibility of reclaiming a future from the damnation of inevitability: a future that, like the past, we might make for ourselves, even if not in conditions of our own choosing.

On the other hand, and against such utopian gestures of political freedom and hope, there is the as yet incomplete, or at any rate unpublished, official history of Lebanon, which, if it were to be completed, would serve as one of the central ideological building blocks of the postwar state. This kind of official history would attempt to impose a kind of order from above, and in straightening, homogenizing, and sterilizing the multiplicity and heterogeneity of memories, stories, accounts, and recollections of the war and of the rest of modern Lebanese history, would summon into being a new kind of ideologically homogenized and conceptually or historically sterilized citizen—quite the opposite of the kind of audience sought for by the most challenging and interesting of the postwar experiments in writing, music, and performance, which, in preserving the possibility of a different and as yet nonexistent audience, also keep alive the possibility of a different and more hopeful future.

Between the hitherto unrealized official narrative and the experimental historical refashionings of history and the present, there is a third narrative that, against all odds, asserts with a fanatical conviction that there can be historical progress, that there can be redemption, that the war can be said to have reached a blissful fulfillment. It is this third narrative to which I will now turn. This is a narrative in which all the difficulties, problems, uncertainties, and hesitations that I have just been discussing are swept aside in a gesture of triumphalism in which the narrative of progress and the narrative of redemption have been woven into each other, in which the past and the future redeem each other while sidestepping the anxieties of an unstable and deeply uneven present. I am referring here to the project to reconstruct central Beirut. I do not have the space here to explain in any detail the nature and background of the reconstruction project (which I have discussed in other contexts: see S. Makdisi 1997, 2002), but suffice it to say that it has involved, first, the cordoning off of a section of Beirut, an area around the traditional city center, which had not previously been thought of as dramatically discontinuous from the rest of the city; second, the demolition and clearing away of the rubble left by the war, as well as a large number of buildings whose destruction was a financial and commercial requirement—was a key to profits—rather than a structural one; and third, the selective reconstruction of some of the remaining buildings.

The project has centrally involved a transfer of property from a widely heterogeneous community of property-rights holders (renters as well as owners) to a private company acting nominally on behalf of the state but animated by its own profit-driven motives. The old downtown had been extremely heterogeneous, unevenly and discordantly combining fruit and vegetable stands, fishmongers, gold markets, clothing stores, and Beirut's famous red light district; mixing together the clean and unclean, the ugly and the beautiful, the smelly and the perfumed; and expressing what Montalbán has referred to in a not dissimilar context as the "legitimate disorder of life." The new downtown, on the other hand, is a formidable outpost of the latest styles, fashions, and brands. There is no red light district; there are no fish markets.

In expropriating the land and properties of central Beirut, this company, Solidere, has essentially reinvented the function and the practice of the city center. On the other hand, it has been driven by an obsessive desire to preserve whenever possible the appearance—for it is only the appearance—of an older heritage. Thus although the company has authorized plans for the construction of fresh designs (such as the new United Nations building, or the al-Nahar building), its priority, aesthetically speaking, has been the restoration and recuperation of old buildings; or, rather, the restoration of the *feeling* of the old. One of the booklets accompanying the international ideas competition for one subproject is called *The Souks in their Memories*. Containing specifically commissioned memoirs of Beirut's old souks, this booklet (together with the *Visual Survey Kit* that includes pages of photographs of the souks as they were before the war), was intended to help participants in the competition to translate collective memory into architectural and material practice; to translate memory and history itself into visual form. "The theme of this Competition," wrote the coordinator, "revolves around the notion of a *souk,* used to mean not only a commercial space, but *an image, a memory, a place that honors tradition and enhances kinds of interaction between merchants and customers.* In light of this, the new souks should provide a familiar and comforting physical environment, one which reinforces the citizens' sense of belonging" (Solidere 1994). One must pause here; what does it means to recreate not belonging as such, but rather a *sense* of belonging? How does one create a sense, or engineer a feeling? Here, the visual field itself creates the *sense* of historical content; it creates and projects feeling—not merely the feeling of comfort and of belonging, but also the feeling of feeling itself.

The souks had been entirely bulldozed by the time Solidere's construction plan began in earnest in the mid-1990s. The demand then was that the new buildings entirely take the place of structures that no longer existed. Elsewhere, wherever feats of engineering have allowed the preservation of old façades, new structures have been cocooned inside the shells of old buildings. "Solidere's success in restoration," the company writes in its most recent annual report (2000),

> comes from combining authenticity with a progressive outlook. The implementation on the ground of the restoration program has confirmed that heritage buildings can survive, provided they are adapted to the needs of contemporary life and business. All restored BCD buildings are fitted with high-tech equipment for functionality, comfort and efficiency. Behind elaborately restored external facades are completely modernized interiors. . . . The final product of restoration is quality space with a special character. (Solidere 2000: 36)

In such a project, we might ask, what does history itself become? Historical features are here reduced to a visual form that gives the new constructions their "special character." Where old structures either could not or have not been saved, many genuinely new structures have been erected in a pastiche of the old architectural styles, endowing them with an approximation of that same "special character." However, that "character" is the same whether the building is a genuine restoration or merely pastiche; in either case, the "special character" is intended to convey feeling.

Throughout Solidere's property, one encounters beautiful old façades painstakingly and faithfully restored, down to the finest detail—which has involved in many cases the resuscitation of building trades and skills that modernization had all but annihilated, particularly in stone- and metalwork. Clearly, the company's discourse of authenticity functions in a strictly visual register, so that what it means by *authenticity* is actually the look—the spectacle—of authenticity, rather than authenticity as such, that is, the kind of authenticity that could come from a genuine engagement with and acknowledgment of historical processes. Indeed, according to the company's discourse, the visual and the spectacular come not merely to dominate and overwhelm all other senses, but to replace them. Thus, just as the authentic is what *looks like* it is authentic, history here is not what actually happened, but what *looks like* it happened. In such usage, history itself has been fully absorbed into the visual field, and it has become the spectacle *par excellence*. In its publications, Solidere is wonderfully frank about its construction of history as spectacle, stressing the role of this spectacle in the marketing of the real estate. In discussing the recently completed residential neighborhood called Saifi Village, for example, Solidere points out that, "drawing on the scale and rhythm of existing buildings, the design gives the impression of small-scale street architecture built up over time, thus reinforcing the sense of place" (Solidere 2000: 31). The spectacle here has assumed for itself, and hence has eliminated, the very function of time; it has taken on the tasks and duties of history: of a history cleansed not merely of pain, but of all kinds of other feelings as well; in short, it has produced a prosthetic history. In their place, new, prosthetic, feelings will be engineered to take the place of the old; new feelings to accompany this sense of spectacular history.

In introducing the question of the reconstruction of central Beirut, I have misleadingly referred to it as a third historical narrative, wedged in between the hitherto unrealized official narrative of Lebanese history and the utopian experiments that, in seeking to reconceive our understanding of history, have sought to invent new ways of imagining the future. In fact it is not a third narrative at all: rather, it not only anticipates the state project to smooth over the historical trauma of the war, but it also brings to a kind of apotheosis the widespread self-induced amnesia that has gripped Lebanon for the past ten or twelve years since the war officially ended. The newly restored buildings are beautiful indeed. But in taking such pains to restore central Beirut to its past—not as it actually was, not as it actually looked and felt, but rather as it ought to have been, as it ought to have looked and felt—Solidere is literally erasing the traces of the war on the city, and this in two ways: first, by substituting image for narrative, and, second, by erasing the last traces even of that messy, uneven, discordant *lived* life that the war itself had destroyed. Its aim is to short-circuit the history of the war by seamlessly uniting the prewar past with the postwar future, and by effecting this unity in false visual terms. History here will be translated not exactly into the spectacle of what happened, but rather into some second- or third-order spectacle; the image of the image; the feeling of the feeling; the look and feel of a past that never really was.

As visually appealing as Solidere is, it ends up representing perhaps a kind of commercial success, but also finally a cultural and political failure. For it is surely not merely more difficult, but also more urgently worthwhile, to try—rather than flatly denying it—to actually engage with the characteristic features of the situation of incomplete modernization in which Lebanon today finds itself. If time and history seem to have broken down—abandoning the fragments of historical memory in a present also unevenly strewn with the detritus of unfinished future possibilities—it becomes essential to conceive of history not as an end in itself but as the foundation of a present more adequate to the challenges facing contemporary Beirut and Lebanon. What this suggests, in turn, is that the task of reconstituting history and memory will flourish most productively in those forms that enable, even require, entirely new understandings of narrative, of community, of temporality and subjectivity. What such projects require, in a sense, is the making of a readership, an audience, fully open to the challenges and rigors of their formal, structural, chronological, and narratological heterogeneity. What is really missing, then, is the right kind of audience, the appropriate reader, viewer, and listener, one whose sensory and cognitive faculties could process a story spoken in dozens of fragmented narratives, told in hundreds of voices, recollected in thousands of images, while sorting out the threads of alternative possible pasts, presents, and futures, all at once.

Notes

1. In 1946, the Lebanese Ministry of Education issued a unified national curriculum, which was modified and to a certain extent decentralized in 1968. As a result, the last centralized history curriculum in Lebanon was defined in 1946 and has not officially been modified on a national scale since then.
2. See Arab Image Foundation website, http://www.fai.org.lb
3. See Walid Raad's work at his website, http://www.theatlasgroup.org. His work has also been installed in various venues, including the Tàpies Foundation in Barcelona and the Witte de With in Rotterdam.

References

Bassil, Karl, Zeina Maasri, and Akram Zaatari, in collaboration with Walid Raad. 2002. *Mapping Sitting: On Portraiture and Photography.* Beirut: Fondation Arabe pour l'Image.
Bloch, Ernst. 1977. "Nonsynchronism and the Obligation to its Dialectics." *New German Critique* 11: 22–38.
al-Daif, Rashid. 1995. *Azizi al-sayyid kawabata.* Beirut: Mukhtarat.
———. 1986. *Fusha mustahdafa bayn al-nuʿas wa al-nawm.* Beirut: Mukhtarat.
Makdisi, Jean Said. 1999. *Beirut Fragments: A War Memoir.* New York: Persea.
Makdisi, Saree. 2002. Beirut/Beirut. In *Tamáss: Contemporary Arab Representations.* Barcelona: Fundació Antoni Tàpies.
———. 1997. Laying Claim to Beirut: Urban Narrative and Spatial Identity in the Age of Solidere. *Critical Inquiry* 23 (3): 661–705.

Makdisi, Ussama. 2001. From Sectarianism to Lebanese Nationalism: Has the Lebanese War Unequivocally Ended? *Adab* 49 (11/12).

Montalbán, Manuel Vásquez. 1992. *Barcelonas.* London: Verso.

Solidere. 2000. Annual Report.

———. 1994. *Visual Survey Kit for the Reconstruction of the Souks of Beirut: An International Ideas Competition.* Beirut: Solidere.

Wettig, Hannah. 2004. "Is Latest Version of National History Fit to Print?" *Daily Star* (Beirut), 2 August.

9 Archaeology, Nationhood, and Settlement

Nadia Abu El-Haj

A "national hobby"—that is how archaeology has often been described in Israeli society. During the early decades of statehood, this historical science transcended its purview as an academic discipline. Archaeological sites and the ancient stories they told galvanized public sentiment. Science and the popular imagination were deeply enmeshed. In the words of one Knesset member describing and defending the Masada myth against a critical historical reading, "Masada is far more than an archaeological or historic site. It is an expression of the independence and heroism of the Jewish people." He could not imagine his national identity "without Masada" (*Qol ha-ʿIr,* 7 February 1992: 37).

A privileged ground for generating and fashioning collective memory for the newly established Jewish nation-state, perhaps that is the most obvious analytic framework from which to discuss the role that archaeology has played in Israeli society, particularly in its early decades. "Collective memory," as Maurice Halbwachs has argued, generates and sustains group identity. In a fundamental sense, it is *ahistorical,* denying the historicity of specific events. Memory (as distinct from "history") upholds the ongoing relevance of "the past" to the present (see also Renan 1996; Davis and Starn 1989). Memories, in essence, never actually *come to pass.* As Steven Knapp argues, "the narratives preserved by collective memory sometimes play a *normative* role—that is, they may in various ways provide criteria, implicit or explicit, by which contemporary models of action can be shaped or corrected, or even by which particular ethical or political proposals can be authorized or criticized" (1989:123).

Recent historical and social scientific scholarship on "national memory" has sought to analyze how memory is produced, what is effaced in the process, and how it is that those "collective memories" become powerfully constitutive of contemporary political possibilities and regimes of rule. Nevertheless, this analytic emphasis on construction stands in tension with the very semantics of the language of memory that frames the debate. As Walter Benn Michaels has asked of collective memory, how can we describe "something we have never known as something we have forgotten"? How is it that such events become "part of our own experience?" (Benn Michaels 1996). There may well be a slippage, in other words, between the language we use to analyze nationalist ideological commitments and the grammar that underlies those very commitments themselves.

Clearly, analyses of nationalism and memory (making) are not promoting Lamarckian notions of racial inheritance. Quite the contrary, to write about nationalism and the construction of memory is to attempt to demonstrate the opposite: how it is that nationalists generate a belief in continuity out of histories of social, political, and cultural ruptures or shifts. Nevertheless, invoking the language of memory in order to analyze specific practices of nationhood does, inadvertently, imply that there is something there, a priori, already *given,* merely awaiting the moment when consciousness is awakened anew. And in so doing, the nation is reified. More specifically, the nation is anthropomorphized, emerging as structurally equivalent to the modern subject. A modern person, after all, as envisioned by John Locke among other philosophers, is understood to be "linked by chains of memory and responsibility," that which "cement[s] identity and difference" (see Hacking 1995) and delineates an individual's continuity and "coherence" through time.

No doubt, there are contexts in which memory is a *category of practice* worth investigating. But in analyzing those practices we may well want to avoid invoking memory in such a way as to imply, albeit inadvertently, that it is a substantial and enduring "thing"—or, that the nation is something, equivalent to *someone,* endowed with the capacity to remember. In ordinary language usage, after all, memory refers to a "faculty" possessed by an individual (or recently, a computer), the "place" where such recollections are stored. It also refers the thing or person *recalled, recollected,* and *commemorated;* something "stored" that *was already known.* And as J. L. Austin and ordinary language philosophers have taught us, a word hardly ever "shakes off its etymology" completely (Austin 1961: 149; Pitkin 1972: 10–11).

In this chapter, I approach the practice of archaeology in Palestine and in the later Israeli state not as an instance in the making of collective memory. Instead, I analyze the contexts in which a certain kind of historical science is articulated quite simply as an instance of a nation "returning home," expressed with a belief in Jewish national return in such a way as to configure territorial claims and to fashion the ideological contours of Jewish settlement in Palestine. Focusing on the pre-state period of British Mandatory rule in Palestine, I examine the processes and projects involved in establishing the discipline of archaeology on the one hand, and the specific research agenda of the Jewish Palestine Exploration Society on the other. In so doing, I consider how it was that archaeological practice, scientific epistemology, and the work of discipline building converged in such a way as to generate specific nationalist, historical sensibilities: a commitment to the archaeological past as *national heritage* and the fact of Palestine as the old–new Jewish national home.

Instituting Archaeology

According to the Anglo-American Committee of Inquiry, Palestine was not colonized by the British because it was inhabited by a "primitive" people in "need of tutelage" but rather because of its "historic significance" and the necessity of it being open to all religions (Anglo-American Committee 1946: 38). In the negotiations between European powers that finalized the Mandate's political framework, that need for "openness" was explicitly extended to the domain of archaeology (Anglo-American Committee 1946: 38). The science of archaeology came center stage under British mandatory rule, and Jewish archaeology gradually emerged as an institutional and intellectual endeavor in its own right.

Securing archaeology as an intellectual pursuit—whether on the part of the Jewish Palestine Exploration Society or British Mandate authorities—involved a series of efforts to define, demarcate, and protect its objects of knowledge. Specific objects and spaces had to be subject to particular regulations and expertise, ensuring a delimitation of archaeology's domain through which entire sections of terrain were remade—legally, aesthetically, and practically. As Timothy Lenoir has argued, the work of discipline building entails reconfiguring epistemological visions and cultural commitments that underpin the social and political order. That labor, in other words, necessitates a struggle to redefine what is to count as valuable (and as valuable knowledge) within the larger social world (Lenoir 1997; see also Latour 1987). It was at the conjuncture of educational projects and legal power (the antiquities law and specific city-planning ordinances) that the British endeavored to instill a general respect for science and a modern conception of heritage among Palestine's Arab (Muslim) population. For its part, the struggle for Jewish archaeology was more specific. In the context of the Jewish Yishuv (the pre-state period of Jewish settlement in Palestine) in which much was esteemed in terms of its contribution to the national interest, Jewish archaeology strove to fashion itself as an integral player in that wider social and political field. The practice of nationhood and the practice of archaeology became deeply entangled, in other words, as a result not of nationalist commitments alone but also, and quite crucially, because of disciplinary need: Jewish archaeologists worked to insert archaeology into the (colonial-)national political project in part to attain their own (emergent) disciplinary goals. Moreover, this effort to institute archaeology was essential not only to defining and stabilizing "artifacts" and "scientific fields" as belonging exclusively within and to the scientific–archaeological domain. It was also constitutive of the legal and ideological transformation of the landscape as a whole.

Configuring National Value

The Jewish Palestine Exploration Society organized and held the first "Knowledge of the Land" (*Yedi'at ha-Aretz*) conference in Jerusalem in October 1943. It was the "first attempt to establish a living connection between those working in the science of the Land of Israel, and the public at large" (Yeivin 1967: 3). As explained by Itzhak Ben-Zvi in his opening remarks, the society was not just an academic institution. It was also a context in which scientists and the public could meet, a society through which "each Jew" could participate in researching the history of the country, and could thus become acquainted with "the homeland" (Yeivin 1967: 4). Ben-Zvi (who later became the second president of the state of Israel) expressed a desire to link the past with the present: a connection signified through the interlacing of the scientific and the popular, one allegedly shared by researchers and "each Jew" of the Yishuv. As articulated repeatedly at its conferences and in its publications, the Jewish Palestine Exploration Society was not simply an academic society but also a popular one. Archaeology was not just a scientific endeavor but, more important, a national–cultural one. As Ben-Zvi pointed out, the society's excavations at Tiberias in 1920 had been carried out by "Jewish researchers and workers." Explaining that many who lived on agricultural settlements had pitched in to help with the work, Ben Zvi noted that "collaboration between researchers and the Yishuv, between the past and present," had thus been created (Yeivin 1967: 4).

Despite this initial optimistic tone, however, the theme that actually dominated the conference's fourth session was quite a different one. What was repeated throughout a discussion on how the society might best structure outreach to its public was the remark that antiquities were being destroyed by Jewish settlers working the land. As was made clear in the exchange that ensued, there was a tension between a priori assertions that *there already existed* an interest in antiquities among Palestine's Jewish public—(modern) nations are, by definition, interested in "their heritage"—and the realities of everyday practice that seemed to fly in the face of that a priori national belief. While the explicit conviction was never abandoned, strategies were devised to teach the value of antiquities to the Jewish public, or in the words of some, to "awaken" its interest in historical objects.

The director of one regional *Yedi^at ha-Aretz* center explained the problem. Upon coming to Palestine, the Zionist movement focused on "redeeming" the land. As a result, "we neglected one of the foundations of our culture—the study of the remains of our past in the country" (Yeivin 1967: 41). "Because of this lack of education," he continued, "every important remain is trampled and cast aside" (Yeivin 1967: 41). This was not the situation in Europe, especially not in Western Europe, which clearly stood, in his eyes, as the model for nationhood: "Every child there knows . . . the value of every ancient shard." In Palestine, by way of contrast, no such sensibility seemed to exist.

The speaker's commitment to these material "foundations of our culture" was not shared by the majority of Palestine's Jewish public—at least not as far as he could tell. And speaker after speaker reported on this rather dire state of affairs. For example, another participant told of a village built right into the foundations of a tell (site of the remains of an ancient settlement) (Yeivin 1967: 44). The youth movements, for their part, felt no connection to the antiquities: "One often hears: Why should we preserve the potsherds for these nuisances (*nudnikim*)? That's a slogan of the Scouts" (Yeivin 1967: 44). While many items had been discovered in recent years, this speaker continued, so too had many been destroyed at the hands of settlers. Throughout the session, it was the actions of Jews living in agricultural settlements about which most concern was expressed. After all, as workers of the land they had become the icons of nationalist mythology. It was they who *should have been* most interested in antiquities if national consciousness necessarily entailed such a commitment. And of course, it was those settlers who were most likely to run into antiquities in the course of their everyday activities and thus to destroy or discard them if not properly educated or suitably concerned.

This debate conveys significant information about the state of archaeology as a national–cultural practice in the 1940s. Despite explicit assertions made by nearly all speakers that there *was* a Jewish interest in antiquities and that (Jewish) antiquities were *intrinsically* recognizable as the foundations of a revived Hebrew national culture in Palestine, the popular regard for such an archaeological or national heritage project does not seem to have been very widespread. Residents of agricultural settlements and even nature/tour guides were depicted as uninterested. Moreover, the formers' everyday practices were understood to be destroying archaeology's objects. Nevertheless, despite all of their own evidence and arguments to the contrary, conference participants continued to assert that the Jewish public of Palestine was interested in "their" antiquities, although that curiosity may have been lying in a dormant state from which it could and should be nourished back to life (paralleling the very project of nationhood).

Many speakers articulated the role of the society in guiding a national educational project. First and foremost, it was the *value* of antiquities that had to be taught. Educational material was needed to teach the most basic question of all: *"What are antiquities"* (Yeivin 1967: 55, emphasis mine)? Antiquities, in other words, were particular kinds of objects whose standing and salience as objects of scientific and national value had to be brought clearly into public view. Various speakers called upon participants to do outreach in their own regions. Others focused on the responsibilities of guides to provide more detailed and accurate information regarding archaeological remains: guides must "know each tell" and make clear to the public that they are "not just passing by a hill but rather by an ancient settlement" (Yeivin 1967: 43). In effect, the landscape *as a whole* and not just discrete, individual artifacts was being cast in terms of its historic value, throwing a perspective across the terrain through which the *moledet* (the homeland) would emerge as existing always, and simultaneously, in the past and not solely in the present.

Educating the proto-state's citizenry about antiquities was promoted in this debate as a role and responsibility the Jewish Palestine Exploration Society must undertake. Nevertheless, assertions—such as "The study of potsherds . . . is one of the important foundations of the history of our culture" (Yeivin 1967: 43)—cannot be taken at face value. They capture only some of the desires and interests motivating this debate and commitments being developed from it. Assuring the proper collection and preservation of archaeology's objects for the purposes of scientific research was the *main concern* for many participants, especially for those members of the society who understood themselves as first and foremost *doing archaeology* (in contrast to the leaders of the *Yediʾat ha-Aretz* movement). For example, one speaker took issue with the vision for the society presented by a director of a regional *Yediʾat ha-Aretz* center who maintained that the society's efforts should focus on public education and, moreover, that the society's scholarly work should be subsumed to the larger project of *Yediʾat ha-Aretz.* *Yediʾat ha-Aretz,* this speaker insisted, was far broader in its focus than archaeology. While he supported public education, it was with a limited goal. Regional branches of the society should be established, which would be contexts in which students, collectors of antiquities, and neighbors of tells could be educated in order to preserve each *as a tell* "for eternity": "If we succeed in this . . . there is a future for *our* existence" (Yeivin 1967: 43, emphasis mine). There would be a future for the Jewish Palestine Exploration Society, which he defined as primarily a "historical-archaeological" society. In other words, what framed this participant's concern and the solutions he proposed had little to do with the question of national value. It was archaeology as a historical and scientific practice whose future he sought to ensure (Yeivin 1967: 43).

The concern with protecting and promoting the society's future as a scientific, archaeological society was articulated and defended by several speakers. Ensuring such a future would require the preservation and protection of its objects of knowledge. But public education would bring other advantages as well. The society's work required funds. Increasing its dues-paying membership was crucial to generating much needed revenue (Yeivin 1967: 49). Moreover, the very value and achievement mentioned by Ben-Zvi in his opening remarks— that archaeological work was being carried out not just by Jewish researchers but by Jewish *workers* as well—was being promoted, by many speakers, as a way of overcoming the financial problems and thus the practical difficulties that the society faced. In other words, the very significance of Jewish volunteers working on archaeological digs (see Ben Yehuda 1995, Silberman 1993) may have its roots not simply in a national–cultural imagination but also in the pragmatic needs of Jewish archaeological work as it struggled to establish itself in Mandate Palestine.

Indeed, it is possible to distill from this debate evidence that complicates the traditional take on archaeology's emergence as a widespread national–cultural practice among Jews of the Yishuv and later among Israeli Jews in the newly founded state. Rather than the emergence of the discipline of archaeology being a simple consequence of an existing national–cultural commitment to investigating the Jewish/Israelite material cultural past, a pervasive national–cultural commitment to Jewish/Israelite antiquities *had to be made* and was forged, at least in part, out of a struggle of and for the science of archaeology itself. In order for archaeology's research projects to be possible at a time when excavating was emerging as the locus of disciplinary distinctiveness and expertise, its objects of knowledge had to be protected from ongoing practices that were precipitating their disappearance. As a *field* science, after all, archaeology's objects are particularly vulnerable; they are never protected and produced within an environment (i.e., a physics laboratory) to which archaeologists alone have access and can lay claim. Particular kinds of material cultural objects and specific kinds of sites have to be recognized as antiquities, as objects of value to be excavated, preserved, studied, displayed, and revered. And in order to do so, a particular set of cultural understandings and commitments need to be forged. In this instance, archaeologists had to generate a belief in the value of antiquities—not just as objects of science, but given the cultural and political realities of the Yishuv, as objects of *national* significance. Simply put, despite commonplace rhetoric to the contrary, there was no widespread, *inherent* identification with archaeology and its objects displayed by the Jewish public of the Yishuv. That identification—the national passion for archaeology so evident by the time of Yigael Yadin's Masada excavations in the 1960s—had to be generated. The society became engaged in a project of educating a Hebrew citizenry that would recognize and be committed to the national–cultural value of antiquities. But the interests that motivated such work were complex. Education was essential if the interests of this incipient scientific endeavor, and not just those of a developing nation, were to be secured.

Legislating Scientific Objects and Terrains

The Jewish Palestine Exploration Society was not the sole institution to engage in teaching the value of antiquities to the general public. The government's Department of Antiquities had long been involved in such a task. It was engaged in "familiarising the fellahin with the existence and meaning of the Antiquities Law, and for generally assuring the obeisance of that law in the district" (PRO CO 733/209/7).

It was not just that the value of antiquities was to be taught. It was also to be legislated, with the force of law imposed. And that law would have to provide an answer to the most fundamental question of all, "What is an antiquity?" In other words, what kinds of sites, monuments, objects, *and spaces* were to be classified as antiquities, and thus be subject to the jurisdiction of the Antiquities Law?

As laid out in the Antiquities Ordinance of 1928:

"Antiquity" includes historical monument, and means
a) any object, whether movable or immovable or a part of the soil, which has been constructed, shaped, inscribed, erected, excavated or otherwise produced or modified by human agency earlier than the year 1700 AD, together with any part thereof which has at a later date been added, reconstructed or restored. (PRO CO 733/159/7: 1)

But as the ordinance then clarified, there was one category of historical object that would not be subject to (most provisions of) its jurisdiction: that is, "antiquities of religious use or devoted to a religious purpose which are the property of a religious or ecclesiastical body," be they monuments or movable objects (Ibid.: 2).

The exclusion of particular kinds of monuments and objects from the full force of the antiquities ordinance was key to fashioning what an antiquity was to be: What kind of a cultural object is it? What is its relationship to the present?

To what kinds of interventions or alterations can it be subjected? Moreover, who is it that the law empowers to make such interventions or alterations? In order to demarcate the legal limits of the antiquity law, I begin by considering the clauses from which objects and monuments in religious use were to be exempted.

Sacred monuments and objects were excluded from two of the main provisions of the ordinance. First, religious monuments and objects in nongovernmental possession could not be subject to either a compulsory lease or to outright confiscation. Second, the government would have no authority in attempting to stop any alterations being made to the structures themselves or to their immediate contexts (PRO CO 733/159/7: 11–13). The latter exemption was important in establishing the distinction between two overarching categories of historical monuments: the sacred and the secular (the "living" and the "dead"). A government memorandum explained the definition as follows:

> It is sometimes also suggested that the Government should be in such a position as would enable them compulsorily to stop, on merely archaeological or quasi-aesthetic and capricious grounds, any work that may be considered by the traditional owners of any shrine (whether Christian, Moslem or Jewish) to be necessary for other than purely archaeological reasons. But it is to be remembered that the monuments in question are not of a merely archaeological character, but are also . . . "living" monuments; that is to say, monuments still in use for religious purposes. (Ibid.: 8)

It was precisely that status of being *in use* that rendered such monuments distinct and that would make restrictions on alterations artificial:

> To take up a rigidly one-sided archaeological, capricious, or "aesthetic" attitude towards such monuments, to lay down that . . . no changes or alterations can, from this date onwards, be permitted, would not be either reasonable or in the interests of archaeology, but would cause that activity to be looked upon as a *deadening influence seeking to arrest the normal current of human affairs.* (Ibid., emphasis mine)

Under the 1928 ordinance, *real* antiquities were, for their part, to be subject to precisely such a "deadening" of the "normal current of human affairs." The question of what could and could not be done to these different categories of "historical monuments" was central to producing the demarcation between the "living" and the "dead," between the sacred and the secular–historical. And in producing that demarcation, these legal provisions delineated a domain of archaeological practice and expertise.

Once placed outside of the Antiquities Law's jurisdiction, it was no longer religious monuments that posed problems for the Department of Antiquities' efforts of historical preservation. It was "monuments of a secular character" not owned by the government on the one hand, and "undiscovered antiquities and antiquities situated on land owned or worked by peasants" (Ibid.: 4) on the other, that became the focus of the department's work. The first category included "monuments of Medieval *art . . . Moslem in origin*," which were found "chiefly in Jerusalem" (Ibid.: 11, emphasis mine). About two-thirds of those monuments were held as private properties, and the department of antiquities aimed to ensure their conservation. And *conservation* is the key word. Although mostly private properties, and mostly (one can assume) private "habitations" (Ibid.: 14), these buildings were understood to be monuments of *art,* Muslim *in origin.* They were no longer "living" monuments allowed to undergo architectural change as may have been precipitated by ongoing practices and quotidian needs. They were now *artifacts*—historical objects subject to scientific inquiry and expert intervention alone.

As legislated by the Mandate's Antiquities Law, all change to such monuments was classified as "damage," which it was necessary to prevent. Section 12(6) of the Ordinance was drafted in order to prevent owners from carrying out renovations or alterations of their properties as they deemed fit. And it was perhaps in efforts to protect Jerusalem's Old City that this clause of the antiquities ordinance was most often invoked. Like all "antiquities"—objects of science and objects of heritage produced at the juncture of legal jurisdiction, archaeological practice and public education—the Old City as a whole and many of its individual buildings were to be protected from any unauthorized works of addition, repair, or alteration. They were to be protected from the ongoing practices of the present.

The Old City as Historical Monument

From the time of Britain's occupation of Jerusalem in 1917, the state of Jerusalem's antiquities was considered to be of prime concern. Beginning with the 1918 town planning scheme, a very specific vision for the city of Jerusalem was pursued, at least in theory if often not realized in actual fact. That plan entailed a strict demarcation of urban space. There were two cities, "the *Ancient City*" and an "adjacent *modern city*" (PRO CO 733/339/4, emphasis mine), paralleling the production of "dual cities" that characterized modernist city planning in various parts of the colonized world (Wright 1997: 328; see also Rabinow 1989). The needs of each of those cities were understood to be radically different. There were to be four planning zones, and the arrangement delineated criteria for development and construction for each of these specific (types of) locales within the singular space of the municipality of Jerusalem as a whole (PRO CO 733/339/3).

The town planning scheme was designed to "preserve the Old City and its immediate surroundings" (Ibid.). In so doing, it promoted a specific aesthetic and endowed archaeology—its institutions, its personnel, and its expertise— with the power to determine and to regulate that historic–aesthetic character. In effect, the urban space was being transformed into an archaeological terrain. It was not enough that *individual monuments* be preserved. Rather, just as French colonial officials had devised a conservation plan for the Moroccan "*madina,*" "a detailed set of aesthetic requirements" were drawn up for Jerusalem's Old City, writ large (Wright 1997: 328). The Old City emerged legally, ideologically, and scientifically as an historic locale subject to sustained expert practice and oversight.

Two principles were to govern construction within Jerusalem's Old City: that the area was to be very limited and that it was to be regulated by a strict sense of an appropriate aesthetic. Its "medieval character" was to be maintained, right down to the style of its arched doorways (PRO CO 733/339/4). After all, the goal of all this work was "the preservation of such *a monument* as the Old City" (PRO CO 733/467/8, emphasis mine), which like all other secular (i.e., "dead") monuments regulated by the Antiquities Law would be subject to strict restrictions regarding any alterations or additions made to them. It was in the adjacent modern city that future development would be allowed to take place (PRO CO 733/339/4).

In the eyes of Europeans and outsiders, the Old City *stood for* the historical in this city planning scheme in relation to which the modern city would and could exist. But in contrast to French colonial cities, for example, in which the *madina* (a term that the French used to designate the old city) was simply a "conservatory" of an unspecified "oriental life" (Wright 1997: 323), Jerusalem's Old City's imagined historical relevance was far more precise. Its existence—its *conservation*—was of principal importance to *Jerusalem's* present and future. It was the Old City, after all, that identified this place as the Holy City, in relation to which the continual (Christian) anxiety regarding its potential destruction made sense. And it was far more than the colonial imagination of (a Judeo-Christian) recuperation that was produced and promoted at this juncture of town planning, legal jurisdiction, and archaeological authority. So too was the very nature of a (secular) historical consciousness: that the present cites and preserves the past in relation to which its own identity is secured; and that the past remains physically distinct, (aesthetically) frozen in time and personified in its physical remains, a distinction between past and present cardinal to the possibility of archaeological practice itself.

Historical Objects in the Hands of Peasants

Existing monuments such as the Old City and its surrounding walls formed but one category of the secular objects in nongovernmental possession. Those "existing or undiscovered antiquities or antiquities on land owned or worked by peasants" produced even more anxiety for officials of the Department of Antiquities (PRO CO 733/159/7: 4). They were considered to be in danger because of the practicalities of peasant life and the limits of peasant knowledge:

> For peasants the all-absorbing object in life must be to gain shelter, food, clothing and fuel for themselves and their families . . . Everything that serves this . . . is used for that end. Stone constructions and rock cuttings, if conveniently situated, are treated as quarries and antiquities that are buried in the ground are, if discovered, treated as things to sell. (PRO CO 733/159/7: 14–15)

Such peasant practices were understood to precipitate "much damage . . . to the legitimate interests of archaeology not merely in Palestine but everywhere else in the world" (PRO CO 733/159/7: 15). In other words, the ongoing uses to which the peasantry had long put material cultural objects, whether through inhabiting old buildings or reusing old stones and quarries, was translated into a form of destruction, one precipitated by need and accompanied by ignorance. But as is made clear in a series of government documents, the protection of antiquities in Palestine needed to proceed by "encouragement" far more than by "threat" (see Ibid.: 1). Proceeding by threat posed a grave danger. It would precipitate the *deliberate* destruction of antiquities.[1]

Proceeding by encouragement rather than by threat, by education rather than by criminalization, the antiquities ordinance hoped to secure these historical objects for the purposes of scientific inquiry, just as had the leaders of the Jewish archaeological community speaking before the first *Yedi'at ha-Aretz* conference in 1943. After all, it was the accumulation of knowledge that was the ultimate objective of the government's (and many of the society's members') interest in antiquities.

The conditions under which this increase in knowledge would be possible necessitated a series of transformations in Palestine—in public consciousness (a public construed, by and large, as Jewish by the Jewish Palestine Exploration Society (JPES) and as Arab-Muslim by the British administration), and in the objects and landscapes themselves. Instituting archaeology set in motion a dynamic that was at one and the same time enclaving (of objects) and expansive (across the terrain). Particular kinds of remains were "defined, segmented, detached" (Kirshenblatt-Gimblett 1991: 388), fashioned legally and culturally as objects of scientific and social value, considered as artifacts to be protected from destruction and sale, to be collected, studied, preserved, and displayed. But archaeology's objects were far from confined to discrete fragments separated from their social or territorial contexts. Larger terrains—tells, rural sites, entire municipal spaces—were also legally transformed into archaeology's domain, albeit never effectively into its exclusive dominion. As a space of scientific production and expertise, in other words, the archaeological field had to be demarcated, defined, and produced, as had the space of the laboratory for experimental science in seventeenth-century England (see Shapin and Schaffer 1985). The landscape of Palestine was divided into discrete zones: historical and modern, archaeological and nonarchaeological, secular and sacred. And in the context of Palestine, shaping that scientific field entailed configuring the colony—fashioning colonial imagination(s)—writ large.

In effect, contemporary Palestine was increasingly saturated with specific historic resonances. From the perspectives of its various colonizers, the objects of archaeology had the power to reach beyond their boundaries to a larger world, "to evoke . . . the complex, dynamic cultural forces from which [they had] . . . emerged and for which [they were] . . . taken . . . to stand" (Greenblatt 1991: 42). For the British, and the broader European-Christian interests they believed themselves to represent, that larger world was a (Judeo-)Christian tradition and history. It was the continued survival of that past that would be evoked in and through the monuments and aesthetic forms conserved in Jerusalem's Old City. The perpetuation—the freezing—of that larger aesthetic-historic "context" ensured that Jerusalem's *true* identity (as the Holy City) remained visible in the now rapidly expanding and changing modern city. For members of the Jewish Palestine Exploration Society promoting public education as, in part, a strategy to secure the survival and centrality of their discipline in the political culture of the Yishuv, it was Eretz Yisrael—an emergent *Altneuland*[2]—of and for a developing settler nation—that would resonate in and through artifacts, tells, and landscapes of (biblical) history, at least once they could be properly delineated and defined, valued and viewed.

Settler-Colonial Configurations: Substantiating a National Terrain

During the pre-state period, the work of discipline building was but one project in which the Jewish Palestine Exploration Society, along with British Mandate personnel and institutions, engaged. Archaeological research also came center stage during this era as large-scale excavations began in earnest. Concerned primarily with the biblical periods, it was sites such as Megiddo and Lachish upon which the European and American archaeological schools focused their attention. However, the material culture studied and excavated under the auspices of the Jewish Palestine Exploration Society and Hebrew University dated by and large to Roman through Byzantine times in the history of Palestine. Given the lack of adequate funding and personnel, they consisted mostly of small trial digs (see Silberman 1993: 225). The work of Jewish archaeology in Palestine concentrated on two kinds of sites: synagogues and tombs. In addition, there was some attention paid to Jewish cities that continued to exist and even flourish after the Romans destroyed the Second Temple or, in a commonly used turn of phrase, "after the destruction" (see Slousch 1925: 8).[3] These material cultural remains were hewn, collected, and classified as signs of Jewishness. Discrete material cultural artifacts, ornamentation, and styles of architecture were interpreted as exemplars of Jewish artistic forms and achievements. They were invoked as emblems of continuity, signifiers of the lasting presence of Jewish communities, mostly in the Galilee, after the fall of the Second Temple.

Examining this work of Jewish archaeology, I consider the relationship between the collection of "discrete particulars" (Poovey 1998)—material cultural and linguistic facts dispersed across the terrain—and the instantiation of a "spatial biography" (Carter 1989), through which a cohesive, historical narrative for the land was given empirical and factual form. In sum, the compilation of ancient Jewish (arti)facts was crucial to substantiating the particular ideological configuration of Jewish settlement in Palestine: that this was an enactment of Jewish national return. In the context of Palestine, after all, the projects of settlement and nation building developed at one and the same time on a singular colonial terrain. Settlement was framed, and legitimized, in terms of a *belief in* and a *commitment to* Jewish national return. Palestine and Israel—the colony and the metropole—were the same place, the former quite rapidly and repeatedly transformed into a cultural and historical space to which the Jewish settlers would lay national claim and over which they would assert sovereign ownership. This effort at fact collecting was, in effect, an "epistemological strategy, a mode of knowing," in and through which Palestine ultimately emerged, visibly and linguistically, as the historic Jewish national home.

Fact Collecting

In discussing Roman and Byzantine Palestine, Shmuʾel Yeivin informed his audience that much of what exists from these periods are remains of religious buildings: churches, monasteries, synagogues. This was, after all, an era of "heightened religious sentiment" (Yeivin 1935: 42). As became clear with the discovery and analysis of more and more synagogues, they were all oriented toward Jerusalem: "in the Galilee, southwards, in the Jordan Valley—westwards." Moreover, "they belong to two types" (Yeivin 1935: 43).

It was precisely the question of typology and its relationship to chronology that research on ancient synagogues engaged: archaeological practice was structured by the detailed description and classification of discrete artifacts and architectures plotted across the terrain. As E. L. Sukenik (one of the founding figures of Jewish archaeology in Palestine) reported to the first *Yediʾat ha-Aretz* conference, the German synagogue excavations of 1903–1907 "discovered for us for the first time the exact structure of the Galilean synagogues," providing "archaeological-artistic examination" on the basis of which artistic and architectural patterns could be identified and the eras to which specific synagogue remains belonged could be determined (Yeivin 1967: 30, see also Maisler n.d.).

Such investigations and typological classifications of Jewish art and architecture were not limited to considerations of synagogues but also characterized the larger edifice of Jewish archaeological practice. Individual remains (ornamental and architectural) were classified along a chronological–typological grid; the development of Jewish art and architecture was mapped and the continued presence of Jewish communities in ancient Palestine, from the time of the Second Temple period through the Byzantine era at the very least, was charted and substantiated. As recounted by Nahum Slousch with respect to his work at the Tomb of Avshalom and other ancient remains in its vicinity (in the village of Silwan just outside Jerusalem's Old City walls), "This structure, certainly the most original if not the most artistic of the early buildings near Jerusalem, is familiar to all, with its lower part hewn in the form of a cube out of the rock of the Mount of Olives" (Slousch 1925: 9). Aaron Mazié, considering the Tomb of Jehoshaphat "in relation to Hebrew art," wrote of this monument as additional proof of "an early independent Hebrew style of art" (Mazié 1925: 68).

Beyond engaging questions of artistic merit, providing descriptions of the structures of each of the tombs and monuments (the Monument of Avshalom and the Tomb of Jehoshaphat, the Tomb of Zechariah and the Tomb of the Sons of Hezir) and identifying them, Slousch emphasized two issues: chronology and function. The question of chronology charted artifacts along a linear temporal grid that tracked national history, or presence, through time. Slousch dated the origins of the Monument of Avshalom to the period between the "later Maccabeans and later Herods," names understood to specify significant moments in ancient Jewish history. Moreover, he concluded that it was not a tomb at all, but a cenotaph constructed as "an integral part of the Tomb of Jehoshaphat" (Slousch 1925: 25). As argued by Benjamin Maisler, this "systematic" examination of tombs "from the point of view of their architectural structure" and through the examination of "individual finds" discovered within them (mostly pottery and glass shards) has been of "great value." It has enabled scholars to understand "the burial customs that our fathers followed in the days of the Second Temple—in the Hasmonean era and that of Herod—and also . . . the architectural skill . . . in which they achieved a high artistic level" (Maisler n.d.: 116). In addition, the inscriptions were of particular (national) importance. Epigraphical analysis revealed names in widespread use amongst "our fathers in the days of the Second Temple," a discovery that has clarified the development of the square Hebrew script. It has also provided insight into "the history of noble families who lived in Jerusalem in the last generations before the destruction (Maisler n.d.: 117). Deciphering individual and familial names, in other words, emerged as one means for tracing a national genealogy incarnated in the "familial-form" (Stevens 1999: 158).

This research into synagogues and tombs comprised what could be described, in Thomas Kuhn's words, as "pre-paradigmatic" science.[4] The collection of ever more facts, cumulative instances of Jewish art and architecture, of Jewish presence and (familial–national) history were never quite integrated into a cohesive historical vision or scientific method. Rather it was the very *collection process itself* that seems to have been significant. As evidenced in the bulletin of the Jewish Palestine Exploration Society (*Yediʾot ha-Hevra ha-ʿIvrit le-Hakirat Eretz Yisrael ve-Atiqoteha*), the examination of specific tombs and particular synagogues was governed by the quest for signs of (ancient) Jewishness continuous in and dispersed across the land of Israel. This work had all the characteristics of butterfly collecting, an amassing of sometimes seemingly inchoate data not limited to what would later be defined as archaeology, strictly speaking. The work of the JPES concentrated as much on historical–geography (relying on linguistic inferences and facts as well as textual sources) as upon what would subsequently delimit archaeology per se (the survey or excavation of material cultural objects). There was, moreover, a broad effort at fact collecting about the past *and present* in the Land of Israel, which converged upon signs of Jewishness, albeit not exclusively so. While archaeology, and the work of the society, was progressively defined with reference to the excavation of specific tells and, hence had a focus on the ancient past, those parameters of a specifically archaeological–historical practice did not yet decisively define and delimit the field.

As becomes apparent by perusing the JPES Bulletin,[5] the discovery of more and more tombs was chronicled, and additional (potential) remains of ancient synagogues were reported. In effect, reading the journal is like reading a list of an ever-accumulating collection of (primarily) Jewish material cultural remains. In 1923, a tomb (later dated to the Second Temple period) was discovered on the property of a Mr. Yahya Aruri; the society then excavated the site (Mayer 1925: 40–41). Another tomb came to light on premises of the Hebrew University in May 1924 (Sukenik 1925) and in the Mahanaim Quarter of Jerusalem in September of the same year. In January 1934, Brasalawski, who traveled the Galilee on behalf of the Society, reported the possible discovery of a synagogue (Brasalawski 1934). Another ancient synagogue was discovered in the village of Samu'a and identified via linguistic similarity as Eshtemoa. It was excavated in the winters of 1935 and 1936 (Mayer and Reifenberg 1942). The Synagogue of Abraham in Hebron was reported on in 1939 (Pinkerfield 1939). And the discovery of a synagogue in the village of Fahma was made in 1947: "It is apparent then, that in the third and fourth centuries there existed a Jewish settlement in Fahma. Its ancient name is not yet known, its current name symbolizes the existence of forests around the village in ancient days whose trees were burned as coal. The Arab name Fahma is older than the days of the Crusades." He dated Jewish settlement in the area to perhaps as early as the Hasmonean period, and at least to the days of the Second Temple and afterward: "This new discovery widens the area of the district and adds another dot to the map of ancient Jewish settlements in the country" (Avi-Yonah 1947: 155).

It was precisely such a perspective that this labor of fact collecting helped to assemble: viewing the (present) land by way of the dots that mark locales of ancient Jewish presence. The Land (ha-Aretz) emerges as recognizable, as visible, and as integrated through the very process of connecting those dots, which were scattered across its terrain. This work of fact collecting needs to be understood as part of a wider cartographic project, one that was not limited to map-making but was very much about "world-making" (Haraway 1997). And in that work of world-making, the point of view of the archaeological relic—here, linguistic alongside material-cultural—was fundamental. Archaeological relics were fetishized as unmediated empirical evidence, "inhabit[ing] a semiotic domain [of a] culture of no culture" (Haraway 1997: 136), compiling facts of ancient Jewish history through the perspective claiming that the land was fashioned as an old–new Jewish national home. This material-symbolic (re)inscription of the land connected the dots not only in space but also through time.

Excavating Galilean Jewish cities (Tiberias, Bet She'arim, Bet Yerah) alongside synagogues and tombs was fundamental to this cartography of continuity. Such sites—cities, synagogues, necropolises, family tombs—were neither dug nor treated in isolation. They were mapped into a larger temporal–geographic grid. Benjamin Maisler's map of the area surrounding Bet She'arim marks the locales of existing settlements and cities, tells, and ruins. Sites with ancient ruins *and* contemporary settlements were also highlighted: Tsiporri (the Hebrew name for the Arab town of Saffouriyah) and 'Afula, for example. Those old–new places are indicated on the map alongside the names and locations of ruins, such as Megiddo and Tell Abu-Shoushah and contemporary Jewish settlements with no known antecedent in the ancient past, for example, Mishmar ha-'Emeq. It was that perspective that was mapped onto the land, producing landscapes that came to *stand for* the Land of Israel, specific locales through which the (ancient, now "revived") homeland as a whole was given concrete and visible form.

By the 1940s, Israeli archaeological practice was intimately entangled with the practice of settler nationhood. It was a cardinal site for the making and continuous reinscription of a particular historical consciousness, which as Paul Silverstein and Ussama Makdisi argue in the introduction to this volume, "entails codes of temporality intrinsic to the production of particular subjectivities." That code of temporality entailed linking the (Jewish) past—via the objects and landscapes made to signify and embody it—to the present now revived Jewish nation on the basis of which a national future would be built. Modern Israeli-Jews—the new Hebrews—worked to *re*-build their nation state on the landscape once occupied by and ruled over by their forefathers.

If one thinks of the work of archaeology as producing and projecting a future and not just a past, the question of the violence and memory, or the violence of historical amnesia, can be seen to occupy but one possible perspective on discussions of history, historical consciousness, and contemporary forms of politics and subjectivity. The work of archaeology can be understood as much through what it produces as through what it erases. Erasure, after all, is but one way in which pasts and thus presents and futures are made. The work of archaeology in Palestine and Israel was not a mere reflection of an ideology and political project already in place. More accurately, it helped to generate and extend "common-sense" understandings of past and present, of the nation and its homeland. The practice of archaeology was essential to substantiating nationalist sensibilities and claims in this settler colony. In producing artifacts and landscapes as embodiments of (Jewish national) heritage, it incrementally reformulated political, geographic, historical, and epistemological truths and in so doing, engaged in the "work of extending" (Pickering 1995: 14) the very parameters of what was imaginable and plausible, rendering as *given* that which in fact *had to be made*.

But as I have argued, the history of Israeli archaeology's emergence as a domain of national–cultural concern and practice is complex: a public interest in the ancient Hebrew and Jewish past had to be created and the interests and motivations behind the work of fashioning archaeology as national heritage were far more complex than existing accounts—and nationalist beliefs—suggest. We must consider the requirements of archaeology as a field science if we are to understand how it was that this discipline became one cardinal site for the production of (national) politics and its attendant historical imagination. It was, after all, in large part out of a concern for *archaeology's future* that this scientific discipline was produced as a national–cultural pastime, as the site of so much state and public concern and commitment, which by the early decades of Israeli statehood had come to seem quite transparently to "make sense": Israeli Jews, a nation returning home, would *of course* be interested in "their" national past. That fact required no historical or analytic explanation.

Notes

1. See PRO CO 733/159/7: 17. See also "Revisions of Antiquities Ordinance," 11 May, in the same file.
2. The term "Altneuland" was coined by Theodor Herzl, widely regarded as the founder of political Zionism.
3. Jewish archaeologists, as well as the Hebrew University and the Jewish Palestine Exploration Society as institutions, participated in excavations that focused on sites of biblical importance, but those large-scale excavations were carried out, for the most part, under the auspices of European and American institutions. The mainstay of the work of Jewish archaeology in Palestine focused on the kinds of sites and the post-biblical eras that I discuss here.
4. According to Kuhn, "in the absence of a paradigm or some candidate for a paradigm, all of the facts that could possibly pertain to the development of a given science are likely to seem equally relevant." But, as he subsequently clarifies, even such seemingly random fact collecting has to be governed by some kind of interpretive framework, even if far less developed than a paradigm (Kuhn 1971: 16–17). For further clarification, see his postscript to the volume.
5. See issues of *Yediʾot* from the 1930s and 1940s. See also the *Bulletin of the Jewish Palestine Exploration Society* 1925 [English].

References

Abu El-Haj, Nadia. 2001. *Facts on the Ground: Archaeological Practice and Territorial Self-Fashioning in Israeli Society.* Chicago: University of Chicago Press.

Anderson, Benedict. 1991. *Imagined Communities. Reflections on the Origin and Spread of Nationalism.* New York: Verso.

Anglo-American Committee. 1946. *Report of the Anglo-American Committee of Inquiry on Jewish Problems in Palestine and Europe.* London: His Majesty's Stationery Office.

Austin, J. L. 1961. *Philosophical Papers.* Oxford: Clarendon Press.

Avi-Yonah, M. 1947. Sridei Bet-Knesset ʿAtiq be-Kfar Fahma. *Yediʾot ha-Hevra ha-ʿIvrit le-Haqirat Eretz-Yisrael ve-ʿAtiqoteha* 8 (3–4): 154–155.

Ben-Yehuda, Nachman. 1995. *The Masada Myth: Collective Memory and Mythmaking in Israel.* Madison: University of Wisconsin Press.

Ben-Zvi, Itzhaq. 1934. Le-Qadmut ha-Yishuv ha-ʿIvri be-Kfar-Hanania (On the Antiquity of the Hebrew Settlement in Kfar-Hanania). *Yediʾot ha-Hevra ha-ʿIvrit le-Haqirat Eretz-Yisrael ve-ʿAtiqoteiha* 2 (2): 57–60.

Bernstein, Richard J. 1976. *The Restructuring of Social and Political Theory.* New York: Harcourt Brace Jovanovich.

Brasalawski, Y. 1934. Heʾarot la-Topografia ha-Historit ba-Galil (Notes on the Historical Topography of the Galilee). *Yediʾot ha-Hevra ha-ʿIvrit le-Haqirat Eretz-Yisrael ve-ʿAtiqoteha* 1 (4): 20–23.

Carter, Paul. 1989. *The Road to Botany Bay: An Essay in Spatial History.* Boston: Faber and Faber.

Davis, Natalie Zemon, and Randolph Starn. 1989. Introduction. *Representations* 126: 1–6.

Greenblatt, Stephen. 1991. *Marvelous Possessions: The Wonder of the New World.* Chicago: University of Chicago Press.

Hacking, Ian. 1995. *Rewriting the Soul: Multiple Personalities and the Sciences of Memory.* Princeton: Princeton University Press.

Haraway, Donna J. 1997. *Modest_Witness@Second_Millenium: FemaleMan_Meets_OncoMouseTM Feminism and Technoscience.* New York: Routledge.

Kirshenblatt-Gimblett, Barbara. 1991. Objects of Ethnography. In *Exhibiting Culture: The Poetics and Politics of Museum Display,* ed. I. Karp and S. D. Lavine, pp. 386–443. Washington, D.C.: Smithsonian Institution Press.

Knapp, Steven. 1989. Collective Memory and the Actual Past. *Representations* 26: 123–149.

Kuhn, Thomas S. 1970 [1961]. *The Structure of Scientific Revolutions.* Chicago: University of Chicago Press.

Latour, Bruno. 1988. *The Pasteurization of France.* Trans. Alan Sheridan and John Law. Cambridge, Mass.: Harvard University Press.

Lenoir, Timothy. 1997. *Instituting Science: The Cultural Production of Scientific Disciplines.* Stanford: Stanford University Press.

Maisler, Benjamin. n.d. *Toldot ha-Mehqar ha-Arkheologi be-Eretz Yisrael (The History of Archaeological Research in Eretz Yisrael).* Jerusalem: Jewish Palestine Exploration Society.

Mayer, L. A. 1925. Tomb in the Nahalath Ahim Quarter, Jerusalem. *Proceedings of the Jewish Palestine Exploration Society* 1 (1–2): 40–41.

Mayer, L. A., and A. Reifenberg. 1942. Bet ha-Knesset be-Eshtemoʾa (The Synagogue in Eshtemoa). *Yediʾot ha-Hevra ha-ʿIvrit le-Haqirat Eretz Yisrael ve-ʿAtiqoteha* 5 (1): 10–12.

Mazié, Aaron. 1925. The Tomb of Jehosophat in Relation to Hebrew Art. *Proceedings of the Jewish Palestine Exploration Society* 1 (2–4): 68–71.

Pickering, Andrew. 1995. *The Mangle of Practice: Time, Agency, and Science.* Chicago: University of Chicago Press.

Pinkerfield, Y. 1939. Bet ha-Knesset shel Avraham Avinu be-Hevron (The Synagogue of Abraham Our Father in Hebron). *Yediʾot ha-Hevra ha-ʿIvrit le-Haqirat Eretz Yisrael ve-ʿAtiqoteha* 6 (2): 61–65.

Pitkin, Hanna Fenichel. 1972. *Wittgenstein and Justice: On the Significance of Ludwig Wittgenstein for Social and Political Thought.* Berkeley: University of California Press.

Poovey, Mary. 1998. *A History of the Modern Fact: Problems of Knowledge in the Sciences of Wealth and Society.* Chicago: University of Chicago Press.

PRO CO. Public Records Office, Records of the Colonial Office, Palestine Original Correspondence Series, London.

Rabinow, Paul. 1989. *French Modern: Norms and Forms of the Social Environment.* Cambridge, Mass.: MIT Press.

Renan, Ernest. 1996. *Qu'est-ce qu'une nation = What Is a nation?* Trans. Wanda Romer Taylor. Toronto: Tapir Press.

Shapin, Steven, and Simon Schaffer. 1985. *Leviathan and the Air Pump: Hobbes, Boyle, and the Experimental Life.* Princeton: Princeton University Press.

Silberman, Neil Asher. 1993. *A Prophet from Amongst You: The Life of Yigael Yadin: Soldier, Scholar and Myth Maker of Modern Israel.* New York: Addison-Wesley.

Slousch, Nahum. 1925. The Excavations around the Monument of Absalom. *Proceedings of the Jewish Palestine Exploration Fund* 1 (2–4): 1–30.

———, E. L. Sukenik, and Itzhaq Ben-Zvi. 1925. Tomb Discovery in the "Mahanaim" Quarter (Jerusalem). *Proceedings of the Jewish Palestine Exploration Society* 1 (2–4): 57–61.

Stevens, Jacqueline. 1999. *Reproducing the State.* Princeton: Princeton University Press.

Sukenik, E. L. 1934. *Ancient Synagogues in Palestine and Greece.* Schweich Lectures of the British Academy, 1930. Oxford: Oxford University Press.

Sukenik, E. L. 1925. The Tomb on the Hebrew University Premises. *Proceedings of the Jewish Palestine Exploration Society* 1 (2–4): 43–47.

Wright, Gwendolyn. 1997. *The Politics of Design in French Colonial Urbanism.* Chicago: University of Chicago Press.

Yeivin, Shmu'el. 1967. *Ha-Kinus ha-Ri'shon li-Yedi'at ha-Aretz (The First "Knowledge of the Homeland" Conference).* Jerusalem: ha-Hevrah ha-ʿIvrit le-Haqirat Erets-Yisra'el ve-ʿAtiqoteha.

———. 1935. Hessegei ʿAssor (The Achievements of a Decade). *Yedi'ot ha-Hevra ha-ʿIvrit le-Hakirat Eretz-Israel ve-ʿAtiqoteiha,* 41–48.

Contributors

Nadia Abu El-Haj is Assistant Professor in the Department of Anthropology at Barnard College, Columbia University. She is author of *Facts on the Ground: Archaeological Practice and Territorial Self-Fashioning in Israeli Society.*

Glenn Bowman teaches in the anthropology department of the University of Kent, where he coordinates the M.A. program in the Anthropology of Ethnicity, Nationalism, and Identity. He is the author of many articles on Palestinian and Yugoslavian violence and nationalism and editor of the *Journal of the Royal Anthropological Institute.*

Saree Makdisi is Professor of English at the University of California, Los Angeles. His books include *Romantic Imperialism: Universal Empire and the Culture of Modernity* and *William Blake and the Impossible History of the 1790s.*

Ussama Makdisi is Associate Professor in the Department of History, Rice University. He is author of *The Culture of Sectarianism: Community, History, and Violence in Nineteenth-Century Ottoman Lebanon.*

James McDougall is Assistant Professor of History at Princeton University. He is editor of *Nation, Society, and Culture in North Africa* and author of articles on modern Algerian history and historiography.

Anja Peleikis is a postdoctoral fellow at the Max Planck Institute for Social Anthropology in Halle, Germany. She has worked on Lebanese transnational migration and multiconfessionalism in postwar Lebanon and is author of *Lebanese in Motion: Gender and the Making of a Translocal Village.*

Gabriel Piterberg is Associate Professor in the Department of History, University of California, Los Angeles. He is author of *An Ottoman Tragedy: History and Historiography at Play* and *Myths, Politics, and Scholarship in Israel.*

Shira Robinson is Assistant Professor of History at the University of Iowa. Her work on Israeli–Palestinian violence and history has been published in the *International Journal of Middle Eastern Studies* and *Middle East Report.*

Paul A. Silverstein is Associate Professor of Anthropology at Reed College and a member of the editorial committee of *Middle East Report.* He is author of *Algeria in France: Transpolitics, Race, and Nation* (Indiana University Press, 2004).

Benjamin Stora is Professor of History of the Maghreb at the Institut National des Langues et Cultures Orientales (Paris) and Directeur Scientifique at the Institut Maghreb-Europe (Université de Paris-VIII). His many books include *La gangrène et l'oubli. La mémoire de la guerre d'Algérie; Imaginaires de guerre. Algérie—Viêt-nam en France et aux États-Unis;* and *Algeria, 1830–2000: A Short History.*

Yael Zerubavel is Director of the Allen and Joan Bildner Center for the Study of Jewish Life and Chair of the Department of Jewish Studies at Rutgers University. She is author of *Recovered Roots: Collective Memory and the Making of Israeli National Tradition.*

Index

Galilee (Israel), 110, 119, 226–227, 229
Gaza Strip (Palestine), 5, 27, 85–86, 92, 121
Geagea, Samir, 6, 137
Geertz, Clifford, 6, 46n15
Gemayel, Bashir, 149n4
Giscard d'Estaing, Valéry, 164
globalization, 134
Goren, Asher, 183
Gouri, Haim, 80
grassroots protest: amongst Palestinians, 110–
    111. *See also* strikes
Groupes de Légitime Défense (GLD) (Alge-
    ria), 69n36
Gulf War, 3
Gur, Batya, 88

Haddab, Mustapha, 61
Hadj, Messali, 69n35
hagiography, 31–32
Haifa (Israel), 110, 181–182
Halbwachs, Maurice, 9, 136, 215
halutzim (Hebr. Zionist pioneers), 177, 191,
    193, 196
Hamas party (Palestine), 7
Hameiri, Avidgor, 75
hamula (Ar. clan), 7, 35, 45n1, 46n19, 47n25;
    and social structure, 27–28, 31
hara (Ar. village quarter), 134–135
Haram al-Sharif (Temple Mount), 15
Hariri, Rafik, 202
Harkis, 59–60, 65, 69n25, 151, 162–163,
    171n2
Haupt, Paul, 147
hegemony, 27–28, 43, 182; cultural, 4; and
    memory, 12–13, 115, 178, 195–197; and
    nationalist myths, 182
Hendel, Yehudit, 88–89,
Herzl, Theodor, 231n2
historical consciousness, 195, 199n33; and ar-
    chaeology; 224, 230; and the Enlighten-
    ment, 179; and memory, 10–11
historical imagination, 11, 62–64, 231
history, 9–10, 18; Algerian, 50–67; Lebanese,
    203–204, 209–210; official history, 6–7,
    17, 106–107, 115, 201, 209–210; Zionist,
    192–196
hizb fransa (Ar. party of France), 70n37
Hobeika, Elie, 15–16
Holocaust, 19n4, 78, 89
homeland, 27, 75–77. *See also* Israel; Palestine
housing: as memory site, 140–141
Hrawi, Elias, 146
human rights, 4, 146–147
Hussein, Saddam, 3

ibn Badis, ʿAbd al-Hamid (Ben Badis), 52, 57,
    69n31
Ibn Khaldun, 51
Ibn Zayyad, Tariq, 120, 128n60
Ibrahimi, Ahmed Taleb, 63
identity, 6–8, 31, 40, 43; communitarian, 7–8,
    33, 65, 155, 158, 163, 170; cultural, 66; Pal-
    estinian, 19n1, 31–34, 104, 180, 189–190;
    production and maintenance of, 33–34, 133–
    135, 143–144; sectarian, 7–8, 31, 134–136,
    138, 141, 148n1
imagined community, 1, 7, 43, 120, 199n33
immigration: to France, 151–152, 159–164;
    and violence, 161–164; and xenophobia,
    151, 164–166, 169–170
Indochina, 156
intifada, 15, 27–35, 42–44, 45nn2,7, 85–86, 91–
    92; and Christian-Muslim relations, 42; and
    group identity, 10–11, 29–30, 32–35, 95n36;
    and martyrdom, 18, 29, 31–32. *See also*
    al-Aqsa *intifada*
Iraq, 116; U.S. occupation of, vii, 1–4
islah (Ar. reform), 52
Islam: in France, 152, 163–167
Islamic Salvation Army (AIS) (Algeria), 5, 66
Islamic Salvation Front (FIS), 66, 70n38
Islamism, 3–4; in Algeria, 51, 64, 67, 68n22,
    70n39, 156
Israel, 3–6, 8, 9, 12, 18, 177–197, 215–230;
    and ethos of patriotic sacrifice, 73–92; and
    master-narratives/foundational myths, 91,
    178–180, 189, 194
Israeli, Benzion, 192, 194
Israeli Defense Forces (IDF), 5, 11, 28–29,
    33, 43, 104–109, 128n64, 182, 185; and as-
    sassination, 7, 29, 104–106, 119; and patri-
    otic sacrifice, 73–92. *See also* Arab-Israeli
    conflict; military rule; Six-Day War

Jaffa (Israel), 190
Japan, 16–17, 19n4
Jenin, 41
Jerusalem, 45n11, 217, 223–224, 228
Jewish National Fund (JNF), 182, 188
Jewish Palestine Exploration Society (JPES),
    216–221, 225–226, 231n3; and educa-
    tion, 217–220; and historical-geography,
    228–229
Jewish Yishuv, 184, 217–218, 220–221, 226
jihad: discourse of 4, 64, 66
jokes, 78–80, 93n20; *See also* violence, and po-
    litical satire
Jospin, Lionel, 164, 167–168, 171n1
Joxe, Pierre, 164

Démocratiques (MTLD) (France/Algeria), 68n16, 69n35
Muʾnis, Shaykh, 184–185
mujahid(in) (Ar. religious fighter[s]), 4, 59, 65
multi-confessionalism, 133–148
museum, 6, 11
myth of return: and Jewish settlement, 216, 226–227, 230; as a master narrative, 177–179, 189, 194

nakba (Ar. catastrophe), 177, 196
narratives: hegemonic, 17–18, 207; image-based, 205–206; in Lebanese literature, 208–210; narrative strategy, 10–11, 42–44, 145–146; and nationalism, 20n9, 157–159; subaltern, 6, 178; Zionist, 17–18, 178–179, 183–184, 193, 196
Nashin be-Shahor (Women in Black) (Israel), 85–86
national heritage, 216–221, 230–231
National Liberation Front (FLN) (Algeria), 6, 53, 58–66, 67n8, 68n16, 69n35, 168
nationalism, 4, 9–11, 19n2; in France, 157–159; in Israel, 215, 230; in Palestine; 43, 178, 181, 191
nationalist mythology, 1–2, 5, 10; in Algeria, 51; in Israel, 76–80, 218–219, 230
naturalization: of history, 10, 65–66, 67n4
Nazareth (Israel), 110
New Hebrew Man, 75
New Profile (*Profile Hadash*) (Israel), 86
Nigeria, 15
nokheihim nifkadim (Hebr. present absentees), 187–189
Nora, Pierre, 140, 199n33
Northern Ireland, 9
nostalgia, 134, 141–142, 193, 203
Nuremberg Trials, 13

occupation: of Algeria, 158. *See also* Palestine; West Bank, Israeli occupation of
Occupied Territories, 27–44, 65, 177. *See also* Palestine
October Events (Israel), 121–122
October 1988 demonstrations (Algeria), 51
October 17, 1961 massacre (France), 161–162, 167–169, 173n22
Old City (Jerusalem), 33, 223–224, 226–227
Operation Danny (Israel), 181
Operation Refugee File (Israel), 185–187
Oran (Algeria), 160
Organisation Nationale des Anciens Mujahidin (ONM) (Algeria), 68n23

Organisation Nationale des Enfants de Chouhada (ONEC) (Algeria), 68n23
Organisation Nationale des Enfants de Mujahidin (ONEM) (Algeria), 68n23
Organization of the Secret Army (OAS) (Algeria), 152–153, 155, 157, 159, 163–165, 168, 171n6, 172nn16,17,18
Orientalism, 182, 192–193
Orthodox Christianity, 29–31, 45n4, 46n15
Oslo Accords, 5, 7, 45n11, 32–33, 35, 43
Ottoman Empire, vii, 1, 3, 18, 30, 68n13
Oz, Amos, 83

Palestine, 8–9, 18, 27–44, 177–197, 197n1, 205; archaeology in, 216–219, 225–227; Israeli occupation of, 4, 17, 31, 44, 86, 178
Palestine Liberation Organization (PLO), 32, 35, 46n13
Palestine (National) Authority (PA/PNA), 7, 28, 32, 34, 38, 41, 43, 47n24
pan-Arabism, 116
Papon, Maurice, 167–169, 173n22
Paris, 156–157, 162
Parti du Peuple Algérien (PPA) (France/Algeria), 68n16, 69n35
Partition Plan (Israel/Palestine), 181
patriotic sacrifice, 63, 73–92
Peace Now (Israel), 85–86
Pélégri, Jean, 160
Phoenicians, 56, 201
Pied-Noirs, 151–152, 154–155, 165, 171n2; and literature, 157, 159–161
Pinochet, Gustave, 14
poetry, 77, 80–84, 128n61
police: in France, 161–162; in Israel/Palestine, 113–116, 119, 121–122, 127n54
politicide, 34
Popular Front for the Liberation of Palestine (PFLP), 30, 32, 116
postcards, 202–205
post-coloniality, 1, 7–8, 11–12
Progressive Socialist Party (PSP) (Lebanon), 137
Propaganda, 182–187
prosthetic devices (of memory), 203
public sphere, 143–144

qadi (Ar. judge), 37–39, 46n21
Qur'an, 151

Raad, Walid, 206, 213n3
Rabin, Yitzhak, 31, 86
racism: in Algerian historiography, 55–56; anti-

violence, 5–9, 12–13; naturalization of, 51–52, 64–65; and political satire, 79–80, 93n20; religious, 7

Vircondelet, Alain, 160, 172n15

watan (Ar. national homeland), 66

Weitz, Yosef, 181–183, 187, 197n7

West Bank (Palestine), 5, 27, 85; Israeli occupation of, 4, 27, 29, 31, 121. *See also* Palestine

widowhood, 89–90, 95n35

World War I, vii, 30

World War II, 2, 16, 19n4, 60, 89, 156

Yavetz, Zvi, 184–185

Yedi'at ha-Aretz (Heb. "Knowledge of the Land") conference (Israel), 218–220, 225, 227, 229

Yehoshua, A. B., 83, 94n25

Yeivin, Shmu'el, 227

Yemeni Jews, 11, 177, 191–196

Yesh Gevul (Israel), 85

Yom Kippur War, 78–79

Young Algerians, 54, 68n12

youth culture, 143–144, 153

Yugoslavia, 147

Zionism, 17, 74–75; and antiquity, 92n6; foundation of, 231n2; and the occupation of Palestine, 178–181, 194, 198, 218

Zohar Commision of Inquiry (Israel), 112, 125n24, 126n38

www.ingramcontent.com/pod-product-compliance
Ingram Content Group UK Ltd.
Pitfield, Milton Keynes, MK11 3LW, UK
UKHW041846270225
455670UK00001B/53